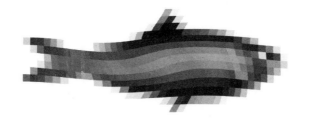

THE
RED
HERRING
GUIDE
TO THE
DIGITAL
UNIVERSE

THE
RED
HERRING
GUIDE

TO THE
DIGITAL
UNIVERSE

**THE INSIDE LOOK AT TECHNOLOGY BUSINESS—
FROM SILICON VALLEY TO HOLLYWOOD**

**BY THE EDITORS OF
THE RED HERRING**

**DESIGNED BY
BART NAGEL'S BRAIN**

WARNER BOOKS

A Time Warner Company

Note

At the time of publication the information in this book is as up-to-date and reliable as possible. However, it is published with the understanding that the rules, regulations, and alliances in the industries covered change very rapidly. The reader is advised to seek professional legal and investment advice regarding specific questions. The author and publisher specifically disclaim any liability that is incurred from the use or application of the contents of this book.

Warner Books, Inc.
1271 Avenue of the Americas
New York, NY 10020

 A Time Warner Company

Printed in the United States of America

First Printing: April 1996

10 9 8 7 6 5 4 3 2 1

Library of Congress Cataloging-in-Publication Data

The Red Herring guide to the digital universe : the inside look at
technology business—from Silicon Valley to Hollywood /
the editors of The Red Herring.
    p.   cm.
Includes index.
ISBN 0-446-52018-7
1. Computer software industry—United States.   I. Red Herring
(New York, N.Y.)
HD9696.C63U564 1996
338.4'70053'0973—dc20   95-48779
                                                         CIP

Dedication

To our hero, Laurence J. Kirshbaum, who came up with the concept for this book, and to all of the intrepid entrepreneurs who keep creating companies for us to write about.

—The Herring Editors

A c k n o w l e d g m e n t s

THE RED HERRING was barely a year-and-a-half old when we received a phone call from one of the biggest hitters in the media business, Laurence J. Kirshbaum, president and CEO of Warner Books. He had two reasons for his call. The first was to commend us for our work with the magazine, which he'd been reading since the first issue rolled off the presses in May of 1993. The second was to explore the idea of our editors writing a book that would bring together, in "THE HERRING style," a comprehensive analysis of the three industries we cover as a regular part of our beat: computers, communications, and entertainment. While there clearly is a plethora of business information out there on these converging sectors, Mr. Kirshbaum felt that creating a "guide" that brought together our research on the technologies, strategies, and companies driving the convergence would offer serious professionals a valuable tool for staying ahead in today's fast-changing media-centric world.

Writing any book takes the special guidance of a careful editor, in our case Rick Wolff, who's been supportive and encouraging at every turn. And we'd be remiss if we didn't thank our agent, Esther Newberg at International Creative Management (ICM), here, who helped translate Mr. Kirshbaum's idea and our enthusiasm into a real-live book deal. Ms. Newberg has been described as "the Madam of the non-fiction literary circles," a title she may or may not embrace, but one we now understand and appreciate.

"Big Six" accounting firm KPMG Peat Marwick helped select and evaluate the 250 companies profiled in these pages by setting up criteria and matching every nominee against them. Roger Siboni, Andrea Gregg, their team, and all the partners who offered input did a great job.

At THE RED HERRING, special thanks is due to Michael Perkins, who refined the concept and wrote each chapter of this book, always meeting his deadlines, compiling THE HERRING's prior research (often doing more on his own), and making this the most up-to-date and informative guide possible. Anne Linsmayer tirelessly built and edited company profiles—she called investor relations departments all over the globe, dug up information from obscure sources, and waded through stacks of paper and layers of hard-to-reach executives and busy entrepreneurs to get whatever could be gotten, incorporated, and updated into each profile. Nina Davis edited or copy-edited every word, fretted over deadlines, played liaison to our production team, coordinated the reviewing of each chapter by outside experts, and was of general support to everyone involved in this project.

And we appreciate the feedback on content and correctness that those outside experts gave us. The help of Jim Breyer, Sandy Climan, Kevin Compton, Fred Davis, Pierre Lamond, Gary Lauder, Bob Metcalfe, Avram Miller, Steve Milunovich, Carl Rosendahl, and Tom Waldrop was invaluable.

So, to everyone mentioned above, and to all others who helped, but have not been mentioned, particularly the entire HERRING team of editors and interns, and our fearless and prolific design and production team, our heartfelt thanks. It's been a blast. As Steve Jobs once said when talking about the spirit it took to start Apple Computer, "The journey is the reward." We understand what he meant a bit better now.

SPECIAL THANKS TO **KPMG** Peat Marwick LLP

THE RED HERRING GUIDE TO THE DIGITAL UNIVERSE

Table of

Contents]

PART THREE | COMPUTERS

PART FOUR | COMPANY PROFILES

00_INTRODUCTION

TIM BROCK

When we published the first issue of THE RED HERRING in May of 1993, the hype surrounding the impending "Information Superhighway" was at an eardrum-piercing pitch. From the back lots of the biggest studios in Hollywood to the cloistered offices of venture capital firms in Silicon Valley, everyone was scrambling to get in on the next big bonanza—the communications, computer, and entertainment industries looked as though they were crashing together.

Interactive television seemed to promise interactive entertainment nirvana in no time at all. The big players found a reason to embrace this medium: to the telcos, interactive television seemed a natural extension to their original two-way communications device, the telephone; to software and hardware developers it promised an entirely new market to develop for, conquer, and create; and to media conglomerates it represented a whole new way to sell (or resell) their libraries of creative content. Well, if Ross Perot had our job, you could just imagine how he would describe the last couple of years in technology and entertainment. "You hear that big sucking sound?" the little billionaire with the big ears would ask us sarcastically. After a short pause, he would happily explain it to us, "That's the sound of some of the biggest companies in America dumping huge amounts of cash into big black holes."

Two-and-a-half years later, the three sectors have fallen back on their butts, although there are plenty of failures and successes from this world to point at. Nowadays, the buzzword for these industries is "consolidation." The entertainment sector is forming mega-mergers in content and distribution. The interactive entertainment business has grown into a $10 billion industry. Most of this market is dominated by Sega and Nintendo, the twin dragons from Japan, and a slew of U.S.-based companies, such as Acclaim and Electronic Arts. Media conglomerates, however, are now opening up their own gaming divisions rather than farming out videos to third-party developers. In communications, ATM and wireless have taken off, indicating the trend toward an increasingly remote, mobile techno-society.

The networking potential of the Internet and the World Wide Web caught everyone by surprise. "It's like we were all struggling to build the high-capacity links to the TV set, and the Internet happened in the meantime," admits Bill Joy, co-founder of Sun Microsystems. As Don Valentine of Sequoia Capital, famous in the venture capital business for his obsession with only backing startups selling into large existing markets, pointed out, "At least there is an installed base to support the Internet phenomenon. How many people do you know who own a set-top box?" More recently, industry reports indicate that the number of PCs sold into the home has surpassed the number sold to businesses, and a Nielsen survey found that there are now over 17 million people surfing the Net. The real Information Superhighway has come into clear focus.

In the midst of this ferment, there's no doubt that 1995 will go down in history as the year of the entertainment mega-mergers. Jack Welch at Westinghouse served up $5.4 billion to snatch up CBS. Not to be outdone, Disney's Michael Eisner acquired Capital Cities/ABC for $19 billion to create the largest media conglomerate in the world. Viacom CEO Sumner Redstone outbid the slicker, savvier Barry Diller for Paramount with $10 billion and swallowed Blockbuster for $8.4 billion, then turned around and sold his $2.25 billion cable business to TCI. Seagram heir Edgar Bronfman Jr. bought MCA for $5.7 billion. And for the grand finale, Time Warner bought Turner Broadcasting Systems in an $8 billion stock deal.

Most media analysts claim it wasn't just testosterone driving this mania—it was survival. The new mission of the media moguls is to own the entire entertainment food chain, from content creation to distribution. Not to do so, they fear, means running the risk of getting squeezed out. The Time Warner/Turner deal is a classic example of the potential competitive power behind such a consolidation.

The ability to skillfully deliver entertainment across multiple media and own the means of both production and distribution will certainly be a competitive advantage in the next year, but this trend will only continue while there is money to fuel it. "Once the money dries up, because of an advertising recession or something else like that, which is certain to happen, you'll see things thrown overboard for survival," argues Barry Diller. And he will probably be right. The reality of these combinations is that they are usually fraught with financial and management challenges. A prime example is AT&T's return to its core business, which throws into question phone and cable companies' extravagant efforts to rapidly bring 500 channels to your living room. Invariably, many executives will get discouraged, jump ship, and start their own media companies. It also became clear that trying to coordinate and manage projects such as the failed interactive TV trials between industry behemoths wasn't going to be that easy, either. "The communications, game, and computer companies all started crashing into each other, and no one company really owned a big enough piece of the market to bring it all together. The whole thing became one big gridlock," recounts Bill Joy.

Content is king, but what conduits and platforms consumers will use to access e-mail, databases, and movie-clips on their shrinking laptops or communicators is still uncertain. Desktop computers are becoming more and more powerful, creeping into the market of high-end graphics workstations, and it is said that any company that does not have an Internet strategy is doomed. The rise (and perhaps eventual fall) of empires such as Apple, Microsoft, America Online, SGI, and Intel has been avidly watched and eagerly imitated by hungry entrepreneurs. The moral to this story is that industry consolidation doesn't necessarily imply the ultimate dominance of only a few players.

As the U.S. completes its shift away from its industrial footing toward an information-based economy, the technology tool makers and entertainment

15

content creators—both big and small—are destined to emerge as the dominant players driving the world economy. During this era, shakeups in the business environment should continue at an even more accelerated pace, spurred by slicker and more powerful production and communication technologies. For the serious player in computers, communications, and entertainment, it will be an exciting time, but one increasingly hard to predict.

Eleven informative chapters on today's most compelling high-tech sectors, and profiles on 250 of the hottest companies in those sectors help sort out the hype from reality. Insights from such luminaries as rock-musician Peter Gabriel; Microsoft's Bill Gates; Jim Clark, founder of Netscape; UNIX-pioneer Bill Joy; Jeff Berg, head of International Creative Management; Larry Ellison, the CEO of Oracle; trend-setting venture capitalist John Doerr, Intel founder Gordon Moore, and networking-pioneer Bob Metcalfe are included. This book serves as a briefing document—it adds perspective, gives information, and helps the reader to better understand the business of high-tech.

November 10, 1995
San Francisco, California

01_ENTERTAINMENT
& EDUCATION
SOFTWARE

Mortal Kombat, Doom, Myst, SimCity, Where in the World is Carmen Sandiego?; these entertainment and education software products have achieved a name recognition is beginning to approach that of Barbie and Monopoly. This trend grows as aging video game players, entering the 25 to 35 age bracket, play games on their personal computers and encourage their children to do the same. According to PC Data, a market research firm based in Reston, VA, educational software was the fastest growing software category in 1994, with sales increasing by 50% over the previous year. For 1995–1996, Robertson, Stephens & Co., a San Francisco–

based investment bank, projected a growth rate of between 38% and 45% for entertainment software and 30% for education software developed for the personal computer. Sales of set-top video games were expected to reach $2.5 billion in 1995 and sales of PC games, $840 million. Educational software sales were expected to be more than $330 million.

Robertson Stephens also made some predictions for 1996. Sales for TV set-top video games were forecast as $2.7 billion. The forecast for entertainment software for the personal computer is $1.1 billion, another $430 million is projected for home education software, reference programs will account for $160 million and the school market will provide an additional $525 million.

With major companies like Microsoft, Viacom, and Time Warner jumping into these markets alongside Sega, Nintendo, and Electronic Arts, the competition for customers and sales promises to become even more intense.

Entertainment Software

Historically, video games have been delivered through cheap game units that hook up to televisions through set-top boxes. Until recently, these set-top players were based on 8-bit and 16-bit technology. The number of bits in the computer processor determines the quality of the game graphics and the speed of play. The more bits the better. A new generation of set-top technology is coming into play based on 32-bit and 64-bit computer processors. In addition to new machines from Sega, Nintendo, and video game dinosaur Atari, Sony and upstart game player 3DO are offering new boxes. The new graphics are impressive, but the quest to become the top-selling game machine promises to be a dogfight.

The personal computer is emerging as a major gaming platform, although the CD-ROM technology that many games require has particular problems discussed in a special section on CD-ROM later in this chapter. At this point, it is enough to say that personal computers do not provide the "plug-and-play" convenience of set-top video machines.

Creating Hit Titles

Perhaps more important than the hardware used are the games that run on these machines. But what exactly makes a game a hit (sales of 100,000 units or more) remains somewhat of a mystery, as much of a mystery as what makes a movie a blockbuster, or a book a bestseller.

However, Keith Benjamin, senior media analyst at Robertson Stephens, suggests at least six factors necessary to make a game a true hit.

1. Buzz—Recommendation by friends goes a long way in promoting a game. An estimated two-thirds of video game buyers rent or borrow titles before purchase.

2. Gameplay—Hit games are challenging, fun, and, most of all, addictive. A hit game's key elements can be used for successful sequels, as in the case of *Doom II* from Id and *Mortal Kombat II* from Acclaim Entertainment.

3. Depth—Multiple levels or "episodes" mean a lot of bang for the buck. Consumers will pay as much as $60 for a game if it translates into a cost of no more than $2 or $3 per hour of entertainment. The *Doom* titles are so popular because they offer numerous episodes and lots of playing time.

4. Demographics—Developing games that appeal to the main audience is crucial. On personal computers strategy games, simulations, and adventures have the broadest appeal to a large gaming audience that includes many adults. These games tend to be more intellectual and less concerned with dexterity, like *Myst*. On video game machines, action/adventure, fighting, and sports games have the biggest appeal to a core audience of young boys and male teens. For these games, "the cool factor and playability are the keys to success," says Mr. Benjamin. *Mortal Kombat II* is a good example of this kind of game.

5. Uniqueness—Sometimes a game that is simply different from anything else out there will have a strong appeal, so long as it has good gameplay. *SimCity* (Maxis) is a good example of a best-selling game in a category all its own.

6. Marketing—Some of the biggest video game companies, like Nintendo, will spend as much as $10 million in television advertising to push a game title such as *Donkey Kong Country*. Brand and game awareness are becoming more important. However, for personal computer games, the outlay of advertising dollars is not as high because the companies are smaller and the competition less cut-throat.

Sega, Nintendo, Acclaim, Capcom, Virgin, and Electronic Arts will remain major sellers of video games. Major sellers of personal computer games include Id, LucasArts, Sierra On-Line, Spectrum Holobyte, Maxis, Brøderbund, and Electronic Arts.

Hollywood Gaming

An important trend in entertainment software is the incorporation of Hollywood elements into game development (a.k.a. "Siliwood," from Silicon Valley + Hollywood). A prime example of this trend is Rocket Science Games, a company that brought together Hollywood designer Ron Cobb, Industrial Light and Magic designers Mark Sullivan and Rich Cohen, *Rising Sun* screenwriter Mike Bakkes, and superstar Mac programmer Peter Barrett—all under the aegis of CEO Steve Blank, a computer hardware industry veteran from SuperMac. Rocket Science touts its convergence of Hollywood-Silicon Valley professionals as "a gathering of some of the best talent from both worlds."

Rocket Science started with some $20 million in funding from venture and corporate investors and gained a $70 million valuation in August 1994. The Rocket Science budget is $1 million per game title because in keeping with the Hollywood model, each title requires an all-star team of programmers, producers, directors, film crews, and actors. Add to this the costs for manufacturing, product royalties, distribution, corporate overhead, and marketing, and Rocket Science has to sell an average of 500,000 units of each title in order to break even.

Rocket Science CEO Steve Blank takes off

STEVE CURLEY

22

One of the company's first game offerings was a title called *LoadStar*, an action program built around a movie script Mr. Cobb originally wrote with John Wayne in mind. It attempts to bring together Hollywood movie drama with Silicon Valley high resolution graphics and gameplay. The verdict is still out on whether this synthesis really works. Some reviewers don't think so. Jim Breyer, a general partner with venture capital firm Accel Partners, an outfit that has consistently invested in entertainment and education software, states, "The real question is going to be how their games rate in creating atmosphere, whether they can elicit the emotional responses necessary to create a runaway hit like *Mortal Kombat* or *Tetris*. At the end of the day, the intangible immersion experience will be the deciding factor in how well they do."

The larger question is: who will consistently produce the hits? New, independent game producers like Id, the heavily funded "Siliwood" companies like Rocket Science and Crystal Dynamics, or the more established players like Electronic Arts, Spectrum Holobyte, Nintendo, and Sega? Many veteran analysts, like Lee Isgur of Jefferies & Co. and Charles Finnie of Volpe Welty, bet on the established players.

Education Software

Education software (sometimes called "learning software") is aimed at a different market from video games. It is purchased by adults, usually parents or educators, for children, mostly under age 13. It is also delivered almost exclusively on personal computers rather than on game machines.

Link Resources, a market research company, estimates that 42% of American households with children own personal computers, and that 60% of the seven million computers sold in 1994 went to households with children.

According to SIMBA International, a research company that covers the school market, the installed base of personal computers in kindergarten–twelfth grade schools reached 4.23 million in 1993. Robertson, Stephens & Co. forecasts an installed base of 8.5 million computers in schools by 1996.

The School Market

The school market has traditionally been considered the most likely market for learning software. Indeed, SIMBA forecasts a growth rate of 103.4% for standalone software (the individual software packages that run on personal computers) by 1998, with $600 million of these sales going into schools. This figure does not include sales of CD-ROMs, which SIMBA predicts will grow 606.5% by 1998, with sales of $325 million, or of integrated learning systems (networked hardware and courseware), expected to reach $420 million in sales by 1998.

These forecasts are built on certain key assumptions:

- Reforms in education will encourage technology purchases
- Home education software sales will help stimulate school sales
- Business use of technology will stimulate school sales
- Cost of technology will continue to decline
- Hardware purchased by schools in 1993 will still be usable in 1998
- Partnerships between textbook publishers and software companies will create greater demand for integrated packages that use both print and electronic media
- Corporate partners will help underwrite the wiring of schools with online services

It is unlikely, however, that computers purchased in 1993 will be able to run the latest and greatest learning software in 1998. The number of technology purchases required to make up-to-date computers significantly accessible to most students puts a serious strain on school budgets. Another key factor is the teacher variable. Even for those teachers who are not technophobic or otherwise resistant to using technology in the classroom, a shortage of time becomes critical in carrying out the complex task of integrating educational software with the curriculum.

SIMBA itself states, "The next five years [1994–1998] will be critical for schools and for technology providers. Schools face key issues in terms of reform, management shifts, and continued concerns about overall funding. They are ready for new technologies, but cautious about investing in unproven teaching tools. Similarly, publishers and content providers are cautious about jumping into markets or formats unfamiliar to them." Software publishers and technology providers who target the school market, especially for the first time, should be cautious and recognize that the barriers to entry are higher than those for the general consumer market.

What Makes for Good Learning Software

As Michael Perkins and Celia Núñez, authors of *KidWare: The Parents Guide to Software for Children* (Prima Publishing, 1995) point out, the primary difference between learning software and video games is that it's not the hit of the moment that will find a market and make money, but so-called "evergreen products"—programs like *Oregon Trail, Just Grandma and Me,* and *KidPix* that constructively engage children and will to last in the midst of the glut of mediocre software currently on the market.

Most parents and educators see children's software primarily as a learning tool. This means software publishers have to incorporate solid content into their programs. On the other hand, if children lose interest in a program after a few sessions, consumers will feel they've wasted their money. So the challenge is to create programs that have both meaningful content and engaging formats.

According to Mr. Perkins and Ms. Núñez, an evergreen product first of all has to be computer-specific. That is, it must make full use of the computer instead of treating it as a glorified flashcard or reading system. It can't be the same boring drill-and-practice software so much in vogue as recently as the early 1980s. For a program to successfully present its content, it must use a far more innovative format, and weave the contents into the dynamic of the program. Simulation programs are a great example. These programs let children step into another world, where they can role-play as engineers, architects, trail-blazing pioneers, or masters of their own universe. In the process, children investigate new subjects and learn new ways to think. Good examples of these programs are

Freddi Fish and the Case of the Missing Kelp Seeds (Humongous Entertainment) and *SimTown* (Maxis).

Brand Equity

Davidson, Brøderbund, and SoftKey's subsidiary The Learning Company are still the big three in learning software. But other consistent producers of quality learning software include Edmark, Humongous Entertainment, Knowledge Adventure, Maxis, MECC, and Mindscape. Microsoft has also produced some good products for children under its *Microsoft Home* label.

According to Volpe Welty, these companies, with their established brand equity, will continue to prosper in the learning software market. Both retailers and consumers are turning to established companies for quality product. In the fourth quarter of 1994, sales of learning software were $200 million; shelf space was scarce, so most retailers went with known brands, as did consumers. In their report on *Edutainment Software* (1995) Volpe Welty states, "Consumer software is still relatively expensive, and parents with kids who already enjoy a product by one of these companies felt more comfortable buying another product from the same company." As an example, the report cites *Reader Rabbit's Interactive Reading Journey* from The Learning Company, a "runaway hit," in spite of its $79 to $99 retail price tag. For the learning software sector as a whole, Volpe Welty expects an annual growth rate of 30%+ at least through 1997.

Brøderbund's attempted acquisition of The Learning Company for $440 million was an effort to solidify its position in the edutainment market. Although Brøderbund reached new heights as a result of publishing the best-selling game title *Myst* (selling 1.5 million copies by summer 1995), and is scheduled to release *Myst II* in 1996, it is still much more at home in the familiar edutainment market. As of September 1995, 15-year-old Brøderbund had revenue of $160 million and earnings of $25 million in the previous fiscal year, with a market capitalization of $1.86 billion. Instead, The Learning Company was acquired by SoftKey, which made it the leader in the educational software market. SoftKey's strategy is to sell software like any other commodity; inexpensively and in huge volumes.

CD-ROM

According to Dataquest, a market research firm that specializes in technology data, in 1994 more than 70% of personal computers sold had a CD-ROM drive, bringing the installed base of these drives to a total of 7.8 million in

American homes and 23.6 million worldwide. Dataquest projects that by 1996 the installed base will have grown to 57.1 million worldwide. These purchases are all part of the trend toward multimedia computers equipped with special sound and video capability.

CD-ROM itself, however, is best understood as a storage medium, something that represents a much greater capacity than the old floppy disks. The typical CD-ROM can hold as much as 660MB of information—equivalent to several hundred floppies. Many publishers use this increased storage space to provide enhanced graphics, audio, and sometimes video.

The Shakeout

By the end of 1994, more than 2,000 CD-ROM titles were on the market. While some of these titles demonstrated an impressive use of CD-ROM capacity, most did not. Many titles were nothing but shovelware—that is, dry facts, statistics, literary texts, and gratuitous video dumped onto a CD-ROM. Indeed, by early 1995, a serious shakeout in the CD-ROM market was already underway. According to PC Data, nearly 20% of CD-ROM titles sold 10 copies or fewer in December 1994. And 90% only sold one copy. Many companies couldn't even get their products on the shelf. According to Gistics, a consulting firm in Larkspur, CA, 96% of all multimedia software developers were unprofitable in 1994. In 1995 many of these companies scaled way back, were bought out, or closed their doors. High development costs, distribution problems, and low quality were the three main reasons for lack of profitability.

The Quality Issue

According to Mr. Perkins and Ms. Núñez, there are three types of CD-ROM titles that especially benefit from the enormous storage capacity and superb audio capabilities made possible by CD-ROM: early learning programs, reference works, and music appreciation titles. Early learning programs that effectively integrate text, animation, and audio work well and sell because parents and educators will pay for a product that younger children can use independently on the computer. And for children to use the program independently, the program must make extensive use of audio and graphics. The Living Books programs from Random House/Brøderbund, such as *Ruff's Bone* and *The Tortoise and the Hare*, are good examples of successful early learning programs.

Reference works also require a great deal of storage space, making them obvious candidates for CD-ROM. If publishers can incorporate quick and useful search mechanisms, as well as some illustrative graphics, animation, and audio, the result can be a highly useful and interesting reference work. Good examples of these include *The New Grolier Multimedia Encyclopedia* and the *Encarta Encyclopedia* from Microsoft.

CD-ROM has also created a new market for music appreciation programs. A program like *Multimedia Beethoven* lets consumers listen to Beethoven's Ninth Symphony, in its entirety, while getting expert running commentary in text form as they go. The CD-ROM also provides other background information on the composer and the piece as well as an illustrated course in important musical concepts.

CD-ROM and Gaming

Many game developers, like Rocket Science, Digital Pictures, and Crystal Dynamics, hoped to use CD-ROM capacity to integrate real video into the action. But even before these companies released any products, the multimedia software division at Media Vision released some video-laced game titles like *Critical Path* and *Quantum Gate*. These programs were criticized for lacking good gameplay dynamic—that is, too heavy on the gratuitous video and bells and whistles, and too light on interaction. In spite of rosy sales forecasts of 100,000 to 200,000 units for *Critical Path*, only 20,000 actually sold according to PC Data.

Other developers hoped they could somehow improve on Media Vision's offerings, so Rocket Science released *LoadStar*, Crystal Dynamics proffered *Off-World Interceptor*, and Digital Pictures came up with a children's program called *Kids On Site*. When reviewing these titles, THE HERRING game editors immediately realized that the extra capacity of the CD-ROM was filled up with a disproportionate amount of weak video—fluff before and after the games—at the expense of playability. As one editor put it, "It seems that game developers think if you put insultingly poor video in a marginal game, then somehow the whole will be greater than the sum of its parts. Not so." About both *LoadStar* and *Off-World*, the editors said, "We believe that game developers should stop trying to differentiate their games by production value and worry more about fundamental playability and depth." Meanwhile, *Kids On Site* was critiqued by Mr. Perkins and Ms. Núñez as too passive, with a lot of movies and limited activities (for example, children simply put three loads of dirt into a dump truck and they are done with that activity). At the moment, the verdict is still out on whether adding video to games will make these programs more attractive to consumers.

Pricing

Another important issue for CD-ROM is pricing. According to Nick Donatiello of Odyssey, a San Francisco research firm that specializes in new media, many CD-ROM publishers are building their long-range business models on price levels that might not last. Says Mr. Donatiello, "There's an assumption that the industry will increase in volume and at the same time stay at the current price level. History would indicate that this is not the way it works." With almost 2,000 titles now on the market, there is increasing competition for attention and shelf space. Prices will have to drop in the face of this kind of competition.

Furthermore the estimated $360 million CD-ROM market may be illusory, since most CD-ROMs aren't purchased but are given away with multimedia computers. According to Dataquest, of the 53.9 million CD-ROMs sold in 1994, about 66% were included with computers. Some computers came with as many as 50 CD-ROM titles. This means publishers are swallowing millions of unrecouped development dollars.

Compatibility Issues

According to Richard Zwetchkenbaum, research director of International Data Corporation, 5.8 million personal computers were shipped in the last quarter of 1994. About three-quarters of them came equipped with CD-ROM drives. Many of the computers were purchased by first-time buyers. These consumers also got to experience bugs, crashing, and incompatibility for the first time. And even experienced computer users had a tough time. For example, *Time* magazine (January 9, 1995) reported the case of the owner of a computer outlet who brought home a fully-configured multimedia PC (what he called a "Cadillac") to discover that only a dozen of his new collection of 45 CD-ROMs actually worked on his computer.

The problem was particularly acute on Windows systems, on which the top-selling home education CD-ROM for the holiday season, *The Lion King StoryBook* from Disney, also had the most problems. Disney pumped almost 300,000 of these CD-ROMs into outlets like Wal-Mart and K-Mart, and more than 200,000 were sold. But, according to a report in *The Wall Street Journal* (January 23, 1995), when Disney's expanded technical support lines opened the day after Christmas 1994 they were instantly overloaded with calls concerning serious technical problems with the *Lion King* CD-ROMs. In the wake of its re-release of the Lion King movie and pressed by the approach of Christmas, Disney had gone ahead and released the CD-ROM in spite of many known bugs in the program. And many consumers simply didn't have the required equipment, like 16-bit sound cards—a designation that did not mean anything to many new computer owners. These problems have not been limited to Disney alone; according to Paul Kagan Associates, the return rate on CD-ROM sales since Christmas 1994 already approaches 40%. According to Bishop Cheen, an analyst at the firm, "It's almost a crisis. If Saks Fifth Avenue had a return rate of 40%, they'd be out of business."

OUT**TAKES**

Peter Gabriel

Founder, Real World

Once the leader of the rock band *Genesis*, and now well known as an innovative performer, Peter Gabriel has always been interested in the inherent interactivity of the rock medium. Mr. Gabriel's company, Real World MultiMedia, published the critically acclaimed CD-ROM *Xplora*, which merges his music with the interactive qualities of CD-ROM to promote creative expression. During his distinguished career, his ten solo albums have sold 20 million copies worldwide, his album *SO* won a Grammy, and he wrote and produced the soundtrack for *The Last Temptation of Christ*. Mr. Gabriel is also the co-creator of the Real Experience theme park in Barcelona, Spain, and he co-founded WOMAD (The World of Music, Arts, and Dance), a series of festivals combining traditional and modern music and dance around the world.

BART NAGEL

How did you get involved in technology?

Over time, we just kept acquiring computer tools we could play around with and use to enhance photographs and music videos and things like that. I have always fancied myself a designer of experiences. Both the WOMAD festivals and the theme park we've been working on in Barcelona are examples of experiences you can create. So for me, learning how to implement technology in my work has been a slow process of experimenting with different ways to create new and interesting experiences for people.

STEPHEN LOVELL–DAVIS

Some would argue that CD-ROM technology is a rough medium—that it is difficult to leverage as an art form. How do you create a quality, satisfying experience for people with CD-ROM technology?

With *Xplora*, we tried to make the look and feel very pleasing. We used images of the earth, the sky, and some other elements to create a natural experience. *Xplora* is also designed to invite people into the experience and make them participants. Users can actually mix their own music, for example—which I think is going to become very popular. That's the great thing about interactivity; it allows us to step inside and work on the interior, instead of standing on the outside as an observer. But I would agree that CD-ROM technology still has certain limitations. I think it is only an intermediate technology until online fully develops. But we think a lot more can be done with CD-ROM technology, and we've only scratched the surface of its capability so far.

31

How do you think interactive technology will change the role of the artist?

Traditionally, the artist has been the final arbiter of his work. He delivered it and it stood on its own. In the interactive world, artists will also be suppliers of information and collage material, which people can either accept as is, or manipulate to create their own art. It's part of the shift from skill-based work to decision-making and editing work—where choice becomes as important as the actual construction of the piece of work. That's what's so exciting—the fluidity and flexibility of technology is a good complement to the human artistic spirit. In other societies, it's assumed that all people are born artists who can express themselves through visual art, music, and language.

Jeff Braun

Chairman and CEO, Maxis

As a kid growing up in Los Angeles, Jeff Braun was a toy nut. He loved anything that buzzed, flashed, beeped, roared, or had buttons. When people asked him in high school what he wanted to do when he grew up he replied, "It hasn't been invented yet." He "went bananas" when he saw his first calculator, and "lost it" when he played with his first personal computer. "It's sort of an addiction or a habit—I always want to play with the latest technology," Mr. Braun admits. After college, he moved to San Francisco and eventually met his future business partner, programmer Will Wright. In 1987 they founded Maxis.

Anne Knudsen

Since its founding, Maxis has achieved tremendous growth, leading to revenues of roughly $35 million in 1995. An interactive and learning software company, Maxis is known for its innovative simulation programs *SimCity Classic*, *SimEarth*, *SimAnt*, *A-Train*, *El-Fish*, *SimFarm*, and *SimCity 2000*. Maxis' first release, *SimCity*, broke the molds of both entertainment and learning software by providing a creative, open-ended "edutainment" experience that has resulted in millions of sales worldwide. New product releases include *SimTown*, *SimTower*, and *Widget Workshop*.

You've always had a special interest in technology, but what kind of machine is going to be necessary to make personal computers accessible to all those neophytes out there who have problems plugging in a toaster?

To me a true consumer personal computer is something like a car, Nintendo machine, Walkman, or VCR. My grandma should be able to use the device without going nuts. But even the VCR isn't what a consumer machine should be because you still see a lot of flashing "12:00"s, a sign that VCRs are still too

32

complicated to use. In the end, the consumer device that will win is the one the consumer prefers.

From a consumer standpoint, what is your vision for Maxis?
We wanted to build games that yuppies could play. People who use our software are more interested in experiencing something that doesn't talk down to them or require quick reflexes. We give people the opportunity to express their creativity through simulation. People can create their own life form, farm, city, or earth, and grow it and change it any way they want. We give them ownership. With our stuff, there's no right or wrong, good or bad, it just goes. It works because no one wants to be told what to do, I don't care how old a person is. We recognize that we have a whole generation of megalomaniacs, and we're going to use the computer to keep them intrigued.

What makes your product different from other types of software products?
The nice thing about focusing on simulations is we don't get knocked off. Most of our competitors who try to imitate what we do actually come up with very different products. They are distinct artistic expressions. It's dynamic, non-linear entertainment. It's not like the spreadsheet game, where people compete with you in a feature-by-feature dogfight.

02_DIGITAL
HOLLYWOOD

J. GARETT SHELDREW

Jurassic Park, Forrest Gump, The Mask, Terminator 2...the list of successful special effects movies goes on and on. But more than just special effects, these movies represent the convergence between Hollywood and digital technology—digital Hollywood. This joining of high-tech and classic pictures is not just becoming an integral part of movie-making, but also of TV and video production, and multimedia game-making—areas in which studios are increasingly getting involved. Digital Hollywood not only promises to deepen the impact of special effects, but some hope it might even alter the structure and economics of traditional Hollywood.

The Economics of Traditional Hollywood

Theater release movies are still making money for traditional Hollywood. In 1994 consumers in the United States spent $5 billion on movies. Yet theater movies are not the only profitable form of entertainment. In that same year, consumers also spent $5 billion on video games, $10 billion on videotape rentals, and $10 billion on recorded music.

Studios are more dependent than ever on blockbuster hits to make a profit. From 1992 through 1994, approximately eight films per year grossed more than $100 million in the domestic market. *Jurassic Park* alone made a cool $1 billion. On the international market, *The Flintstones*, *Forrest Gump*, and *Schindler's List* each pulled in more than $200 million in 1994. Yet almost half the revenues of most films typically derive from video rentals and pay-TV showings. Some companies have become very dependent on these revenues. Of the $480 million in cash flow at MCA in 1994, about $150 million to $200 million came from the home video release of *Jurassic Park*.

In addition to relying on critical revenues from video rental and pay-TV, the studios depend heavily on producing programs specifically for television. According to a report in *The Economist*, after movie bombs like *Geronimo* and *Last Action Hero*, Sony would have had to shut down its Columbia Pictures if it weren't for TV properties like *Wheel of Fortune* and *Jeopardy*.

At the same time, the cost of movie-making has soared. The average cost of making and marketing a movie jumped 15% in 1994, to $50.4 million. In 1995 overhead continued to escalate. The average cost of the negatives for a movie made by a Hollywood studio was $31 million. On top of that, another $29 million was paid for print making, marketing, and advertising. With overhead around $60 million, it's no surprise that two out of three Hollywood releases are financial flops. A studio's successful movies must gross upwards of $120 million to cover costs, pay off theater owners, and compensate for failed films. Of the 300 or so full-length features Hollywood turns out each year, only a dozen make it into nine figures.

It's no surprise that studios can experience wide swings in its fortunes. Paramount Pictures went from the top of the box-office hill (*Top Gun*) to the bottom (*1492: Conquest of Paradise*) in just a few years, before recovering in 1994 with *Forrest Gump*. The pretax operating income of MCA's film business tumbled from $200 million in 1993 to $130 million in 1994. Time Warner's film group had an excellent year in 1994, generating $565 million in pretax operating income on $5 billion in revenues. (By contrast, however, its music labels churned out $720 million in operating income on just $4 billion in revenue.)

Then there's the case of Sony. In 1989 it paid $3.5 billion to buy Columbia Pictures from Coca-Cola. Over the next five years, Sony pumped another $1 billion into the studio, but to no avail. Sony had to make a $2.7 billion write-off and absorb a $510 million fourth quarter loss—a total $3.2 billion charge—in 1994.

In 1995 another Japanese company, Pioneer Electronic, had to write off $90 million in two American film companies. Pioneer had a 41.2% stake in Carolco Pictures, an unprofitable movie studio, and a 50% stake in the home video distributor Live Entertainment. Pioneer had invested $170 million in the businesses. Although Carolco had hits such as *Basic Instinct*, *Total Recall*, and *Terminator 2*, it ran into trouble in 1994 with cost overruns on two other films, *Cutthroat Island* and *Show Girls*. In October 1994 Pioneer had to supply Carolco with $8 million in emergency financing after the film company ran out of money.

These economics also create an environment in which Hollywood outsiders like Sony, and Matsushita—which bought MCA in 1990 for $6.1 billion, then sold an 80% stake to Seagram for $5.7 billion in 1995—typically overpay for studios. Harold Vogel, an analyst with Cowen & Co. in New York and author of *Entertainment Industry Economics,* says, "People overpay for studios because they are overwhelmed by the glamour and want to hobnob with movie stars and go to the Oscars. And they think it is a better business than it really is."

In an attempt to increase the odds of producing hits, the studios have pumped up their output. The total number of pictures rated by the Classification and Rating Administration grew from 342 in 1983 to 608 in 1993. Most mainstream studios plan to increase their output even more in the coming years. The one exception is Disney, which in 1994 netted $1.1 billion on revenue of $8.5 billion—with filmed entertainment accounting for more than half of both earnings and sales. Because of Disney's hit rate, it doesn't need to increase the volume of its output. But most of Hollywood's top studios make only modest profits with a rate of return of only 8.7%, according to *Variety* magazine. Jonathan Taplin, the producer of *The Last Waltz* and other films, offers an explanation, "It's very simple: the inflation of production costs in movies is out of control."

Going Digital

Against this backdrop of escalating costs, some hope digital technology can help transform the economics of movie-making, leading to lower overhead and bigger profits.

Boss Film Studios is an award-winning visual effects studio with numerous movie and TV credits. Its CEO, Richard Edlund, told THE HERRING that filmmaking has changed so dramatically from its photochemistry days, that even going back to 1992 would mean a return to "the dark ages." The difference is that digital processes are far more central to the grammar of filmmaking. Sci-fi and action/adventure films are no longer the only ones using special effects. In *Forrest Gump*, for example, digital effects were used to make star Tom Hanks play superhuman Ping-Pong and shake hands with former American Presidents Lyndon Johnson and John F. Kennedy.

Given this trend, *The Economist* posits two ways in which some hope digital technology could turn Hollywood on its head. First, it could break the hold the unions have over staffing on a production set. Instead of using teams of carpenters, decorators, and electricians to build and light sets, entire scenes could be synthesized on the computer and then digitally composited with live-action shots of the actors playing their roles against a blue screen.

And second, digital designers could develop "virtual actors" with personalities and attitudes all their own. This might save on the huge salaries and royalties granted to top stars. Mel Gibson, for example, gets up to 15% of a movie's gross earnings, which can mean as much as $20 million in some cases. Kevin Costner's asking price is a straight $12 million. Sylvester Stallone gets $20 million.

At the lower end of the acting scale, one actor can be digitally duplicated, turning five extras into a stadium full of people, at a fraction of the cost of using real people. And some films have effectively combined the appeal of a human actor with the power of special effects, at a reasonable cost. New Line's *The Mask* was produced for less than $25 million but brought in $120 million. This assumes that the human actors' salaries are reasonable.

Then there are movies like *Casper* from Universal Studios, in which the stars are digital performers who talk and show emotion. The "lifelike" Casper the Friendly Ghost and his three obnoxious uncles—Stretch, Stinkie, and Fatso—appear to be more than mere animations (although each image of the characters was "painted" by an animator at a high-resolution Silicon Graphics workstation). The characters cast shadows and refract light and exhibit subtle facial impressions and body language. The ghosts are onscreen for 40 minutes, almost half the movie. Using this kind of technology, it's easy to foresee movies that will be somewhere in-between traditional animation and typical live-action productions.

But how realistic extensive cost-savings from technology are remains to be seen. Meanwhile, in some ways Hollywood is slow in catching up with the new technology precisely because of the human—not the digitized—element. Some aren't quite as optimistic about sudden transformations. Roger Stone, a developer and engineer-designer of digital studios, told THE HERRING, "Union biases die hard. Proprietary systems are big investments, and systems standards are set according to power politics, not reason. So much of Hollywood is the good-old-boy network that is impenetrable to new ideas."

In spite of this resistance, it is estimated that the independent digital studio industry is growing at a rate of 25–50% a year. Meanwhile, some forecast that movies using state-of-the-art digital techniques will cost only half as much to make as analog-based movies.

Technologies and Companies

A fact Hollywood can't ignore is that seven of the ten highest grossing films have been special effects films. And a very profitable movie, like *The Mask*, can be a big draw largely because of its effects. There's no question that movie-going audiences feel a strong attraction for the escapism of "synthetic reality."

But special effects production has come a long way since the days of the matte paintings and handmade creatures used by Industrial Light & Magic (ILM) in the original *Star Wars* trilogy. In fact, at the time, ILM had to invest in huge, expensive systems to create the desired effects: hulking animation cameras, room-filling optical printers, and enormous motion-control photography systems. Even in 1984, director James Cameron still used traditional animation techniques to make *The Terminator*. By 1991 when Mr. Cameron shot *Terminator 2: Judgment Day*, and introduced the liquid metal cyborg that played opposite Arnold Schwarzenegger, he was harnessing the new digital wizardry of ILM. Now ILM founder George Lucas looks forward to going even farther, with a kind of "virtual backlot," where everything will be computer-generated and all sets and props exist only in cyberspace.

Even now digital artists use computers to do much that used to be done with paint and props. Many of the production techniques and elements—graphics, simulated cel animation, 3D computer-generated imagery, lighting, digital painting, image processing, compositing, and editing, as well as music and sound effects—have moved down to the affordable, yet powerful desktop workstation.

In the process, the old style "black boxes" from companies like Quantel are giving way to what the techies describe as the "general purpose, programmable, resolution-independent, open architecture, white-box systems"—known to many as high-powered workstations. Quantel has dominated the black box market with a series of proprietary, hardware/software combinations, each designed with a specific purpose in the post-production process. But the workstations fast approach the old black boxes in terms of speed and capability. And they are considerably less expensive than many of the high-end black box alternatives.

One of the main suppliers of these workstations is Silicon Graphics (SGI), a company that originally sold image-processing computers to scientists and engineers in the mid-1980s and now does the same for movie producers. SGI's Indigo^2 Extreme workstation is a particularly flexible and powerful system that can produce images for a wide range of venues, including theatrical motion pictures, television, billboards, magazines, interactive multimedia, and large-format, location-based entertainment. One of these workstations partnered with Kodak's Cineon software yields a system capable of high-end digital film editing. This set-up rivals a black-box alternative such as Quantel's Domino product. Artists can also use the SGI Power Challenger to receive 3D image data over a computer network, render those images using the system's vast number-crunching resources, and send the final renderings back over the network to a production company or an independent artist.

To solidify its position in digital Hollywood, SGI has taken some major steps in recent years. It established a subsidiary, Silicon Studio, dedicated to providing a special environment for the creation of entertainment content; a service and support structure for the authoring community that includes collaboration and training; and a defined set of tools that will let filmmakers take original digital source material and repurpose it for CD-ROM, interactive TV, and location-based entertainment. It has opened up a training center in Santa Monica, CA, to be closer to the film industry operations in Hollywood.

SGI has also acquired two major digital media software companies, Alias Research and WAVEFRONT Technologies. Both companies offer 2D and 3D graphic design software that runs on SGI workstations. Alias specializes in rendering and special effects applications, and WAVEFRONT has excellent technology for compositing, especially the process of layering streams of video on top of each other.

SGI has contracted with DreamWorks SKG to develop a computer animation system named DAD (Digital Animation Dreammachine) for the DreamWorks Digital Studio. DAD will be developed in alliance with Cambridge Animation Systems, an animation software company based in Cambridge,

England. Silicon Studio markets DAD to the larger entertainment industry and ultimately expects a $1 billion market for the technology. SGI's arrangement with DreamWorks resembles the one it made with Industrial Light & Magic (ILM) in 1993 to create a production plant for the creation of digital imagery in entertainment. All the SGI tools are complementary: the systems developed for ILM are compatible with DAD.

Other companies that offer special effects software for desktop computer systems include the Microsoft-owned SOFTIMAGE, Adobe, and Autodesk.

In the $4 billion video and audio editing systems market, the "product retooling" shift from analog-based to digital-based systems has also opened up the market for a number of vendors providing leading-edge editing systems. Companies such as Avid Technology, Data Translation, and ImMIX have become leading suppliers of digital editing systems for industry professionals.

But the digital effects houses epitomize the new digital movie business—companies like ILM, Discreet Logic, Sony's Imageworks, Digital Domain, Rhythm & Hues, (Colossal) Pictures, Pacific Data Images, and R/GA Digital Studios.

Digital Domain was founded and is run by Scott Ross, the former head of ILM; Academy Award–winner Stan Winston; and James Cameron, the producer and director of *Terminator 2*, *The Abyss*, and *True Lies*. Like other digital studios, Digital Domain uses many of the technology tools from companies associated with digital Hollywood. It has SGI workstations using the SOFTIMAGE Digital Studio product line for animation work, Alias Research's PowerAnimator system for 3D modeling, Parallax Matadors for paint effects, Pixar's Renderman for rendering, and Discreet Logic's Flame for compositing, as well as some proprietary software tools of its own.

R/GA is another good example of a special effects company that has effectively employed digital technology in movie projects, such as *In the Line of Fire* and *The Shadow*, and in commercials for Diet Coke, Shell Oil, and Reebok. Rhythm & Hues, (Colossal) Pictures, and Pacific Data Images have worked on several movies, commercials, and music videos, and each company plans to produce games and theme park or location-based entertainment material.

Up to this point, the digital production studios have been 100% internally owned and have not used much outside capital. Instead they have financed themselves on a project-by-project basis. Generally they have not been seen as good investments by venture capitalists. Jim Breyer, a general partner with venture capital firm Accel Partners, summarizes many venture capitalists' thinking on this matter: "Many digital video editing studios and effects houses are unattractive because the Hollywood model is to throw a lot of money at producing content." Mr. Breyer sees this as being particularly true of those studios that want to make their own films. "The typical independent film company today sets out to raise $100 million to get started, which by definition puts them out of a venture capital firm's normal strike zone."

DreamWorks SKG

The promise of digital Hollywood in many ways is symbolized by the "new establishment" studio founded by Steven Spielberg, Jeffrey Katzenberg, and David Geffen—DreamWorks SKG. DreamWorks has five primary business sectors: film, animation, television, music, and interactive media.

To get DreamWorks started, Mr. Spielberg's Amblin Entertainment and Mr. Geffen's Geffen Films were folded into the new studio. Mr. Katzenberg runs the company, Mr. Geffen oversees financial matters, and Mr. Spielberg makes script decisions and directs. Other key figures on board include Ron Nelson, former COO of Paramount; Michael Montgomery, former treasurer at Walt Disney; and Helen Hahn, former Disney vice president.

Feudalism or Federalism?

As DreamWorks unfolds, will it operate in the style of Silicon Valley federalism or traditional studio feudalism?

Hollywood feudalism is characterized by the people with creative talent in and around the entertainment industry working for union wages. This is quite different from the Silicon Valley model, in which the people who provide the artistic value become partners in the enterprise and are rewarded accordingly. These rewards might take the form of better cuts of the revenue and profits and/or equity participation in the venture.

DreamWorks could operate in either a contract labor service environment or a product-development culture friendly to the talent. Mr. Spielberg has said, "I want to find ways to ensure that filmmakers, both established and new, are free to explore their art and share success. So many studios are about competition and talking behind backs and lying and double-dealing and gouging out the eyes of the artist."

DreamWorks intends to eventually employ more than 500 people, paying $40 million per annum in administrative costs and salaries. And the three founders plan to distribute shares in the company to all employees. Yet Mr. Spielberg also had his eye on a 75-acre property—the old Hughes Helicopter site in Playa del Rey where Howard Hughes built the *Spruce Goose*—as a site for a campus-like studio. While the other partners resist this kind of purchase, Mr. Spielberg still might get his wish for a customized lot complete with production facilities. One insider told *Vanity Fair*, "Steven wants to drive through his own studio gates," and that he is susceptible to "the glamour of a studio in the old-Hollywood sense of it."

Yet DreamWorks could out-maneuver older studios with their notoriously steep hierarchies, bloated staffs, and inefficient use of technology, by operating a "virtual studio," leasing soundstages and other facilities as needed. It might also benefit from using a flat business model typical of today's most competitive technology companies. This flexible structure, epitomized by the mighty Microsoft, fosters independent, project-based units, motivated by the team's success. Instead of trying to be everything to everybody,

ERIC WHITE

DreamWorks SKG's famous founders

DreamWorks could focus on its strengths—ideas, story development, talent, connections, and capital management—and farm out other work, such as special effects, to outside partners.

Capitalization and Partnerships

DreamWorks plans to release 24 live-action feature films by the year 2000. An estimated investment of $800 million to $900 million will be necessary before the films begin generating net cash. The music division will require an additional $25 million investment.

43

The studio anticipates that a significant piece of its revenues will come from animation, as Jeffrey Katzenberg will attempt to duplicate the success he had at Disney with animated movies and videos. But the first animated effort is not expected before Christmas 1998.

A major early investment in DreamWorks came from Paul Allen, co-founder of Microsoft. Mr. Allen agreed to invest $500 million to acquire an 18.3% stake in the studio. At the time of his investment, Mr. Allen told *The New York Times*, "I am on the board of the directors, I have a chance to work with three incredibly talented individuals who have a track-record of producing. Based on the business plan and everything that is part of it, I am very optimistic about the returns." Other investors with smaller stakes include Microsoft CEO Bill Gates, IBM, and Silicon Graphics.

To kickstart its TV franchise, DreamWorks formed an alliance with Capital Cities/ABC to develop TV content. Both sides plan to put up as much as $100 million as part of a seven-year pact, making it ABC's largest production investment. The two sides agree to evenly split any revenues their programs generate. The joint venture plans to air five prime-time series and four first-run syndicated shows by the year 2002.

DreamWorks has also reached an exclusive 10-year licensing agreement with Home Box Office (HBO). The deal calls for several films over the 10-year span of the agreement, beginning in 1996. HBO will pay an average license fee of about $10 million per movie. All the movies will be shown on HBO, after appearing first in movie theaters. Ultimately, the deal could yield $1 billion in revenue for DreamWorks.

Microsoft also got into the act by forming a software company with DreamWorks to produce interactive and multimedia entertainment products. Each partner initially invested $15 million in the venture, called DreamWorks Interactive. It is based in Los Angeles, where about two-thirds of the employees work, but has a sister development and production facility at Microsoft's headquarters in Redmond, WA. The initial focus is CD-ROM adventure games and interactive stories; the first titles will be available by Christmas 1996. Part of the plan is to develop interactive products based on films and television series produced by DreamWorks. The company expects to produce as many as two dozen titles a year. Like Rocket Science [see chapter 1], Dream-Works Interactive will employ talent from the software, animation, and film industries.

But the marriage of Hollywood and software companies has not always been a happy one. Strauss Zelnick, the former president of 20th Century Fox, joined video game maker Crystal Dynamics in mid-1993, intent on bringing Hollywood production glitz to game programming. Little more than a year later, after the disappointing rollout of its *Crash and Burn* title, Mr. Zelnick bolted. Another startup venture, Catapult Technologies, co-founded in March 1994 by a former Sony Pictures executive, Adam Grosser, and one of Silicon Valley's premier technicians, Steve Perlman, also ran into trouble within a year. The Viacom-backed Catapult developed a modem and online service that lets video game players use the telephone lines to play against each other from different locations live. But Mr. Perlman and another senior executive suddenly resigned. And then there's Da Vinci Time and Space, a startup dedicated to interactive television programming. One of its co-founders, the movie producer Jeff Apple (*In the Line of Fire*) also abruptly resigned and returned to the movie business after fewer than two years at Da Vinci.

OUT **TAKES**

Jeff Berg

CEO, International Creative Management

After spending a couple of hours getting the inside perspective from Jeff Berg, one of Hollywood's most powerful dealmakers, THE HERRING could see clearly that the 47-year-old head of International Creative Management (ICM) would not be satisfied until his firm is solidly on top. ICM is engaged in a fierce and often brutal battle with Creative Artists Agency (CAA) and The William Morris Agency to reign as the dominant talent and literary agency in the world. "The competition is constant and endless and doesn't bother me at all," Mr. Berg says. "I like being in the ring." But he also adds, "We respect our competitors."

Mr. Berg and his partners have built ICM into a global franchise that includes offices in Los Angeles, where most of its television and motion picture work is done; New York, where it has one of the largest literary agencies in the world; and London, where it is the largest agency in the U.K. ICM's client list of 2,500 writers, directors, and actors is stunning. To name a few: Arnold Schwarzenegger, Julia Roberts, Mel Gibson, Michelle Pfeiffer, Jodie Foster, Denzel Washington, Nick Nolte, Richard Gere, authors Colin Powell and Margaret Thatcher, director Spike Lee, and Joe Eszterhas, at $2 million a pop Hollywood's highest-paid screenwriter.

Talking with Mr. Berg in his gadget-filled office, it also became clear to THE HERRING that his agenda is to march his firm headfirst into the digital revolution. On his desk, stacks of CD-ROMs sit between movie scripts and contracts. "Jeff genuinely likes and uses technology," says Bill Block, ICM's other power agent focused on digital media. "I think this gives us an advantage over other agencies that try to court interactive content creators." Indeed, Mr. Berg proved extremely conversant on a wide range of technology subjects and business issues.

46

How is technology impacting the entertainment business today?

In production. In the pre-production process, everything from budgeting to storyboarding is handled on a computer. In post-production, if you use an Avid or Lightworks system, you can actually edit a film digitally. Technology has streamlined the whole moviemaking process tremendously. Over the long term, I think technology will have the most impact on the publishing and distribution side of entertainment. If you think about it, reformatting content has been a critical part of entertainment economics for years. It has been most pronounced in the music business in the last 20 years, where we have seen LPs, cartridges, cassettes, CDs, and now mini CDs. New delivery systems have constantly driven the music catalogue, and each title can be sold all over again. The same thing is now happening in film. Just 15 years ago, there was no such thing as home video. Movie cassettes now share shelf space with laser disks, and eventually we'll see online delivery. Technology will always provide artists with new outlets for their work.

With the growing impact of the cut-and-paste power of technology, however, the issue of who owns what content becomes increasingly cloudy. What are the rights of the creators?

I feel intellectual property is the private property of the authors and creators of the material, and as such, has to be subject to the laws and regulations of the market. Fundamentally, I am free-market oriented, but I don't think a developer's hard work should be subject to piracy.

So what is exactly is ICM's commitment to interactive media?

We have four people in the company devoted to this area, including Bill Block and me. We view software content as material delivered in digitized form, and we help the creators of this material, the designers and software developers, to license the rights to their work. We believe this is important because, if you think about it, CD-ROM, online, and interactive television technologies really have no purpose unless they deliver something of value. Something has to fill up those 500 channels. Interactive content creators, therefore, sit at the front of the value chain, and that's exactly where ICM likes to be. We focus on helping artists protect their intellectual property. We also bring together businesses that work on different aspects of interactive media.

03_THE INTERNET &
ONLINE SERVICES

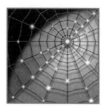

The hot new technology trends in 1995 were the Internet and online services linked to the Internet. Like interactive TV and CD-ROM before it, the Internet promises to be the next great new interactive medium that will open the way to mass consumer use and provide great prosperity for businesses and investors. Yet the question remains: what online path makes the most sense to consumers and businesses—direct Internet access or a subscription to a commercial online service?

At the end of 1994, the online services market represented a modest business of about $1.2 billion, driven by several national services, including America Online

(AOL), Prodigy, CompuServe, Delphi, and GEnie, with Microsoft Network (MSN) looming on the horizon. All were expanding their offerings to include shopping and information, and outfitting their interfaces with graphical browsers to make Internet access easier and more advertiser-friendly. Yet the services were still primarily communication rather than transaction environments, driven by electronic mail, information retrieval, and the ability to access chat forums.

Meanwhile the Internet boasted 20 to 30 million users, although the number of regular users, especially on the consumer side, was closer to 2 million. For the Internet to become a viable medium for a mass market, several issues have to be addressed, including improved data compression, security, search tools, and access speed.

The Internet

Beginning in 1969, the forerunner of the Internet, called the ARPAnet, was developed by two dozen engineers and scientists (a.k.a. Arpanauts) and funded by the Pentagon's Advanced Research Projects Agency (ARPA). Their mandate was to link distant computers into a national computer network system. One of their main achievements was developing packet-switching network technology so the ARPAnet could work like a phone network rather than like a mainframe system dependent on a single link [see chapter 7 for more information on computer networking]. In September 1969 a network between UCLA and SRI International was successfully forged. By 1971 more than 20 sites were hooked up; a year later the first electronic mail was sent. In 1988 the ARPAnet was officially decommissioned in favor of what is now known as the Internet.

Today's commercial and technical challenge is to complete the transformation of the Internet from an academic forum into a global service accessible and useful to mainstream businesses and consumers. Two major needs must be met for this to happen: infrastructure and applications.

The infrastructure needed includes those technologies necessary to make the Internet functional for the mainstream—access provision, security systems, browsers and interfaces, search engines, server software, pipelines, and hardware. Applications range from online commerce to news services and other content.

Many consumers and businesses access the Internet through a relatively newer part of the Net called the World Wide Web. The Web is a collection of linked onscreen documents (or pages) that provide information that can include words, pictures, audio snippets, and video clips. Clicking on highlighted words—which represent links to other Web pages—allows users to jump easily to related information, even if the computer (server) storing the data is many miles away. The Web lets general users and businesses bypass the arcane procedures of the Internet's older avenues, such as typing in long, abstruse commands, and allows them to more easily get to the information they want. Many businesses set up Web pages that offer packaged and frequently updated sets of information that users can regularly access.

Hardware, Access, and Interfaces

The first companies to profit from the Internet were the hardware providers—the makers of servers and connectivity devices, including industry stalwarts such as Cisco Systems, Hewlett-Packard, DEC, IBM, and Sun Microsystems.

The next wave of prosperity came to the Internet access providers, involving young companies like NETCOM, Performance Systems International (PSI), and UUNET Technologies. On the strength of the Internet trend, all these companies went public at good valuations. According to Forrester Research, in 1995 the revenues of access providers topped $125 million, up more than 40% from 1994.

NETCOM serves mostly individual users. PSI serves both organizations and individuals, offering a combination of hardware, software, and communications facilities that provides value-added services such as electronic mail and access to newsgroups, bulletin boards, and directory services. UUNET offers round-the-clock network support and World Wide Web services, security, a user interface, and training. Microsoft took a minority interest in UUNET to build and maintain an Internet link for the MSN.

Also out of the gate fast were browser companies such as Spry, Netscape, and Spyglass. A browser is a graphical, point-and-click navigational tool that makes it easier for non-technical users to move around the Internet, in particular the World Wide Web. CompuServe acquired Spry for an astounding $100 million as part of its Internet access plan. Spry sells Internet in a Box, a browser and Internet connection package. And Microsoft, AT&T, DEC, and IBM licensed the right to provide customers with the Spyglass Web browser.

The strategy of Netscape, another browser provider, is to create an installed base for the browser in the business market by offering it for low cost or no cost and then try to create feature-rich, higher-priced server software to sell to companies. On the consumer side, Netscape sells its browser as an off-the-shelf product.

Pipelines and Bandwidth

A big viability issue for Internet and interactive services is bandwidth—the combination of speed and data capacity required to carry online offerings. Downloading information into one's computer from an online source can be a slow process. Downloading one megabyte of data (roughly equal to eight million bits of data, or a full second's worth of uncompressed video) can take 4.6 *minutes* with a traditional telephone modem connection and 2.6 *seconds* with a cable-modem connection. There are also specialized phone lines that provide transmission speeds somewhere in between, such as integrated services digital network (ISDN) with a rate of 2.1 minutes for one megabyte, and the T1 phone circuit which has a rate of 5.2 seconds.

Cable companies have shown a special interest in becoming high-speed carriers of online services. Even the traditional coaxial cabling used for cable TV is good enough to reach a data transmission rate of 2.6 seconds or less. Until the telephone companies put fiber-optic cabling in place, a process expected to take several years, cable companies will have the edge in providing the pipeline for high-bandwidth data transmission.

One of the first definitive efforts by a cable company to deliver ultra-fast online services is @Home, a joint effort of Tele-Communications Inc. (TCI) and the venture capital firm Kleiner Perkins Caufield & Byers. @Home plans to build a network that can deliver at 10 million bits per second (about 1,000 times the speed of a traditional phone connection). Greater bandwidth also makes the online transmission and downloading of graphics and video more attractive to consumers. Using traditional phone lines, a single page of a catalog can take an entire minute to load, whereas the cable connection could display a whole catalog almost instantaneously. Besides providing access to the Internet and the World Wide Web, @Home would carry commercial online services such as Prodigy, AOL, and MSN.

For @Home to be feasible, the company must construct a nationwide communications data-artery known as a backbone, which connects high-speed long distance lines to high-speed wires in each local cable system. This process will have to include a digital switching system that provides a connection to the Internet and routes customer data. Locally, the cable that now goes into the TV set would be split. One branch would continue to the TV, and the other would go to a cable-modem hooked up to the PC.

The first cable-modems were around $600 each. Some analysts doubt consumers would spend that kind of money on hardware in addition to monthly fees. Intel, Motorola, and General Instrument are all working on cable-modems they hope to sell somewhere in the $100 to $150 range.

Search Engines

After e-mail, information retrieval is the most popular Internet application. While surfing the Net allows users to access information on a whim, the ability to perform deliberate searches are another matter. Effective search engines are an important part of the evolving infrastructure, especially if the Internet will have any value for businesses, schools, and libraries.

There are navigators providing a table of contents or index to the World Wide Web, functioning as a sort of Web untangler. These navigators include the Whole Internet Catalog, Yahoo! (a growing index with more than 30,000 entries), and the World Wide Web Virtual Library. Search services that let users scour the Net using key words including Lycos (from Carnegie-Mellon), WebCrawler, Gopher, and Archie. In addition, Wide Area Information Servers (W.A.I.S.) offers a full text-retrieval system for the Net. But none of these navigators or services has completely solved the search-and-retrieval puzzle for the Internet.

A next-generation search-and-retrieval text engine is needed. Companies like Con-Quest Software, InfoSeek, Personal Library Software, and Architext are actively trying to solve this puzzle. Their goal is to become the de facto standard for information retrieval on the Net and then to sell their tools to information providers and online services.

Architext, in particular, seems to have solved many of the key math problems necessary for the breakthrough development. Its software functions in a highly distributed (i.e. large network) environment, allows concept-based queries, and performs automatic hypertext linking to cross-referenced and group-related subjects and topics. The goal is to help users find the specific information they are looking for.

53

BART NAGEL

Clockwise from top left: Architext founders Mark Van Haren, Ryan McIntyre, Ben Lutch, Joe Kraus, Graham Spencer, and, hidden behind the couch, Martin Reinfried.

Security

Security is an important issue for online services and on the Internet, both for message and information exchange (e-mail, the sending of documents, etc.) and for any form of online commerce, especially those using credit card numbers.

Unless information is properly encrypted, it's an easy target for hackers when it moves from one system to another. And these types of attacks are especially hard to track, since they are generally "passive" attacks. (That is, the hacker merely eavesdrops on the "conversation" between the two systems, without taking or modifying anything.) This method is a great way for hackers to copy passwords and other valuable information.

While much has been made of how military and institutional computer systems need to be better secured from the prying eyes of hackers, little has been said of how this same lack of security will affect the prospects of online commerce. Many companies are setting up electronic shops on the Internet, trying to lure new customers with the ease of buying wares from their home computers. Will credit card numbers and electronic cash belonging to these consumers be safe?

Peter Neumann, principal scientist at SRI International, says, "There are probably no secure systems on the Internet. Some are just administered better than others and are harder to break into." The Computer Emergency Response Team reported that the Internet averaged more than six "security incidents" per day in 1994, nearly double the number in 1993. This pattern continued into 1995—in the week following the jailing of the notorious hacker Kevin Mitnick, there were 30 serious breaches of security on the Internet. Also in 1995 Citibank revealed that a Russian hacker had breached its computer system and illegally transferred $10 million to various bank accounts around the world.

Some of this activity has undoubtedly been stimulated by the fact that cracking algorithms, the programs for finding and collecting passwords (called sniffers and Trojan horses), and the basic tools for breaking and entering most online security systems have been posted on the Internet by hackers.

"With electronic commerce, the opportunities for fraud are on a potentially greater scale than they have been with traditional commerce," cautions Dr. Neumann. Proponents of electronic commerce argue that fraud exists in current forms of commerce as well. Credit card companies, for example, know they can expect a certain percentage of fraudulent charges, and keep reserves on hand for those cases. But Dr. Neumann says, "The loss could be significantly greater on the Internet." Credit card numbers need to be encrypted before transmission, so that if they are stolen they cannot be read. This is not easy to do.

Part of the problem is that the data encryption systems legally exported from the U.S. are not as secure as they could be, because the federal government limits the power of the systems to a level that the FBI and National Security Agency can crack. This law goes back to the Arms Export Control Act, enacted just after World War II, that put encryption codes on a national security list along with bombs and explosives. The fear is that without restrictions on encryption, criminals and terrorists could create unbreakable codes to hide plots from the authorities. Consequently, stronger encryption standards, like RSA Data Security's RC2 and RC4, which employ encryption key lengths over 52 bits (full-strength encryption), are generally not exportable. In fact, key lengths usually must be limited to 40 bits or under to be exportable.

In summer 1995, as if to highlight the problem, a hacker in France breached the encryption scheme of Internet access provider Netscape. Because of export restrictions on encryption, Netscape's overseas software uses only a 40-bit scheme, making it vulnerable to the hacker's attack. In the United States, Netscape employs a 128-bit encryption scheme, which is virtually uncrackable.

Then there is the need to prevent unauthorized access to computer systems. A hacker can break into a computer system by using a method known as Internet Protocol Spoofing (IPS). Spoofing takes advantage of an Internet design flaw that lets hackers fool computers into believing that a message is coming from a known or trusted computer. By pretending to communicate from a friendly computer, a hacker can sometimes take over an otherwise secure system. Spoofing allows hackers to easily bypass traditional firewalls, the secure gateways between private networks and the Internet.

Interestingly, computer experts have known about this Internet flaw for almost a decade. Little was done to guard against this type of intrusion because in the early days of the Internet, when this network of networks was used almost exclusively by scientists and other professionals, hacking was not a significant threat. Internet users by and large adhered to a protocol that scorned unauthorized entry into a colleague's system. With the Internet's popularization, this protocol has been increasingly violated. Consequently, there is a growing need to protect systems from unauthorized access.

Checkpoint Software Technologies, for example, has developed a firewall product that came under attack by a group of hackers. It repelled over 60,000 access attempts in one night and was never breached; yet such attempts highlight the growing threat. These security issues will have to be resolved before serious and secure online commerce can occur.

Online Commerce

An obvious question is: once the infrastructure is in place, what are businesses and consumers going to do with it? Many companies want to fill this void with a wide variety of services and content. Early offerings ranged from Virtual Vineyards (an online seller of fine wines) and FTD florists selling flowers, to electronic magazines and newspapers. Other attractive offerings include music and travel information.

In spite of the serious security issues described above, some analysts and entrepreneurs predict that online shopping will be the killer application of online. Some even envision strip malls in cyberspace.

Neil Blackley, an analyst with Goldman Sachs, points to the current electronic retailing market on television—home shopping channels and infomercials—as an indicator of the potential of online commerce. Revenues for television shopping in 1994 were $5 billion. Mr. Blackley believes an online offering, especially if it includes high-quality graphics and video, could be even more effective than the current television offerings. He anticipates greater timeliness (the ability to update information for the consumer by the second); a larger database of product information that the consumer can access (beyond what is being shown on a given infomercial or shopping network at the moment); search tools that will allow users to find whatever they want; and the ability to make payment online. Consumers may even be able to employ an intelligent agent search device to scour online malls for the products they desire.

Steve Reynolds, managing director of the Consumer New Media Practice at market research firm LINK Resources, agrees that the online market will eventually mimic infomercials: product will be offered, testimonies will be given, and orders accepted—all online. Putting this in place will take time. The challenge will be to avoid the great boondoggle of 1982—Videotex. Heavy hitters such as the TV networks, American Express, Warner Brothers, the Tribune Company, Times Mirror, *The New York Times*, Chase Manhattan, and AT&T joined forces to create this interactive system to deliver communications, entertainment, shopping, news, and education to the home via a special terminal hooked up to the television. According to Mr. Reynolds, "It got skunked," losing over $1 billion.

News Services and Publishing

The report on the traditional newspaper is a mixed story. Advertising revenues hit a record high in 1994, reaching $34.2 billion—up $2.3 billion or 7.25% from 1993, representing the largest percentage gain in eight years. Yet newspapers' share of all advertising dollars in the U.S. continued to shrink: 22.8% in 1994, down from 23.1% in 1993. The number of Americans who read newspapers also continued to shrink: 61.5% of all adults read a newspaper every day, compared with 77.6% in 1970. Weekday circulation of 9 of the 10 largest metropolitan newspapers, and that of *The Wall Street Journal*, has dropped. The cost of newsprint continued to go up, by as much as 40% in 1995. Declining circulation and advertising revenues and escalating costs have caused some newspapers to shut down or fold into the operations of cross-town rivals.

These trends have newspaper publishers running scared. In a quest to capture new readers and advertisers, many publishers have decided to go online. Of America's 1,500 newspapers, about 60 have developed electronic editions, and another 30 to 40 plan to offer services by the end of 1995. Newspapers and magazines pour more than $100 million a year into electronic editions. Some companies such as Knight-Ridder, publisher of *The San Jose Mercury News* and other papers, and Times Mirror, publisher of *The Los Angeles Times*, are hiring special reporters and editors—"digital journalists"—for the electronic editions of their publications. There are also online offerings for *The New York Times, The Wall Street Journal*, and *The Washington Post.* And eight of the largest newspaper publishers, including Hearst, Gannett, Cox, Knight-Ridder, and the Tribune Company, have formed a cooperative effort called the New Century Network designed to help local newspapers publish on the Internet.

Magazines such as *Newsweek* have also gotten into the act with online versions. And Condé Nast has developed its own Web site, CondéNet, designed to offer material from its 14 core magazines. Time Warner also has a Web site, Pathfinder, that features articles from *Sports Illustrated, Fortune, Time,* and other magazines, as well as the ability to order home videos from HBO. *Mr. Showbiz* is an electronic magazine specifically designed for online. It offers a mix of movie reviews, entertainment news, celebrity gossip, tabloid headlines, and chat forums.

The profitability of online news may prove elusive. Publishers face two questions: First, how do we get paid? Second, how do we protect our assets from getting stolen? Billing services will have to be developed that can charge by the number of printouts made, the time spent online, or the amount of information accessed. The protection of intellectual property becomes very difficult once information is digitized. Right now there is not much protection. Bob Ingle, vice president of new media at Knight-Ridder, has said, "We're all looking at losing money for a hell of a long time." Yet many publishers feel they have no choice. The fear is that aggressive Information Superhighway providers—like the cable and online service companies, the telcos, and even Microsoft—will grab readers and advertisers and further cut into the fortunes of newspaper publishers.

Will Hearst—editor and publisher of *The San Francisco Examiner* for 10 years, grandson of William Randolph Hearst, and now a general partner with the venture capital firm Kleiner Perkins Caufield & Byers—has a unique perspective on these issues. Coming from the publishing industry, Mr. Hearst is especially aware of the practical issues involved in online implementation. "It was all the issues that arose from trying to put the *Examiner* online," Mr. Hearst told THE HERRING, "that made me aware of the problems that need to be solved for this medium to work well as a publishing forum." He says, though, that "traditional print newspapers still make sense—they're portable, convenient, browsable, and cheap. CNN-on-demand might be more to the point. To be able to select the news broadcast clips you want when you want them and to skip the rest, would be truly useful."

Interprise Groupware

One form of online communication and publishing that could fill some lucrative niches is interprise groupware, the linking together of interrelated enterprises into online communities. A good example is Physicians Online, a collaborative network linking physicians to each other, and to several databases of medical information. It also offers a program for continuing education. The basic service is free to practicing physicians, but it charges for premium services and has paid advertising. Physicians Online built its subscriber base to 50,000 in one year, with corresponding revenues of $10 million.

Information Retrieval

Along with e-mail, information retrieval is the most popular use of the Internet. Yet unless one is an astronomer, a physicist, or a member of Physicians Online, it's not always obvious exactly what kind of useful information one can access on the Net. As hobbyist-skeptic Chris O'Malley put it, "It is fuzzy satellite weather maps, canned audio clips from the President, unfettered access to obscure college journals...the Internet is one big Gumpism: You never know what you're gonna get."

Even Vice President Al Gore's romantic notion about plugging every schoolchild into the Library of Congress to "explore a universe of knowledge, jumping from one subject to another" is a fairy tale. All of the Library's books would have to be digitized and made available on computer for this to happen—the Library has some thirty million records. Digitizing even a small fraction of these archives would be a huge and expensive task. Realistically, the best students can hope for is to see an online card catalog of the Library's holdings. But the Library of Congress doesn't lend books, so students would actually have to go there to read anything they were interested in!

Then there's the Usenet. The Usenet is home to the Internet's newsgroups, or online discussion forums, with topics ranging from every conceivable hobby to alternative lifestyles. Net surfers can also access the Congressional Record, the Shakespeare Homepage, the National Science Foundation server, and the Cheese Page (where one can view full-color pictures of cheeses from around the world).

These fragmented offerings, while amusing, show the need for more definitive content. Music is one possible killer application. As one analyst says, "It is browsable, salable, findable, and most importantly, entertaining." Other potentially attractive content could come from travel agencies, real estate firms, and investment firms, all supported by advertising. There's also the need to bring online business services to the Net. The old LEXIS-NEXIS legal information and news service could be updated and made available on the Internet.

Netscape

Netscape is a company building its whole business around the Internet. In addition to providing its Web browser to businesses, it also sells it retail for about $40 as the Netscape Navigator Personal Edition. It features one-button access to four Internet gateways: MCI, NETCOM, Portal, and UUNET.

Netscape also focuses on the back-end technology and services of the Net, including the server, software, billing and payment systems, database integration, and subscription management. It sells server versions of its Navigator to companies that offer Web sites. The company also sells technical support for each copy of this software. Netscape is banking on numerous content providers needing to use its product to provide access to the Web for information exchange and online commerce.

The attraction for the providers is that in this model a much larger share of the cash-flow goes to providers than if they work through a traditional online service. Providers also maintain direct access to their subscriber lists. Knowledge of subscriber demographics creates the opportunity both to target products and information more effectively and to garner paid advertising. Providers can also look forward to incorporating multimedia elements in their offerings, rather than being limited to the text and simple graphics found in some traditional online services.

In 1995 individuals and businesses paid anywhere from $30,000 to $200,000 to have Web sites designed, built, and maintained.

Online Services

While most entrepreneurs and investors are still waiting for big profits from the Internet, conventional online services aren't exactly amassing huge fortunes either. America Online (AOL), the fastest-growing service as of early 1995, earned only $6 million on $104 million in sales in 1994. CompuServe, a subsidiary of H&R Block, had more impressive profits—$102 million before taxes on sales of $429 million in 1994. But most of the profit came from business users rather than consumers. Prodigy, a joint venture of IBM and Sears, has been a big loser. The two companies together have poured more than $1 billion into it since 1984, and never made a profit until early 1995.

Traditionally, the conventional services have run their own kingdoms. Each creates and distributes the software customers use to log on and navigate online; each controls the computers customers dial into and the content they view. Each service hosts electronic bulletin boards and runs chat rooms and conference areas in which subscribers meet electronically. Each operates as an information aggregator that makes deals with content providers and publishers to offer their material on the service. The bulk of the revenue of online services comes from subscriber and usage fees.

Yet many consumers who log on soon log off. The churn rate—the number of subscribers who quit each year and must be replaced for an online service to stay even—is a big problem for all services. Jupiter Communications, a research firm specializing in the online services market, estimates the average churn rate for online services at more than 40% a year.

And the online industry is in flux. Various technologies and business models are colliding: consumer-oriented online services, value-added networks, corporate local-area networks and wide-area networks, the information retrieval business, and other components of the knowledge economy. Most conventional services are trying to hedge their bets by providing Internet access. In the midst of this flux, the two services attracting the most attention are AOL and the nascent Microsoft Network (MSN).

America Online

Steve Case, president and CEO of AOL, says he's primarily out to capture market share. Consequently, he's not concerned about AOL's small profits. The main thing, he contends, is to build a critical mass of subscribers and a powerful brand identity. As market share grows, profits will grow, he predicts.

Like others betting on this market, Mr. Case counts on his online service developing more offerings attractive to consumers. In THE HERRING, Mr. Case wrote that larger electronic markets will come about "by combining the medium's ability to distribute large volumes of detailed information with its intrinsic communications capabilities, and then link that with transaction capability."

Mr. Case also hopes to leverage multimedia. As he builds his digital franchise, Mr. Case sees the market as driven by four components: 1) breadth and depth of content; 2) the packaging and presentation of content with genuine visual appeal; 3) attractive pricing that is "simple, affordable, and predictable"; and 4) the creation of a sense of community online.

To push AOL forward, Mr. Case has organized the company into four divisions: America Online Services, its flagship online service; America Online Technologies, which develops and maintains the technology architecture that delivers the online offerings; AOL International, which seeks to bring AOL's products and services to the international markets, especially Europe and Japan; and the Internet Services Company (ISC), which manages AOL's Internet offerings.

AOL continues to bring in new content partners and make acquisitions to expand its business. A particular area of focus is the ISC. In fall 1994 AOL paid $30 million for BookLink Technologies, a company that makes Web-browsing software. In spring 1995 AOL acquired Global Network Navigator (GNN) for $11 million. GNN was the first major electronic publishing site on the Web, offering topics ranging from personal finance news to travel information. It organizes and catalogues the information in an easily navigated system, as a type of advertising-supported guidebook. GNN had 180,000 registered subscribers and 400,000 regular viewers. The GNN serves as an Internet-only offering for those not interested in subscribing to the traditional AOL service. Mr. Case describes it as his "second brand."

Microsoft Network

While companies like Netscape see the Internet as synonymous with the Information Superhighway, and in turn pooh-pooh the traditional online services as "walled cities," Russell Siegelman, general manager of online services at Microsoft, prefers to talk about "packager services," like Microsoft Network (MSN), that provide comfortable "gated communities" for subscribers who aren't necessarily interested in surfing the Net. And for those who want to access the Net, gateways in and out of these communities will still be available.

Yet MSN's strategy is not only to package services, but to develop content and software. MSN also serves as a platform for its own content and for that of third-party providers. The MSN software includes user interfaces, security, billing, and search tools. And to expand the online market, packagers like MSN will seek new sources of revenue in advertising and transactions.

MSN offers two tiers of service: a basic service that provides standard functions like e-mail; and an extended, à la carte service in which content providers set their prices, as in cable television, and consumers can pick and choose what they want.

Around the time of MSN's debut in 1995, Microsoft's chairman and CEO Bill Gates told THE HERRING:

The Microsoft Network is evolving into a branded community on the Internet. We are going to experiment with a number of very focused content services; some of them will be advertising supported, for some of them we will try to charge a subscription. This model is not unlike that being followed by other branded communities. And the proliferation of these communities is really quite amazing! Basically, we are seeing almost every magazine, TV channel, newspaper, newsletter, and other important information source putting their stuff up on the Net. And the competition to get people's attention on the Net will be incredible, and the competition for ad and subscription revenue will be pretty unbelievable. So over the next three to four years, we have no doubt that the level of investment required to be successful will *greatly* exceed the income that will be available for Internet services. It will therefore be imperative for publishers to be willing to take the long-term approach here, to continue investing in building a large community.

Steve Reynolds of LINK Resources, meanwhile, foresees a protracted price war as a result of MSN's entrance into the market. This puts pressure on the various providers to recognize their main revenue not from basic monthly fees, but from premium service, advertising, and transaction fees. The push will be to increase the volume of users, even as per-subscriber revenue falls.

OUT **TAKES**

John Doerr

General Partner
Kleiner Perkins Caufield & Byers

Although the return-on-investment (ROI) performance of venture capital funds is closely held, observers need not look too hard to figure out that Kleiner Perkins Caufield & Byers (KPCB) has experienced spectacular returns. As of 1995 KPCB had raised $961 million to help create 76 public companies out of the total of 240 privately-held companies they have invested in. As co-founder Tom Perkins put it, "Our companies have created hundreds of thousands of jobs and billions of dollars in wealth."

THE HERRING paid a visit to John Doerr, the KPCB partner who heads up the firm's investments in information technology, to tap into his thoughts about the emerging online services market. Mr. Doerr, who joined the firm in 1980, attained his stature by sponsoring the firm's investments in Compaq, Cypress Semiconductor, Intuit, Lotus, Sun Microsystems, Symantec, and Xilinx. Mr. Doerr has also invested in Netscape, the Internet browser and services company started by Silicon Graphics founder Jim Clark. "In five years, everyone will have an e-mail address," says Mr. Doerr, "This could be bigger than the PC revolution."

In what way do you expect the online revolution to help businesses prosper?
Smart companies will provide customers with both productivity tools and value-added services over the Internet. In the early 1980s the PC was driven by spreadsheets and word processing, and by lowering costs in businesses. But the killer online applications will lever the top line—helping us inform, sell, educate, entertain, inspire, even govern. At first, I thought Al Gore was nuts when he talked about information highways, on-ramps, off-ramps, and road-kill. But I was wrong. We can use online networks not just to lower costs but to improve communications and build communities.

What current opportunities are you looking at?

We are backing several vertical, online transaction ventures: MNI Interactive and its MusicNet for entertainment, Preview Media for travel, and Individual for business information [also, the @Home joint venture with TCI; see above]. But I also believe in the year 2000 the Internet could be decisive in who is elected President. It's a sea change. The network really is the computer. The Net may be as important as the microprocessor and the PC. That's why we are really, really excited and active in online education, entertainment, shopping, travel, financial services, health care, and the infrastructure hardware and software that will make it happen.

And in the future, all businesses will be using the Net?

That's what Netscape is all about—providing the tools businesses need to create their own services on the Net. I believe small businesses and individuals will run their own servers. If you're not on the Net, you're losing an advantage. Imagine conducting business without a fax machine.

Jim Clark

Chairman and Founder
Netscape Communications

THE HERRING first mentioned "The Internet Opportunity" in the April 1994 issue of the magazine, when Netscape Communications [then called Mosaic Communications] was barely two months old. At the time, Netscape founder Jim Clark

announced, "I have become convinced that the Internet *is* the Information Superhighway, and that Marc Andreessen's vision is right on."

Netscape emerged as a market leader, went public at an astounding valuation, and by fall 1995 boasted ten million customers. Thousands of small companies formed to build the browsers, servers, languages, programming tools, and services that transformed the Internet and World Wide Web into a booming commercial business.

As we all should have expected, Microsoft jumped into the game in a major way. Bill Gates stated, "The surging popularity of the Internet is the most important single development in the computer industry since the IBM PC was introduced in 1981. Like the PC, the Internet is a tidal wave. It will wash over the computer industry and many others, drowning those who don't learn to swim in its waves."

To get some more insight, THE HERRING asked Alex Serge Vieux, one of our founding editorial advisors, to interview Jim Clark.

Why do you think the Internet will be widely embraced as a new model to distribute content and software?

First of all, the Internet is low cost. We proved that by using the Internet to distribute our first product, and we built a customer base of ten million users in just about nine months. Our only expense was the engineering cost of making the program. There is no other distribution system in existence that would have allowed that. Currently, you have to pay money up front to distribute software either through conventional retail channels or through the large distributors that sell into corporations. On the Internet you don't need these intermediate distribution mechanisms. So we see this potential for low cost of distribution of any kind of intellectual property—whether it be software, or pictures, or movies, or CDs, or anything that can be represented as bits—as one of the most revolutionary aspects of the Internet.

It sounds as though this new distribution system means that out-of-the-garage software companies could essentially compete with huge, established companies, if they can come up with better, cheaper products.
Exactly. I know of a small company that has developed an office suite product that is compatible with Windows, competing with Microsoft Office, and its strategy is to sell this product over the Internet for $30 or $40, instead of the $400 Microsoft charges. When you consider that 70% of Microsoft's profits come from its Office suite, small companies, such as the one I am talking about, could potentially put real pressure on Microsoft's biggest revenue stream. And this is truly a threat for any big company. So the Internet as a new distribution model sort of disables the current distribution system, or bypasses it, and allows small companies to compete even with Microsoft in its core markets.

Does Netscape's own business model include any transaction fees, or will your revenues come solely from software license fees?
We think the idea that *anybody* should be allowed to charge a fee for every transaction over the Internet is absurd. We think that Microsoft, in trying to do that, is setting itself up for failure. It's just not going to be possible. It would be like paying France Télécom a percentage of a wire transfer over the telephone. That's ridiculous. The only way this could happen is if some company had an absolute monopoly on the Internet, and no one will, if we can help it.

Under this emerging Internet paradigm, what happens to the private online services such as AOL, CompuServe, Prodigy, and Delphi?
A lot of people think of these types of private networks as the future of data networking, and I think that is completely wrong. But if each of these online services becomes a site—an information aggregator—on the Internet; that is, using the Internet as a switch for users to get to their sites, then they could continue to do well. But the network is *not* equivalent to those services. It is my understanding that Bill Gates views the Microsoft Network in this way—as just another publishing community on the Net. I think he is smart to push the Microsoft Network in this direction.

Jerry Yang, David Filo, Tim Brady

Yahoo!

In 1995 Yahoo! had become the most popular directory on the World Wide Web. With over a dozen employees and financing from Sequoia Capital, Chief Yahoos

Jerry Yang and David Filo had gone from engineers to entrepreneurs. Tim Brady joined them as director of marketing.

Yahoo!'s value is obvious to anyone who's surfed the Web, because it categorizes and creates paths to all the pages fit to read. With some new sponsors, and a new look, Yahoo! has gone commercial. But the online services, and many Web-based directories, are also entering these waters. Yahoo! must sink or swim.

How did Yahoo! get started?

We jumped on Mosaic at the beginning of 1994. We wrote some software to combine our hot-lists. It started out as a collection of computer-related sites we were interested in—very much what the Web was designed for: to share documents with many people. Initially we collected some of the friskier, weirder sites on the Web, and it took off by word of mouth. We were in a unique situation in the summer of 1994 to experience that kind of grass-roots growth, fueled by a lot of interest that was not our doing, and then just sit back and watch access logs go up. I don't think that could happen today.

How will the advertising work?

We're committed to a free service, and we'll pay for it through sponsorship. It's going to involve learning to steal money away from the other advertising media, like TV and print. Companies aren't going to increase their ad budgets just because the Web's out there. It will stay the same, and we'll have to take a portion. We're charging $20,000 a month per advertiser, and those pages get around 250,000–300,000 hits a day. That's pretty conservative when Netscape's Platinum program is $40,000 a month and they aren't offering much more than we are.

67

What's the potential for advertising?

We have 13,000 categories at the moment and about 20,000 pages. But for right now, we're just going to sell five pages. We'll rotate them daily. We're taking a big risk by having five charter advertisers. We hope we can give them enough to satisfy their needs. Our next step is working on more context-sensitive ads. The more qualified a demographic we can provide, the better.

How will your users react to advertising?

We're very concerned about it. The increased download time may start to bother people. We're putting a lot of time into making the ads unobtrusive and interesting, and trying to intelligently integrate them. There has to be a separation between our content versus the advertising content. At least for the short term, unless this business model doesn't work, you won't see advertising inside the directory. There will be a section above it or it will be clear that it's commercially sponsored.

How do you see your product developing?

The goal, which is fairly modest, is to make the Internet intuitive for the user and to act as a starting point, not as an end. It's kind of a discovery experience. Our vision is to provide different ways of viewing that content, whether it's through hierarchy or through a search or through customization.

What do you see as your competitive advantage?

Primarily we're a brand. We're trying to promote the brand and build the product so that it has reliability, pizzazz, and credibility. The focus of all the business deals we are doing right now is not on revenues, but on our brand. Our strategic goals are to get advertising and get in front of every browser, in as many channels as we can. We want to build strategic relationships with two types of people: the ones who own the eyeballs—the online services, the PSIs, and the Netscapes of the world—and the content providers. A lot of the publishers realize they should be developing relationships with us. How we manage those content relationships is really the core of our business.

BART NAGEL

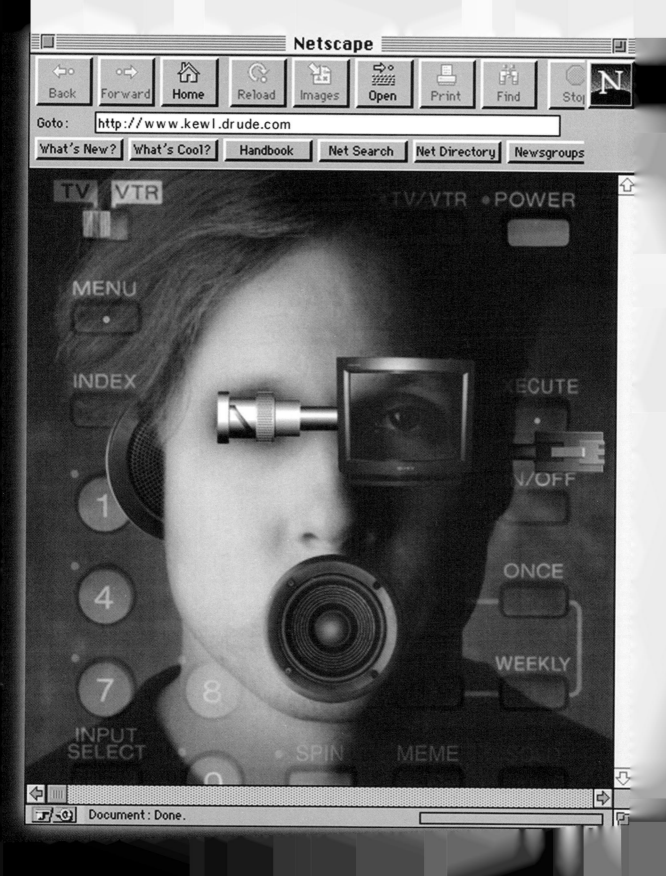

CKS|Partners

MARK KVAMME

Salomon Brothers

RAY LIGUORI & JACK GRUBMAN

FUTUREVISION

ROBERT SCHENA

IKONIC
INTERACTIVE, INC.

ROBERT MAY

VICE PRESIDENT AL GORE

DAVE CLAUSEN

REDGATE

TED LEONSIS

Ogilvy & Mather Direct

MARTIN NISENHOLTZ

POPPE TYSON

DAVE CARLICK

04_BUILDING THE
INFORMATION
SUPERHIGHWAY

The race to build the Information Superhighway (ISH) is on. Multibillion-dollar cable and telecommunications companies are scrambling to create the infrastructure that will become the ISH. But what form will it take? Will it be some kind of interactive TV (ITV) that will fulfill all the promises of video-on-demand, interactive shopping, and educational services, or will these be delivered to the personal computer over expanded versions of on-line services? Or will it be some combination of ITV and the PC?

Right now, the interactive services most often cited as auguring the birth of the ISH amount to little more than pay-per-view movies, additional voice communication services, and more home shopping channels. Beyond these, the ISH has only produced some interactive television trials and certain fledgling attempts at interactive advertising. It is too early to tell what other services and technologies will emerge, but this isn't preventing industry heavyweights from investing some serious money to find out.

Highway Builders

The first chapter of the ISH story considers whether cable companies will provide phone services or whether phone companies will provide content and cable services. Eventually the cable industry, the phone industry, satellite companies, and broadband wireless companies may all compete to provide interactive services.

Many of the existing services that will be part of the ISH are already very lucrative. Wired local telephone service brings in $88 billion annually, and revenue growth is 3–5% a year. Cellular services collect $11 billion annually, with revenue growth of 25–35% a year, and cable TV brings in $20 billion a year.

Cable Companies

Cable companies are consolidating their holdings. What was once a fragmented industry is coalescing into the hands of a few giant companies eager to build empires that will let them go head to head with telephone companies in the ISH race. The leaders in the cable race are Time Warner and Tele-Communications Inc. (TCI), both of which have been on massive acquisition sprees. At the end of the first quarter of 1995, each company served roughly one out of six cable subscribers in the United States. And both claimed to be the biggest cable provider. Other emerging titans that have snapped up properties include Comcast, Continental Cablevision, Cox Communications, and Cablevision Systems.

So far, this consolidation has resulted in regional empires formed through "clustering"—the grouping of cable services in a single region under the aegis of one cable provider. Clustering increases efficiency in marketing, advertising, and purchasing programs and equipment. It also offers a block of customers that can be sold phone services more easily. Alan Mutter, CEO of Intermedia Partners, a provider of cable services in the southeastern United States, said, "As business evolves from plain old cable TV to the new telecommunications services of the future, it's important for a cable company to have a large body of customers in a single region." Time Warner owns large clusters in New York, Florida, and

North Carolina. It also controls 33 clusters of 100,000 subscribers or more in other parts of the U.S. Time Warner's total subscriber base adds up to 11.5 million homes. TCI claims a subscriber base of 11.65 million.

As a potential impediment to growth, cable companies face the specter of competition from the regional Bell operating companies (RBOCs), and the regulation of cable rates. According to John Waller, chairman of Waller Capital, a broker of cable deals, the ISH race "will be a handful of cable companies competing against a handful of phone companies." The lure for these companies is the promise of controlling the pipelines that will send video, phone calls, and interactive services to America's homes. Commenting on competition with the RBOCs, Mr. Mutter of Intermedia says, "We're moving toward the telephone business, and they're moving in our direction."

And regulation has started to ease. Since most local cable companies already enjoy local monopolies, regulators have concluded that stringing together sets of adjacent monopolies presents no real threat to a free marketplace. Regulators also anticipate fierce regional competition between cable companies and RBOCs.

As cable companies compete with the RBOCs, one big hurdle they will have to jump over is a reputation for poor service. The Federal Communications Commission logs some 9,000 complaints per month from cable subscribers. Busy signals, service interruptions, unwanted "upgrades," and installation appointment no-shows have plagued the service offering of many cable companies.

Telecommunications Service Providers

The other big contenders in the ISH race are the telecommunication service providers—the RBOCs, as well as AT&T, Sprint, MCI, and GTE.

According to Jack Grubman and Raymond Liguori, telecommunications analysts at Salomon Brothers, the seven RBOCs—Ameritech, Pacific Telesis, BellSouth, Bell Atlantic, SBC Communications, and U S WEST—are already changing themselves from high-margin, monopolistic providers of regional telephone service to companies addressing larger market opportunities on the ISH. To pursue these opportunities, the RBOCs will need to acquire more customers (expand out of region), upgrade their networks to offer broadband services, and significantly increase their marketing efforts.

Some have already taken steps to expand their business offerings. In 1994 SBC Communications bought two cable systems that serve the Washington, DC, area, and in 1995 it won government approval to build consumer video networks in Massachusetts and Rhode Island. NYNEX has also formed a video consortium with Bell Atlantic and Pacific Telesis, called TELE-TV, designed to compete directly with cable and direct satellite companies by providing programming services to the home. They not only plan to offer programming that includes sports, news, games, and shopping, but also video-on-demand. They hope to reach over three million homes by the end of 1996. Pacific Telesis also acquired a wireless television company, Cross Country Wireless, for $175 million. Owning the company will let Pacific Telesis offer video services to five million customers before the end of 1996. And in a separate deal, Bell Atlantic has joined with NYNEX to invest $100 million in CAI Wireless Systems, another provider of wireless TV services.

CAI and Cross Country Wireless beam cable channels from transmission towers to special antennas on the rooftops of houses. The signal is then delivered through coaxial cable to the television set, where it is decoded by a converter box. Investment in this technology and the video consortium by the RBOCs signifies that they do not want to wait until they have sophisticated fiber-optic networks in every neighborhood before they break into the video market. The RBOCs have repeatedly pushed back their timetables for completing their fiber-optic networks. Bell Atlantic, in particular, has asked the FCC to disregard its application to offer video services to its customers over fiber-optic cables. The company said it wanted time to rethink its strategy for upgrading its networks.

In another kind of partnership, Sprint joined with cable companies TCI, Comcast, and Cox to form a venture that would offer both wireless and wired local telephone service. The objective is to marry local cable lines to Sprint's huge switching centers and long-distance network. The marketing of the local telephone services will be packaged with Sprint's long-distance services and each cable company's cable TV and video services. This venture is the first to offer combined local/long distance and telephone/cable/video services under a single brand name (Sprint), glued together by single switching architecture, with combined billing and customer service. Sprint owns 40% of the joint venture, TCI 30%, and Comcast and Cox each 15%. These companies also successfully completed a joint bid of $2.1 billion in the FCC broadband auctions for licenses in 29 metropolitan and regional markets [see chapter 5 on Wireless Communications & Mobile Computing for more detail].

Sprint and the cable companies have powerful incentives to make their partnerships work as they counter AT&T's strength, especially after its acquisition of McCaw Cellular (subsequently renamed AT&T Wireless), as well as compete with the RBOCs, which seek to add long distance and cable/video services to their offerings.

News Corp.

In many ways, Rupert Murdoch's News Corp. is the business model most of the ISH builders would like to follow. News Corp. is the first media empire to achieve globalization through its extensive distribution system, which includes a movie studio, broadcast station group, cable network, British and Asian satellite television services, and newspapers. According to Jessica Reif, entertainment analyst at Merrill Lynch, "The company has landed in its enviable strategic position as *the* global player, because Rupert Murdoch is capable of thinking in unconventional ways."

In America News Corp. owns and operates Fox TV and the Fox Children's Network as well as movie studio 20th Century Fox. It also owns *TV Guide*, the HarperCollins book publishing company, and *The New York Post*. In Mexico News Corp. has a production joint venture with the media powerhouse Grupo Televisa. In the U.K. News Corp. operates a satellite operation, BSkyB, and several newspapers, including *The Sun*, *The Times*, and *The Sunday Times*. In Germany News Corp. controls Vox, a cable channel that reaches 8% of all German TV households. In Asia News Corp. owns Star TV, a direct broadcast satellite operator, with a footprint that covers two-thirds of the world's population and 350 million TV households, as of 1994. Star TV provides both English- and local-language programming for sports, music, film, and general entertainment shows targeted especially at India, Taiwan, Indonesia, and the Philippines. News Corp. also has a joint venture with Australian Telecom to deliver pay TV via satellite and wireless cable.

Time Warner is the only other major media company as diversified as News Corp., but it does not have comparable global distribution channels. Viacom and Disney have focused on being content providers on the ISH rather than owners of infrastructure, although Disney's $19 billion acquisition of Capital Cities/ABC makes it a far more serious ISH player than it used to be.

Even with its distribution advantage, News Corp. is far from having a lock on all the markets and sectors in which it has a strong presence. Fred Moran, an analyst with Salomon Brothers, believes that News Corp.'s BSkyB satellite operation in the U.K. will face serious competition from various cable/telephone hybrid operations that will offer better technology and more attractive programming packages.

Interactive Television

The ISH conduit that many are hoping for and banking on is interactive TV (ITV). Proponents of ITV argue that to make the ISH truly compelling for a mass market, it has to effectively deliver content that includes video and audio as well as text. Compared to TV, the Internet and the PC are considered lacking in the delivery of quality video and audio.

Advocates of ITV such as Robert May, president and CEO of Ikonic Interactive, a company that has developed user interfaces for ITV, and Robert Schena, president of FutureVision of America, an information provider for ITV, like to point to TV's superior installed base compared to that of PCs: 89 million or 97% of the homes in the United States have TVs; television cabling runs past 95% of the U.S. households with TV; more than 60% of TV households are connected to a high-bandwidth coaxial cable capable of delivering high quality video. This is in contrast to an installed base of approximately 15 million multimedia capable computers. The estimated market for ITV is said to be somewhere between $6 billion and $12 billion.

The Content

Proponents of ITV envision the repurposing of all forms of information for the medium. Game shows will invite viewers to play along, sporting events will offer sidebar explanations of rules and allow users to purchase team memorabilia at the touch of a button. And video-on-demand will allow users to scroll through menus of movies and television programs, stocked and updated by various vendors. Pushing a remote control button will call a movie to the screen and automatically bill the viewer. Armchair video shopping will also emerge, offering a whole range of consumer products and services.

Industry consensus says "content is king." This is why U S WEST paid $2.5 billion for access to Time Warner's video library, and paid $1.2 billion for access to the video libraries of Viacom and Paramount. Three other RBOCs—Ameritech, SBC Communications, and BellSouth—cut a $500 million deal with Disney to create and deliver entertainment and interactive programming over the RBOC pipelines. Later in 1995, GTE also joined the consortium. Cable channels are eager for new content as well, as shown by the exclusive 10-year licensing agreement Home Box Office (HBO) has with DreamWorks SKG. It calls for several films over the 10-year span of the agreement, and requires HBO to pay an average license fee of about $10 million per movie.

The Economics

But is there really a market for ITV? "To believe is to be happy, to doubt is to be wise," is an old saying that might apply. The economic feasibility of ITV is far from certain.

Take the case of ITV pioneer Interactive Network (IN). Despite a cash infusion of $42 million in 1994 from backers like TCI, NBC, Motorola, and Sprint, IN had to delay the roll-out of its new subscription-based, play-along television service, cut its workforce by 17%, and see its president and COO, Peter Sealey, resign after only nine months at the company. IN operates in four markets—the San Francisco Bay Area, Sacramento, Chicago, and South Bend—but has only 5,000 subscribers. IN hoped to improve its prospects by no longer manufacturing its own hardware and instead folding its services into set-top boxes provided by TCI and others. Despite IN's problems, Thomas Weigman, Sprint's president of Multimedia Strategic Services, said, "It is obvious to us that Interactive Network is the leader in play-along interactivity in the home, and it is a virtual certainty that residential interactive services will be a significant market in the 1990s." IN had to declare bankruptcy in 1995.

And the question remains: what will people use interactive TV for anyway? The "killer app" most often cited is video-on-demand, allowing consumers to see a film whenever they want it without paying extra or making a trip to the video store. ITV vendors like to talk about people rewinding a baseball game to see the homer again, or watching an HBO movie they'd like to see whenever they want to, or downloading *NYPD Blue* to watch it at any time. Yet these advantages are already available with a VCR. And many are skeptical of the economics of ITV. Bill Gates says, "People talk about video-on-demand because it's one of the few things in multimedia for which you can predict a revenue stream. But it won't generate enough revenue to pay for the infrastructure." And it is not necessarily accurate to forecast revenue using the current video rental market as a model; of its $12 billion in annual revenues, some $3–$4 billion comes from penalties for late returns, a source of income that would not necessarily be accessible to ITV providers. According to one financial projection, a successful nationwide video-on-demand service for the United States would need to generate as much as $20 per week per subscriber to provide a reasonable return on investment over a ten-year period. This would mean persuading each family to watch five or six films a week, thereby spending four times more on video-on-demand than they spend now subscribing to cable TV.

The Technical Challenges of the Delivery System

Some important technical challenges must also be faced to implement ITV. Systems that can effectively store, transport, and organize video, voice, and other data must be developed to deliver content to ITV households. Digital compression technology (the ability to squeeze lots of data into a small information package) will be essential to any ITV system. No one has yet built a video server that can economically deliver the necessary ITV content. Companies such as Digital Equipment, IBM, and Intel have tried but have not succeeded. Some companies have made claims that their servers can send video signals to somewhere between 30,000 or 50,000 homes at once, but this has not been publicly demonstrated.

Meanwhile numerous ITV trials have occurred around North America. Most of these experiments have been joint efforts, involving RBOCs, telcos, as well as hardware, software, and content companies. In Omaha, NE, U S WEST teamed up with Scientific-Atlanta and DEC to try to bring ITV services to 60,000 subscribers. Similar partnerships have attempted to implement ITV trials in Richardson, TX; Rochester, NY; Canada; and a number of midwestern communities.

Most of these trials ran up against some kind of technical snag. Bell Atlantic announced in August 1994 that its $11 billion effort to build an advanced video network over the next five years had been delayed by technical problems and pricing differences with its main equipment provider, AT&T. About the same time, Time Warner announced that its 3,000-home trial in Orlando, FL, would be delayed because of technical difficulties encountered by its partner Silicon Graphics. Insiders say that the boxes Silicon Graphics made for the Orlando trial each cost several thousand dollars to manufacture and are only a little less complex than some of the company's workstations. Most of the technical problems still wait to be solved, and many trials have closed down without fanfare.

In August 1995 U S WEST formally announced the end of its experiment with ITV. John O'Farrell, president of U S WEST Interactive Services Group, said, "The technology to create two-way television and sophisticated programming production is years away, and more expensive than we originally thought." In fact most of the RBOCs have scaled back their ITV plans, focusing instead on traditional cable-TV opportunities, as well as defending their hold on local phone service against potential competitors.

Interactive Advertising

When THE HERRING first considered digging into the world of interactive advertising in the last quarter of 1994, our intuition told us that it was too early in the game to be interesting. Then we read a rather bold comment made by Intel's vice president for corporate development, Avram Miller: "Advertising is probably going to be the killer app for the information highway." When the smoke cleared, we found that interactive advertising was indeed seen as one of the main promises of the ISH. We found that some advertising firms, such as CKS Partners and Redgate Communications, have already committed to interactive media and see it as key to their strategy. Other firms, such as Ogilvy & Mather and Bozell, Jacobs, Kenon, & Eckhardt, have created special divisions to explore interactive advertising opportunities.

Companies and advertisers hope that interactive media will let them reach consumers through entirely new avenues of communication, where users can experience interactive advertising and directly order products and services. The two most talked-about venues for interactive advertising are Web sites on the Internet [see chapter 3 for more detail] and ITV. Other vehicles include on-demand fax, CD-ROM (which stores and delivers video, audio, and animation along with text), and private networks via satellites.

Companies and Strategies

Two young companies that epitomize the pursuit of the emerging opportunities in interactive marketing are Redgate Communications and CKS Partners.

Redgate is a new media company that merged with America Online (AOL) in 1994 and is now a subsidiary of AOL. Redgate manages multimedia databases and delivers advertising and sales content via CD-ROM, cable, fax, satellite networks and other means. Redgate developed some of the first shopping catalogs delivered on CD-ROM. It also pioneered the use of video press releases as part of Interactive Information Networks (INN), its joint operation with Electronic Data Systems. The goal, according to Redgate founder Ted Leonsis, is to provide new media advertising that is "highly targeted, personal, and granular."

Whenever Redgate is hired by a client, it first performs a content and new media audit, analyzing the state of the company's advertising, marketing, and technical content. The goal is to come up with recommendations to create specific, interactive, and customized ways for clients to connect with their primary target audiences. Redgate advises clients to set up a special database system where they can digitize their content and prepare it for delivery on various media such as CD-ROM, online services, and eventually, ITV. This system makes clients more accountable because it requires daily updating, response-tracking, and regular dialogue with the customer.

Redgate also wants to help clients develop interactive shopping environments. For this service, it will ask for "a piece of the rock"—Redgate will forgo the production fee in exchange for a share of the income stream generated by the product.

CKS Partners of Cupertino, CA, described by *The Wall Street Journal* as "the ad agency of the future," provides a wide range of interactive services for its clients. On the low end, it produces CD-ROMs that deliver information about a company's products or services. CKS considers CD-ROM the low end because CD-ROM offers a fixed and one-way interaction—there is no way for users to get more information from the technology after they have viewed everything on the CD-ROM. On the higher end, it offers services within online environments. On one level, they can create an electronic forum for their clients within an existing online environment like AOL or the Internet. Clients can go in and change and update the information on the forum at any time. Another level of service is where clients actually have live operators standing by, monitoring the online activity and helping customers navigate to the information they need. CKS foresees a third level that will incorporate interactive videoconferencing between company and customer. To increase its resources for growth, CKS has formed a strategic partnership with The Interpublic Group, the second-largest advertising agency holding company in the world.

Which Strategy?

In spite of the discussion about lucrative cable and telephone services, and the promise of ITV and interactive advertising, Ken Leon, a communications analyst with Lehman Brothers, believes that most of the ISH builders are pursuing the wrong strategies. Rather than flirting with video-on-demand and other TV services, Mr. Leon thinks that telecommunications companies should be building online services to compete with America Online, CompuServe, Microsoft Network, etc. Because of the low barriers to entry in the online services market and the tremendous technical, marketing, and financial resources of telecommunications companies, they could dominate the online market.

Even mighty Microsoft does not have the nationwide distribution plant or broadband capability of an AT&T or a Sprint. The telcos, including the RBOCs, also have impressive brand identities associated with quality, service, and reliability. For some of the database content, the telcos could subcontract to news services, advertising firms, and specialized vendors. They could also build state-of-the-art networks from scratch for interactive multimedia, rather than trying to upgrade existing systems or build on top of other operating systems.

Meanwhile, during the rest of the 1990s, it will cost GTE and the RBOCs $150 billion to roll out the broadband networks necessary to provide next-generation video services—while the market penetration of cable services is starting to slip— from 64.5% in 1993 to 62.8% in 1994. In contrast, online services are just getting started, with fewer than 5% of households hooked up as of early 1995, leaving lots of room for market growth.

The main telco exception is MCI. Like its cousin, Deutsche Telekom, Germany's dominant telecommunications service company, it recognizes the potential for online information and interactive services. MCI's networkMCI program was the first integrated information and communications services package offered by a telephony network. The product integrates electronic mail, Internet access, and fax services without resorting to dependence on outside vendors and is marketed under the widely recognized MCI name.

AT&T and Ameritech have also made forays into online services, but in a less coherent fashion than MCI. AT&T has a stake in four unrelated online services: Interchange, PersonalLink, ImagiNation Network, and Multex Systems. Interchange offers content owners like Washington Post, Reuters, and Grolier Publishing an online publishing forum. PersonalLink is a messaging system developed by General Magic that is designed to gather news and shopping information based on the preferences of individual users. ImagiNation Network is an entertainment service that features chat lines, games, and educational information. Multex Systems has partnered with AT&T to sell an online publishing system that helps financial service firms to electronically distribute research reports as they become available. AT&T announced in August 1995 that it intended to offer Internet access service, but the announcement contained very few specifics and no detailed timetable.

The RBOC Ameritech also has disparate holdings in online services. It has an equity position in Peapod, an electronic shopping service for groceries and other products available to 10,000 customers in the Chicago and San Francisco areas. It has partnered with Random House Publishing to invest in Worldview, an online travel and entertainment guide. Ameritech has also acquired SecurityLink, a company that provides an online security monitoring system, and has invested $472 million in an alliance with General Electric to develop and market electronic commerce programs on a worldwide basis.

But these services, according to Mr. Leon, do not add up to the full-fledged online strategy he thinks the telcos ought to pursue. He thinks the cable companies are not pursuing the right ISH strategy either. If the telcos are making a mistake chasing the TV business, the cable companies are equally mistaken in their pursuit of phone business, as exhibited in the alliance of TCI/Cox/Comcast and Sprint and Time Warner's alliance with U S WEST. Instead of entering the already crowded and competitive field of telephony, cable companies should leverage their resources to enter the far less competitive field of online services. The best ISH strategy, says Mr. Leon, is to begin with hypertext databases like those of the current online services, then evolve to video programming capability later down the line.

OUT **TAKES**

Where is the Information Superhighway going? Convinced that consumers want a whole array of services like news, games, home shopping, video-on-demand, and mail delivered electronically to their homes, technology heavyweights are casting about for a system to make the Information Superhighway a reality for many Americans. So far there are two "naturals" that could serve as receptacles for these information services: the PC and the TV—a choice that's been described as "the den or the living room."

Some are betting that interactive TV (ITV) will be the medium of choice. The assumption is that most consumers are already comfortable with TV, so the challenge is to develop a set-top controller (a cable-converter box that sits atop the TV) that will deliver all the services that American consumers are supposedly dying to get. Others, like IBM, Microsoft, and TCI, are hedging their bets, hoping to get a big chunk of either the PC or TV version of the Information Superhighway or both.

THE RED HERRING talked to two industry luminaries to get their perspectives on the building of the Information Superhighway, Don Valentine of the venture capital firm Sequoia Capital, and Bill Gates, chairman and CEO of Microsoft.

83

Donald Valentine

Managing Partner, Sequoia Capital

ANNE KNUDSEN

Since the venture capital firm Sequoia Capital was founded in 1972, it has provided funding for over 200 companies, including Apple, LSI Logic, Electronic Arts, Radius, Cypress Semiconductor, Oracle, Cisco, and more recently, C-Cube, a manufacturer of video compression chips that could serve as an important technical component in building the Information Superhighway.

Will the PC or the TV be the primary communications device of the future?

I have stated on the record, along with Andy Grove [CEO of Intel], who has perhaps, more self-serving reasons for his opinion, and George Gilder, who may also have book-publishing-related incentives behind his position, that the PC will be the primary communications device, *not* the TV with the pizza box sitting on top. The PC is the established interactive product today, and has been in the home for a long time. And the evidence suggests that interactive people *like* to use their PCs, and they are generally *not* television watchers. Converting television watchers into interactive players who will want to change the ending of movies and play interactive games is pure *2001* fantasy. HAL will have to be there verbalizing how to operate the interactive TV set before the couch potatoes in Des Moines, IA, will learn how to use it.

And while the press and the White House may have just recently discovered the Internet, it has also been around a long time and has a large and growing number of users. So the highway exists, the interactive product exists, and millions of people are happily operating on the information highway today.

So you are wondering if there will ever be a market for an ITV set-top box?
If you really look at it, the TCIs and Time Warners have all pushed out their target dates for their ITV services. The trials have been a disaster. I don't know when anybody is going to figure it out. With my satellite hook-up at home, I have had 500 channels for ten years, and there's nothing to watch! So when you eventually have all this whiz-bang interactive stuff in place, what are people going to watch?

How about using your television to video-conference with your mom?
No, I don't think that will happen. We will have voice command and control of PCs before we have a television that is interactive for the traditional television watcher. Traditional television viewers watch four or five hours of 30-minute, commercial-intensive network programs every night from 6:00 PM to 11:00 PM. I don't think these people could be easily trained to use a digital television, *if* there is ever such a thing.

William H. Gates

Chairman and CEO
Microsoft Corporation

Jim Clark of Netscape Communications likes to say that the Internet is the Information Superhighway. But the Internet does have at least one big limitation—its lack of affordable bandwidth. If the Internet is to be a viable alternative to interactive TV, how should this problem be addressed?

Currently, the personal computer is being hooked up over a narrowband telephone structure, which does have a lot of shortcomings. We are big believers in the move to midband technologies, which covers both ISDN (integrated services digital network) and PC cable-modems [see chapter 3 for more details]. Both technologies have been much maligned for their high prices. But I say with confidence that the infrastructure companies—the cable and TV companies—will be providing these services for around $20 a month. Once these technologies come into play, users will benefit from a data-rate almost ten times greater than what's currently available. So we'll move from the narrowband world, where text comes across at an excellent speed and pictures come across at an adequate speed, to the midband world, where pictures come across at a great speed and video comes across with an adequate quality—at least good enough to do videoconferencing.

What about movies on demand?
I don't think that content such as movies and rich educational experiences will really be available until we move into the full broadband generation, which will take a number of years. But on a business-to-business basis, video capability should be affordable within two to four years.

Will the telecommunications business be unsettled by Internet companies providing users with unlimited access, even to other countries, without charging for long-distance phone calls?
I think the unspoken, underlying assumption is that communication is

85

costly and that it should be billed on the basis of time and distance. But government-sanctioned monopolies and other governmental involvement around the world have driven this cost basis. The beauty of the Internet is that it challenges these assumptions. The price paid by a corporation to connect to the Internet is determined by the size of its "on-ramp," not by how much the connection is actually used. Usage isn't even metered, and it doesn't matter if you connect to information stored nearby or halfway around the globe. The Internet is growing so quickly that the latest, least-expensive technology is being incorporated into it as rapidly as possible. Telecommunications switches installed a few months ago to keep the Internet running didn't even exist a year ago. Internet providers lease communications lines on a commodity bid basis, which continues to drive prices down. In short, the Internet is the only public network of which the economics reflect the latest advances in communications technology and the full benefits of competition. It isn't happpenstance that the Internet's World Wide Web became popular now instead of a few years ago. If millions of people had tried retrieving graphics across the Internet at the beginning of the decade, the overtaxed system would have smoked out of existence. It's right on the edge, as it is.

86

Will Sir Bill conquer the Information Superhighway?

With the emergence of the Internet, is the vision of the Information Super-highway finally coming clearly into focus?

Well, we don't really like to use the term "highway," because it suggests that the government should build it, which is certainly not necessary. It also suggests that everyone will be going to the same place, which is really the opposite of what the Internet achieves. It is more about people going wherever they want. Highway also implies traffic jams and a sense of distance, which is also opposite of what we have here. What we have is a revolution in communications—the ability to find people with common interests and share common tools and common interfaces. And for Microsoft, the beauty of this revolution is that it will drive PC usage to a new level, particularly in the home.

BART NAGEL

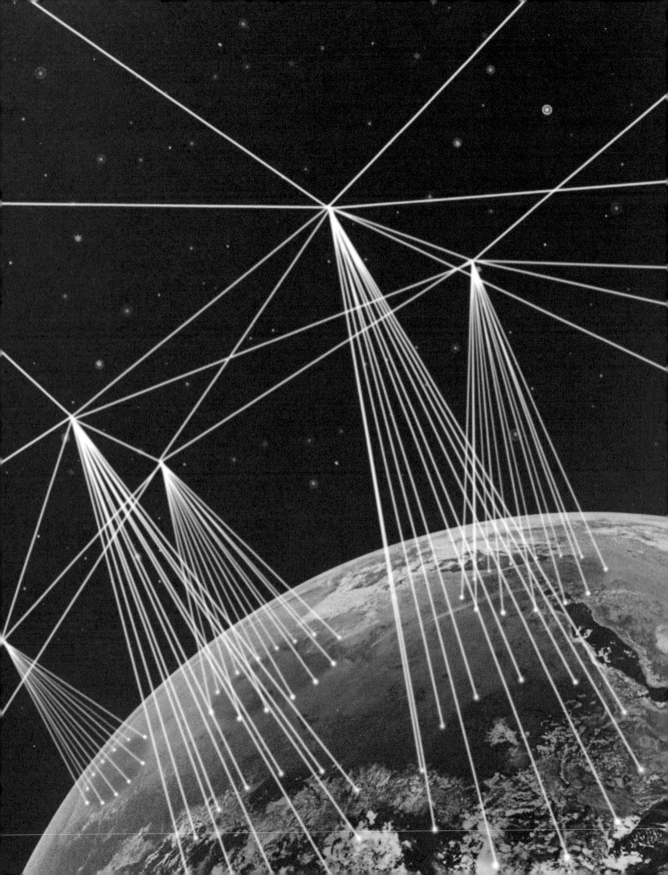

05_WIRELESS COMMUNICATIONS & MOBILE COMPUTING

STEVE CURLEY

Wireless communications and mobile computing offer a panorama of services and technology that includes cellular phones, paging devices, wireless fax, mobile radio, personal communicators, and satellites. Two important questions emerge: how viable are these various technologies, and how big is the wireless market?

Until three years ago, the wireless industry was largely synonymous with cellular telephone services. Commercial cellular services were introduced in 1983, and over a 10-year period grew to a market of approximately 19 million users. By 1995 the market had grown to 25 million customers.

Yet the cost of equipment and services has continued to make cellular unaffordable for the mass consumer market, and cellular providers have yet to make a profit.

In addition to cellular, developers, investors, and consumers face with a bewildering array of acronyms that represent competing wireless technologies and devices—PCS, CDPD, ESMR, and PDA, to name a few. Just how viable any of these technologies are remains an open question.

Meanwhile, large companies have paid big bucks in Federal Communications Commission (FCC) auctions, to buy slices of the broadcast spectrum they hope to use to deliver wireless services to huge anticipated consumer and business markets. Many providers also hope for large international markets, some of them based on global satellite networks.

The FCC Auctions

In 1994 for the first time, the FCC held an auction to sell the rights to use the public airwaves. This narrowband auction raised $617 million from the sale of 10 licenses for nationwide advanced paging networks. For two-way, high-capacity channels, Paging Network, for example, paid $80 million each for two licenses, as did KDM Messaging. Another company, Mtel, also paid $80 million for a license. For two-way, lower capacity channels, BellSouth Wireless, Mtel, and AirTouch Communications each bought one license at over $47 million a pop. For one-way channels, Page Mart II paid $38 million for one license and Paging Network paid $37 million for another. Mtel was also granted a pioneer's preference license in the one-way category, for which the government wants it to pay several million.

This was just the beginning. More license auctions involving the broadband capacity needed for personal communications services (PCS) were held in late 1994 and early 1995, and brought in $7 billion for the Federal Government. In this instance, PCS was defined to include potential markets for a new generation of cellular services and two-way wireless links for portable computers and electronic notebooks.

The participants in the broadband auctions—bidding for higher capacity airwaves—were even bigger companies than in the narrowband auctions. The telecommunications service company Sprint led the way, by successfully bidding $2.1 billion for licenses in 29 metropolitan and regional markets, including New York, San Francisco, Detroit, and Dallas-Fort Worth. Sprint's bidding group included the cable companies TCI, Comcast, and Cox Communications, which are eager to get into telephone services and other communications services. AT&T finished second, successfully bidding $1.7 billion for 21 markets. A consortium led by three regional Bell operating companies (RBOCs)—NYNEX, Bell Atlantic, and U S WEST—came in third, bidding $1.1 billion for licenses in 11 markets. Although it was the fourth-place bidder, Pacific Telesis acquired the single most expensive license, covering the southern California megalopolis region of Los Angeles and San Diego, for $493.5 million. To accompany these new licenses, the RBOCs also won a ruling in 1995 that allows them to enter the long-distance cellular market.

When asked if smaller players were unfairly frozen out of the FCC auctions by the high bidders, Barry Nalebuff, a professor of economics at the Yale School of Management and adviser to one of the small bidders, told THE HERRING, "Actually it would be a cruel trick to have smaller companies get into this business anyway. It's an enterprise that depends on a huge volume of customers in order to succeed. You need at least 100,000 subscribers just to get started. It's a bit like the story of how sharks must keep swimming or die. Companies in this business will have to keep doubling their subscriber base or die, and in the end it may be that it's not only the shark that keeps swimming but also the one that swims the fastest and eats the most that will prevail."

Paging Services

Paging services include one-way messaging and both low and high capacity two-way messaging. Motorola has been the dominant provider of paging services for some time. Other prominent suppliers include AirTouch Communications, PageMart, Paging Network, and Mobile Telecommunications Technology (Mtel), including its Destineer subsidiary which is developing two-way messaging technology. One cut on the paging market is by the incorporation of messaging into personal computers and possibly personal digital assistants (PDAs) through the PCMCIA receiver card technology.

Personal Communications Services (PCS)

In spite of the huge outlay of cash for PCS licenses, questions remain about the viability of personal communications services. Some analysts believe that PCS technology will do almost nothing that cellular service can't already do. "There is nothing that the new PCS spectrum can be used for that the old spectrum can't offer," says Jerry Waylan, executive vice president of the PCS group at GTE. And PCS does not necessarily mean cheaper wireless phones or lower calling costs.

Rather than a revolutionary technology destined to replace cellular, PCS may at best be a strategic supplement. Long distance carriers such as Sprint and AT&T hope to reduce the $21 billion they pay each year to the RBOCs for access to local phone networks by developing PCS networks that bypass the RBOCs. Cellular companies, including the RBOCs, see PCS as a way to fill in the gaps in their cellular networks.

Yet the cost of building PCS networks promises to be staggering. Sprint had to pay $442 million just for a license that covers the New York metropolitan area. And it will have to spend at least that much again, and maybe twice as much, to build the PCS system and absorb all the startup costs. All the winners of the PCS auction bidding are likely to accrue similar costs in building their systems, which adds up to a total expenditure of at least another $7 billion and probably closer to an additional $14 billion.

PCS operates at a higher frequency than cellular (two gigahertz vs. 800 megahertz), but the higher the frequency, the smaller the range of transmitters. Like cellular, PCS bounces radio signals through the air using a series of transmission towers, but PCS requires four to five times as many radio towers to provide the same service to the same region. It took cellular providers a decade to install about 11,500 cell cites. PCS providers must build many more transmitters in a much shorter time and at a much higher cost in order to compete with cellular. To cover the United States, PCS providers will have to build 100,000 cell sites, including thousands of towers.

Meanwhile cellular phones are getting smaller and cellular providers are moving toward PCS-like digital technology. And many of the claimed special promises of PCS—such as a single phone number that follows a user everywhere—are already available from cellular providers. Michael Blumberg, an analyst of the wireless industry for D. F. Blumberg & Associates, told *The Wall Street Journal*, "I haven't seen anyone present a distinctive PCS application that would generate large amounts of revenue in a reasonable amount of time."

In addition to "follow me" capability, in which calls placed to users' personal numbers will always find their way to them—at home, at work, or on the road—cellular technology offers many other services supposed to be unique to PCS. Wireless data applications, including electronic mail messages traded over untethered (i.e. wireless) laptop computers, and wireless faxes, are available using the basic method of connecting a laptop with a cellular phone and a dial-up connection.

Pacific Gas & Electric already uses traditional telephone lines for remote meter reading for 2,500 of its large commercial users. And PG&E will not wait for the PCS implementation of a wireless system that could help them provide this service to a broader base of customers. Instead, it is talking with cellular operators about designing a more sophisticated and efficient system. James Pope, vice president of technical and construction services at PG&E, indicates, "I can foresee that by the end of this century we'll have remote reading, predominantly wireless, for all our customers."

Cellular has already captured the early adopters and big users of wireless services. By the time PCS gets off the ground, the cellular industry will have invested $20 billion in the infrastructure required to serve these customers.

The one area in which PCS has an advantage over traditional cellular is in transmitting video images over the airwaves. Video signals require the greater bandwidth PCS frequencies provide. Yet video applications are still a phantom market. Meanwhile, it is possible to transmit video images over the older analog cellular networks.

CDPD

CDPD stands for cellular digital packet data and is billed as an alternative to traditional cellular for wireless data communication. The traditional form of cellular is a circuit-switched analog technology that many users already find cost-effective for file-transfer applications like faxes and e-mail. CDPD is a digital packet-switched technology that overlays existing cellular networks and requires special equipment to intermittently transmit small packets of data.

With market projections for wireless data communications of somewhere between $4 billion and $8 billion by the end of the decade, lots of money is being spent on CDPD and other new wireless technologies. The market research firms Yankee Group and BIS Strategic initially predicted annual market growth of 50% for CDPD, while AD Little forecast 70% growth, and Probe Research 100%, but most have recently backed off from these predictions. CDPD has a small installed base and is still being tested in many markets. Delays in infrastructure roll-out have impeded progress. So far, the lack of inexpensive, easy-to-use devices and the high cost of deployment have prevented CDPD from becoming a feasible alternative to traditional cellular technology.

SMR and ESMR

SMR stands for specialized mobile radio and is a technology originally developed for radio dispatch. An enhanced version—ESMR—is supposed to reach larger wireless markets.

The biggest company involved in ESMR technology is Nextel. Nextel founded the ESMR industry by combining many frequencies used for low-tech dispatch systems, such as those used for taxi cabs, into a nationwide network meant to compete with the cellular industry. The network is active in Los Angeles, San Francisco, and Denver. A major shareholder in Nextel with a 19% stake is Motorola, a wireless communications and mobile computing pioneer.

In September 1994 MCI Communications withdrew a bid to invest $1.36 billion for a 17% stake in Nextel. The deal purportedly collapsed because of differences between MCI and Motorola, but MCI also had some concerns about the quality of Nextel's product. Nextel's network is all digital, based on Motorola technology known as MIRS—mobile integrated radio system—which allows voice, messaging, and dispatch over a single handset. MIRS technology has had several problems, including poor voice quality (one critic said it sounded as if users were talking underwater) and reliability, causing MCI to conclude that MIRS could not effectively compete with cellular telephones.

Mobile pioneer Craig McCaw flying to Nextel's rescue

MCI hoped an alliance with Nextel would act as at least a partial counter to AT&T's acquisition of wireless giant McCaw Cellular Communications (subsequently renamed AT&T Wireless). In turn, Nextel hoped to benefit from MCI's brand identity as well as from its money. MCI was noticeably absent from the FCC auctions for wireless spectrum.

To strengthen its position, Nextel acquired two ESMR operators: OneComm and Dial Page. It is also merging with American Mobile Systems. Nevertheless, Nextel experienced a net loss of $51 million in the fourth quarter of 1994 and posted a loss of $149.7 million for the entire year. The company has spent $720 million to build infrastructure for its ESMR network that covers 30% of the U.S. The plan was to spend an additional $2.4 billion to expand to 85% coverage by the end of 1997.

Nextel's funding for its network expansion was running about $800 million short until cellular pioneer Craig McCaw came to the rescue in early 1995 with a personal investment of $300 million in Nextel increasing to as much as $1.1 billion over a six-year period. If Mr. McCaw exercises all his options, he could own about 23% of Nextel and become its largest shareholder. Meanwhile, Nextel scaled back its plan to build the equivalent of a nationwide cellular-telephone network, and instead will focus on the narrower task of building private dispatch networks for business customers who want to link mobile workers, such as construction crews, airline mechanics, and truck drivers.

Motorola says it is determined to fine-tune its MIRS technology and make it an open system that other equipment manufacturers could license to build their own systems. Nextel wants to use the technology in its microphone radios used for dispatch so that they can act like telephones for private person-to-person conversations as well as in its broadcast communications devices for reaching several users at once.

Dedicated Data

Ardis and RAM Mobile Data are two important companies providing dedicated wireless data services within special niches. Ardis, a unit of Motorola, uses a combination of rooftop antennas and traditional telephone lines to offer its wireless services mainly for internal use in large corporations. RAM Mobile Data, a joint venture between Bell-South and RAM Broadcasting, allows users to send e-mail from laptop computers.

But general purpose wireless data providers, such as Metricom, are expected to take a bite out of the dedicated data market. At Stanford University, for example, through a service offered by Metricom, students and faculty can use laptop computers anywhere on campus to tap into the university's in-house computer network and access the Internet. Users of Metricom's service must have a wireless modem which sends and receives signals to and from tiny, low-powered transmitters located on top of light and telephone poles.

Satellite Networks

The leading company in two-way, mobile satellite communications and the tracking system market is QUALCOMM. The company's specialized devices, based on its proprietary code division multiple access (CDMA) technology, are used primarily by transportation companies. The service provides broad coverage, with voice quality and capacity 10 to 20 times greater than analog cellular systems, but at a high cost.

In a separate investment, Craig McCaw joined with Microsoft's Bill Gates to form Teledesic Corporation, a $9 billion venture that promises to link users around the world to a global satellite network supposed to provide 95% coverage of the planet at all times.

The network seeks to put 840 satellites into orbit, pole to pole, 435 miles above the earth. Each satellite will circle the earth every 99 minutes and communicate with strategically placed gigalink and resident terminals that could transmit not only ordinary phone calls, but also large bandwidth transmissions like high resolution medical images and two-way video conferences. These types of transmissions will be made possible by using digitized signals and a special broadcast band the FCC has put aside for new video transmission technology. (The quest for these new broadcast bands has been characterized as an "electromagnetic land rush.") Teledesic wants to offer services by the year 2001.

Some concerns about the feasibility of this project remain. Teledesic still has to complete about $1.5 billion worth of research and development. Its goal is to build all 840 satellites by the year 2000 and launch every one of them by the end of the following year. This would mean over 100 rocket launches in fewer than two years, a rate never before achieved. Teledesic also needs to get regulatory approval from many countries that have state-owned phone systems and might be reluctant to give up revenue from these systems. Teledesic ultimately would compete not only with other satellite projects, like Motorola's $3.3 billion IRIDIUM system, but also with telephone and cable companies in urban business centers where the highest volume of wireless communications traffic and the greatest number of customers are found.

Personal Digital Assistants

One possible wireless device is the personal communicator or personal digital assistant (PDA), broadly defined as some sort of battery-powered, handheld combination of computer, fax machine, pager, and phone. Early PDAs such as the Envoy, the Simon, the Zoomer, and Apple Computer's Newton MessagePad did not have wireless capability but served more as electronic address books and notepads.

When Apple first introduced its Newton MessagePad in 1993, it was widely ridiculed because of its fickle handwriting recognition technology and $699 price tag. THE HERRING believes it is destined to be ranked with the Edsel as one of the all-time turkeys. And in July 1994 AT&T shut down EO, its maker of pen-based personal communicators. AT&T had a 52% stake in EO and had invested some $40 million to $50 million in the company, but EO reportedly sold fewer than 10,000 units.

A subsequent entry in the PDA market was the Sony Magic Link PIC 1000. This PDA is supposed to be for "mobile executives," allowing them to send and receive e-mail, make airline reservations, log appointments, and check stock quotes. The device incorporates General Magic's Magic Cap operating system and has a user-friendly interface. The device can record, but not translate, hand-writing, much like a fax machine does. To create computer text, users tap on a key-board that appears on the screen. But there are problems, like a dim screen and small memory. It was introduced with a high price of $995, which went up to $1,500 when several essential "accessories" were added, like more memory, a pager card, a carrying case, and a rechargeable battery. The device is also fat and heavy, a bit like

STEVE CURLEY

PDA angst

lugging around an unabridged copy of *War and Peace* all the time. The Magic Link has two problems that prevent it from being a viable consumer item—it's overpriced and it's not very portable.

General Magic, founded in 1990, has lined up such major corporate backers as AT&T, Philips, Matsushita, Sony, Motorola, and, ironically enough, Apple, to the tune of $20 million. France Télécom, the French phone company, as well as NTT, Fujitsu, and Toshiba, also jumped on board. These companies hope that General Magic will provide the software that will become the global standard for wireless, hand-held computers.

General Magic has two products, Tele-script and Magic Cap. Telescript is the software language designed to move information in a variety of digital formats across networks. The language will use "smart agents" that search networks, collecting and sorting the types of data spec-ified by the user. Magic Cap is the operating system and interface used in personal communicators like the above described Sony Magic Link. Telescript is included in Magic Cap.

Some optimistic analysts see a kind of historical pattern in the fits and starts of the product development and consumer acceptance of the PDA.

Betty Lyter, a New Media analyst at Montgomery Securities in San Francisco, believes personal communicators will follow a pattern similar to that of other electronics products that had relatively lackluster beginnings. It took three years for sales of camcorders and audio CD players, seven years for VCRs, and nine years for color televisions to exceed 1 million units. Moreover, in the initial year, none of these products sold more than 250,000 units.

Yet a product on the market since 1991 meets the requirements of mobile executives better than any PDA: the H-P 100 LX palmtop computer. It has a real keyboard and can run standard applications like Lotus 1-2-3. When connected to a cellular phone, it can send e-mail and wireless faxes. It delivers what it promises, has a lucrative niche, is reasonably priced, and is truly portable. By the end of 1994, it had sold more than 300,000 units.

Whether a real market exists for this generation of personal communicators or PDAs, wireless or not, remains to be seen.

Market Prospects

One of the most talked about opportunities in wireless is the international market, especially in developing countries. It has been estimated that half the people in the world have never made a telephone call. In Nigeria, there is a 10-year waiting list for a telephone. There is an enormous latent demand, worldwide, for wireless telephone services. Bypassing much of the old tethered infrastructure, developing countries would instead deploy wireless as their general communications infrastructure. But some investors and communications companies avoid developing countries because of civil, political, economic, and regulatory risk. India is a good example of a country that represents both the promise and peril of technology investment in a developing arena that could include wireless [see outtake from interview with Bill Draper of The Draper International Fund].

For the wireless market as a whole, many forecast huge growth, yet thus far, some predictions have not panned out. CDPD is a good example. Early estimates predicted annual growth ranging from 50–100%, with the implication that this "market" was going to explode, and that cellular carriers and others should be there to get their share.

Wireless data departments sprang up in cellular companies, and hundreds of millions of dollars were invested in these markets. Among the most aggressive investors was McCaw Cellular. Even though the cellular business has averaged 45% growth in recent years—without ever making a profit—no one questioned the implicit assertion that everyone would get rich with CDPD technology at a growth rate of 50% a year. But in the first quarter of 1995, there were fewer than 200 paying CDPD users.

Another technology given expansive forecasts is PCS. Organizations have spent more than $7 billion on licenses from the FCC and do not want to hear that it will be anything but a blazing success. In reality, it is not possible to forecast PCS revenue and growth, because no one can really define PCS functionality, its target markets, or its distribution channels. This uncertainty has not prevented predictions of a rosy future for PCS. Yankee Group analysts say there will be at least 400,000 PCS customers by the end of 1997. Telecator's *PCS Market Demand Forecast* goes much further, projecting 8.5 million PCS subscribers by 1998 and 31.1 million by 2010. In the 1995 update to its PCS forecast, the Personal Communications Industry Association predicts 14.8 million PCS subscribers by the year 2000 and 39.5 million by the year 2005.

One reasonable possibility is that PCS might serve as the broadband conduit the cable and telecommunications companies will need to offer wireless video services; it could also help them fill in some of the gaps in their phone services [see chapter 4 for discussion of the Information Superhighway strategies of these companies].

A bizarre twist in the cellular market is concern over the impact of cellular technology on electronic pacemakers for the heart. Research by the Wireless Technology Group found evidence that in some cases a pacemaker will recalibrate itself or stop and restart when a digital cellular phone is placed near the chest, as is the case when a user carries a pocketphone model in a shirt or jacket pocket. About six million pocketphones were sold in the U.S. in 1994, approximately 375,000 of them digital. There are about two million pacemakers in use worldwide; 130,000 are implanted each year. The pacemaker problem comes on the heels of eight lawsuits that claim that cellular phones cause brain cancer.

The division and viability of the market for the various wireless technologies—cellular, PCS, ESMR, satellite links, dedicated data, etc.—remains an open question. Convenience and low cost are key factors in reaching a mass market, especially with consumers.

OUT **TAKES**

Bill Draper

Principal
The Draper International Fund

One of the most talked-about opportunities in wireless is the international market, especially in developing countries. But some investors and communications companies avoid developing countries because of civil, political, economic, and regulatory risks. India is a good example of a country that represents both the promise and peril of technology investment in a developing arena.

Bill Draper joined with partners Robin Richards and Kiran Nadkarni in 1995 to form the Draper International Fund, a $40 million venture fund focused on India. It is the first venture effort with a presence in both the U.S. and India. It has several high-profile Indian advisers and investors.

Mr. Draper served as chairman of the Export-Import Bank for five years during the Reagan administration. He then served as head of the United Nations Development Programme (UNDP), the largest source of multilateral development assistance in the world. Before embarking on his international career, he founded his own venture capital firm, Sutter Hill Ventures, where he worked for 20 years.

The new era of multinational business in India comes in the wake of a history of resistance by Indian nationals to outside investment. In the 1970s the socialist Indian government pressured Coca-Cola and IBM to abandon their operations in India (both have returned). More recently, a regional Indian government voted down the development of a power plant in Dabhol, a $2.8 billion joint venture of Houston energy giant Enron and minority partners Bechtel Enterprises and General Electric. Nevertheless, the country is privatizing much of its state industry sector, and the demand for new infrastructure has created a huge need for project financing. The opportunity for wireless infrastructure is large: India has only nine million telephone lines for at least 900 million people.

100

ANNE KNUDSEN

Mr. Draper discusses why he chose to invest in India, with all its possibilities and risks.

Why India?

Actually at first we looked at Chile, then China, Vietnam, and Indonesia. But we finally decided to focus on India, because it has a large English-speaking population, and its current movement toward democratic capitalism is stimulating rapid growth in the economy. India also has a compatible business culture, with legal and accounting practices similar to those in the U.S.

Meanwhile, India's per capita income is only $330 and the economy is only growing about 4% annually.

Well, you're right. But India is just now beginning to be freed up and allowed to grow. The other thing to remember is that the government still owns much of the industry, so that an overall GNP growth rate of 4% hides the fact that the privately-owned side of the economy is probably growing at 12% and the companies we will invest in will grow at a rate of 40%. India still has weak infrastructure and bad communications, but an inefficient market is often the best place to invest and make a lot of money.

101

Is wireless communications a potentially strong growth industry for a developing country like India?

Definitely. It's a huge opportunity, because developers can skip the last 30 years of laying in all the old wired infrastructure, like they've been doing in developed countries, and more quickly implement wireless technology instead. Several of the enterprises we are looking at funding in India right now are in wireless communications.

Could India produce the next Silicon Valley?

I want to make it clear that there are a lot of risks in what we are trying to do. But we are betting that the economic changes India has made over the last few years will stay in place, even if there is a change in government. But it is a risk. The government has to maintain its momentum toward privatization and foster a system where entrepreneurs can be rewarded for working hard and being innovative. We can't forget that the Rao government is up for re-election in 1996, so anything can happen.

06_SEMICONDUCTORS

TIM BROCK

T he semiconductor industry is one of the fastest-growing sectors in the world today. In 1980, the semiconductor market was just under $15 billion worldwide. By 1994, according to Dataquest, revenues reached the $111 billion. According to the Semiconductor Industry Association, the industry grew an estimated 32% in 1994, and was expected to grow another 40% to over $140 billion in 1995.

This boom has been fueled by the continuing surge in personal computer shipments and by the spread of semiconductors into huge new markets, including telecommunications, consumer electronics, and automobiles. Computer chips are so pervasive that they are even put into decoder rings, identification cards, hospital bracelets, and key chains. Dallas Semiconductor manufactures the memory buttons containing such chips, which hold the software that gives owners access to secret computer files and locked rooms or whatever other storage area they want to keep secure.

According to Ernie Ruehl and Mike Wishart of investment bank Lehman Brothers, the rapid growth of the semiconductor market has translated into large market capitalizations for many semiconductor companies, as well as for the industry as a whole. As of June 30, 1995, they report, the publicly traded semiconductor companies in the United States had a collective market capitalization of over $160 billion. For 1994 the leading semiconductor companies worldwide ranked according to revenue were Intel, NEC, Toshiba, Motorola, Hitachi, and Texas Instruments.

Breaking the Pattern?

Historically, the semiconductor industry has been very cyclical. While the 1970s showed steady growth, the 1980s and early 1990s were roller-coaster rides. Analysts and many investors expect the current upward trend to last longer and have an even greater impact than past highs.

John Lazlo, senior technology analyst with PaineWebber, points out that the current upcycle is the longest and most enduring ever, with each year of it showing growth. Furthermore, this expansion is being driven by products that were in their infancy only ten to fifteen years ago—computer networking systems, electronic games, wireless communications equipment, and personal computers. This market growth has also persist-

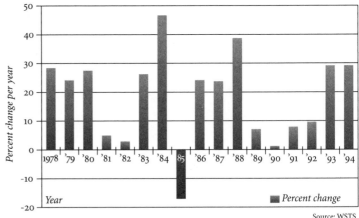

Annual growth of worldwide semiconductor industry revenues

Percent change per year

Year

■ *Percent change*

Source: WSTS

ed through general economic downturns in the past decade in the United States, Europe, and Japan.

In the 1985 to 1995 period, semiconductor technology drove the change and growth of the worldwide electronics industry. From 1996 to 2005, semiconductor development will continue to drive technology change and market growth in the form of wireless communications, networked personal computers, home PCs, and consumer electronics. For the year 2000, Dataquest forecasts a $1 trillion global electronics equipment market with semiconductor revenues totaling $275 billion. Dan Klesken, senior analyst at Robertson Stephens, is even more optimistic, forecasting semiconductor revenues of $350 billion by the year 2000, and a whopping $850 billion by the year 2005. According to Mr. Lazlo, new geographic markets, such as China, India, Malaysia, Latin America, and Eastern Europe/Russia could need up to $100 billion worth of semiconductors by the year 2005.

Types of Chips

Semiconductors can be divided into two groups: digital and analog. Analog chips are used in many electronic devices such as audio amplifiers, microwave ovens, and cellular phones. Digital chips are used in all computers and are divided into two groups: logic chips (microprocessors, microcontrollers, etc.) and memory chips (RAM and ROM). As the digitization of information grows, digital chips are replacing analog chips in many devices.

It's also important to know that microprocessors are made according to two main designs (or architectures): reduced instruction set computing (RISC) and complex instruction set computing (CISC). The current Intel chips have a base CISC architecture but incorporate some RISC features. RISC architectures have been adopted by most other microprocessor suppliers and developers, including Digital Equipment Corporation (DEC), Hewlett-Packard, MIPS (a subsidiary of Silicon Graphics), IBM/Motorola/Apple, and Sun Microsystems/Texas Instruments. Proponents of RISC claim that the chips are cheaper to design and build, operate at higher speeds, and provide greater price-performance advantages than CISC. Intel states that it has addressed all these issues with its Pentium chips.

In the personal computer market, the PowerPC RISC chips produced by the IBM/Motorola/Apple alliance seemed especially well-suited to compete. Power PC desktop and notebook computers, priced below $3,000, were said to be up to 50% faster at number-crunching tasks and graphics programs than comparably priced Intel CISC-based models. But as Price Waterhouse points out in its 1995 *Technology Forecast*, when it comes to dominating the semiconductor market: "Technology alone will not be the deciding factor. [The market] will be determined by a mix of factors: technology, volume, availability of software, extent of alliances, perception of market strength, promotion, and compatibility." So far Intel, strong in all these areas, has successfully made its chips the standard for PCs.

The Manufacturing Challenge

The big challenge for Intel and other chip manufacturers is maintaining profitability despite escalating manufacturing costs. Each successive generation of semiconductor technology requires an increase in the amount of capital needed to build state-of-the-art manufacturing facilities. Building a typical fabrication plant in the 1980s cost $250 million; in 1995 it costs more than $1 billion.

The fabrication process itself is also moving toward smaller geometries and larger silicon wafers. This trend means more output and better profit margins based on greater efficiency, because more semiconductors can be manufactured per wafer. The long-term goal is 12-inch wafers and sub 0.20 micron line geometries. (A micron is a millionth of a meter.) The most recent production process reduced the lines of circuitry to a width of 0.35 micron, about half its previous width, on an 8-inch wafer. Motorola plans to build a semiconductor factory that will use 12-inch wafers by the end of the decade. Intel could start a 0.25 micron manufacturing process by late 1997. This plant would cost as much as $3 billion to build. Dataquest estimates it will cost the semiconductor industry a total of $15–$30 billion to put its new manufacturing infrastructure in place.

This trend reflects the realities of Moore's Law, coined by Gordon Moore, chairman of Intel [see interview outtake], in 1965: the number of transistors that can be packed on a semiconductor chip doubles roughly every 18 months. In 1975, Dr. Moore amended his Law, saying that every two years silicon components on the chip would double in complexity. The result is not only cheaper but faster chips that consume less energy and are more reliable. With Intel's new P6 chip, the amount of computing power that $100 can buy has risen 254-fold since IBM selected Intel's 8086 chip for the PC it launched in 1981.

But silicon capacity has its limits. Every doubling of chip power results from doubling chip density; ultimately the chip surface becomes too crowded to be workable. According to the Semiconductor Industries Association, the limit for the chip etching process—photolithography—is 0.18 micron. At that point, serious technical problems come into play, such as the inability to properly focus the light used in the etching process and an overheating of the chips that leads to melting. Some long-term alternatives to the current process include the use of gallium arsenide instead of silicon, and the development of laser chips through optical circuit technology. But cost and technical problems would still have to be solved with these other processes.

American Companies

Intel is the world's leading semiconductor company. Texas Instruments has emerged as the fifth-largest producer of dynamic random access memory (DRAM) chips and is also the dominant supplier of digital signal processor chips. Micron Technology has pulled ahead of Advanced Micro Devices (AMD) as the fifth-largest U.S. semiconductor supplier. Other important American companies include Cyrix, NexGen, Atmel, Xilinx, Cypress Semiconductor, LSI Logic, Alliance Semiconductor, Cirrus Logic, Zilog, and various designers and manufacturers of specialized multimedia chips.

107

Micron Technology

By the end of its 1995 fiscal year, Micron Technology's profit had doubled to more than $800 million on sales of $2.8 billion, and the company had become a Wall Street favorite.

Along with Texas Instruments, Micron Technology has led a remarkable American comeback in the market for DRAM chips, partly attributable to continued growth and broadening of the personal computer market, since PCs require more and more RAM. This demand became even greater with the introduction of the Windows 95 operating system which requires 16 MB of RAM to run comfortably on a PC.

Analysts at investment bank Robertson Stephens forecast growth of the worldwide DRAM chip market at 60% to $37.1 billion in 1995 and 35% more in 1996 to $50 billion. Increasing demand coupled with shortages of DRAM chips has kept prices high.

One reason for the shortages is that a recession in Japan, starting in the early 1990s, has forced Japanese manufacturers to pull back from building more factories to increase capacity and gain market share. The let-up in Japan, combined with strong demand, meant that DRAM chip prices have held steady in the 1990s, instead of dropping 30% annually as they had for years before.

New memory chip factories are being built to cash in on the suddenly lucrative DRAM market. In addition to the United States, and again in Japan, new factories are going up in South Korea, Taiwan, Malaysia, and China. In 1995 14 new factories started production, increasing the supply of DRAMs by 46%. Another 16 factories were expected to start producing chips in 1996. But with demand rising 70% yearly, analysts predict that DRAM chips will still be in short supply through 1996 or 1997.

Micron Technology has doubled its production capacity since 1991. It plans to add capacity of another 30% in 1996, including a $1.3 billion chip factory in Lehl, UT. However, Micron is prospering because of its increased capacity, but also because it has been an innovator in chip design, shrinking the size of its chips and making them easier to package for makers of personal computers such as Dell Computer, Samsung, and Toshiba.

Intel

Intel has the greatest market share in semiconductors because of its dominant position in microprocessors and its huge financial muscle. In recent years the company has spent almost $10 billion on capacity expansion and research and development. Intel owns 75% of the microprocessor market. Because Intel is top dog in the burgeoning semiconductor market, *The Wall Street Journal* even speculates that it could achieve "the totally unexpected: becoming the most profitable company on earth."

Intel has ridden the PC boom to huge prosperity. Sharply falling PC prices have opened up the consumer market. Dataquest forecasts sales of 107 million PCs worldwide in the year 1999, compared with sales of 50 million in 1994. Many analysts think that only Intel has the resources to meet such feverish demand, propelling the company to $8–$11 billion in annual earnings by the year 2000. This is in line with Intel's annual earnings growth rate of 37% in the 1990s.

Meanwhile, with its introduction of the P6 chip, Intel continues to maintain its aggressive schedule of introducing a new microprocessor every two years. Such speed of development, combined with tremendous economies of scale and high barriers to entry, puts Intel in a very strong position for some time to come.

As discussed above, one major barrier to entry is the increasing cost of manufacturing. A corollary to Moore's Law is Rock's Law, coined by the distinguished venture capitalist and Intel director Arthur Rock: The cost of semiconductor manufacturing plants and equipment doubles every four years. Intel's latest

ANNE KNUDSEN

Arthur Rock

plant opened in Rio Rancho, NM, cost $1.8 billion, or 600 times as much as Intel's original $3 million factory. In 1995 Intel's total capital investment in manufacturing was $3.5 billion, a 45% increase over 1994's capital outlay.

But there is also the danger of overcapacity. Dataquest estimates that the Rio Rancho facility alone could eventually produce more than 61 million P6 chips per year. The entire microprocessor market for 1995 was 65 million and is expected to grow to 100 million by 1998. Intel obviously banks on continuing to dominate the market.

Intel also plans to add more multimedia capability to its microprocessors through what it calls native signal processing (NSP). This addition is part of Intel's contribution to industry-wide multimedia, communications, and network server standards. Intel hopes that such standards will reduce system complexity, increase ease-of-use, lower overall system costs, and expand the use of PCs.

Multimedia Chips

109

Intel's efforts in NSP could clash with the strategy of companies like Analog Devices, AT&T, Motorola, Texas Instruments, and C-Cube, which are developing specialized digital signal processor (DSP) chips.

DSP chips convert video and audio data from analog into digital formats and can store this digitized data or send it over computer network links. Because digital processing is used more and more for fax transmission, data compression, videoconferencing, wireless computing, and most multimedia applications, DSP chips are increasingly important components in computers. DSP chips are also used in other electronic devices such as home stereo music systems and mobile phones.

Intel's NSP strategy for personal computers is to take some DSP capability and add it to its own microprocessor. The idea is that if the main processor can take over some of the functions of DSP, then perhaps cheaper DSP chips can fill in the rest of the functionality. Or perhaps the DSP chip can be eliminated altogether, at least for the lower-end machines. Intel's NSP provides baseline multimedia functionality for little or no added cost to consumers. NSP also gives independent software developers a more consistent and compatible multimedia platform for which to develop.

But where does this leave developers of DSP chips such as C-Cube? Some analysts and investors feel that Intel's sucking more functionality onto the microprocessor means a shrinking market for C-Cube and other DSP chip makers. Others think the reverse is true; that the demand for multimedia will actually expand the market for DSP chips. While NSP provides baseline multimedia functionality, specialized DSP chips would still be required to provide enhanced multimedia functionality. Applications that require enhanced functionality include videoconferencing, 3D graphics acceleration, and audio and video compression.

Meanwhile in mid-1995, C-Cube's technology was selected by both Sony and Sharp Electronics for use in its entertainment products. Sony will use C-Cube chips in a new line of video compact disc players, and Sharp will put them in a new portable entertainment system. C-Cube also won an Emmy Award for best technology for its work with MPEG (Motion Picture Experts Group) software used for video compression.

OUT **TAKES**

Gordon Moore

Chairman and Co-founder, Intel

The story of Dr. Gordon E. Moore and Dr. Robert N. Noyce suddenly bolting from Fairchild Semiconductor, the division of Fairchild Camera and Instrument Corporation that the two co-founded in 1957, to start Intel, is well-entrenched in the annals of Silicon Valley. But not everyone remembers how challenging the task of creating and building the world's dominant semiconductor company actually was for the ambitious and hard-driving team of entrepreneurs that founded Intel in July of 1968. In the early seventies Intel had to sell some of its core technology to a Canadian concern to generate needed revenues; the economic downturn caused by the oil crisis in the mid-seventies forced the company to shrink its staff by a third; and privateering Japanese companies undercut Intel's market share in the early 1980s, forcing the company to turn to Big Blue for a handout. Many people also forget that Intel was founded with less than $5 million in total venture capital—using a two-page business plan written by legendary venture capitalist Arthur Rock—and that Dr. Moore is known for more than just being co-founder of a semiconductor powerhouse. He is also famous for "Moore's Law"—which correctly predicted in 1965 that the transistor density of semiconductor chips would double every eighteen months until 1980—and for purportedly coining the phrase "vulture capitalist."

ANNE KNUDSEN

111

George Gilder romantically observed that back at Fairchild, you used the three most common elements on earth when you first designed the major parts of the semiconductor device.
Yes, we were really looking for materials that were inherently inexpensive, and generally available. Oxygen is the most prevalent, but it's a gas, so we couldn't

use that directly. But we learned that when you combine oxygen with the earth's second most common element, silicon, at about the ratio they occur in nature, you end up with silicon dioxide for an insulator. And for the conductor, we added aluminum, which is the third most common element. But, of course that kind of drama is always recognized after the fact. [Laughs]

When did you first come up with what is historically referred to as "Moore's Law"?

I published the original premise of Moore's Law back in 1965, in the fairly early days of the integrated circuit, when I was asked to predict what was going to happen to semiconductor components over the next ten years. Because I had observed that the few integrated circuits we were building at the time were roughly doubling in density every year, I merely extrapolated that trend over the following ten years, and it turned out to be a very accurate prediction. Things have changed a little since then, and now, of course, Moore's Law is used to predict almost everything in the computer industry, and I'm happy to take credit for all of it. [Smiles]

When did you realize what a huge impact the semiconductor would eventually have on society?

It was a realization that came gradually. At Fairchild, we had no appreciation of the magnitude of the opportunity we were working on—we were frankly amazed that people were buying what we made. But by the time we started Intel, we had already created a company that was doing $200 million in business and had some 30,000 employees, so we had some inkling of the potential for the semiconductor business. It wasn't really until the PC came out that this became a big business for us.

I suppose that is another place where luck played a role. If IBM had designed another process in their PC, Intel would be a very different— most likely much smaller—company.

You are absolutely right.

Silicon Valley lore is that Intel's board was initially skeptical about the concept of producing and selling a general purpose microprocessor.

We started with the idea that we wanted to make complex silicon circuits. But at the time, there were only 10,000 computers manufactured a year, so there wasn't enough demand for the kind of complicated chips we wanted to design. So the first product we focused on was semiconductor memory, which was a general purpose function that existed in all digital systems. Next, we focused on the calculator market. But by the time we were exploring this market, all the name-brand calculator companies had chosen their semiconductor partners, so we were left doing business with this obscure, third-tier, Japanese manufacturer called Visicom. They presented us with the logic design for some thirteen complex chips they wanted us to build. Well, our engineering team at the time wasn't big enough to design two chips, never mind thirteen! That's when Ted Hoff came up with the idea to design all of these chips into one general purpose computer architecture. This design could also be used in other general purpose applications, such as elevator controls and traffic light controls.

What are the necessary factors for success in today's semiconductor industry?

Well, we feel like the fox being chased around by a bunch of wolves. One of the significant ways we try to run faster is by running parallel development programs. About five years ago, we set up two different sites, one in Santa Clara, CA, and one in Oregon, and we have overlapping leading edge technology development programs going at the same time, so we can bring out products more rapidly. This, of course takes a lot more people and a lot more money.

113

The framed Pentium chip design behind you is signed by the two dozen principal members of the engineering team—half of whom have international surnames.

Today, half the engineering students that graduate from American universities are foreign-born. When you go down to our cafeteria, it looks like the United Nations. It really goes back to our basic education system and the motivations in our society. Not many young Americans want to go into the technical field. We no longer emphasize the hard sciences anymore, and once you drop out of math, it's hard to get back into it.

Pierre Lamond

Partner, Sequoia Capital

Pierre Lamond's résumé reads like a history of semiconductors. In 1962, soon after immigrating to the United States from France, Mr. Lamond joined the industry's progenitor—Fairchild Semiconductor. Its employees included the future founders of companies like Intel, Advanced Micro Devices, and LSI Logic. Mr. Lamond and his boss, Charles Sporck, started Fairchild's entrepreneurship trend by leaving in 1966 to found National Semiconductor.

Since 1981 Mr. Lamond has been with venture capital firm Sequoia Capital, where he has helped build some of the most important semiconductor companies of the 1980s and 1990s, such as Cypress Semiconductor, C-Cube Microsystems, and Microchip Technology. At times, he has done this by taking leave of his venture capital post to temporarily assume an operating position with a portfolio company.

114

Was it luck or foresight that led you to the infant semiconductor industry of the early 1960s?

I have to give great credit to one of my professors from France. He predicted that semiconductors would replace vacuum tubes. That convinced me to look for a job in the area.

One of the first companies you got involved with at Sequoia was Cypress Semiconductor, of which you are still chairman. What caused the company to get into trouble?

A tremendous amount of effort and money was being spent on SPARC chips for Sun with very little return. We thought that a Sun-sponsored RISC chip would lead to a huge market, but it hasn't, and it won't. If I could go back in time, I would have said we should develop an Intel clone rather than a RISC chip, but that is 20/20 hindsight.

The other Sequoia company where you played an operating role was Microchip Technology. What was your strategy there?

Microchip was originally a supplier of commodity devices. Some of the products had negative gross margins—they cost more to make than they were sold for. That's without considering the costs of sales, marketing, development, and overhead. Then we focused on microcontrollers, the company has very successfully gone public, and annual sales are up around $350 million.

With investments like CommQuest Technologies, NeoMagic, and NVIDIA, Sequoia is clearly still optimistic about semiconductors. Nearly four decades after the industry was born, why do you believe these opportunities continue to emerge?

Sales of semiconductors hit approximately $100 billion worldwide in 1994, and the industry is still growing at a 20% rate. A market with that size and that growth still presents startup opportunities. I have been proven wrong before in passing on investments like Alliance Semiconductor, when I thought there wasn't room in semiconductor markets to support new companies.

Some people say that circuit lines on semiconductors can't get much thinner than what's starting to be achieved now. Would that reduce the opportunities for startups to innovate?

I doubt it, because if line widths reach around 0.35 microns, a third dimension will come into play with more and more interconnect. It's already happening in memory chips like DRAMs, with storage capacitors sitting on top of the circuit. You move from two levels of interconnection to three to five, and everything changes.

115

What about your friends at Intel? Do their native signal processing efforts limit the opportunities for semiconductor companies developing functions outside of the microprocessor?

When there are millions of transistors on the microprocessor, you can do a lot on it. But consider C-Cube. You can say that a few generations after the Pentium, a decompression chip will be unnecessary. But C-Cube has a chance to improve that function on a peripheral chip while Intel improves the microprocessor. The process can be accelerated or the resolution can be enhanced. Consider other areas. People want faster and faster input/output. That won't happen if it all goes on the microprocessor. Adaptec and others will continue to push I/O benchmarks. It's also true in graphics. A microprocessor will be able to render what we look at today, but what about 3D? There will continue to be many opportunities for new companies to drive the semiconductor industry.

07_INTERNETWORKING

TIM BROCK

Unless you are an engineer, computer networking is probably not the kind of thing you spend your spare time dreaming about. Yet networking is a critical aspect of the communications boom. Electronic mail, file-sharing, the Internet, and teleconferencing are only some of the applications and resources made available by networking technology.

Computer networks enable the digital transmission of information from one location to another. In recent years, networking has evolved from the older-style computer systems based on mainframes, known as host computing, to the so-called client/ server computer architecture, sometimes called distributed or peer-to-peer computing.

Today there are three primary segments of networking: host computing, local-area networks (LAN), and wide-area networks (WAN). Host computing focuses on the products used to connect the traditional mainframe systems to other computers or peripherals. WANs are systems that connect far-flung regions into a computer network. Internetworking is concerned with the hardware devices that connect users on local-area networks within and across organizations. Internetworking is the fastest growing and most important area of computer networking. It allows PCs to share files and printers and connects a large numbers of workstations and PCs into a corporate-wide computing environment.

Elements of Internetworking

A LAN is a local-area computer network that links PCs together so that they can communicate and share information. The LAN has at least one server computer connected to several PCs designated as client computers. The LAN market has developed rapidly over the last several years, as users required the ability to share peripherals across LANs and communicate among PCs. Internetworking is largely concerned with the interconnectivity and interoperability of LANs.

There are several key components and devices that enable networks to function effectively. The most important networking companies provide at least some of these technologies, often integrating them into a complete networking solution for the customer. Following are some of the most important:

Adapter card: Provides the interface between a desktop computer or server and a LAN.

Hub: A network device that provides connectivity between users on the same LAN.

Bridge: An internetworking device that can handle data traffic exchange between similar LANs or different LAN types.

Router: An internetworking device that routes traffic among LANs.

Ethernet switch: A type of hub that dedicates LAN wiring to all attached computers and moves packets of information among the computers based on their addresses.

ATM switch: ATM stands for Asynchronous Transfer Mode. The ATM switch is a network device that uses cell-based technology to switch data traffic across networks through dedicated lines. ATM is currently under development at several networking companies and, though as yet not fully implemented, is expected to be faster than Ethernet switching and able to handle more data, including audio and video information.

As bewildering as all of these components might seem, these are some of the main devices network providers use to make internetworking possible, and in the process, make large profits in the industry. The assumption is that while personal computers and workstations might make individuals more productive, networking is what enhances what networking companies call workgroup and enterprise productivity.

Internetworking Trends

Personal computers are the driving force behind many current internetworking trends. According to the Yankee Group, a market research firm specializing in technology, by the end of 1994 there were 19 million PCs connected to LANs in the United States. The goal of the internetworking industry, according to the Group, is to reach a point where "virtually every white-collar worker has a PC, receives electronic mail every day, and is connected to a network." At the same time, networks are growing, becoming more complex, and needing greater power, memory, and connectivity.

Long-Term Issues and Customer Requirements

Morgan Stanley, an investment bank that has worked on several networking company financings and mergers and acquisitions, foresees customers making the following requirements of networking technology:

- Commitment to open standards (i.e. no closed or proprietary systems)
- Global distribution and service capabilities
- Hub as well as routing technologies
- Commitment to switching as a next-generation enabling technology
- Migration path to ATM
- Ability to provide remote LAN access for remote offices
- Network management interoperability

To these customer requirements the Yankee Group adds the following customer needs as forces driving the network market:

- Increasing speed in the LAN
- Building networked applications
- Empowering the mobile worker
- Building wide-area infrastructure

119

- Managing the network
- Building electronic commerce applications

In this atmosphere, every networking company is scrambling to be more important to its customers than the next company. They are trying to combine several functions in one networking solution, in what the Yankee Group calls "a networking version of the Swiss Army Knife."

Despite the nature of these customer needs, networking has historically been a technology-driven market. The feasibility of the technology determines the feasibility of the applications available for the customer.

Technology Developments

In the wake of the transition from the mainframe, host-based model of computer networking to internetworking, there have been successive waves of technology that included bridges, hubs, and routers. The recent transition trend within internetworking is from shared to switched connection models. Historically the network was constrained by the capacity of its conduits—more data traffic meant lower performance. In a traditional Ethernet network, for example, if two PCs broadcast data over a network simultaneously, the system protocol was to prevent a collision by having both PCs hang up and try again. If too many users try to send data at once, the network slows dramatically. New protocols like Switched Ethernet and ATM allow communications to occur over dedicated lines so that each connection can utilize the full bandwidth capacity (i.e. transmission speed) of the network.

Ethernet

Ethernet already has a large installed base, is relatively simple and cheap to implement, and offers a large group of vendors from which customers can choose. The Yankee Group forecasts sales of almost $7 billion in Ethernet products for 1997. According to the Group, "For the great majority of users, Ethernet switching will satisfy their needs for several years." The key question will be how to provide the network capacity required to tie together all those Ethernet switches. This illustrates a larger point made by the Yankee Group:

It is one problem to get the lowest-cost widget to support a workgroup. It is quite another to tie the widgets together into a coherent, global network.

While driving that coherent, global network is the goal of network planning, it remains more of a goal than a reality.

ATM

Though still in its incubation period, ATM is seen by many technologists and investors as the next great networking technology. ATM features variable speed capabilities and fixed cell length, which translates into standardized protocols. Useful for multimedia networking, it also expedites high performance and the creation of larger networks. The main obstacle to adoption of ATM by businesses is the high cost of investing in new equipment. Many businesses already face strained network budgets. As a result, network vendors are developing systems that will support current networking protocols, such as Ethernet, but will allow users to slowly and economically implement ATM. The assumption is that ATM adoption will be gradual.

One example of a company pursuing the gradual ATM adoption strategy is privately-held Agile Networks. The firm is headed by William Seifert, founding chief technical officer of Wellfleet (now part of Bay Networks). Mr. Seifert describes Agile's network concept as a "Relational LAN." The term describes the company's goal of providing geographic independence to workstations on a network. Users are placed in logical rather than geographic groupings. The network uses an ATM backbone but has Ethernet running to the desktop computers. The evolutionary path foreseen by Agile is from Shared Ethernet to Switched Ethernet to ATM. The product is software intensive, what Mr. Seifert describes as "a next-generation router."

121

Another privately-held company developing ATM technology is First Virtual Corporation, founded by Ralph Ungermann, founding CEO of UB Networks (formerly Ungermann-Bass and now a Tandem Computer subsidiary). First Virtual Corporation provides desktop multimedia applications, including elements of video and audio, through ATM networks. As a "virtual corporation," the company outsources much of its work, and its product is developed through partnerships. The ATM technology, for example, is licensed from Advanced Telecommunication Modules, an Olivetti spinoff company based in Cambridge, England. The media server that First Virtual is using is being developed with Conner Peripherals of San Jose, CA. First Virtual is hoping for a $2 billion multimedia networking market by 1997.

Another pioneer in the ATM market is the publicly-held Fore Systems of Warrondale, PA. Fore was first to market with complete ATM networking solutions, from switches to adapter cards and software. By 1995 its market share was nearly double that of its nearest competitor.

According to the Yankee Group, more than $550 million in research and development was spent on ATM in 1994. Potential new networking applications based on ATM include desktop videoconferencing and computer/telephony integration. Dataquest forecasts a 75% growth rate for ATM equipment, reaching approximately $1.4 billion by 1997.

The Networking Oligopoly

According to George Kelly, senior securities analyst covering data networking for Morgan Stanley, the industry is essentially dominated by a power block of dominant manufacturers. This oligopoly consists of four companies—Bay Networks, Cabletron, Cisco Systems, and 3Com. These companies have achieved so much success in recent years that they have amassed vast product portfolios, installed bases, research and development (R&D) staffs, and channels of distribution. The difference in scale between the oligopoly companies and the other networking companies is best illustrated by looking at the comparative outlays on R&D. Through August 1994 the top four companies had R&D expenditures ranging from $130 million to $180 million each. The next closest company had outlays of approximately $65 million, with most companies spending well below $50 million.

Many of these smaller companies are counting on ATM technology to level the playing field with the oligopoly, since the big four have largely built their success on adapters, Ethernet hubs, or routers. The problem, according to Mr. Kelly, is that the big companies are just as committed as their smaller competitors to exploiting ATM as the next wave of networking. And the huge R&D budgets of the four power players will enable them to do substantial work to develop ATM, and in the process defend themselves against the array of ATM startup companies. The oligopoly wants to prevent a repeat of what happened to companies like IBM and DEC in the networking market—displacement as the market leaders, from ignorance or preoccupation with their installed bases, resulting in a lack of attention to new technologies. As a result of innovation, aggressive product development, close customer contacts, open standards, and account control, the big four thrived, and they want to keep it that way.

In addition to big R&D budgets, another way the oligopoly has thrived is through mergers and acquisitions (M&A). Bay Networks itself is a product of the merger of two companies that were already big players in the networking market—Wellfleet, a manufacturer of routers, and SynOptics, a maker of intelligent hubs. Some months after its merger, Bay acquired Xylogics for $330 million in stock. Xylogics filled a critical hole in Bay's product line with its hardware and software products that allow users of laptop computers to dial into corporate networks from remote locations. In 1987 3Com combined with Bridge Communications in the networking industry's first important merger. The combined company is headed by a former Bridge executive, Eric Benhamou, who has overseen the successful integration of the complementary product lines. 3Com went on to make several acquisitions including BICC Data Networks, which provided critical mass in the hub market, and companies providing switching, remote access, and ATM technologies (Synernetics, Centrum Communications, and Nicecom, respectively). In summer 1995 3Com also entered into a $775 million agreement to acquire Chipcom, a maker of high-end products for large networking requirements, including intelligent hubs. Through this strategy, Mr. Benhamou has changed 3Com's position from a company once completely dependent on adapter cards—"The Workgroup Computing Company"—to one with a complete product line—"The Global Data Networking Company." Meanwhile, Cisco, the leading vendor of routers, bought Crescendo Communications, a leader in fast switching technology, and Newport Systems, a privately-held supplier of software-based routers. Cisco also acquired Kalpana, an Ethernet switching company. And to expand its business into new areas, Cisco acquired Combinet in August 1995. Combinet makes equipment that lets small offices and telecommuters connect their computers to headquarters over high-speed phone lines known as Integrated Services Digital Network (ISDN) circuits.

123

The M&A hyperactivity of the big four, like its extensive R&D outlays, is based on the assumption that long-term networking solutions will require a combination of adapters, routing, switching, ATM, remote access, and sophisticated network management from one source. Analysts expect the pattern of M&A in the networking industry to continue almost unabated for some time to come.

Oligopoly notwithstanding, there is still room for highly innovative and flexible smaller companies, such as Agile Networks and First Virtual, to develop new technologies and fill certain niches in networking. Morgan Stanley analyst George Kelly states, "The advantage that startups enjoy of being able to take a fresh new look at customers' near- and long-term requirements, without the encumbrance of supporting and enhancing legacy systems, cannot be underestimated." Larger companies, like ALANTEC, Ascend Communications, Cascade, Chipcom, Digital Link, Newbridge Networks, and Network Peripherals, will also prove to be important players in the market.

The Information Technology Paradox

Oligopoly or not, many businesses primarily face the problem of implementing networking technology as part of their infrastructure. Into the 1990s, the low return on this technology has presented one of the greatest macroeconomic mysteries ever. U.S. companies have invested tons of money in technology to streamline business procedures, but there has actually been little in the way of lower business costs or greater efficiency. And no one has been able to genuinely measure the ROIT—Return On Information Technology. This "information technology paradox" continues to puzzle business executives and economists.

During the 1980s, somewhere between $860 billion to $1 trillion was spent on information technology, but in white collar services (banking, finance, health care, insurance, telecommunications, etc.) productivity increased by only 0.8% annually, compared with the historical norm of 2.5% a year. Part of the problem, according to Stephen Roach of Morgan Stanley, is that "companies today probably have ten times as much processing power as they need."

In his report, *America's Productivity Revolution* (Morgan Stanley, March 8, 1995), Mr. Roach examines the situation again. In the 1990s productivity gains have averaged 2% a year, double the anemic 1% pace that prevailed in the 1970s and 1980s. Some analysts assume that this increase is primarily due to a more efficient use of technology. But Mr. Roach argues that the answer is a little more complex than that. On one level, there's been the need to pare the excesses of bloated cost structures through layoffs, plant closings, outsourcing, and other forms of downsizing. Meanwhile, for those employees who remain, more capital is spent on giving them new tools and new technologies, yet this technology will be of little benefit if employees aren't trained to use it to work smarter. But Mr. Roach remains optimistic. He writes:

> The problem was never the "machine" itself, but more the manner in which it was managed. As America leapt headlong into the Information Age, technology acquisition was both indiscriminate and misdirected. In the new competitive environment of the 1990s, the user community can no longer afford such complacency. The restructuring of back-office, sales, and managerial functions has been tied explicitly to more focused, strategic applications of information technology. And the improved productivity results of the 1990s suggest that the service sector is now turning the corner in resolving the fabled information technology paradox.

But Mr. Roach goes on to say that ultimately, ideas and knowledge-based solutions drive productivity, not technology. Meanwhile, the ubiquity of laptop computers, cellular phones, wireless modems, and home fax machines may be as much a curse as a blessing, because it obligates people to work longer hours. Mr. Roach calls this "the ugly little secret of America's productivity-led recovery—a stretched work force that is delivering more, but only because it's working more." In other words, increased productivity cannot automatically be credited to more technology or even improved technology, but rather to greater intellectual effort and more work hours in using the technology.

For the purchaser of networking technology then, the challenge is to come up with a clear plan for implementing the technology that enables people to work smarter, not just harder. In the end, the tools are only as good as those who manage them.

OUT **TAKES**

Robert Metcalfe

Executive Correspondent
InfoWorld

When the history of the information revolution is written, Robert Metcalfe will go down as the inventor of Ethernet and the founder of 3Com. To THE HERRING, he is

also a fellow technology journalist with a passion for new ideas and insightful commentary. For two years, Mr. Metcalfe served honorably as CEO and publisher of *InfoWorld,* one of the computer industry's most powerful weekly news publications. Mr. Metcalfe says *InfoWorld*'s mission "is to help information system managers move their mission-critical applications down from their mainframes to internetworked client/server systems." Mr. Metcalfe now serves as *InfoWorld*'s executive correspondent and continues to write his weekly column, which gains new readership each time it's published. "My favorite job," says Mr. Metcalfe, "is to explain things that are being hyped, because the people who are busy hyping things don't do a good job at explaining them, because they are generally busy lying about them."

Two of the hottest and most hyped-up areas in networking are Ethernet switching and ATM. Are these the right areas to focus on?

Yes. The switching phenomenon is the sweet spot in the market, where the growth and upside exist, and this will continue at least through 1996. But this technology does not change what is on the desktop. ATM is the big play, but it's a long-term play. The problem with ATM is that there is no standard. So it won't be a volume opportunity until the market and technology get sorted out a little more. But ATM will sell in volume someday.

George Gilder says the law of the telecosm tells us that when you take any *n* number of computers and connect them, you will get *n²* in exponential performance and value. Mr. Gilder also says that was your idea [Metcalfe's Law].

George is being a little generous here. Back in the late 1960s, when I was working on the ARPAnet, the prevailing view was that if you had a smart computer terminal, you would need less communications ability because you could do everything yourself. I woke up one morning thinking that theory was backwards. I realized that the more capability your terminal or PC has, the *more* communications ability it would need. That is why I was driven to develop networking technology. But the law of the telecosm is quite an old formula. Look at the telephone network. It didn't take long for the idea to penetrate that hooking several phones together so they could talk to each other was the most valuable strategy.

What is the story behind the development of Ethernet?
At Xerox we were building a new personal computer called the Alto, and it was my job to network them. The first thing the computers had to connect with was a laser printer which could print a page per second at a resolution of 500 dots per inch. If you do your arithmetic, that's a lot of bits per second. We all had disks that we wanted to share too, so the network had to be fast enough to accommodate this locally. So I took what I had learned on the ARPAnet, and from there, it was a very small step to come up with the idea of the Ethernet, on May 22, 1973. I remember the day, because I knew someday someone would ask when it was invented.

I might add that we also invented a router at Xerox! I've been kicking myself for a long time for not being Cisco. A lot of people are kicking themselves for that.

Eventually you left Xerox to start your own company. Why?
In Silicon Valley everybody starts their own company. 3Com's founding in June 1979 was based on the assumption that with the momentum in that market behind the Ethernet standard, driven by DEC, Xerox, and Intel, there would be a demand for Ethernet-compatible products. 3Com was founded to promote, serve, and exploit that market opportunity. 3Com stands for "computer communication compatibility"—which is connecting things together. At this point, the n^2 idea Mr. Gilder talks about came up first. When you connect computers together, the cost of doing so is n, but the value is n^2 because each one of the machines you hook up gets to talk to all the other machines in the network. When you graph that, you see that your costs grow slowly compared to the value of the network. Building on this concept, we peddled three ideas at 3Com: one, that LANs were a good idea; two, that they should be standard; and, three, that the standard should be Ethernet. And, oh yes, that you should buy your Ethernet from 3Com.

127

Craig Benson

Chairman, COO, and Treasurer
Cabletron Systems

When Craig Benson and Robert Levine started Cabletron in a garage in 1984, they raised money by mortgaging their homes and borrowing heavily from commercial banks. "We knew we had a business model that none of the professional venture capitalists would like," says Mr. Benson. "Nobody was stupid enough to invest in us." Cabletron went public in 1989 and has since completed five public financings that raised more than $500 million. On Wall Street, Cabletron is recognized for having the most consistent revenue growth and profitability in its industry category. In the networking world, Cabletron is known for its guerrilla sales tactics and its commitment to customer service.

How did Cabletron develop and what is behind your growth?
We started with cabling, evolved to installation, then to test equipment, and finally, to components for networks. The key to becoming an integrated company is that at the outset, we sold services rather than products, and we've kept that service orientation. We have about 180 outside salespeople in the company, but in the sales support and customer service area we have over one thousand people. We break it down into a multiple-step process so customers have access to specialized experts who help them with their networks every step of the way.

Fast Ethernet, Switched Ethernet, and ATM are causing big stirs in networking. How will these factor in your future?
These will be huge opportunities for the whole industry. Our challenge is to provide a migration path, because customers don't like to make big technology leaps overnight.

In the midst of these changes, is there still room for a two-man cabling shop that focuses on the right technology trends?

I don't see the two-man shop being successful in networking. When we started out, it was a lot easier because there were no major companies that were exclusively focused on internetworking. This is not to say that small companies cannot succeed in niche areas, but in general, customers want a large entity to provide their network with long-term support.

129

08_CLIENT/SERVER
COMPUTING

C lient/server computing has both hardware and software components. In a client/server network personal computers are linked together so that they can communicate and share information. The network has at least one server computer connected to several PCs, designated as client computers. The server houses many of the main applications and databases for the network that can be accessed by the individual client computers. Client/server software includes databases, operating systems, analysis tools, development environments, and programs that enable connectivity and network management.

J. GARRETT SHELDREW

The Client/Server Landscape

At the optimum level, client/server computing combines the performance, centralized data administration, and security of a mainframe network, with the flexibility, ease-of-use, and pricing of a personal computer network. Analysts see the development of client/server computing as representing the convergence of the previously distinct personal computer, minicomputer, and mainframe computing models into one integrated, networked, and coherent enterprise-wide model.

Client/server computing used to be limited to smaller networks within departments or workgroups. The trend is to expand the client/server structure to include whole companies or enterprises. The goals, as always, are to improve productivity and to lower costs. Meanwhile, users can more easily access needed data and communicate more freely through electronic mail and other forms of data exchange. Ultimately client/server networks include not only tethered, or wired, computers, but also mobile, wireless computer devices (laptops, personal communicators, cellular handsets, etc.) that can communicate with the network.

According to the market research firm Forrester Research, the market for client/server software jumped from $187 million in 1991 to $5.9 billion in 1995.

Companies and Strategies

Client/server computing is increasingly seen as a more flexible and productive alternative to using mainframes for company-wide computing functions, including mission-critical applications such as accounting. As a result, mainframe vendors, like Computer Associates, are stepping up their efforts to provide client/server products.

Computer Associates (CA) is the largest dedicated software vendor for mainframes, but it has seen its mainframe-related percentage of revenues go down in recent years, while its CA-Unicenter client/server software products have brought increasing revenue. Unicenter had $300 million in sales in its first 18 months and is a leading tool for managing networked computer systems. CA jointly markets Unicenter with two Microsoft products: Windows NT Server and SQL Server. CA offers three other corporate applications: CA-Manman, a manufacturing management program; CA-Masterpiece, a financial management and accounting application; and CA-Hrisma, a human resources management system. CA also acquired a major competitor, Legent, in 1995 for $1.78 billion. This merger combined the two largest independent suppliers of mainframe software into a giant with $3 billion in revenues, and added Legent's client/server products to the CA lineup.

One of the most important companies in the client/server market is Oracle Systems, headed by president and CEO Larry Ellison. Its corporate-database software products, along with those produced by competitors Sybase and Informix, have been mainstays of the client/server boom. Oracle provides pre-packaged applications for general services such as human resources, accounting, and manufacturing, as well as programming tools for customizing its software. Oracle's products have generally been used at the upper tiers of corporate

Oracle president and CEO Larry Ellison

computing, but the company is making a push into the lower end of network computing—workgroups, departmental users, small businesses—where users have less technical training and require simpler applications. While the higher-end products have more functionality and require extensive training and service support, the lower-end offerings must be cheaper, less complex, bundled solutions. As Oracle moves into the lower tiers, it will inevitably clash with Microsoft, which is trying to push its way up from personal computing and smaller networks.

Oracle, Sybase, and Informix are all offering low-end workgroup versions of their database management systems and new programming tools for client/server computing. Oracle currently has about a 50% share of the corporate-database market. And with only about 15% of the client/server transition completed—what the analysts call the computer-downsizing movement—there is still plenty of room for market growth.

This growth potential prompted two important players in the client/server market, Sybase and Powersoft, to merge. This acquisition, valued at $875 million, brought together Powersoft's programming tools with Sybase's database management and connectivity software.

Lotus Development, acquired by IBM in 1995, has also participated in the client/server market through its groupware product Lotus Notes, a program that allows all network users to see and work on the same file simultaneously. Like Lotus 1-2-3, its trailblazing spreadsheet program, Lotus Notes is seen as a "killer app" that helped create a fundamentally new and different use for the computer, spawning a new market. By the end of 1994, there were over one million users of Notes. Lotus also has a joint project with AT&T—AT&T Network Notes—in which AT&T is developing an infrastructure that will provide the dial-in connectivity, administration, support, and billing services to help broaden the market for the Notes product and gain wider industry support from developers.

Nevertheless, Novell is still the market leader in groupware with its GroupWise product, which as of fall 1995 had three times as many users as the better-known Lotus Notes. Serious competition in the groupware market is also expected from Microsoft and Oracle.

Other important companies include PeopleSoft, French-based Business Objects, and the German company SAP. PeopleSoft offers software applications for human resources management and corporate accounting and financial packages. Business Objects provides decision support, query, and report-writing software used with client/server relational database management service (RDBMS) packages offered by Oracle and others. SAP offers software that gives companies a way to link data from their finance, sales, and manufacturing departments. If sales change, for example, factory data will automatically be updated. Other important companies include Baan, Tivoli, Platinum Technology, BMC, and Compuware. Data warehousing companies such as Red Brick Systems, are another important part of the client/server market. Data warehousing involves the creation (or consolidation) of a database into a unified resource for an entire corporation to aid in decision support.

As client/server computing grows, demands for customer training, consulting, and support will also grow. Servicing client/server networks will be a big source of revenue for Oracle and the other software providers. And systems integrators and consulting companies, such as Cambridge Technology Partners, BSG, Computer Sciences, EDS, Ernst & Young, KPMG, and Andersen Consulting, could garner a good deal of business from the client/server boom.

The Cost of Implementation

In spite of its promises, implementing a client/server network can be costly. And estimating the cost of implementation over a typical five-year period must take into account expenditure for hardware, software, maintenance, upgrades, and labor. Hardware costs include not only the desktop client computers and servers, but all the components required for network connectivity. Labor costs include the time users spend learning, operating, and maintaining their desktop systems, as well as providing server and network support.

The Gartner Group, a leading research firm and provider of information technology advisory services, estimates that labor constitutes more than 70% of the total cost of a owning a client/server system over a five-year period. Hardware, software, upgrades, and maintenance make up most of the remaining costs, with most of it spent on the desktop systems rather than on the server. In contrast to stand-alone PCs, client/server systems are a long-term investment: $50,000 to $65,000 per end-user over a five-year period.

Like most sophisticated technology, a client/server system is complicated to implement. Customers must deal with a variety of hardware, networking, and software elements that theoretically interoperate, but actually have a hard time working together smoothly. Because there is generally a skill gap in most organizations, where the complex knowledge required to implement client/server is lacking, service and maintenance support, as well as training, remain important parts of the whole client/server package.

Caveat Emptor

A good example of implementation problems on a large scale is the series of massive computer automation projects for the state of California which suffer from mismanagement and poor design and could cost taxpayers well over $1 billion in the end. While only one of these projects involves client/server networks, they do represent the kind of data management services that client/server networks are supposed to handle.

One computer project, a program to automate the welfare system, is so plagued by mismanagement and so overpriced that it is not likely to be implemented until the year 2000—five years behind schedule—and it may cost more than $1 billion, twice the original estimate. Other computer boondoggles include an uncompleted $152 million program that would allow counties to share information on child support cases; a child welfare tracking system that has cost $10 million to date and might be abandoned; a $49 million Department of Motor Vehicles information system that had to be dumped; and a $37 million student financial aid automation system that may also have to be abandoned.

These debacles illustrate the perils of poor planning and design leading to incompatible systems that simply can't talk to each other. The state has so many electronic mail systems, for instance, that state senators can't count on successfully sending messages to colleagues in the Assembly. State officials have had

135

to face the fact that the poorly designed systems came about because although departments had little computer expertise, they still tried to create their own networks and ended up with muddled plans and dysfunctional systems.

Trends

According to Steven Milunovich, an analyst with Morgan Stanley & Co., an important trend affecting client/server computing, and information technology as a whole, is scalability—moving PC technologies up into enterprise-wide computing. This means that a computer that once served as only a personal desktop system can now be a high-powered workstation, a departmental server, or an enterprise (i.e. company-wide) server.

Mr. Milunovich believes that smaller computer technology will eventually conquer the computer industry from the desktop up. With the PC as the engine, scalable computing means that the network becomes the computer. The result is the commodization of computers—the PC becomes a low-price, high-volume commodity interchangeable anywhere in the network. Scalability also means more compatible computers that become universal standards.

The implication is that because networks are moving away from mainframes and minicomputers toward client/server systems, an economy of scale (buying the largest computer) is being replaced by economies of volume (buying the most compatible and prevalent computer). Increased standardization also means greater uniformity and compatibility of interfaces, operating systems, applications, storage technologies, and microprocessors. The biggest beneficiaries of these trends toward standardization and scalability, says Mr. Milunovich, are Microsoft and Intel (sometimes lumped together as "Wintel") and the PC vendors such as Compaq Computer. The potential losers are the maker of workstations, like Sun Microsystems, and the database companies discussed above. The Microsofts and Compaqs will prosper more by moving up into client/server networks as a result of scalability, says Mr. Milunovich, than the Oracles or Suns will benefit by trying to move down to the lower end of these networks.

136

OUT **TAKES**

Charles Wang

Chairman & CEO, Computer Associates

Computer Associates (CA) has an immense mainframe and minicomputer application, database, and system software business, and has aggressively moved into the client/server market. Its client/server revenue more than doubled in the fiscal fourth quarter of 1994, while its mainframe business grew by just a little over 10%.

CA has largely built its business through acquisitions, completing more than 50 over the last two decades. The company made a major move in June 1994 by purchasing the ASK Group, which included the Ingres client/server database developer, for $330 million. It then bought a major competitor, Legent, in 1995 for $1.78 billion. The merger with Legent combined the two largest mainframe software companies into a giant with $3 billion in revenues. It also adds Legent's client/server products to the CA lineup and in turn opens the way for CA to sell its client/server products to Legent customers. CA has also expanded its own client/server products through the development of its Unicenter system management tools.

THE HERRING talked with Mr. Wang about business technology trends that touch on both the promises and pitfalls of client/server computing.

As both a businessman and a technologist, what do you see as the main challenge for implementing technology in business?
A serious disconnect has developed between technology people and business people. Most business people don't understand technology's issues and terms, or even its role in their companies. On the other side, technology people can get so wrapped up in their alphabet soup of acronyms that they forget their reason for being: to serve business. My advice to business people is to understand that they can use technology to gain a competitive advantage. My advice to technology people is to get out of their ivory towers and become part of business. This is

137

because the two sides have to work together to make technology a competitive tool. The CEO should learn the fundamentals of technology and should include the chief information officer at the highest levels of management. That person should talk to the CEO about the impact of technology decisions the same way the company's lawyers, accountants, and other advisors talk to the CEO about their responsibilities.

But isn't there a lot of hype in the technology industry?
Most technology companies are run by technologists who think they have a panacea for everything. Every four or five years they call for a revolution where we have to throw out everything and redevelop. If you go to the trade shows and see their great new gizmos and advances, you must remember that these things won't fundamentally change the way we use technology overnight. A better approach is intelligent evolution: business people should understand the role of technology, preserve their investments in it to run their businesses, and embrace those new developments that make sense.

What about all the discussion about empowering workers through the use of electronic mail and accessing the Internet?
In most cases, electronic mail is an abused tool. Managers do not have time to read all their messages, and some people spend all their time sending them. It's become a cover-your-ass tool, where someone says he copied you on a message he knows you'll never have time to read. At CA, we restrict its use in order to give employees more time to do exciting things like visit clients. Even though we've had a lot of whining, it's worked out wonderfully. One issue with some of the Ingres people who joined us as a result of our acquisition of ASK was that they were shocked that we wouldn't allow them to surf the Internet. I'm sorry, but I pay them money to produce computer code and serve clients, not surf.

09_PERSONAL PRODUCTIVITY SOFTWARE

Until recently, it was personal productivity software—word processing, spreadsheet, and database programs—that drove the desktop computing market. People were buying personal computers to write, crunch numbers, and track data more efficiently. Although personal productivity is still a major reason individuals buy computers, much has changed in the market in the last few years.

In 1989 PC users had numerous options in word processing and spreadsheet software that included products not only from Microsoft but from companies like WordPerfect, Lotus, Software Publishing, Borland, and Ashton-Tate. Today,

Microsoft alone owns about 80% of the corporate word-processing and spreadsheet markets, and has almost as big a share of the consumer market. Meanwhile the Macintosh market continues to shrink, with a worldwide PC market share of just 8.5% in 1995.

Application Suites

A lot of personal productivity software is sold in suites—collections of programs grouped together at a single price. Microsoft Office is a suite that includes Word, Excel, Powerpoint, and a client license for Mail. ClarisWorks is another suite, developed for the Macintosh, that contains word processing, graphics, database, and spreadsheet programs. Lotus offers SmartSuite, which contains Word Pro, Organizer, ScreenCam, Approach, Freelance Graphics, and 1-2-3. Novell's PerfectOffice includes WordPerfect, Quattro Pro, Presentations, InfoCentral, Envoy, and GroupWise.

Before 1990 Microsoft was mostly a desktop operating system company, but with the triumph of its Windows operating system, its way was paved to dominate in personal productivity applications as well. In both stand-alone applications and suites, Microsoft is the market leader with its Office suite, Word word processor and Excel spreadsheet because all of its competitors were late in providing Windows versions of their applications. Applications bundling also took its toll on competitors. Software Publishing, developer of Harvard Graphics, one of the first graphics presentation programs, owned 70% of the market until Microsoft began bundling presentation software in its Office suite. By 1995 Software Publishing had only 8% of the market.

Upgrades

For some years now, in order to bring in new revenue, software companies have relied on selling product upgrades to old customers. Never mind that the 4.0 version of a program may have been good enough—what you need now, they say, is version 5.0. In some cases, the upgrade treadmill has led to a point of diminishing returns. A once elegant and easy-to-use program begins to suffer from feature overload. The user is confronted with rows of meaningless icons, useless layers of dialogue boxes, and a program that hogs memory and runs miserably slowly. Additional features also mean more bugs. More features also mean manufacturers have to spend more time explaining to consumers how to use the programs.

A perfect example is Microsoft Word 6.0 for the Macintosh. Tests done by *Macworld* magazine in 1995 showed that Word 6.0 took more than 7 minutes to start. Counting words in a long document took 5 minutes and 48 seconds using 6.0, compared to 33 seconds for the same document in Word 5.1. When fully installed, Word 6.0 required more than four times the hard disk storage space 5.1 required. As one technical expert put it, "This is a particularly ugly example of how much worse an upgrade is than a previous version. But I think there should be a moratorium on upgrades anyway. Besides being slow and full of features no one wants, they require more memory, and the computer memory required to run these upgrades isn't getting any cheaper."

The greater hardware demands of application upgrades and revised operating systems like Windows 95 promise more sales for the makers of computer chips, PCs, and software that runs with the upgrades; yet feature bloat not only means greater hardware cost for the consumer, but also leads to the need for more technical support, especially for beginners.

Service Support

As of 1995, according to the market research firm Odyssey LP of San Francisco, about 58% of PC owners had their computer two years or fewer, making the PC market a very young one with many novice users. Most of these users expect their computers to be like other consumer electronics products; plug-and-play items that are supposed to work right out of the box. Since this is not always the case, technical support for computer products owned by beginners is especially critical.

The gap between what computer owners know about their machines and what the software industry expects them to know is widening, especially with the advent of multimedia machines with their more complex configurations that include sound cards, more memory, and CD-ROM drives. This was dramatically illustrated during Christmas 1994 in the case of Disney's *The Lion King StoryBook* CD-ROM. Not only did many consumers not have the required equipment, like 16-bit sound cards, such designations did not mean anything to them anyway. And these problems have not been limited to Disney.

Because these inexperienced home users do not have the training and the in-house technical support that corporate users have, software and hardware companies have had to add thousands of technicians to handle the huge increase in calls to their help lines. According to Dataquest, the average call volume increased by 20% annually in 1993 and 1994. The average call length also increased by 20% in each year. Robert Johnson, an analyst at Dataquest, says, "It's a double whammy. And nothing undercuts a company's reputation more quickly than lousy service." For some companies the numbers are even greater. Compaq Computer, for example, averaged 25,000 calls a day in 1995, up 50% from the year before.

Dataquest found that of the PC users who called technical support, 67.5% called a software publisher first. According to The Learning Company, a children's software subsidiary of Brøderbund, about one-third of the customer service calls they receive are not directly related to their products. Instead, the callers want basic advice on how to set up and run their computers.

As the market for PCs expands and some of the personal productivity software gets more complex, the need for service support will only increase. With the continued drop in prices for personal productivity software, there is more pressure on profit margins because of the concurrent increase in the costs of service support for these programs.

Integrated and Customizable Applications

Beyond the traditional personal productivity applications, another new battlefront for the PC desktop could be customizable applications and "applets."

Not surprisingly, Microsoft has already fired the first shot with its OLE—Object Linking and Embedding—utility. OLE allows Windows applications to tap easily into each other via live "hot" links in the software. On the simplest level, these inter-application links mean different applications could share the same spellchecker. On a more complex level, OLE could make it easy for a user to create a presentation using graphics generated by a graphics program linked to data in a spreadsheet with text created by a word processor, all rolled into one electronic document.

The main competition to OLE comes from OpenDoc, a linking utility jointly developed by Apple and IBM, supported by Novell and promulgated through the CI Labs consortium. OpenDoc eliminates the need to launch separate applications (word processors, spreadsheets, etc.) or to move back and forth between them. It also supports the use of "applets," small application modules—such as spellcheckers, charting or graphics capabilities, and dictionaries—that can be plugged into existing applications. Applets promise to add specialized functionality, help automate repetitive tasks, and make applications easier to use.

The net result of linking capabilities and applets could be customized applications. The WordPerfect word processor, for example, sells very well in the legal market, but has many functions never used by lawyers. It is also missing a legal dictionary and an online link to legal databases like LEXIS. Using a utility like OpenDoc, developers could create "WordPerfect for Tax Attorneys," eliminating the useless features and containing the ones lawyers use most. Users could develop their own customized applications by searching the Internet for applets, paying for them, downloading, and folding them into their application programs.

Going Mobile

Personal productivity nirvana will not arrive, according to Michael Kwatinetz, research analyst at PaineWebber, until mobile professionals can carry their applications with them in a way that will allow them to continually update and communicate information anytime, anywhere. This means using truly portable computers to plan appointments, update phone books, take notes, send e-mail, make presentations, take sales orders, send and receive faxes, update financial analyses, and tap into remote databases and online services.

Current notebook computers can be outfitted to perform most of these functions. But Mr. Kwatinetz would like to see a genuinely practical personal digital assistant (PDA) that incorporates these applications along with a built-in cellular phone and fax/modem. Mr. Kwatinetz feels that a successful PDA market could swing the applications market momentum away from Microsoft to developers of PDA-specific applications.

On the PC front Mr. Kwatinetz predicts a greater installed base in the home, growing from a 35% penetration level in 1994 to 57% in 1997 or 1998 in the United States, and from 15% to 45% worldwide in that same time frame. This growth will result not only from falling prices, but from the expanded use of productivity software in the home. Growing software categories will include financial software (tax preparation, budget, and bill paying programs, etc.), printing, desktop publishing and design programs, and scheduling software.

Mergers and Acquisitions

One way software companies have tried to cope with increasing costs and more intense pressure from Microsoft is through mergers and acquisitions. The most stunning deal in recent years was IBM's 1995 acquisition of Lotus. The other big deal was the merger of Novell and WordPerfect in 1994.

Novell-WordPerfect

The stock swap of Novell and WordPerfect was valued at $1.4 billion. Novell also purchased the Quattro Pro spreadsheet program from Borland for $145 million as well as one million copies of its Paradox database program. This purchase combined Novell's powerful networking operating system with recognizable brands of personal productivity software.

Novell had revenues of $1.12 billion in 1993. WordPerfect was privately held and 1993 revenues were estimated at $700 million, although its profits of only $10 million gave it a margin of just 1.4%. WordPerfect had high overhead, supporting a payroll of 7,000 employees, with a per capita revenue of $100,000 but profit per capita of only $1,500. Combined revenues for the new company and product line was $1.9 billion, still leaving it way behind Microsoft, which had annual revenues of $4 billion in 1994. Lotus was third, with annual revenue just below $1 billion.

Not everyone was impressed with the Novell/WordPerfect merger. Commenting on the deal at the time, analyst Mary McCaffrey of Alex. Brown & Sons said, "I am very surprised Novell is moving into the applications side of the business. There will be many digestion problems as Novell swallows WordPerfect. I see this as a distraction. Novell is not very familiar with applications software, and it's going to take some time to integrate everything together into the kind of applications suite they'll be competing against. It would've been better for Novell to focus on getting the next release of its networking software to work well."

By summer 1995 Ms. McCaffrey's predictions had already come true. Although Novell's earnings for its fiscal third quarter ending July 29 were up 33% compared to the same quarter the year before, revenue from its major applications programs had declined sharply. Sales of the company's WordPerfect and PerfectOffice applications, in particular, declined about 35% in the same period. Revenue from Novell's personal productivity segment, composed almost entirely of the two applications, fell to $88 million in the third quarter from $135 million a year earlier.

Meanwhile, Novell had stumbled badly in the introduction of the latest version of its networking software—Netware 4.0. Gaps and bugs in the product caused customers to more actively consider alternatives like Microsoft's Windows NT product. Some analysts felt this meant a loss of market momentum for Novell as well as of customer mindshare, despite Netware's superiority over Windows NT in most ways. One important difference is Novell's Directory Services feature, which allows a user to log on to a corporate network and gain access to files and services without having to search through cryptic lists of electronic addresses or enter numerous passwords.

Novell is the market leader in groupware with its GroupWise product, which as of fall 1995 had three times as many users as the better-known Lotus Notes.

Novell has several other products in the works, including wireless networks and a technology that would allow users to exchange information over ordinary electric power lines, turning electric outlets into potential Netware connections.

IBM/Lotus

IBM acquired Lotus in spring 1995 for $3.5 billion, the largest software deal of this kind ever. IBM bought Lotus primarily for its groupware product Lotus Notes, a program that allows networked users to see and work on the same file simultaneously. Like Lotus' trailblazing spreadsheet program Lotus 1-2-3, Lotus Notes is seen as a "killer app" that helped create a fundamentally new and different use for the computer. Sales of Notes doubled annually, and by the end of 1994 there were over one million users of Notes. IBM's expectation was that Notes could be marketed through its global sales force, which operates in 140 countries.

This acquisition is a definite gamble for IBM. By some estimates, IBM paid an additional $2.8 billion over and above the historical value of Lotus. Naturally, the advisors to the deal generated several million dollars in fees. IBM's investment bank, CS First Boston, netted $12 million on the transaction. Lotus' bank, Lazard Frères, collected an additional $8–$9 million. And not to be forgotten were the lawyers. IBM's outside firm collected $2–$3 million in fees, and the law firms for Lotus and Lazard Fréres collected in the neighborhood of $1 million to $2 million each.

The Jolly Blue Giant of IBM, CEO Louis Gerstner

Joseph Bentzel, president and CEO of Green-Soft, a company that sells paperless document-managing software, points out that examining the Lotus annual report for 1994 reveals that 51 cents of every dollar Lotus spent went to marketing and sales. Microsoft's annual report for 1994 shows that 29.7 cents of every dollar it spent went to marketing and sales. While Lotus spent more on marketing, it had less of the

147

market. Mr. Bentzel concludes, "So I think buying Lotus was an absolutely necessary move for IBM. It's like the Cold War: it's better to have two nuclear superpowers than one."

Looking Ahead

Why has there been such a concentration of the personal productivity market into the hands of a few superpowers? Eric Schoenberg and Scott Sedlacek, respectively senior associate and managing director with the investment bank Broadview Associates, say the huge, upfront research and development expenditures make it hard for the smaller, less capitalized companies to compete. Meanwhile, as the price of software drops, this puts more pressure on the profits of retailers, who will therefore only want to carry recognizable brands. Products from the larger, brand-name publishers like Microsoft virtually guarantee retailers a big volume of sales.

But this does not mean that the software market is closed to new companies. History shows, according to Messrs. Schoenberg and Sedlacek, that new market niches as well as new technology paradigms will continue to emerge. Smaller, more agile entrepreneurial ventures are better positioned to foster innovation and take advantage of new niches. And technology shifts—"the reshuffling of the deck"—such as the move from stand-alone applications on individual PCs to groupware, open the door to new companies as well.

One trend that can be exploited by new companies is telecommuting. Any application that allows users to operate away from the traditional office environment will become increasingly important. One example is LapLink, made by Traveling Software, which allows users to transfer files between their laptop and desktop computers.

Groupware presents some unique opportunities. In addition to Lotus Notes and Novell's GroupWise, new products are emerging from what someone has called "groundswell groupware"—the spread of collaborative applications from pockets of users inside organizations. Providing direct competition to Lotus is Collabra Software, which offers a groupware platform that focuses on information sharing and conferencing, at a fraction of the price of Notes. Unlike Notes, Collabra's product operates on top of existing e-mail networks and does not require users to import documents. The Internet also provides a promising environment for new collaborative applications.

Not to be forgotten are utility programs. It is true that with each new version of MS-DOS and Windows, Microsoft has continued to bundle more utilities—disk compression, memory management, anti-virus programs, screen savers—but there is still room for more utilities. Symantec has been the industry leader in desktop utility programs for the PC and the Macintosh for some time. To bolster its position, it acquired smaller utility companies like Norton, Central Point Software, Fifth Generation Systems, and Contact Software. More recently it announced a merger with Delrina, a maker of communications utility software, including WinFax.

Another key niche exists for programs that reduce tedious data entry tasks. Watermark Software offers a toolkit that lets users append and integrate scanned documents into their applications. Other niche companies provide tools for embedding voice annotation or scanned images into applications.

OUT **TAKES**

William N. Joy

Co-founder and Vice President for Research
Sun Microsystems

If THE RED HERRING had the job of starting the computer industry all over again and could pick five players living today to pull it off, Sun Microsystems co-founder Bill Joy would be on that team.

In the 1970s, Mr. Joy was the principal designer of the UC Berkeley version of the UNIX operating system. Its networking protocol and implementations helped spawn the Internet. In 1982 Vinod Khosla (now a general partner with venture capital firm Kleiner Perkins Caufield & Byers) convinced Mr. Joy to skip out of academia and join him and a couple of other 27-year-olds—Sun's current CEO, Scott McNealy, and hardware guru Andreas Bechtolsheim—to co-found what has become the world's leading computer workstation company. In the early days at Sun, Mr. Joy spearheaded Sun's "open systems" model of computing; co-designed SPARC, Sun's RISC microprocessor architecture; and developed the Network File System which allows multivendor remote access.

Today, Mr. Joy primarily camps out in his palatial pad in Aspen, CO, and continues as a key contributor to the strategies and technologies that drive Sun's success. He also remains one of the world's leading experts on the UNIX operating system.

How do you see things shaping up in the PC market?
I view the Internet as the real opportunity, not the PC. The Internet is a bigger phenomenon in my mind. I want our stuff to run on PCs, but they are just a clumsy way to connect to the Internet right now. The PC is not a particularly interesting device; it is pretty horrible from almost every vantage point. I guess they are cheap—you can buy them in parking lots across the country. But they don't represent a particularly great use of technology. Microsoft owns all the application categories, anyway, and they have no real interest in doing much innovation, so the whole PC space is just kind of boring. I mean, what's the big new thing

now in PCs? I guess people are getting *Doom* video game chips for Christmas and will have a little animation. Big deal.

Should computer companies just concede the PC market to Microsoft and Intel and move on?

The PC market has been really lucky—it has had a long smooth sail. But one of these days the dogs aren't going to eat the dogfood. It happened already! The business/commercial customers didn't buy Intel's Pentium processors. Maybe Windows 95 will be the same way. People might just say, "Yeah it works, but I really don't see enough advantages to making the change." Maybe a lot of people will just decide they don't want it. There is no guarantee in the long run that Windows 95 is going to work. That's the myth of progress. But things don't always get better. Then again, I'm not a PC user. I use Macintoshes and Suns.

So what about Apple?

I want them to figure out who they are. I don't know who they are anymore. Ultimately, I think that America has only two really great consumer electronics companies: Motorola and Apple. I do think both understand the human factor to creating consumer devices—things like form-factor, color, and packaging—better than any other company in this country.

`151`

Should IBM buy Apple, since both companies use the PowerPC chip, and IBM's OS/2 operating system seems to be up against the ropes in the growing consumer market?

It ain't never gonna happen. IBM is on a mission from Louis Gerstner [the CEO] to go buy whatever pieces they need to attack Microsoft's franchise, using OS/2 as a base. There are rumors all over the place about the things IBM is doing. I respect my sources, and will not reveal them, but it is quite clear that Gerstner has his checkbook in hand, and will be attacking Microsoft's application business. That's why I'm not worried about Microsoft in our market, because it is going to be under fierce attack in its own market. What Bill Gates thinks is sacrosanct—that Microsoft "owns" the corporate desktop, that it "owns" the home market—is just not the case. Windows 95 is the wrong design center. It's just kind of "crufty" stuff. OS/2 is a better product. Now I'm not sure if IBM will succeed, but they are certainly going for it. They have a lot of patents, they have a lot of smart people, and they could do some serious damage to their competition.

Why do you think interactive TV hasn't happened as planned?
It's just taken a lot longer to deploy than everybody thought. By the time companies such as @Home bring digital TV to the home, you will be able to take your Super Netscape version 4.0 Web browser with the latest version of our Hot-Java product [Sun's real-time, interactive World Wide Web browser enhancement], and that will be your animated user interface. It's like the Internet happened in the meantime. Right? The world changed a lot. I mean if you work like hell for two years on a technology, and no one is buying it, it's usually time to move on to your next idea. Look at Microsoft. They spent ten years trying to look like the Mac! They have now successfully stolen the Mac and UNIX, so now they have to do something original. It will be real interesting to see what happens with Microsoft now.

152

10_MULTIMEDIA TECHNOLOGIES

BART NAGEL

In the realm of high technology, multimedia refers to the use of computers to integrate text, audio, graphics, animation, and video into specific programs. Advances in multimedia technologies and increasing compatibility have helped create new and improved applications. These applications range from videoconferencing and enhanced training simulations to next-generation video games. But to make multimedia relevant to businesses and consumers alike, developers must create standards that are easy to use and meet the real needs of customers. This is the main challenge that the multimedia industry faces.

Markets and Applications

Multimedia has caught on in the consumer market largely through video games. A smaller level of penetration has come through education, reference, and edutainment CD-ROM titles although a large number of these titles have been flops [see chapter 1 on Education & Entertainment Software for further details]. Todd Bakar, managing director and senior technology analyst at Hambrecht & Quist, wrote in THE HERRING regarding multimedia for CD-ROM and online services: "The risk to this growth scenario is the lack of creativity that permeates the widening array of applications competing for the consumer's time. Too much content and information has simply been repackaged and repurposed for these new platforms, failing to take advantage of the medium's interactivity."

Meanwhile, other potential multimedia applications for the home, such as interactive TV and videophones, are at least a few years away. As *The Wall Street Journal* put it in mid-1995, "The history of home technology is littered with flops." It is not always easy to know what consumers want, even when providing technologies that could deliver potentially appealing services such as online banking or interactive shopping.

156

Business Applications

Faced with the trial and error, hit and miss of the home consumer market—epitomized by the shifting fortunes of CD-ROM and interactive TV—many developers have turned their attention to the business market. Potential applications include interactive training, distance learning, and increased integration of multimedia into sales, marketing, and business presentations.

Presentation software has evolved from slideshows run from personal computers to programs that allow users to include video clips, sound, and animation. Software packages such as Q-Media, Super Show-and-Tell, and Passport Producer Plus have made it easier to synchronize audio with video or animation. And a program like ScreenCam (Lotus/IBM) allows users to add textual captions to movies. These movies can be distributed as sales demos on floppy disk and CD-ROM, or through online connections.

Videoconferencing promises to be one of the main drivers for business multimedia. Important developers include PictureTel, Compression Labs, AT&T, and Intel. Videoconferencing is expected to work its way down to the desktop computer. As with traditional videoconferencing, the participants will view and hear each other using video and audio capabilities built into the computer.

Working within the same computer environment, users will not only see and talk to each other, but can share and alter text and graphics in tandem with the conversation. Gartner Group forecasts revenues of more than $4.7 billion for the desktop videoconferencing market by 1997.

The integration of multimedia into training applications also has potential. Self-paced courses offering interactive modules can be taken by individual users on personal computers. These courses can be offered on CD-ROM and eventually over local area networks or through online services. Simulation environments using 3D graphics and the immersion experience of virtual reality can put users in even more thorough training environments and situations that will better prepare them for their actual work.

Multimedia Standards

Because of accelerated product cycles, low barriers to entry, interest from large vendors, and the race to set standards, multimedia technologies is one of the most competitive areas covered by THE HERRING. To be successful, companies and developers must form the right business relationships and quickly push products to market that will significantly outperform existing customer options. While some companies will become standard setters and establish large markets for their multimedia products, the risk remains high for most competing companies.

Hardware

To offer more advanced multimedia in personal computers, Compaq Computer and other PC vendors have deployed the Motion Picture Experts Group (MPEG) standard of video and audio reproduction in their systems. The MPEG standard is a high-quality alternative to the jerky, muffled multimedia found in earlier generations of multimedia PCs.

Compaq uses the MPEG chip package developed by S3. MPEG is relatively cheap to employ because the chip package adds only about $100 to the typical price of a multimedia PC. The hope is that MPEG will help make CD-ROM titles and online offerings more visually compelling. It is also one more step toward the integration of interactive multimedia with the World Wide Web. The combination of multimedia technology with high-bandwidth online access would create a Broadband Web. MPEG technology is also employed in videoconferencing and has been endorsed by Microsoft.

157

Many multimedia technologies are incorporated into computer boards or add-in boards for upgrading the multimedia capability of PCs. Sound Blaster sound boards from Creative Technology can be added to many PCs. Diamond Multimedia offers boards that include graphics and digital video accelerators. At the same time, many of these functions are migrating to the motherboard as standard components. Intel is a big force in this process; it has aggressively moved to establish standards that influence every aspect of multimedia, including peripheral connections, interfaces, and videoconferencing. Many of these can be incorporated into either the central processing unit (CPU chip) or on the motherboard [see chapter 6 on Semiconductors for more on Intel and the incorporation of multimedia capability into microprocessors].

Systems Software

As multimedia pervades more of the computer industry, operating systems (OS) will have to provide better coordination of multimedia components and configurations. These capabilities will increasingly be built into both the Windows and Macintosh operating systems. Historically, the Macintosh OS has offered the most seamless multimedia capability. The challenge is for Windows to meet or surpass this standard.

As computers are used more and more as communications and collaboration tools, multimedia-friendly operating systems will need to provide smoother network integration and more efficient use of shared information. The increasing demand for videoconferencing is rapidly bringing network integration to the forefront of multimedia development. Network transmission of multimedia is particularly difficult, as it requires carefully timed delivery of sound and video information. This process contrasts with typical data networking, which has relied predominantly on imprecise and "bursty" delivery of data. Both Apple and Microsoft, as well as Novell, are racing to incorporate elements in their operating systems that will help solve these problems.

Development Tools

Development tools fall into two areas: first, production and editing tools, used to create video, sound, and animations for multimedia; and second, presentation and authoring tools, used to put together multimedia programs.

Production and editing tools include painting, drawing, visualization, simulation design, animation, and video and audio editing software. Publishers of these programs include Adobe, Autodesk, Corel, Fractal Design, Alias

Research, WAVEFRONT, SOFTIMAGE, MultiGen, and Xaos Tools. Although some of their programs can be used by amateurs to develop their own multimedia effects, most are used by professionals in sophisticated development processes [see chapter 2 on Digital Hollywood for a discussion of software tools used to develop special effects].

Meanwhile, presentation and authoring tools help expand the user base beyond the "techie" realm of cutting-edge game development and special effects movies into the more mainstream arena of commercial applications. Presentation tools are used primarily for sales, marketing, and business communications. Authoring tools allow users to implement more advanced multimedia functionality in business and entertainment applications.

Authoring tools bring together video, graphics, text, and sound into one seamless presentation. This process involves assembling the pictorial presentation, matching and interweaving the soundtrack with the visual elements, and fully developing the interactivity of the multimedia production.

Examples of popular authoring tools include Macromedia's Director and Authorware, AimTech's Icon Author, Oracle's Media Objects, and Multimedia ToolBook from Asymetrix.

Kaleida Labs, a joint effort of Apple and IBM, hopes to establish a new standard for multimedia development. Kaleida offers what it calls a cross-platform, object-oriented authoring language (ScriptX), as well as its own platform (Media Player). ScriptX is designed to let developers customize more of the features that affect how the multimedia application operates. Although some competitors want to characterize Kaleida as simply offering another authoring tool, the company rejects this notion. Executives there told THE HERRING, "Kaleida views itself as pursuing a platform business. We're not an authoring tool company, which is a misperception that a lot of people have in the multimedia community, as well as in the business community at large."

159

Mergers and Acquisitions

The really big deal in multimedia enabling software companies was the merger of Adobe and Aldus in 1994. In a stock swap valued at $525 million, these two desktop publishing giants together became the fifth-largest software firm.

Both companies were part of the original desktop publishing revolution. Adobe provided the Postscript software language, which enabled the Macintosh to translate images into digital maps that could be output by a laser-printer; Aldus provided the PageMaker application that lets graphic artists do page layouts on computer screens. The merger gave the combined company annual revenues of more than $500 million as well as a comprehensive product line in document creation, desktop publishing (DTP), pre-press production, and electronic document delivery.

In addition to Postscript, Adobe also offers Photoshop, a tool for scanning and manipulating images used in newspapers, catalogues, brochures, and periodicals; Illustrator, a program for creating drawings; and Acrobat, an application for translating and communicating electronic documents between different computer platforms. In spite of early success with PageMaker, Aldus had lost ground in desktop publishing to Denver, CO-based Quark and its more designer-friendly Quark XPress program.

The goal of the technically integrated Adobe/Aldus product line is to allow designers to work in the various applications in an almost seamless fashion, creating a layout in one program and bringing in graphics, photos, and typography using other programs without any hidden conflicts.

OUT **TAKES**

Carol Bartz

President & CEO
Autodesk

Autodesk has historically been known as the domain of the "cowboy coders"—a computer-aided design (CAD) outpost dominated by software engineers pursuing pet projects on their own schedules. In 1992 when Carol Bartz arrived from Sun

ANNE KNUDSEN

Microsystems to take the helm, her mission was to lead a transition to a more disciplined and market-driven Autodesk, an organization like the one she had left. By 1995 Ms. Bartz had presided over a new release of Autodesk's flagship AutoCAD product; a streamlining of the company to increase responsiveness to customers; and the growth of annual net income from $44 million to $57 million.

Ms. Bartz now contemplates sources of new revenue for Autodesk. As the CAD market matures, the company is looking for additional markets in which it can leverage its strengths. Multimedia is a natural. Driven by AutoCAD spin-offs Animator Pro and 3D Studio, Autodesk's multimedia business is growing 30–50% annually. THE HERRING spoke with Ms. Bartz at her company's San Rafael, CA headquarters.

161

As Autodesk pays more attention to specific customer segments, do you expect the traditional CAD markets to represent a smaller share of total revenues?
Absolutely. High-end CAD is definitely on a very slow growth curve. Autodesk was founded on the principle of bringing CAD to the mass market. Now the explosive growth potential for us is in more general design software, as opposed to CAD in particular. In the next decade, we intend to bring 3D to the mass market. Our motto is that we create products that transform people's ideas

into reality. I find that very compelling because everything we use, wear, or live in is an idea turned into a product.

How essential will multimedia technologies be to the company's future?

Multimedia will be very important. We are becoming increasingly exposed to it on the CAD side because people want to experience and visualize the products they are going to manufacture and the buildings they will build. Multimedia has a lot of synergy with our strengths in geometry and rendering. And some markets not directly connected to CAD, like videography, authoring, kiosks, and games, are very high-growth markets.

Will these trends eventually take Autodesk into the home market?

I believe so. As products become easier to use, they will migrate down from the design engineers to more general designers, and then to high-end home users. Our Animator Studio is a package that could be used by people who get into creating images and animation and playing with sound. In another five years, it could be someone like my six-year-old doing that sort of thing.

Larry Ellison

President & CEO
Oracle Systems

Larry Ellison enjoys the notoriety his ascent to the top of the information management software industry has brought him. You can see it in his eyes. Oracle, the company he founded with Robert Minor back in 1977, has emerged as the world's largest vendor of software that helps large corporations and governments better manage their information. Now Mr. Ellison is gearing up the company for the biggest battle of the information age. "Skeptics may disagree, but I believe the sheer impact of the interactive network into the home will rival that of the electric light, the telephone, and the television. We won't just talk or shop on the information highway; we will live on it," says Mr. Ellison. "An information highway is, in many ways, like a great library that comes to you. It has the same potential to enhance our lives as the Library of Alexandria stimulated the intellectual development and prosperity of the Greek and Roman civilizations," he prophesies.

163

Oracle is developing one of the main multimedia technologies needed to make Mr. Ellison's vision of the information highway a reality—the Media Server. This Media Server is a digital "multimedia library" that will store, retrieve, and manage all forms of digital information ranging from video to text. Oracle's specific goal is to make the Media Server the most popular tool for bringing video to the Internet, commercial online services, and eventually to interactive TV. To achieve this end, Oracle has entered into numerous strategic alliances with some of the top telephone, publishing, and computer companies in the world. One of the most important alliances is with Intel, which is collaborating with Oracle to develop technology for video-on-demand to personal computers via digital phone lines called ISDN (integrated services digital network). In particular, the effort would combine Intel's Proshare videoconferencing technology with Oracle's Media Server to allow users to record, store, and retrieve video messages, the same way they use e-mail and other data from corporate networks and online services.

So you are very optimistic about the Information Highway?

In my opinion, this is the dawn of the real information age. With the broadband service to everyone's home, the sun is really rising. The opportunities are enormous.

And where does Oracle fit in?

The information highway has to be a very low-cost, high-speed, two-way networking service available to consumers. Oracle's strategy is to provide a complete set of software for the delivery of on-demand consumer services. We believe that we will deliver the stream servers at a cost of a couple of hundred dollars per active stream, and that includes both hardware and software. We expect competition to drive prices down like a rock.

What about Microsoft's offering?

It's very expensive and it isn't here. We are years ahead of Microsoft. We are winning most of the deals because Oracle is the only company that has technology that works today. We have proven that! So we not only have to take this technology and couple it with services, but we have to help the phone companies actually install and build these systems.

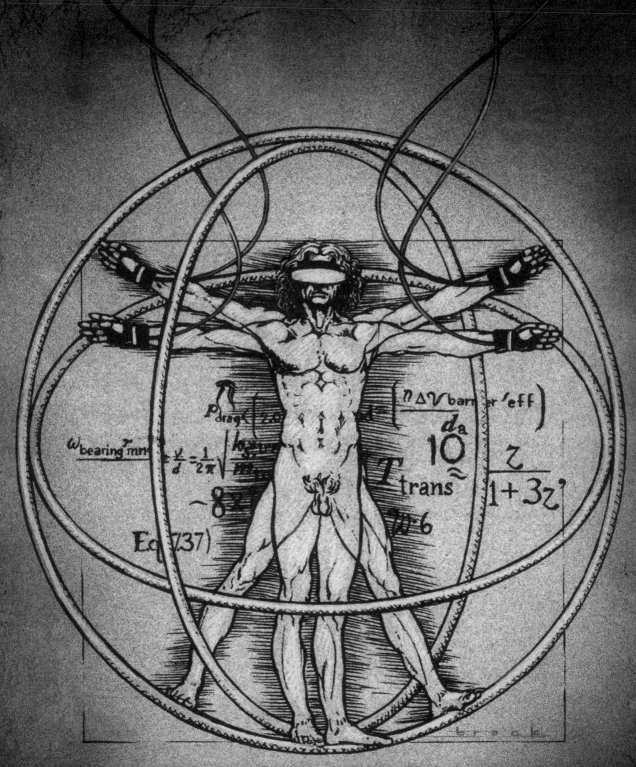

Bleeding Edge Technologies

11_BLEEDING EDGE
TECHNOLOGIES

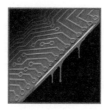

TIM BROCK

Virtual reality simulations, neural networks, speech and image recognition—these are some of the bleeding edge technologies that will become widespread applications in the not-so-distant future. Most of these technologies are being developed beyond the fringe of commerce at universities and research labs around the world. Even further out are developments in fuzzy logic, telemedicine, and nanotechnology. What all these technologies have in common is the challenge of moving from the realm of pure research to practical application. Increasingly, this is the quest of many scientists and engineers who are allied to business.

167

Product Development Challenges

To transform a new technology from its research and development (R&D), pre-market phase into a successful product is a big challenge. The timing and size of the potential market are often unclear. Some of the new technologies that are migrating or have attempted to migrate into the mainstream in recent years include asynchronous transfer mode (ATM) network technology [see chapter 7 on internetworking], desktop 3D graphics, object-oriented database management systems (OODBMS), and pen-based computing. The results have been mixed. There are many more technologies that researchers hope can emerge from the commercial R&D facilities, as well as from the back labs of universities and out of the proverbial garages, to become the cutting-edge products of tomorrow. But there are some important hurdles to get over.

Sometimes bleeding edge technology in the R&D phase does not develop, develops too slowly, or turns out differently from what was anticipated. Artificial intelligence (AI) is a good example. Early assumptions about the nature of intelligence were naïve. Consequently, computer systems that use AI to reason over a wide range of topics in a human manner remain a distant goal.

Sometimes products based on new technology claimed to be bleeding edge are too expensive to justify the purchase or adoption. The personal digital assistant (PDA), especially when claiming handwriting recognition capability like the Apple Newton, exemplifies this problem.

To thrive and prosper, a new technology must either become the standard in an emerging market or be adaptable to a prevailing standard. Sony's Betamax VCR is the classic case of a failed attempt to set a standard. The effective development and adoption of high definition television (HDTV) has, at least in part, also been thwarted by the standards issue.

Incubators of Applied Technology

Until the late 1960s, many large businesses were funding risky new technologies internally. General Electric, IBM, and RCA were among those companies willing to invest in basic technology research long before its commercial viability. As Harvey Poppel and Mark Toole of Broadview Associates point out, IBM poured tens of millions of dollars into technology like its Josephson junctions before admitting failure. In the 1970s venture capitalists moved in to provide most funding for bleeding edge ventures. Yet more recently, many venture capitalists have shifted their investment focus to later-stage products or technologies. Once again large corporations such as AT&T, IBM, Xerox, and 3M have stepped in to fund new technologies, usually by creating or backing early-stage companies.

One of the reasons the big companies got back into the act is that shifting market conditions in technology require firms to stay on top of new developments. As Messrs. Poppel and Toole put it, "Existing markets with short or shrinking product life-cycles require constant development, as the players try to hit the sweet spot of constantly shifting competitive zones. Aspiring winners have to walk the bleeding edge, as they are not afforded the luxury of waiting for standards to develop or for market demand to be clearly defined."

Xerox PARC

Xerox Palo Alto Research Center (PARC) has been a cradle of Silicon Valley innovation for 25 years. The pure research done at Xerox PARC has often been on the bleeding edge, too far out to be commercially viable. But the work is funded by a large multinational corporation increasingly focused on bringing to market the discoveries made at the center.

Xerox PARC has the reputation of developing a lot of great technology that it let get away. Among the cutting-edge technologies developed at PARC that mushroomed into new industries worth billions of dollars, without direct benefit to Xerox, were breakthrough developments that include the icon-based graphical user interface later implemented in Apple's Macintosh computers, the Ethernet technology now used in local-area networks, the modem, and the mouse. But the current directors of Xerox PARC say this has changed. "PARC missed some market opportunities," they state, "but it also hit a few, such as laserprinting [today a multibillion dollar Xerox business]. PARC and its parent made some mistakes, but we learned and moved on."

Most PARC technology flows directly into Xerox business divisions. But if a technology developed at the research center does not fit into a division at the parent company, Xerox may start a new company, put together a joint venture, partner with an existing startup, or license the intellectual property.

Xerox PARC is researching and developing technologies in a number of areas. For the Internet, Xerox PARC is working on a World Wide Web browser that can simultaneously display hundreds of pages and their hyperlinks using what it calls hyperbolic projection. PARC has also developed Network Video, one of the first videoconferencing tools used for multicasting (i.e. selectively broadcasting) video on the Internet. Xerox PARC also developed the basic infrastructure for all Internet multicasting, the Multicast Backbone (MBONE). PARC's Jupiter project is developing a collaborative multimedia environment in which authors can use a simple scripting language to create dynamic objects and virtual rooms for user interaction. And there is the Information Visualizer (IV), which provides a 3D animated interface. Another product is Tab, a wireless palm-top PDA used for note-taking, file-browsing, e-mail, and selectively downloading information from the Internet.

Bell Laboratories

Bell Laboratories was formed in 1925 by the Bell System. At the height of its influence in basic scientific research, from 1937 to 1978, scientists at the lab won seven Nobel Prizes. Bell Labs has done inventive research and development in transistors, lasers, fiber-optics, solar cells, light-emitting diodes, communications satellites, cellular mobile radios, negative feedback principles for controlling processes, code systems for the National Security Agency, control systems for antiballistic missiles, and much more. The lab has been awarded more than 25,000 patents, an average of one a day over its 70-year history. Under AT&T's reign, Bell Labs had an annual investment of $3.5 billion and employed 25,000 people in eight states and 21 foreign countries.

Like others, Bell Labs operates in an atmosphere of depressed financial support for basic scientific research. Dr. Arno Penzias, Nobel Prize winner and vice president of research at Bell Labs, indicates that the result is an increasing emphasis at Bell Labs on the development of commercially useful devices and systems, not on the pursuit of scientific knowledge. In a 1995 interview with *The New York Times*, Dr. Penzias said, "It's true that changes have been made to benefit the shareholders and customers, not basic science. But that's as it should be, because the world has changed. Science has already won many of its goals, and a lot of today's basic research goes far beyond any commercially interesting objectives."

This new climate has also affected Bell Labs' sister institution, Bell Communications Research Company (Bellcore), owned by the seven regional Bell operating companies (RBOCs). When the Bell System broke up in 1984, AT&T retained Bell Labs and renamed it AT&T Bell Laboratories, and the RBOCs pooled their resources to create Bellcore to conduct applied research and computer software development. According to Dr. Robert Lucky, Bellcore's research director, "Basic research is not affordable in this environment." In 1995 the RBOCs put Bellcore up for sale. This move does not bother Dr. Penzias. "The change in research priorities," he says, "is not a nice message for fundamental science. But the opportunities in applied science are greater than ever. We have to meet the changing needs of our companies and of society." It seems that like Xerox PARC, Bell Labs will have to become more practical and entrepreneurial, and less theoretical, if it is to survive and prosper.

Universities and Technology Centers

Each year, MIT conducts more than $750 million in sponsored research, 80% of which is paid for with federal funds. Because of this level of research universities like MIT, Stanford, and Harvard have technology licensing offices. Stanford has a full-time staff of 21 people in its Office of Technology Licensing, while MIT devotes 23 people to this task. These offices receive as many as three or four applications for new and potentially patentable ideas per week. Approximately 10–15% of these discoveries are selected for patenting. As holders of intellectual property, these universities as well as research plants like NASA's Jet Propulsion Laboratory and Lawrence Livermore National Laboratory try to sell their ideas. They use press kits, advertisements, Web sites, and databases to actively market their breakthroughs to corporations, entrepreneurs, and venture capitalists. In FY 1993–94, for example, Stanford's Office of Technology Licensing earned licensing revenues of $38 million on an operating budget of $2 million.

171

Then there are consulting firms and technology centers that focus primarily on helping businesses adopt the latest technology. Andersen Consulting, for example, runs a Center for Strategic Technology (CST) in Palo Alto, CA. "CST's mission," according to Joe Carter, an Andersen Consulting partner and the Center's director, "is to accelerate the uptake of advanced information technologies into business." The Center helps reduce the lag time between when new technologies first come out and when customers adopt them. CST accomplishes this by offering workshops that educate executives on how to implement technology in their businesses. Another CST strategy is to present case studies and demonstrations that show how technology can be applied. Case studies cover applications ranging from object-oriented programming and interactive training to multimedia teleconferencing and remote customer service interfaces.

The CST also studies how workers of the future will operate from their homes. It is experimenting with a hypothetical home of the future—the Home Lab—set up with high-speed computer networks and other emerging computer technologies. CST is also teaming up with Xerox PARC to test the Live-

Board, a computerized whiteboard that, along with videoconferencing, can be used real-time for collaborative projects among groups of employees working from different locations. Other areas of research at CST include corporate education and training, broadband trials, multimedia banking, interactive home shopping, field sales support applications, and practical applications for personal digital assistants and virtual reality.

New Technologies

Several companies, public and private, are trying to commercialize bleeding edge technologies. Bell Labs has been developing neural networks since 1986. Other companies such as National Semiconductor, of Santa Clara, CA; Nestor of Providence, RI; HNC Software of San Diego, CA; and Infobased Systems of La Jolla, CA, are also working on various neural network applications. Centigram, a San Jose, CA-based company, has patented a text-to-speech technology. Excalibur Technologies of San Diego offers an application that uses fuzzy logic and neural networks to learn the pattern of a document and create an index. Dragon Systems of Newton, MA, offers a multilingual, discrete speech recognition software package. High Techsplanations of Rockville, MD, sells virtual reality real-time software and tools for surgical simulations and pre-operative rehearsals that include tactile feedback to differentiate the textures of different organs. This is only a small sampling of the many enterprises trying to capitalize on new technologies.

Virtual Reality

Virtual reality (VR) ranges from simple sensory enhancement in video games to full immersion products that simulate the feel, touch, and even smell of an alternate virtual world. VR visualization is exemplified through the classic helmet, sometimes called the head-mounted display (HMD). With an HMD, the participant can see and control a simulated race car, a virtual human being or other representative (avatar), or walk through different environments that appear three-dimensional. Many of the early commercial uses of VR have been offered by companies like Iwerks Entertainment and CyberMind, which provide location-based entertainment (LBE) in the form of specialty theaters and immersive gaming environments.

The key to VR is computer processing power. More processing power translates into more realistic lighting and shading, the ability to handle multiple entities in the simulated environment, or a combination of both features. The U.S. Army has constructed an interactive simulation with these features that represents an entire battle occurring in a virtual arena. Simulating all the facets of a battle—landscape, troops, vehicles, firearms, enemy movements—requires a staggering number of computer calculations. The computer must calculate more than 50,000 actions to simulate the speed and movement of a tank moving across the frozen tundra.

Companies like Integrated Computing Engines (ICE) have created low-cost, high-performance platforms called superstations with enormous visualization and processing power. While 1.5 hours of calculation and production went into every animation frame of the movie *Jurassic Park*, ICE can reduce the aggregate amount of time spent on these visualizations to a matter of minutes.

Neural Networks

Neural networks are loosely modeled on certain properties of the human brain. Like the brain, neural networks are designed to train themselves to discover patterns if given enough time and data. These systems are useful for risk evaluation, consumer credit analysis, and other pattern analysis. This discovery and extraction of data, based on regularities in large data sets, is known as data mining. When past data is representative of future behavior, neural networks can be used to forecast future trends and to classify individual cases. Neural networks have been built to forecast exchange-rate fluctuations, production yields, and operational loads. Price Waterhouse reports the example of a German motor manufacturer who built a neural network to forecast demands for spare parts, increasing the accuracy of those predictions substantially.

Other examples of commercially-applied neural networks include American Express' use of a supercomputer to manage and run a rule-based system to detect credit card fraud, and to categorize card users for marketing and sales lists. Bloomberg Business News applies neural network technology to multiple data-streams to break apart, assess, and predict key indicators, market points, and securities.

Speech Recognition

New speech recognition devices are developed all the time. Voice-controlled personal computers, telephones, and videocassette recorders are current projects. One main area is the use of speech recognition over the phone. Long distance credit card calls and database access by verbal request are just a couple of the applications that have emerged.

Corona of Menlo Park, CA, is a startup working on high-end speech recognition technology. Its goal, according to CEO Ronald Croen, is to make interacting with computers as easy as using the telephone. Corona is working on human-to-computer speech technologies that will allow one person to connect to another's phone by simply stating the name of the person to be reached; a voice interface that lets customers access their banking records over the phone; and an over-the-phone booking service that lets callers make plane and hotel reservations by talking to the computer. In essence, wherever callers push the buttons on a touch-tone phone, Corona hopes to develop a speech recognition application that will allow customers to use their voices instead of their fingers. Corona's main competitors in this market are Texas Instruments, Voice Control Systems, and Voice Processing Corporation.

Pattern Recognition

In addition to speech recognition systems and the data mining used in neural networks, other candidates for pattern recognition technology include shape, color, and handwriting data.

Handwriting recognition efforts have thus far proven unsuccessful, highlighted by some notable failures in this area, such as the Apple Newton MessagePad and the pen computing products of the now defunct GO Corporation. Shape and color recognition technology is used on some assembly lines to see if the wires on computer circuit boards are in the right place and have been soldered correctly.

Top 10 Technologies for AD 2005

1. Genome mapping—gene probes that will predict who will get what disease.

2. Supermaterials—rugged, adaptable materials used for communications, energy, and transit.

3. Compact energy sources—powerful, long-lasting fuel cells and batteries.

4. High-definition TV—digital TV and video and better computer imaging.

5. Handheld electronic devices—portable phone, fax, and computer all in one.

6. Smart manufacturing systems—sensor-driven assembly lines.

7. Anti-aging products—creams to cover wrinkles and gene tinkering to slow aging.

8. Targeted medical treatments—focused treatments that reduce side effects.

9. Hybrid-fuel—lower gas use and emissions with higher performance.

10. Edutainment—3D educational games and simulations for children.

According to the Battelle Technology Management Group, the hot technologies for the next decade will bring pocket-size computers, insulin pumps embedded in the bodies of diabetics, and anti-aging creams that really work. The most striking feature of these technologies will be advances in miniaturization applied to fields ranging from medicine to electronics.

175

OUT **TAKES**

Eric Drexler

The Foresight Institute

Eric Drexler currently heads the Palo Alto, CA–based, non-profit organization called the Foresight Institute, which, in his words, "gathers and distributes information and holds conferences on technologies that are clearly going to have a large impact on society, with a particular focus on nanotechnology." This makes sense, as Mr. Drexler first introduced the word "nanotechnology" to the English language back in 1981 when still a graduate student at MIT. Nanotechnology, also known as advanced molecular engineering, is the science of creating machines at an atomic level. "Somebody recently completed a computer-based study on the use of the term 'nanotechnology,' and the results followed a pretty steep exponential curve after the publication of my first book, *Engines of Creation*. I think the curve is getting even steeper as we speak," Mr. Drexler told THE HERRING. People generally take one of two distinct views on nanotechnology. Some view it as a serious scientific endeavor that could lead to the creation of atomically precise manufacturing systems, where programmed atoms serve as the building blocks, and productivity and through-put will increase a trillion-fold. According to this school of thought, nanotechnology could provide, among other things, a personal computer that packs a trillion transistors, and has a current CPU's power in every transistor. Others view nanotechnology as a novelty that a few scientists are a little over-enthusiastic about because it works on a nanometer scale.

ANNE KNUDSEN

Whether the nanorevolution will occur remains to be seen. But we do know from talking to Intel founder Gordon Moore, and other leading semiconductor industry executives, that the photolithography technology used to build today's semiconductors will ultimately hit the wall, and the number of transistors that can fit on a single chip will cap off. What then? Well, listen to Eric Drexler—he just might have the answer.

So what turned you on to nanotechnology, anyway?
I was a student at MIT back in the 1970s doing research on building manufacturing systems from scratch in outer space. When I studied molecular biology and biochemistry, I could see that people were, indeed, using molecules to make a lot of things, including copies of nature. Workers in the field were basically taking raw material, putting it together, and building what they referred to as "molecular machines." Wondering where this was all going to end up, I started to imagine what advanced systems would look like, and what kind of new industrial technologies might result.

What part of your work has been most controversial?
Well, the fact that "nanotechnology" is a nice-sounding word that excites funding sources to provide money for research has, of course, been embraced with great vigor. [Laughs] The general notion that technology is heading toward atomic precision, and that this precision will ultimately be achieved through some form of mechanical manipulation of individual atoms and molecules, was slower to take off than some of us thought, fueling some cynicism. The serious controversies surrounding nanotechnology concern how long the development will take, how much it will cost, who will get there first, and what we should do about it. The spurious controversies have to do with whether it makes physical sense or not. And I don't know of any informed person who would argue that it doesn't make sense. This science is really taking off. There is a growing community of people who view nanotechnology as a critical component to any study of science in the future.

When do you think that nanotechnology will really take off?
When you have molecular machine systems that will take molecules and put them where you want them. From an engineering perspective, if you can build molecular systems like those I've been talking about, you will be able to build very complex, precise structures that can serve as parts for the molecular machines. And the characteristic speed of operation for these machines will be something on the order of a billion cycles per second, which will lead to enormous through-put and higher productivity. At this point you can design computers in such a precise way that every atom is carefully placed and optimized in all three dimensions.

Nathan Myhrvold

Senior Vice President of the Advanced Technology Group Microsoft

In 1992 Bill Gates decided to make Microsoft the first software company with an internal division fully dedicated to the commercialization of advanced research.

To lead this cerebral effort, Mr. Gates found a logical candidate within his company in Nathan Myhrvold—a holder of five degrees and a former postgraduate assistant to Cambridge University astrophysicist Stephen Hawkins. Mr. Myhrvold had been in Redmond, WA since Microsoft's 1986 acquisition of a small windowing systems company he led.

Microsoft's Advanced Technology Group has grown and consists today of its initial Microsoft Research effort; Advanced Consumer Technology, which focuses on interactive television and other broadband network applications; and Microsoft Online Services, the umbrella division for Microsoft Network. We spoke with Mr. Myhrvold about how Microsoft—historically known for exploiting technologies rather than developing them—is staking its claim at the bleeding edge of software development.

What motivated Microsoft to establish the Advanced Technology Group?
Microsoft's goal has always been to deploy as much technology as possible in products. We initially did this through advanced development, in which there is a defined product goal. A few years ago, we decided to get into basic research. The goal is no more precise than exploring new technologies. If you are smart about it, you focus your work so that it leads to great products. We thought it made sense to start investing in this area because our visions for personal computing require a variety of new technologies. The computer science research community—a resource to the whole industry—develops some of those, but there are always things we want done that other people aren't focusing on. Microsoft Research was formed as the beginning of the Advanced Technology Group. It now has more than 100 people and is doing work that compares favorably with computer science research done anywhere.

178

The business thinking that goes into our efforts is just as important as the technology thinking. The ultimate goal of this group is to find commercially viable applications of advanced technologies. That can be done through in-house development or by incorporating work done elsewhere.

Are you using any of your advanced research efforts in interactive television development?

Sure. We are investigating the use of artificial intelligence in the user interface. Let's say you're using video-on-demand and you want help picking movies based on what you've watched in the past, including consideration of what you have turned off in the middle. This is a question that deals with uncertain information. Computers are very good at dealing with certain information. But there are lots of problems for which certain information is not available and adaptive behavior and inference must be exercised. We are studying the Bayesian approach, which incorporates probability theory to represent uncertainty. If we build great Bayesian inference engines, we will be able to use them in different areas, such as user interfaces and smart operating systems for interactive television and other applications. I expect it will become a very important technology over the next five years.

Let's talk about some other basic research efforts. What are you doing in speech recognition?

Recognition-based input is often touted as a panacea. But until now, the technology has not been mature enough. The required computation load has been too much and the error rate too high. Very powerful processors and tons of memory are required. We're working on making the systems better, smaller, faster, and more practical. Combine this with processors and memory still getting cheaper, and expect to see some interesting applications in the next few years.

What about natural language interfaces?

Once you recognize somebody's speech, the next step is to understand the person's language well enough to perform a command. That's the user interface side of natural language processing. There's another side concerning the content of a file being built by a user. Natural language technology can be used to monitor grammar, meaning, and other areas. Today, a wordprocessor will let you hack away even if you are creating nonsense. Natural language technologies can create much more powerful tools for people who work with documents.

00_FOREWORD TO COMPANY PROFILES

Roger S. Siboni

When the editors of THE RED HERRING asked KPMG to help identify 250 shining stars in the Digital Universe, we knew it would be a daunting task, and our experiences with this research and analytical process in the past months have most definitely proven this the case.

We quickly realized that traditional methods of evaluating companies, by looking at such criteria as their earnings growth, market share, balance sheet strength, and stock performance, while important, were inadequate for this kind of analysis—particularly because many of the most interesting companies are still private and in their early stages of development. To evaluate these companies we needed methods that better describe their mastery of the continually changing environment that characterizes the digital world. In essence, we needed to establish a new performance metric for the '90s.

We started with a pool of nearly 1,000 companies, identified in interviews with venture capitalists, investment bankers, industry analysts, and high-tech executives from all over the world. We then devised metrics that would assess performance along a number of new dimensions and which allowed young startups and mature corporations to be evaluated on an equitable basis. It was difficult to come up with perfect criteria for companies operating in such diverse industries, but we gave it our best efforts. Our final selection criteria included:

Contribution to a paradigm shift—a company's current or potential influence in the following areas:

> Technology
> Marketing
> Organization
> Finance
> Alliance activity
> Business model

Management team—the companies we selected had to have outstanding leadership. We examined their:

> Vision
> Strategic thinking
> Execution
> Attracting and retaining top people
> Charisma
> Grounding in reality

Financial resources—we assessed the following areas to judge financial strength:
> Cash-flow
> Debt burden
> Proportion of revenues from recurring sources
> Revenue and earnings consistency

Market dominance—we looked at the relative position of companies versus their competitors by taking into account:

      Ability to set the terms of competition

      Market share/proportion of businesses either

            number one or number two in their markets

Market potential—who will dominate tomorrow's markets? We examined some potential indicators:

      Proportion of revenues that comes from products

            introduced in the last five years

      Technology leadership

      "First-to-market" ability

The following pages present profiles of the 250 companies that KPMG and the editors of THE RED HERRING believe scored best overall in the categories listed above. We admit that this evaluation has not been a perfect science, and expect, upon the publication of this book, to hear from countless entrepreneurs who will contend that their companies should have been included on our list. (Many will probably be right.) We also appreciate that in this technology business, things change fast. Today's bright star could be tomorrow's supernova. But at the time of this writing, we feel confident that the companies we selected should be among those most closely watched by industry executives, as they strive to stay informed and maintain leadership in their respective industries.

      Roger S. Siboni

      National Managing Partner

      Information, Communications & Entertainment Practice

      KPMG Peat Marwick LLP

      rsiboni@kpmg.com

How the Digital Universe Companies Stack Up

General Industry	Total Companies	Percent of Total
Computers	91	36.40
Communications	59	23.60
Entertainment	100	40.00

Industry Sector	Total Companies	Percent of Total
Broadcasters	9	3.60
Computer Networking	24	9.60
Consumer Electronics	5	2.00
Design Automation Software	6	2.40
Desktop Computers/File Servers	5	2.00
Enterprise & Client/Server Software	26	10.40
Enterprise Computers	2	0.80
Entertainment/Education Software	25	10.00
Film & Entertainment Production	20	8.00
Information Highway Equipment	5	2.00
Information Highway Services	18	7.20
Information Providers	5	2.00
Information Services	7	2.80
Newspaper/Magazine Publications	4	1.60
Online Services	23	9.20
Peripherals	6	2.40
Personal Productivity Software	16	6.40
Record Companies	1	0.40
Recording Studios	1	0.40
Semiconductor Equipment	3	1.20
Semiconductors	25	10.00
Storage	3	1.20
Wireless	11	4.40

Geographic Location	Total Companies	Percent of Total
West	154	61.60
Midwest	9	3.60
Southwest	13	5.20
Mid-Atlantic	43	17.20
Southeast	7	2.80
Northeast	22	8.80
Europe	1	0.40
Canada	1	0.40

Ownership Status	Total Companies	Percent of Total
Private	107	42.80
Public	143	57.20

Annual Revenue Level	Total Companies	Percent of Total
Over $5 billion	35	14.00
$1 billion to $5 billion	31	12.40
$500 million to $999 million	11	4.40
$250 million to $499 million	18	7.20
$100 million to $249 million	15	6.00
$50 million to $99 million	11	4.40
$10 million to $49 million	33	13.20
Under $10 million	15	6.00
No revenues/Wouldn't disclose	81	32.40

Combined Annual Revenues of all companies: **$24,469,790**

185

Year Established	Total Companies	Percent of Total
Prior To 1940	29	11.60
1940 to 1949	1	0.40
1950 to 1959	6	2.40
1960 to 1969	7	2.80
1970 to 1979	25	10.00
1980 to 1989	101	40.40
After 1990	77	30.80
N/A	4	1.60

Number of Employees	Total Companies	Percent of Total
Over 100,000	14	5.60
50,000 to 99,000	19	7.60
10,000 to 49,000	19	7.60
1,000 to 9,999	51	20.40
100 to 999	72	28.80
Under 100	75	30.00

Total of numbers of people employed by all companies: **4,558,666**

3COM

Address:	5400 Bayfront Plaza
	Santa Clara, CA 95052-8145
Telephone:	408/764-5000
Fax:	408/764-5032
E-mail:	info@3com.com
Web site:	http://www.3com.com
Industry:	Communications
Sector:	Computer Networking
CEO:	Eric A. Benhamou
CFO:	Christopher Paisley
Stock Exchange:	NASDAQ
Stock Symbol:	COMS

Product Description

3Com is a global data networking company that evolved from a supplier of discrete networking products (Ethernet adapters) into a supplier of LANs and enterprise-wide networking products. It is one of the "Big Four" internetworking companies in the three merging areas of routing, switching, and hubs. 3Com's products include routers, hubs, switches, and adapters for Ethernet, Token Ring, and high-speed networks.

Market Strategy/Positioning

3Com has strategic relationships with Primary Access, Sonix Communications, ASTRAL Token Ring Alliance, Madge, Hewlett-Packard, and Bay Networks. Significant customers include most major *Fortune* 500 companies. The company's competitive advantages are its timeliness in addressing the fastest-growing networking sectors—remote access and ISDN connectivity (the company has a large presence)—and its critical mass to succeed in the global data networking market. 3Com primarily competes against Cisco, Bay Networks, and Cabletron. Additional challenges and risks include competing in several emerging growth areas simultaneously.

Other

3Com was founded in 1979 and has continually grown through acquisitions, including Synernetics and Nicecom. It announced its tenth acquisition, high-end hub maker Chipcom, last year. CEO Eric Benhamou co-founded Bridge Communications in 1981; previously, he worked at Zilog for four years. CFO Christopher Paisley was formerly vice president of finance at Ridge Computers and worked for five years at Hewlett-Packard.

KEY FACTS

Year Established:	1979
Employees:	2,300
Fiscal Year End:	May
Revenues FY '94:	$827.1m
Revenues FY '95:	$1.3b
EPS '94:	$(0.53)
EPS '95:	$1.73
Shares Outstanding:	5.0b
Five-Year Growth Rate:	29%

186

3DFX INTERACTIVE

Address:	415 Clyde Avenue
	Suite 105
	Mountain View, CA 94043-2228
Telephone:	415/934-2400
Fax:	415/934-2424
E-mail:	info@3dfx.com
Web site:	n/a
Industry:	Entertainment & Information
Sector:	Film & Entertainment Production
CEO:	Gordon Campbell
CFO:	Gary Martin

Product Description

3Dfx Interactive is focused on bringing advanced 3D technology to electronic entertainment. The company's products deliver high-quality, low-cost 3D graphics for video games played on PCs. Its first product will provide 3D video game applications at quality levels and frame rates currently available on high-end Silicon Graphics Reality Engines. 3Dfx designs VLSI chips and software for PC platforms and is staffed by VLSI designers, systems engineers, and marketers. A PC-based software developer's kit is in development. 3Dfx plans to market its products at all levels of integration (chip, board, and subsystem level products) via distribution partnerships.

Market Strategy/Positioning

The company's mission is to provide new levels of interactive 3D electronic entertainment for the mass market. The company's competitive advantages are its sole focus on the electronic entertainment market, where it intends to deliver the most realistic game-play at affordable prices. 3Dfx Interactive primarily competes against 3Dlabs, NVIDIA, Rendition, and Chromatics Research. Additional challenges and risks include meeting the demand for increasingly "realistic" games and the need for affordable visualization technology—which is highly dependent upon PCs becoming the electronic entertainment platform of choice. 3Dfx Interactive is unique in bringing 3D graphics to end-users without the need to buy a costly workstation.

187

Other

3Dfx was founded in 1994 by Silicon Graphics veterans, with the mission to bring new realism to video games. CEO Gordon Campbell previously founded Chips & Technologies, Seeq Technolog; he is also founder and president of TechFarm. In addition, he sits on the board of directors of 3Com and Bell Micro. Co-founder and vice president of sales and marketing Ross Smith formerly worked for Media Vision. He was also director of OEM sales for Pellucid and OEM sales manager of MIPS. Other executives hail from Apple, Silicon Graphics, MIPS, Sun Microsystems, Mediavision, Sega, and DataEast.

Primary VCs/Outside Financing

Venrock Associates, Charter Ventures, U.S. Venture Partners, and Mitsui Comtek.

KEY FACTS

Year Established:	1994
Employees:	35
Fiscal Year End:	December
Revenues FY '94:	n/a
Revenues FY '95:	n/a
Date of Next Financing:	n/a
Date of Last Financing:	March 1995
Size of Last Financing:	$5.5m
Total Capital Raised:	n/a
Post Round Valuation:	n/a
Expected IPO Date:	n/a

3DLABS

Product Description

3Dlabs develops chips and software to integrate 3D graphics into boards and systems for multimedia, simulation, virtual reality, interactive TV, and games. The company expects markets to broaden from professional to personal use, with industry shipments of two million 3D graphics rendering chips in 1996. 3Dlabs is differentiated from its competitors through its focus on professional and productivity use and not just on entertainment.

Address:	2010 North First Street Suite 403 San Jose, CA 95131
Telephone:	408/436-3455
Fax:	408/436-3458
E-mail:	osman.kent@3dlabs.com tom.donohue@3dlabs.com
Web site:	http://www.3dlabs.com
Industry:	Computers
Sector:	Semiconductors
CEO:	Osman Kent
CFO:	Tom Donohue

Market Strategy/Positioning

The company's mission is to make its GLINT architecture for 3D graphics acceleration pervasive in many market areas through a combination of selling merchant silicon, licensing its 3D technology, and forming strategic partnerships. 3Dlabs has strategic relationships with Alias, Creative Labs, IBM Microelectronics, Microsoft, Intergraph, Komatsu, and S3. Significant customers include Creative Labs, Fujitsu, and NEC. The company's competitive advantages are market leadership for professional-class 3D on the PC, strong software skills, and the chance that 3Dlabs will set the platform standard for 3D games on the PC. 3Dlabs primarily competes against NVIDIA and Lockheed Martin. Additional challenges and risks include volumes of 3D chip shipments that need industry standards and infrastructure to evolve first. 3Dlabs is unique in being the only chip vendor focused on 3D graphics chips with strong software skills and having a range of chip solutions, from workstation class accelerators to games platforms and consumer devices.

Other

The company was founded in 1984 and acquired by DuPont in 1988 to become DuPont Pixel. A management buyout in April 1994 eventually formed 3Dlabs. CEO Osman Kent previously founded DuPont Pixel. The company has a very stable management team and strong experience in the 3D market.

Primary VCs/Outside Financing

Management.

KEY FACTS

Year Established:	1994
Employees:	45
Fiscal Year End:	December
Revenues FY '94:	$0.0
Revenues FY '95:	n/a
Date of Next Financing:	n/a
Date of Last Financing:	n/a
Size of Last Financing:	n/a
Total Capital Raised:	n/a
Post Round Valuation:	n/a
Expected IPO Date:	n/a

@HOME

Product Description

@Home plans to bring Internet access to customers through cable TV lines. @Home partners will provide consumers with broadband cable-modems which they will connect to the PC. The company promises to provide information faster than phone lines. Telephone modems deliver information at 14,000 bits per second, and @Home says it will offer connection speeds of 10 million bits per second. Enhanced connection will make viewing of graphics and video and listening to audio more practical. The company is forming relationships with content providers to build information resources. It will provide broadband connections to online services, including Microsoft Network, with commercial service scheduled to begin in 1996 in trial cities and a national rollout following in two or three years.

Address:	101 University Avenue
	Suite 240
	Palo Alto, CA 94301
Telephone:	415/833-4950
Fax:	415/833-4955
E-mail:	info@home.net
Web site:	http://www.home.net
Industry:	Entertainment & Information
Sector:	Information Provider
CEO:	William R. Hearst, III (acting)
CFO:	n/a

189

Market Strategy/Positioning

The company's mission is to provide Internet access, a nationwide Internet backbone, and many other services to consumers and businesses who want to tap into the Internet. The company's competitive advantages are its superiority over regular phone lines, (which do not have @Home's bandwidth), its combination of speed and data capacity, and its delivery of interactive services including video and graphics. @Home will primarily compete against major cable and telecommunication providers. Additional challenges and risks include technical limitations and consumer acceptance of Internet services.

Other

@Home was founded in 1995 by Kleiner Perkins Caufield & Byers principal Will Hearst III to offer high-speed access to the Internet through existing cable systems. Once senior management is in place, Mr. Hearst will return to venture capital firm Kleiner Perkins Caufield & Byers. Will Hearst was publisher of *The San Francisco Examiner* from 1984 to 1995. He currently serves as a director of the Hearst Corporation, Preview Media, MicroUnity Systems, Sun Microsystems, and Longfellow Pictures.

Primary VCs/Outside Financing

Kleiner Perkins Caufield & Byers and TCI.

KEY FACTS

Year Established:	1995
Employees:	50
Fiscal Year End:	December
Revenues FY '94:	$0.0
Revenues FY '95:	$0.0
Date of Next Financing:	n/a
Date of Last Financing:	n/a
Size of Last Financing:	n/a
Total Capital Raised:	n/a
Post Round Valuation:	n/a
Expected IPO Date:	n/a

ACCLAIM
ENTERTAINMENT

Address:	1 Acclaim Plaza
	Glen Cove, NY 11542-2708
Telephone:	516/656-5000
Fax:	516/656-2040
E-mail:	n/a
Web site:	n/a
Industry:	Entertainment & Information
Sector:	Entertainment/Education Software
CEO:	Gregory Fischbach
CFO:	Anthony Williams
Stock Exchange:	NASDAQ
Stock Symbol:	AKLM

Product Description

Acclaim Entertainment is a publisher and developer of interactive entertainment products for Nintendo, Sega, and Sony entertainment systems, as well as for PCs. Acclaim publishes its products under the Acclaim, LJN, Flying Edge, and Area labels. The company's best-selling titles are *Mortal Kombat*, *Mortal Kombat II*, and *NBA Jam*. It has developed digital actor motion-capture technology that was used by Warner Bros. for *Batman Forever*. Acclaim has a strong worldwide distribution and is the leading publisher of entertainment software abroad, selling directly to 85% of the European market. Acclaim has offices in Canada, France, Germany, Japan, Spain, and the U.K.

Market Strategy/Positioning

Acclaim Entertainment has strategic relationships with TCI, Atari, Nintendo, Philips, Sega, Commodore, Apple, IBM, IBM-compatible PC manufacturers, and 3DO. Significant customers include Toys'R'Us, NeoStar, Babbages, and Wal-Mart. The company's competitive advantages are its strong alliances with large entertainment organizations. Acclaim primarily competes against Electronic Arts, Spectrum Holobyte, Sega, Sony, Atari, Sierra On-Line, and Brøderbund. Additional challenges and risks include timing the decline of 16-bit software and the rise of 32-bit and 64-bit titles, the seasonality of the business, and the need to create a succession of hit titles from both inside and outside developers.

Other

Acclaim Entertainment, founded in 1987 by Greg Fischbach and Jim Scoroposki, was the first independent U.S. company to publish software for the Nintendo Entertainment System. Acclaim and TCI formed a new company headed by MTV creator John A. Lack, and TCI also acquired 10% of Acclaim Entertainment. Prior to co-founding the company, chairman and CEO Greg Fischbach was president of RCA Records International. Since 1979 co-founder James Scoroposki has been president of Jaymar Marketing, Inc., a New York–based sales representative organization. CFO Anthony Williams was previously the executive vice president at Crossocean Trade Finance Corporation and is a native of the U.K.

KEY FACTS

Year Established:	1987
Employees:	300
Fiscal Year End:	August
Revenues FY '94:	$480.8m
Revenues FY '95:	$578.0m (estimate)
EPS '94:	$1.00
EPS '95:	$1.08 (estimate)
Shares Outstanding:	47.9m
Five-Year Growth Rate:	20%

ADAPTEC

Product Description

Adaptec develops intelligent subsystems and associated software and VLSI circuits used to control the flow of data between a micro-computer's CPU and its peripherals. Its solutions range from simple connectivity products for single-user and small office desktops to ATM products for enterprise-wide computing and networked environments. Additionally, Adaptec produces interface cards for disk drives and network interface cards for ATM. Adaptec also introduced ten new NICs (Network Interface Cards) in March of 1995.

Address:	691 South Milpitas Boulevard Milpitas, CA 95035
Telephone:	408/945-8600
Fax:	408/957-6666
E-mail:	info@adaptec.com
Web site:	http://www.adaptec.com
Industry:	Computers
Sector:	Peripherals
CEO:	F. Grant Saviers
CFO:	Paul G. Hansen
Stock Exchange:	NASDAQ
Stock Symbol:	ADPT

Market Strategy/Positioning

The company's mission is to improve microcomputer system functionality and performance through innovative I/Oware hardware and software solutions. Adaptec has strategic relationships with IBM, Microsoft, Sun Microsystems, Novell, Banyan, Apple, and Hewlett-Packard. Significant customers include Acer, AT&T, Compaq, DEC, Dell, Gateway 2000, Hewlett-Packard, IBM, Intel, NCR, Sanyo, Siemens, Sony, and Toshiba. The company's competitive advantage is its leading-edge line of products, in terms of compatibility and performance. Adaptec primarily competes against Future Domain, Bus Logic, Seers Logic, Q Logic (ICs), FORE Systems, and Western Digital. Additional challenges and risks include sustaining the company's technical advantage in the marketplace and leveraging its core competencies into new markets.

191

Other

Adaptec was founded in 1981 by Larry Boucher, Wayne Higashi, and Bernie Neimen. Mr. Boucher was one of the inventors of the Shugart Associates System Interface—the design specifications for products that connect computers to other devices. Chairman John G. Adler was CEO of Adaptec from 1985 to 1995. Prior to founding Adaptec, Mr. Adler was with IBM for 18 years, followed by two years at Amdahl Corp. President and CEO F. Grant Saviers was president and COO from August 1992 and became CEO in July 1995. Before joining Adaptec, he spent 24 years at DEC. Paul Hansen became vice president and CFO in 1988, after four years as corporate controller. Mr. Hansen was previously an assistant controller at Raychem Corp.

KEY FACTS

Year Established:	1981
Employees:	1,700
Fiscal Year End:	March
Revenues FY '94:	$372.2m
Revenues FY '95:	$466.3m
EPS '94:	$1.11
EPS '95:	$1.76
Shares Outstanding:	51.7m
Five-Year Growth Rate:	20%

ADOBE SYSTEMS

Address:	1585 Charleston Road PO Box 7900 Mountain View, CA 94039-7900
Telephone:	415/961-4400
Fax:	415/961-3769
E-mail:	n/a
Web site:	http://www.adobe.com
Industry:	Computers
Sector:	Personal Productivity Software
CEO:	John E. Warnock
CFO:	M. Bruce Nakao
Stock Exchange:	NASDAQ
Stock Symbol:	ADBE

Product Description

Adobe Systems develops, markets, and supports computer software products and technologies that let users create, display, print, and communicate electronic documents. The company has a 50% market share in printer operating systems, graphics applications software, and desktop publishing software. It is also developing new products in emerging growth markets like digital video and electronic publishing. Continued growth is expected, because of a strong consumer base in the growing desktop publishing market.

Market Strategy/Positioning

The company's mission is to make a dramatic impact on how society creates visually rich information and on how it distributes and manages that information. Adobe has strategic relationships with Macmillan Computer Publishing, Hewlett-Packard, Apple, IBM, Netscape, and Electronics for Imaging. Significant customers include Hewlett-Packard, Electronics for Imaging, and Apple. The company's competitive advantage is its existing Adobe tools, designed with the ability to create content as digital media evolves. A new family of Adobe products offers electronic delivery across all platforms, and the company wants to make all products interoperable. Adobe acquired Aldus for $450 million in August 1994. It also bought Premiere from SuperMac and hired its creator. Adobe Systems primarily competes against Frame Technology, Interleaf, Microsoft, Novell, Quark, Sun Microsystems, and Xerox. Adobe is unique in developing products that allow people to create, deliver, and access visually rich information across multiple computer platforms.

Other

The company was founded in 1982 by Dr. John Warnock and Dr. Charles Geschke. The company is named after Adobe Creek, located near the founders' homes. Messrs. Warnock and Geschke originally developed and commercialized the company's Post-Script page-description language. Adobe established PostScript as the industry standard imaging model for the printing of electronic documents. Before founding Adobe, CEO John Warnock and president Charles Geschke were with the Xerox Palo Alto Research Center (PARC).

KEY FACTS

Year Established:	1982
Employees:	1,570
Fiscal Year End:	November
Revenues FY '94:	$597.8m
Revenues FY '95:	$709.5m
EPS '94:	$0.97
EPS '95:	$2.14
Shares Outstanding:	64.0m
Five-Year Growth Rate:	19%

192

ADVANCED FIBRE

Address:	1445 McDowell Boulevard North Petaluma, CA 94975
Telephone:	707/794-7700
Fax:	707/794-7777
E-mail:	don.green@fibre.com
Web site:	n/a
Industry:	Communications
Sector:	Computer Networking
CEO:	Donald Green
CFO:	Daniel Steimle

Product Description

Advanced Fibre develops cost-effective, expandable fiber-optic systems for world-wide applications. Its flagship product is a digital loop carrier for various telephone network topologies that facilitates transitions to fiber-optic networks. Its products are sold directly to telephone companies and are cost-effective for smaller markets that service fewer than 2,000 subscribers. Advanced Fibre's products also support any service (including ISDN, voice, fractional T, video, etc.) across the existing transmission media.

Market Strategy/Positioning

The company's mission is to develop and manufacture communications equipment that connects the telephone subscriber and the central office, and to increase the information transfer rate for access to the telephone network. Advanced Fibre has strategic relationships with Tellabs and Harris. Significant customers include AGT, Ameritech, Telmex, and Time Warner. The company's competitive advantage is its performance and state-of-the-art technology. Advanced Fibre primarily competes against AT&T, NTT, DSC, Fujitsu, R-Tech, and Seiscor. Additional challenges and risks include competition from major telephone companies.

Other

The company sprang from the ideas of John Webley and software engineer Jim Hoeck. Mr. Webley inspired Donald Green, who had just left DSC, to get venture capital and develop a marketing team. Because of Mr. Green's reputation at previous companies, he could pull together the venture capital, while Mr. Webley and Mr. Hoeck developed the company's UMC 1000 prototype. CEO Donald Green founded both Optilink and Digital Telephone Systems. CFO Dan Steimle was previously senior vice president–operations and CFO at the Santa Cruz Operation. Vice president of software development Jim Hoeck was a co-founder and president of Quadrium, the predecessor to Advanced Fibre. John Webley is vice president of hardware development, worked at DSC, and co-founded of Quadrium.

Primary VCs/Outside Financing

B.J. Cassin, Coral Group, St. Paul Venture Capital, Vanguard Venture Partners, Hambrecht & Quist, Harris Corp., and Tellabs.

KEY FACTS

Year Established:	1992
Employees:	125
Fiscal Year End:	December
Revenues FY '94:	19.0m
Revenues FY '95:	40.0m
Date of Next Financing:	n/a
Date of Last Financing:	October 1994
Size of Last Financing:	6.5m
Total Capital Raised:	24.0m
Post Round Valuation:	90.0m
Expected IPO Date:	1996

193

AGILE
NETWORKS

Address:	1300 Massachusetts Avenue Boxborough, MA 01719
Telephone:	508/263-3600
Fax:	508/263-5111
E-mail:	info@agile.com
Web site:	http://www.agile.com
Industry:	Communications
Sector:	Computer Networking
CEO:	William Seifert
CFO:	Michael Rubino

Product Description

Agile Networks develops products that integrate Ethernet and ATM switching to provide customers with a high-performance local backbone network that is easy to manage, scalable in capacity, auto-configuring, and multimedia capable. The company provides an automated solution to problems presented by endstation moves and changes with high software content, while preserving an organization's existing infrastructure by inserting a modular switch between routers and hubs.

Market Strategy/Positioning

The company's mission is to be a leading supplier of local backbone networks for building and campus environments through the application of ATM technology. Agile Networks has strategic relationships with VAR Data Systems and distribution partnerships in the U.K., Germany, Japan, and Australia. Significant customers include Bear Stearns, Boston University, Argonne Labs, and NTT. The company's competitive advantage is its ability to provide a complete solution while preserving existing infrastructure. Agile Networks primarily competes against Bay Networks, Cisco, 3Com, and FORE Systems. Additional challenges and risks include forming/creating an alignment with emerging ATM Forum standards and ensuring interoperability with third-party ATM devices.

Other

The company was founded in 1991 by CEO William Seifert. Mr. Seifert was founder of Wellfleet and inventor of the modern multiprotocol router/bridge before starting Agile Networks. He was also the founder of Interlan, a pioneering manufacturer of Ethernet interface controllers and network terminal servers. CFO Michael Rubino previously worked at Process Software, as vice president of finance and administration. He was also CFO at BICC Communications.

Primary VCs/Outside Financing

Accel Partners, Alex. Brown & Sons, Brentwood Associates, Charles River Ventures, Oak Partners, and Norwest Ventures.

194

KEY FACTS

Year Established:	1991
Employees:	45
Fiscal Year End:	June
Revenues FY '94:	n/a
Revenues FY '95:	$7.5m (estimated)
Date of Next Financing:	n/a
Date of Last Financing:	May 1994
Size of Last Financing:	$7.3m
Total Capital Raised:	$13.8m
Post Round Valuation:	$28.0m
Expected IPO Date:	n/a

AIRSOFT

Address:	20833 Stevens Creek Boulevard Suite 200 Cupertino, CA 95014
Telephone:	408/777-7500
Fax:	408/777-7527
E-mail:	info@airsoft.com
Web site:	http://www.airsoft.com
Industry:	Communications
Sector:	Wireless Communications
CEO:	Jagdeep Singh
CFO:	Kent Jarvi

Product Description

AirSoft offers wired and wireless remote connectivity software. AirSoft features full desktop functionality from mobile node and wireless capabilities with no constant connection required.

Market Strategy/Positioning

The company's mission is to develop the world's fastest, highest-performance, and easiest-to-use software in bandwidth-constrained networks. AirSoft has strategic relationships with RAM Mobile Data, Ericsson, BellSouth, Perot Systems (marketing), and IBM. The company's competitive advantages are ease-of-use, wireless support, and the product's 100% compatibility with all remote node servers. AirSoft primarily competes against Novell, Mobilware, Microsoft, and TSI. Additional challenges and risks include potential competition from big players in the industry. AirSoft is unique in offering the first and only network acceleration software.

Other

AirSoft was founded in 1993 from research started at Stanford University. The founders realized that low-bandwidth networks were becoming more important, since PC users were becoming more mobile. The company shipped AirSoft Air Access1.0 in November 1993 and won the *PC Magazine* 1994 Award for Technical Excellence. Before starting AirSoft, CEO Jagdeep Singh launched, marketed, and managed a high-end desktop workstation at Sun Microsystems, Hewlett-Packard, and Stanford University.

Primary VCs/Outside Financing

Venrock Associates, Greylock Partners, and Redwood Microcap.

195

KEY FACTS

Year Established:	1993
Employees:	20
Fiscal Year End:	December
Revenues FY '94:	n/a
Revenues FY '95:	$1.0m
Date of Next Financing:	n/a
Date of Last Financing:	n/a
Size of Last Financing:	$1.5m
Total Capital Raised:	$5.0m
Post Round Valuation:	n/a
Expected IPO Date:	1996

AIRTOUCH

Product Description

AirTouch provides wireless telecommunications services, both domestically and internationally. The company's products include paging and cellular phone systems, a vehicle location service called AirTouch Teletrac, a credit card verification system, and mobile telephone service. AirTouch is also part-owner of a long-distance telephone company in Japan.

Address:	1 California Street
	17th Floor
	San Francisco, CA 94111
Telephone:	415/658-2000
Fax:	415/658-2286
E-mail:	helpdesk@ccmail.airtouch.com
Web site:	http://www.datahut.airtouch.net
Industry:	Communications
Sector:	Wireless Communications
CEO:	Sam Ginn
CFO:	Lydell Christensen
Stock Exchange:	NYSE
Stock Symbol:	ATI

Market Strategy/Positioning

The company's mission is to enhance people's lives around the world through wireless communications. AirTouch has strategic relationships with U S WEST, Bell Atlantic, NYNEX, AT&T Wireless, Cellular Communications, and Globalstar. Significant customers include Pacific Bell, Pacific Telesis, U S WEST, Cellular One, Nextel, the CA Judicial Council, Seattle Municipal Court, Bay Area Rapid Transit, CALTRANS, LAX, Blue Shield, Blue Cross, Pacific Gas & Electric, Northwest Natural Gas, Tandem Computers, Hewlett-Packard, and UNISYS. The company's competitive advantages are its experience in working with nearly all major wireless technologies and its established operations in markets worldwide. AirTouch primarily competes against Contel Cellular, Sprint, and BellSouth.

Other

AirTouch entered the wireless industry in the mid 1980s as a unit of PacTel Corp. In April 1994 AirTouch spun off from Pacific Telesis Group to become an independent public company. The spinoff has provided AirTouch with greater financial flexibility and potentially greater freedom from regulatory restraints. In July 1995 the company announced a joint venture with U S WEST to combine their domestic cellular operations and to pursue new opportunities in Personal Communications Services (PCS). The joint venture also formed PCS PrimeCo with Bell Atlantic and NYNEX to provide service in areas where none of the four partners have cellular operations. As an independent company, AirTouch expects to benefit from having a management team that can focus entirely on the wireless communications industry. CEO Sam Ginn, previously chairman and CEO of Pacific Telesis Group, became chairman and CEO of AirTouch in March 1994.

KEY FACTS

Year Established:	1994
Employees:	4,580
Fiscal Year End:	December
Revenues FY '94:	$1.2b
Revenues FY '95:	n/a
EPS '94:	$0.21
EPS '95:	$0.32 (estimate)
Shares Outstanding:	493.8m
Five-Year Growth Rate:	25%

ALANTEC

Address:	2115 O'Nel Drive San Jose, CA 95131
Telephone:	408/955-9000, 800/ALANTEC
Fax:	408/955-9500
E-mail:	powerhub@alantec.com
Web site:	http://www.alantec.com
Industry:	Communications
Sector:	Computer Networking
CEO:	George Archuleta
CFO:	Pat Royan
Stock Exchange:	NASDAQ
Stock Symbol:	ALTC

Product Description

Alantec develops networking products that include intelligent switching hubs for Ethernet, ATM, and FDDI LANs, which offer the bandwidth of switching with the functionality of routers. Software-based switching provides virtual LAN functionality and packet-based multimedia support. Sales in the backbone segment of the Ethernet switch market grew 135% in 1994. Alantec owns 20% of the fastest growing segment of the networking market.

Market Strategy/Positioning

The company's mission is to provide "best in the class" LAN switching products and services to resolve network bandwidth problems. Alantec has strategic relationships with Auspex and Network General (technology, marketing, and distribution agreements), and recently licensed ATM software from FORE Systems. Significant customers include AT&T, GE, DHL, LSI Logic, Microsoft, Motorola, Oracle, and Silicon Graphics. The company's competitive advantages are its technical expertise in multiprotocol LAN switches (it pioneered this technology) and true multiprotocol VLAN support across its product line. Alantec primarily competes against Cisco, 3Com, Cabletron, and Bay Networks. Additional challenges and risks include developing and managing the best distribution channels, working to put resellers in place, and enhancing domestic sales forces.

197

Other

The company was founded in 1987, and in 1991 it shipped the industry's first "intelligent switching hub." Alantec went public in 1994, after an 84% increase in revenues from 1993. It completed its secondary offering in April 1995. Before joining Alantec, CEO George Archuleta was CEO of Vitalink Communications and led that company through its IPO in 1988. Executive vice president Dr. John Wakerly formally joined the company in 1990 after doing consulting work for a number of years. Previously, he co-founded David Systems and served as director of architecture. Dr. John Wakerly has published numerous books and reports and holds patents in digital system design. CFO Patrick Royan worked at Crosspoint Systems as CFO before joining Alantec in 1990. He was also a senior accountant at Coopers & Lybrand.

KEY FACTS

Year Established:	1987
Employees:	145
Fiscal Year End:	December
Revenues FY '94:	$25.0m
Revenues FY '95:	n/a
EPS '94:	$0.46
EPS '95:	$0.85 (estimate)
Shares Outstanding:	11.1m
Five-Year Growth Rate:	38%

AMBER WAVE
SYSTEMS

Address:	42 Nagog Park
	Acton, MA 01720
Telephone:	508/266-2900
Fax:	508/266-1159
E-mail:	info@amberwave.com
Web site:	n/a
Industry:	Communications
Sector:	Computer Networking
CEO:	Greg Hopkins
CFO:	Susan Hammond

Product Description

Amber Wave Systems provides LAN switching at hub-level prices. It has workgroup LAN switching platforms for 8 to 32 ports, and its architecture is based on a 5-slot 600Mbps backplane. Amber Wave claims scalability and support of ATM. Its products compete with switching alternatives based on prices as low as $175–$250/port. Amber Wave makes aggressive use of the Internet to promote the company and products though its assertive direct-marketing and advertising programs.

Market Strategy/Positioning

The company's mission is to deliver plug-and-play Ethernet switches at prices competitive with shared LAN hubs. Significant customers include manufacturing, education, health care, and financial service companies that need high performance LAN solutions without the high price. The company's competitive advantages are its breakthrough pricing, which is competitive with shared LAN hubs; its modular design, which expands from 8 to 32 ports; and its cut-through technology, which optimizes latency and reliability. Amber Wave primarily competes against 3Com and Cisco (and its Kalpana subsidiary). Additional challenges and risks include Amber Wave's need to quickly develop market awareness and sales channels in an increasingly competitive market.

Other

The company was founded in January 1994 by Curt Gridley and Paul Chieffo. Greg Hopkins joined the company in November 1994 as CEO; he was formerly vice president of engineering at UB Networks (Ungermann-Bass). Amber Wave received venture capital in January 1995. Both Mr. Gridley and Mr. Chieffo were key architects for Artel's Galactica enterprise switching system.

Primary VCs/Outside Financing

Battery Ventures, Venrock Associates.

KEY FACTS

Year Established:	1994
Employees:	15
Fiscal Year End:	December
Revenues FY '94:	n/a
Revenues FY '95:	n/a
Date of Next Financing:	n/a
Date of Last Financing:	January 1995
Size of Last Financing:	2.5m
Total Capital Raised:	2.5m
Post Round Valuation:	7.5m
Expected IPO Date:	n/a

AMERICA ONLINE

Address:	8619 Westwood Center Drive Vienna, VA 22182
Telephone:	703/448-8700
Fax:	703/448-0793
E-mail:	infor@aol.com
Web site:	http://www.aol.com http://www.blue.aol.com
Industry:	Entertainment & Information
Sector:	Online Services
CEO:	Stephen M. Case
CFO:	Lennert J. Leader
Stock Exchange:	NASDAQ
Stock Symbol:	AMER

Product Description

America Online is a provider of easy-to-use online services. Its offerings include Internet access, computer support, e-mail, bulletin boards, real-time chat groups, interactive newspapers and magazines, software downloading, hardware- and software-specific special interest groups, multi-player games, business/financial information, and educational services. America Online has enhanced its Internet support, giving access to USENET Newsgroups, WAIS, and Gopher databases. In August 1995 NaviSoft, a company started and owned by AOL, announced its product, Navi-Service, to help companies establish and edit Web sites on the World Wide Web. NaviSoft is a complete Internet publishing company.

Market Strategy/Positioning

The company's mission is to lead the interactive services market, and to capture market share and position itself in the battle of major Internet access providers. America Online has strategic relationships with American Express, Bertelsmann, Time Warner, CNN, ABC, NBC, MTV, Knight-Ridder, Tribune, IBM, Apple, Viacom, Comcast, Continental Cablevision, Cablevision Systems, Rogers Cablesystems, Hachette, Intel, and General Instruments. The company's competitive advantages are its annual subscription growth of 200% (1.5 million subscribers at the end of 1994), its gained market share through aggressive marketing, its growth at more than twice the industry rate for the last two years, and its avoidance of content surcharges and its development of new revenue streams by leveraging a growing audience. America Online primarily competes against CompuServe, Prodigy, GEnie, Delphi, Performance Systems International, NETCOM, and UUNET. Additional challenges and risks include managing the higher-than-expected growth rate, which has stressed the company's infrastructure; and maintaining growth and increasing market share by improving subscriber totals, number of paid hours, and customer retention. Increasing competition in the online services market is also a major challenge, with Microsoft Network and AT&T's Interchange Online being introduced in 1995. America Online is unique in its continued focus on its ease-of-use. The company is the largest, fastest-growing online service as a result of its convenience and creative marketing.

199

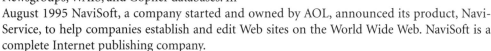

KEY FACTS

Year Established:	1985
Employees:	2,500
Fiscal Year End:	June
Revenues FY '94:	$104.5m
Revenues FY '95:	$387.0m
EPS '94:	$0.20
EPS '95:	$0.43
Shares Outstanding:	23.0m
Five-Year Growth Rate:	47%

AMERICA ONLINE

Other

America Online was originally founded as Quantum Computer Services. In 1992 the company went public and struck an alliance with Apple. A Windows version of its software was introduced in 1993. To increase marketing its presence, the company acquired Navisoft, Booklink, and Redgate Communications in 1994. In 1995 America Online acquired ANS, an Internet access supplier. The company planned to open a service in Europe by the end of 1995. In July 1995 the company announced a partnership with Time Warner Cable to begin a broadband trial. CEO and president Steve Case co-founded the company in 1985. His goal was to create a mass market for online services. He also created AOL Services, AOL New Enterprises, and AOL Technologies. CFO Lennert Leader was previously with LEGENT.

AMERITECH

Product Description

Ameritech offers communications services and products, long distance connections in five states, cellular service, and systems software. The company's products serve voice, data, video, and content communications markets. It has partnered with 30 companies to build a screenphone that will combine voice and text. Ameritech has also formed an alliance with Peapod, a company that will offer a service for consumers to order groceries over the Internet.

Address:	30 South Wacker Drive
	Chicago, IL 60606
Telephone:	312/750-5000
Fax:	312/207-1601
E-mail:	n/a
Web site:	http://www.ameritech.com
Industry:	Communications
Sector:	Information Highway Services
CEO:	Richard C. Notebaert
CFO:	Oren G. Shaffer
Stock Exchange:	NYSE
Stock Symbol:	AIT

Market Strategy/Positioning

The company's mission is to be the world's premier provider of full-service communications for people at work, at home, or on the move, and to increase the competitive effectiveness of the businesses they serve. Ameritech has strategic relationships with The Walt Disney Company, EDS, Tribune, Random House, Philips Home Services, Citicorp, BellSouth, IBM, NYNEX, Scientific Atlanta, Consumer Direct Access, MNI Interactive, Peapod, General Electric, British Columbia Systems, Bell Canada, and Telenet. Significant customers include the Library of Congress, Time Warner, 10.8 million end-users, and one million businesses. The company's competitive advantages are its competitive prices and quality services, its significant investments in content, and its move into long distance, video, and international markets. Ameritech primarily competes against AT&T, MCI, Sprint, Time Warner, TCI, ALC Communications, American Business Information, Bell Atlantic, BellSouth, Cable & Wireless, Contel Cellular, GTE, Metromedia, NYNEX, Pacific Telesis, Southwestern Bell, and U S WEST. Additional challenges and risks include the regulatory challenges to entry into cable, TV, and long-distance markets. Ameritech is unique in being the most productive regional Bell operating company and in building portfolios of interactive services.

Other

Ameritech is one of the seven regional Bell operating companies incorporated after the breakup of AT&T in 1984. Ameritech plans to branch out into all forms of communications and has entered several alliances to develop interactive information services. Chairman and CEO Richard Notebaert previously served as president of Indiana Bell. CFO and executive vice president Oren Shaffer served as president of Virgo Cap and CFO of Goodyear Tire & Rubber Company.

KEY FACTS

Year Established:	1984
Employees:	63,600
Fiscal Year End:	December
Revenues FY '94:	$12.6b
Revenues FY '95:	n/a
EPS '94:	$2.13
EPS '95:	$3.32
Shares Outstanding:	553.0m
Five-Year Growth Rate:	7%

ANSWERSOFT

Address:	3460 Lotus Drive
	Suite 123
	Plano, TX 75075
Telephone:	214/612-5100; 800/896-2677
Fax:	214/612-5198
E-mail:	info@answersoft.com
Web site:	n/a
Industry:	Computers
Sector:	Enterprise & Client/Server Software
CEO:	Jeanne Bayless
CFO:	Chris Apple

Product Description

AnswerSoft develops client/server-based application software that provides a comprehensive solution for call management and control. It provides business process automation applications that tie together applications databases, communications systems, and customers. AnswerSoft's product, SoftPhone, flexibly automates phone activity, provides easy access to hard-to-use phone features, and integrates phone activity with complex office tasks. The company's line of products includes SoftPhone, Sixth Sense Telephony, Sixth Sense Toolkit, and Intelligent Call Router.

Market Strategy/Positioning

The company's mission is to provide business process automation software that increases productivity and customer satisfaction. AnswerSoft has strategic relationships with AT&T, Novell, Inter-Voice, and Northern Telecom. Significant customers include American Mobile Satellite, Pitney Bowes, TGI Fridays, and GeoGraphix. The company's competitive advantage is its "software-only" solution, which uses customers' existing infrastructures, including applications, databases, and communications equipment. AnswerSoft primarily competes against NPRI, Early Cloud, and Digital Systems. Additional challenges and risks include establishing distribution channels and making the most of the market's early stage.

Other

In 1993, CEO Jeanne Bayless and co-founder Gary Young recognized the emerging demand for business software that would offer today's business user unlimited access to data in real-time. Answer-Soft was formed and released its first product, Soft-Phone, in August 1994. In March 1995 it announced Sixth Sense software for business process automation. Jeanne Bayless brings 16 years of management experience to AnswerSoft. Before founding Answer-Soft, Ms. Bayless was CFO and COO for Blyth Holdings, a client/server software development tools company. Gary Young previously spent 12 years with Texas Instruments as product development manager and chief architect.

Primary VCs/Outside Financing

Austin Ventures, Battery Ventures, Gibraltar, TVM,

202

KEY FACTS

Year Established:	1993
Employees:	25
Fiscal Year End:	December
Revenues FY '94:	n/a
Revenues FY '95:	n/a
Date of Next Financing:	n/a
Date of Last Financing:	December 1994
Size of Last Financing:	$8.0m
Total Capital Raised:	$8.5m
Post Round Valuation:	$11.3m
Expected IPO Date:	n/a

APPLE COMPUTER

Address:	One Infinite Loop
	Cupertino, CA 95014
Telephone:	408/996-1010
Fax:	408/974-2042
E-mail:	@applelink.apple.com
Web site:	http://www.apple.com
Industry:	Computers
Sector:	Desktop Computers/File Servers
CEO:	Michael Spindler
CFO:	n/a
Stock Exchange:	NASDAQ
Stock Symbol:	AAPL

Product Description

Apple Computer develops easy-to-use multimedia-ready PCs, servers, peripherals, software, online services, personal digital assistants, and networking and communications products that integrate Macintosh systems into different computing environments. Claris, a wholly-owned subsidiary of Apple, offers application software for a variety of platforms. Apple also offers online services through eWorld. According to Dataquest, Apple's share of the global PC market, where it has been steadily losing ground to IBM compatibles, dropped to 8.1% in 1994 from 9.4% in 1993. In 1994 Apple moved to the PowerPC chip, slashed prices, and agreed to license the Macintosh operating system to clone-makers in an effort to stop the erosion of its market share.

Market Strategy/Positioning

Apple has strategic relationships with Motorola and IBM (joint development of the PowerPC microprocessor). It has also invested in a number of joint development efforts, such as Kaleida (with IBM) and Taligent (with IBM and Hewlett-Packard), and recently licensed its operating system to allow Macintosh clones. Apple primarily competes against IBM-compatible PC makers, including IBM, Compaq, Dell, Hewlett-Packard, and Packard Bell, and Microsoft in operating systems. Additional challenges and risks include the need to increase its market share in order to avoid losing the critical mass required to attract software developers to write applications for its platform.

Other

The company was founded in 1976 by Steven Jobs and Steve Wozniak. In 1984 Apple revolutionized the personal computer industry by introducing the Macintosh. In 1992 Apple lost its suit against Hewlett-Packard and Microsoft claiming copyright infringement on its "look and feel." Michael Spindler joined Apple in 1980 and took over as CEO in 1993 from John Sculley, who had been CEO since 1983. Mr. Spindler previously worked at DEC, Intel, Schumberger, and Siemens.

KEY FACTS

Year Established:	1977
Employees:	14,500
Fiscal Year End:	September
Revenues FY '94:	$9.2b
Revenues FY '95:	n/a
EPS '94:	$2.60
EPS '95:	$4.14 (estimate)
Shares Outstanding:	121.2m
Five-Year Growth Rate:	14%

APPLIED
MATERIALS

Address:	3050 Bowers Avenue
	Mail Stop 1818
	Santa Clara, CA 95054-3299
Telephone:	408/986-7229
Fax:	408/ 986-7115
E-mail:	n/a
Web site:	n/a
Industry:	Computers
Sector:	Semiconductor Equipment
CEO:	James Morgan
CFO:	Gerald F. Taylor
Stock Exchange:	NASDAQ
Stock Symbol:	AMAT

Product Description

Applied Materials is the world's largest producer of wafer fabrication systems. Its products include chemical vapor/physical vapor/ epitixial, and poly-silicon deposition, plasma etching, and ion implementation systems. It is working to commercialize major new products, including a CVD tool for flat-panel display manufacturing, a chemical mechanical planarizaton tool, a sub-micron oxide etch tool, and a dielectric tool.

Market Strategy/Positioning

Applied Materials has a strategic relationship with Komatsu to produce LCD equipment. Its alliance with Komatsu will help diversify its revenues. Significant customers include blue-chip companies that have diversified and global customer bases. The company's competitive advantages are its extensive investment in research and development of both incremental and new process innovations, its global customer support and service infrastructure, and its single-wafer, multichamber process design. Applied Materials primarily competes against LAM Research, Novellus, and Hitachi. Additional challenges and risks include general market fluctuations in the industry. Applied Materials is unique in having a global customer service system that allows the company to support the global semiconductor fabrications systems of the largest semiconductor companies.

204

Other

Founded in 1967, Applied Materials was an early producer of fabrication equipment for semiconductors. It was the first to offer turnkey solutions and to build customer demonstration labs. In 1972 the company went public, and in 1979 it bought the ion implantation business of Lintott Engineering. Its Japan Technology Center opened in 1984 costing $9.2 million. Chairman and CEO James Morgan previously worked with West-Ven Management, a venture capital partnership affiliated with Bank of America, and at Textron.

KEY FACTS

Year Established:	1967
Employees:	6,500
Fiscal Year End:	October
Revenues FY '94:	$1.7b
Revenues FY '95:	$3.0b (estimate)
EPS '94:	$2.51
EPS '95:	$4.46 (estimate)
Shares Outstanding:	89.0m
Five-Year Growth Rate:	25%

ARBOR SOFTWARE

Address:	1325 Chesapeake Terrace
	Sunnyvale, CA 94089
Telephone:	408/727-5800
Fax:	408/727-7140
E-mail:	jdorrian@avs.com
Web site:	n/a
Industry:	Computers
Sector:	Enterprise & Client/Server Software
CEO:	James Dorrian
CFO:	Andrew Stern

Product Description

Arbor Software develops and markets OnLine Analytical Processing (OLAP) database products for mission-critical analysis of current and projected enterprise performance data. Its flagship product is an OLAP database server that allows users to combine and simultaneously share diverse, enterprise-wide data and rapidly analyze it from any perspective and at any level of detail, directly from a spreadsheet or custom application. Managers typically use it to analyze product profitability, sales channels, inventory, forecasting, and budgeting.

Market Strategy/Positioning

The company's mission is to improve the performance of corporations through the development and delivery of innovative software products. Arbor has strategic relationships with Cognos, Comshare, Hogan, Microsoft, Trinzic, Walker Interactive, Intelligent Office Company (IOC), and Hewlett-Packard. Significant customers include 3Com, AirTouch, American Airlines, Bank of America, Compaq, Chemical Bank, Guinness, Intel, LAM Research, Lehman Brothers, NEC, and U S WEST. The company's competitive advantages are its status as a technology leader, its open client/server architecture, and its scalability. Arbor primarily competes against IRI Software, Hyperion Software, Pilot Software, IMRS, and SAS. Additional challenges and risks include building its sales channel, convincing leading relational database systems to add multidimensional layers, and improving scalability to compete with data warehousing alternatives for enterprise-wide applications.

Other

James Dorrian and Robert Earle co-founded Arbor Software in 1991 to address the need for multidimensional analysis of large volumes of business data. The first product was shipped in May 1992. CEO James Dorrian previously served as president of Solutions Technology. Before Solutions Technology, he was Western States director at Thorn EMI Computer Software. Co-founder and CTO Robert Earle was previously president of Sygen.

Primary VCs/Outside Financing

Hummer Winblad, Sequoia Capital, Mayfield Fund, and Accel Partners.

KEY FACTS

Year Established:	1991
Employees:	75
Fiscal Year End:	March
Revenues FY '94:	n/a
Revenues FY '95:	n/a
Date of Next Financing:	n/a
Date of Last Financing:	September 1993
Size of Last Financing:	$3.0m
Total Capital Raised:	$7.5m
Post Round Valuation:	$20.0m
Expected IPO Date:	1996

ARCHITEXT
SOFTWARE

Address:	2700 Garcia Avenue
	Suite 300
	Mountain View, CA 94043
Telephone:	415/934-3611
Fax:	415/934-3610
E-mail:	info@architext.com
Web site:	http://www.architext.com
Industry:	Entertainment & Information
Sector:	Online Services
CEO:	Joe Kraus
CFO:	Ryan McIntyre

Product Description

Architext Software provides navigational services for the Internet. The company has developed software for advanced textual searching and browsing online and is currently developing software for information vendors and consumers. Architext's products allow conceptual searches for information rather than keyboard searches. The company's browsing tools feature query-by-example, automatic subject grouping, automatic abstracting, and automatic hypertext linking. The Architext engine supports multiple data formats, including ASCII, SGML, HTML, RTF, and PostScript.

Market Strategy/Positioning

The company's mission is to be a market leader in the new field of media navigation. Architext has a strategic relationship with International Data Group (IDG). Significant customers include IDG and Leknema. The company's competitive advantages are its advanced proprietary navigation software technology, which is not merely a search-and-retrieval engine; its automatic hypertext linking, which is helpful in browsing; and its dynamic subject grouping, which helps condense a large list of documents into subgroups of related topics. Architext primarily competes against ConQuest, CyberSource, Personal Library Software, Yahoo!, and TBD. Additional challenges and risks include a limited operating history, the increasing competition in new technology, and maturation of the Internet market. Architext is unique in having a strong retrieval power, browsing intelligence, and distributed server architecture.

Other

In 1993 six Stanford graduates decided to build software that would help people more efficiently search through large bodies of data on the Internet. A presentation was made to IDG, and the company won a service contract to complete work on an online service project. The company first shipped products in 1995. Architext's new hires hail from Frame Technology, Sun Microsystems, and Cadence Design Systems.

Primary VCs/Outside Financing

Institutional Venture Partners, Kleiner Perkins Caufield & Byers, Charles River Ventures, and IDG.

KEY FACTS

Year Established:	1993
Employees:	15
Fiscal Year End:	December
Revenues FY '94:	$0.0
Revenues FY '95:	$0.0
Date of Next Financing:	n/a
Date of Last Financing:	August 1995
Size of Last Financing:	$1.5m
Total Capital Raised:	$3.0m
Post Round Valuation:	n/a
Expected IPO Date:	n/a

ARCSYS

Address:	1208 East Arques Avenue Sunnyvale, CA 94086
Telephone:	408/738-8881
Fax:	408/738-8508
E-mail:	info@arcsys.com
Web site:	n/a
Industry:	Computers
Sector:	Design Automation Software
CEO:	Gerald C. Hsu
CFO:	Jon A. Bode
Stock Exchange:	NASDAQ
Stock Symbol:	ARCS

Product Description

ArcSys develops, markets, and supports integrated circuit design automation (ICDA) software for the physical design of high-density, high-performance integrated circuits (ICs). The company's products are designed to solve problems inherent in submicron (less than 1.0-micron) and deep submicron (less than 0.5-micron) IC design. In addition, its architecture and technology are developed to provide faster time-to-market, reduced production costs, interaction of logical and physical design stages, and preservation of customer design investment.

Market Strategy/Positioning

The company's mission is to establish a significant market position as a supplier of physical design software for the ICDA market. ArcSys has strategic relationships with Synopsys and Attest Systems. Significant customers include Alcatel, Cirrus Logic, GoldStar, Matsushita, Motorola, National Semiconductor, Samsung, Sony, Advanced Micro Devices, France Télécom, Mitsubishi, Yamaha, and Trident Microsystems. The company's competitive advantages are its proprietary technology and innovative business model. ArcSys primarily competes against Cadence Design Systems and Mentor Graphics. Additional challenges and risks include a limited operating history, the intensely competitive and rapidly changing ICDA software market, and the fact that the company currently holds no patents on its products. ArcSys is unique in developing technology specifically for "deep submicron" ICs, and in its flexible pricing, designed to meet increased demand.

207

Other

ArcSys was founded in 1991 to develop ICDA software for the physical design of high-density, high-performance ICs. It began shipping its cell-based place and route software in 1994. The company went public in June 1995. CEO Gerald Hsu was vice president and general manager of the integrated circuits division at Cadence Design Systems. Founders Yuh-Zen Liao and Stephen Tzyh-Lih Wuu both served in the IC research and development department at Cadence. In addition, 11 of the industry's top 12 layout technologists—dubbed the "dirty dozen"—reside at ArcSys.

KEY FACTS

Year Established:	1991
Employees:	75
Fiscal Year End:	December
Revenues FY '94:	$6.2m
Revenues FY '95:	$17.5 (estimate)
EPS '94:	$(0.12)
EPS '95:	$0.32 (estimate)
Shares Outstanding:	9.5m
Five-Year Growth Rate:	43%

ASCEND COMMUNICATIONS

Address:	1275 Harbor Bay Parkway
	Alameda, CA 94502
Telephone:	510/769-6001
Fax:	510/814-2300
E-mail:	info@ascend.com
Web site:	http://www.ascend.com
Industry:	Communications
Sector:	Computer Networking
CEO:	Mory Ejabat
CFO:	Robert Dahl
Stock Exchange:	NASDAQ
Stock Symbol:	ASND

Product Description

Ascend's products span a broad range of high-speed digital wide-area network (WAN) access products. These products use bandwidth-on-demand to enhance and extend existing corporate networks for applications such as remote local-area network (LAN) access, Internet access, bulk file transfer, videoconferencing, imaging, and integrated voice, data, and video access.

Market Strategy/Positioning

Ascend has strategic (marketing and sales) relationships with AT&T, British Telecom, Sprint, MCI, PictureTel, VTEL, and Compression Labs. Significant customers include AT&T, GTE, MCI, Sprint, IBM, Hewlett-Packard, Goldman Sachs, Coca-Cola, Johnson & Johnson, Allied-Signal, Toyota, Mobil Oil, Time Warner, and Northern Telecom. The company's competitive advantages are its pioneering efforts in inverse multiplexing and its WAN access switch being the de facto standard among Internet providers worldwide. Ascend primarily competes against Teleos and Promptus in the videoconferencing access market; 3Com, Telebit, Cisco, and Shiva in the remote LAN access market; and Teleos, Newbridge Networks, and Premisys in the integrated access market. Additional challenges and risks include increased competition in target markets, particularly in the remote LAN access and Internet access markets.

Other

Through 1994 Ascend Communications focused on the videoconferencing market with its inverse multiplexor, a market it still owns. The same bandwidth-on-demand technology is now used in its remote LAN and Internet access. Dataquest showed the company's owning over 60% of the combined ISDN market in a May 1995 report. Former chairman Robert Ryan is a co-founder and served as CEO until June 1995. Before Ascend, Mr. Ryan founded Softcom, later acquired by Hayes. Ascend's current CEO, Mory Ejabat, served in various executive management positions at Micom Systems.

KEY FACTS

Year Established:	1988
Employees:	220
Fiscal Year End:	December
Revenues FY '94:	$39.3m
Revenues FY '95:	$117.8m (estimate)
EPS '94:	$0.38
EPS '95:	$0.61 (estimate)
Shares Outstanding:	25.6m
Five-Year Growth Rate:	40%

208

AT&T

Product Description

AT&T is a worldwide provider of communications services and products, as well as of network equipment and computer systems, to businesses, consumers, telecommunications services providers, and government. Interchange Online Network, a division of AT&T, develops and markets a next-generation publishing platform that offers a collection of online information services presented by independent publishers. AT&T has also developed VCOS, a Windows compatible real-time multitasking operating system, to harness the power of DSPs. AT&T's joint venture with BBN Planet aims to provide businesses with secure and reliable Internet access. In August 1995 AT&T announced it would offer access to the Internet for all customers, and the company created three new divisions to compete on the Internet: AT&T Worldnet, Hosting and Transaction Services, and a third that will develop content for Worldnet. AT&T is also the leading company in wireless communications, the fastest growing segment of telecommunications. Last year it launched SafetyNet, a group of public safety programs for communities, and it also successfully bid for 21 wireless licenses in the broadband personal communications services (PCS), at a value of over $2 billion.

Address:	295 North Maple Avenue
	Basking Ridge, NJ 07920
Telephone:	212/387-5400
Fax:	212/841-4715
E-mail:	n/a
Web site:	http://www.att.com
Industry:	Communications
Sector:	Information Highway Services
CEO:	Robert E. Allen
CFO:	Richard W. Miller
Stock Exchange:	NYSE
Stock Symbol:	T

209

Market Strategy/Positioning

The company's mission is to be the world's best at bringing people together by giving customers easy access to each other and to the information they want and need. AT&T has strategic relationships with WorldPartners, an international consortium of telephone companies which AT&T helped create. Other alliances are with Ziff-Davis, Gartner Group, Washington Post, Tribune, and Bolt Beranek & Newman. The company's competitive advantages are its 50% share of the digital switch market and its strong alliances. AT&T primarily competes against ACC, Alcatel, American Express, Ameritech, BCE, Bell Atlantic, BellSouth, Cable & Wireless, Cray Research, EDS, Fujitsu, GTE, Hewlett-Packard, IBM, Intel, MCI, Metromedia, Microsoft, Motorola, NEC, Northern Telecom, NTT, NYNEX, Pacific Telesis, Southwestern Bell, Sprint, Siemens, U S WEST, and Visa. Additional challenges and risks include keeping its costs balanced with those of competitors, and challenges from "nontraditional" competitors in emerging markets.

KEY FACTS

Year Established:	1885
Employees:	304,500
Fiscal Year End:	December
Revenues FY '94:	$75.1b
Revenues FY '95:	n/a
EPS '94:	$3.01
EPS '95:	$3.48 (estimate)
Shares Outstanding:	1.6b
Five-Year Growth Rate:	11%

AT&T

Other

Bell Telephone was organized in 1877, a year after Alexander Graham Bell invented the telephone. The company was incorporated as American Telephone & Telegraph in 1885. J.P. Morgan gained control of the company in the early 1900s. Bell Labs, the research and development unit, was founded in 1925. In 1984 a government suit led to the breakup of AT&T, which spun off seven regional Bell companies. In August 1995 AT&T completed the $12.6 billion purchase of McCaw Cellular, renamed AT&T Wireless Services. Robert Allen has been chairman and CEO of AT&T since 1988. During his 37 years at AT&T, he has served as chairman of Chesapeake and Potomac Telephone, AT&T CFO, chairman and CEO of AT&T Information Systems, and president and chief operating officer of AT&T. CFO Richard Miller was formerly chairman and CEO of Wang Laboratories.

ATMEL

Address:	2125 O' Nel Drive
	San Jose, CA 95131
Telephone:	408/441-0311
Fax:	408/436-4377
E-mail:	info@atmel.com
Web site:	n/a
Industry:	Computers
Sector:	Semiconductors
CEO:	George Perlegos
CFO:	Kris Chellam
Stock Exchange:	NASDAQ
Stock Symbol:	ATML

Product Description

Atmel designs, manufactures, and markets a broad range of high-performance non-volatile memory and logic integrated circuits using proprietary CMOS technologies. The company's non-volatile memory products include EPROMs, EEPROMs (both serial and parallel interface), and Flash memory. Its logic products include programmable logic devices (EPLDs and FPGAs), ASICs, and microcontrollers. The company's core competency is the design and manufacture of low-voltage, high-speed devices. Atmel is currently the only volume supplier of 3 Volt Flash memory. These products, because of their low power usage, are particularly well-suited for use in portable systems where battery life is critical, such as cellular telephones, pagers, notebook computers, and consumer electronics.

Market Strategy/Positioning

The company's mission is to leverage its unique non-volatile memory technology in products for the consumer, telecommunications, automotive, and computer markets. Atmel has a strategic relationship with European Silicon Structures (holds a majority interest), and also has an agreement with Paradigm to manufacture SRAMs for strategic customers. Significant customers include Compaq, Conner Peripherals, Ericsson, Groupe Bull, Honeywell, IBM, Motorola, Nokia, Northern Telecom, Sony, Texas Instruments, Toshiba, and Westinghouse. The company's competitive advantages are its NVM process technology and its leadership position in low-power chips for portable applications. Atmel primarily competes against AMD, SGS-Thomson, Microchip, Xicar, and Catalyst. Additional challenges and risks include its need for expansion capacity and the complications of SRAM technology.

211

Other

George Perlegos founded Atmel in 1984. Initially the company designed chips manufactured by General Instruments and Sanyo Semiconductor in return for a small stake in the company. In 1989 Atmel bought a Honeywell chip-manufacturing plant in Colorado Springs for $60 million, and four years later it built another plant there for $300 million. The company's IPO was in March 1991, and it has had three subsequent offerings, raising a total of $178 million. Founder and CEO George Perlegos was previously a design engineer at Intel and later chief technical officer at SEEQ Technology.

KEY FACTS

Year Established:	1984
Employees:	2,400
Fiscal Year End:	December
Revenues FY '94:	$375.1m
Revenues FY '95:	$580.3m (estimate)
EPS '94:	$1.33
EPS '95:	$1.93 (estimate)
Shares Outstanding:	47.4m
Five-Year Growth Rate:	27%

ATTEST SYSTEMS

Address:	165 North Redwood Drive
	Suite 150
	San Rafael, CA 94903-1969
Telephone:	415/491-7800
Fax:	415/491-7805
E-mail:	76276.1604@compuserve.com
Web site:	http://www.attest.com
Industry:	Computers
Sector:	Personal Productivity Software
CEO:	Herbert M. Gottlieb
CFO:	Herbert M. Gottlieb

Product Description

Attest Systems performs software audits for companies and governmental agencies to prevent the use of pirated software by employees on work computers. Attest's audits can also locate games and pornographic files and help plan for disasters, such as earthquakes, viruses, or sabotage. Attest can perform unannounced "search and seizure" audits if a software company obtains a court order that allows it to search another company's computers for pirated software. Attest has developed "GASP" (Gottlieb Associates Search Program), a PC-compatible software-auditing program. The company's products are marketed to other auditing companies and to systems administrators at large companies. A Macintosh version is currently being developed.

Market Strategy/Positioning

The company's mission is to help customers control the use and cost of existing PC software and hardware resources and make informed decisions on future growth, changes, and purchases. Attest Systems has strategic relationships with Microsoft and IBM to work on its database, and plans to ally with Autodesk to investigate software piracy in South America. Significant customers include AMEX Life Insurance, the Salvation Army, Orrick, Harrington & Sutcliffe, the U.S. Navy, and the U.S. Air Force. The company's competitive advantage is its leadership helping companies conduct independent software audits. Challenges and risks include successfully entering overseas markets to combat software piracy.

Other

Attest Systems was founded in 1993 to provide assistance in making software auditing a standard practice. Its flagship product was developed in 1991 to conduct enforcement audits for the Software Publishers Association (SPA), the Business Software Association (BSA), and software publishers. CEO and CFO Herbert Gottlieb is a CPA with 20 years of accounting, consulting, and software-auditing experience. He has served as a consultant for the SPA and the BSA.

Primary VCs/Outside Financing

100% privately owned by private investors.

KEY FACTS

Year Established:	1993
Employees:	8
Fiscal Year End:	n/a
Revenues FY '94:	$0.0
Revenues FY '95:	$0.0
Date of Next Financing:	n/a
Date of Last Financing:	n/a
Size of Last Financing:	n/a
Total Capital Raised:	n/a
Post Round Valuation:	n/a
Expected IPO Date:	n/a

AUTODESK

Product Description

Autodesk produces, develops, and markets design and multimedia software. Although its computer-aided design (CAD) product accounts for 80% of revenues, the company also offers digital media tools to create, capture, assemble, manage, and play back material on Intel machines. CAD customers account for 40% of Autodesk's 3D product sales. Its products are also used for pre-visualization of film scripts/electronic story-boards and for game development. Autodesk has sold 50,000 copies of its 3D product and holds 63% of the market. Current projects include a 3D product for Windows NT and a developers, kit for virtual reality applications.

Address:	111 McInnis Parkway San Rafael, CA 94903
Telephone:	415/507-5000
Fax:	415/507-5100
E-mail:	jere.k@autodesk.com
Web site:	http://www.autodesk.com
Industry:	Computers
Sector:	Design Automation Software
CEO:	Carol Bartz
CFO:	Eric Herr
Stock Exchange:	NASDAQ
Stock Symbol:	ACAD

Market Strategy/Positioning

The company's mission is to create quality software solutions and support services that foster innovation, creativity, and productivity for customers and partners around the world. Autodesk has strategic relationships with Xaos Tools, HSC Software, Schreiber Instruments, and Parker-Hannifin. Significant customers include Sony and Chevron. Half of Autodesk's customers are *Fortune* 500 companies. The company's competitive advantage is that its products have become industry standards. Challenges and risks include maintaining a leadership role in all markets. Autodesk is unique in being the only software company in the top five that does not compete with Microsoft.

Other

Founded by John Walker in 1982, Autodesk originated in his garage. Mr. Walker is the author of *The Autodesk File*, a book chronicling Autodesk's development. The company acquired its object-oriented multimedia authoring technology through exclusive rights from MediaShare. Carol Bartz became chairman, president, and CEO in 1992. Since then, the company's revenues have grown from $285 million to $455 million in 1995. She was previously with Sun Microsystems as vice president of worldwide field operations. Before Sun, Ms. Bartz worked at DEC and 3M; she currently sits on the boards of AirTouch, Cadence Design Systems, the California Chamber of Commerce, and the National Breast Cancer Research Foundation.

KEY FACTS

Year Established:	1982
Employees:	1,800
Fiscal Year End:	January
Revenues FY '94:	$413.8m
Revenues FY '95:	$457.1m
EPS '94:	$1.27
EPS '95:	$1.13
Shares Outstanding:	47.2m
Five-Year Growth Rate:	20%

AVID TECHNOLOGY

Address:	One Park West
	Metropolitan Technology Park
	Tewksbury, MA 01876
Telephone:	508/640-6789
Fax:	508/640-1366
E-mail:	n/a
Web site:	n/a
Industry:	Entertainment & Information
Sector:	Film & Entertainment Production
CEO:	Curt A. Rawley
CFO:	Jonathan H. Cook
Stock Exchange:	NASDAQ
Stock Symbol:	AVID

Product Description

Avid Technology supplies digital, non-linear editing software and systems for the manipulation of video, film, and audio. Avid also develops and sells digital recording, editing, and playback systems to broadcasters. The company's product bundling integrates C-Cube's video-compression chip, RasterOps' video-processor board, and Digidesign's audio-processor board.

Market Strategy/Positioning

The company's mission is to redefine the art of communications. Avid has strategic relationships with Apple, Silicon Graphics, Ikegami, Pinnacle, and C-Cube. Avid is also a sponsor of Open Media Framework (creating standard interfaces among products). Significant customers include 250 broadcast and production companies that use aspects of Avid's disk-based technology. Avid positions itself as more than a video-editing company—it is considering moving into the digital movie-distribution and digital image-capturing systems market, particularly for broadcast environments. The company primarily competes against Sony, Panasonic, Data Translation, ImMIX, and Sonic Solutions. Additional challenges and risks include the explosive growth of the company, and its future focus on addressing the needs of broadcasters.

Other

Avid Technology was founded in 1987, and it acquired Digidesign for $196 million to strengthen its presence in the audio market. Additional acquisitions include DIVA (to develop video editing and presentation software for non-professionals), SofTech Systems, Parallax, and Elastic Reality. Avid was the first in its business and has a strong technology base and extensive product line. It also does not want to be considered solely as a video editing company. President and CEO Curt Rawley has over 20 years experience in management operations, technology, marketing, and finance. Mr. Rawley previously worked at DEC, Applicon, Pixel Computer, and Racal Electronics. After leaving Racal, he founded Jasper Technology, a consulting firm, and began working with Avid. In February 1989 he became vice president of operations for Avid, and was promoted to CEO in May 1991.

KEY FACTS

Year Established:	1987
Employees:	1,200
Fiscal Year End:	December
Revenues FY '94:	$210.4m
Revenues FY '95:	$410.0m (estimate)
EPS '94:	$1.13
EPS '95:	$1.47 (estimate)
Shares Outstanding:	18.0m
Five-Year Growth Rate:	32%

214

BAAN

Product Description

Baan develops enterprise resource planning applications. These applications provide mission-critical application software that integrates sales forecasting, component procurement, inventory management, manufacturing control, project management, distribution, transportation, and finance across an organization. Baan's seven principal software applications support the entire business cycle. Typically, the company's products can be configured and initiated within a span of three to 12 months.

Address:	U.S. Headquarters
	4600 Bohannon Drive
	Menlo Park, CA 94025
Telephone:	415/462-4949
Fax:	415/462-4952
E-mail:	n/a
Web site:	n/a
Industry:	Computers
Sector:	Enterprise & Client/Server Software
CEO:	Jan Baan
CFO:	David C. Cairns
Stock Exchange:	NASDAQ
Stock Symbol:	BAANF

Market Strategy/Positioning

The company's mission is to help multinational corporations maintain a competitive advantage in the management of critical business processes. Baan has strategic relationships with Hewlett-Packard, IBM, Oracle, Informix, Ernst & Young, KPMG Peat Marwick, and Origin. Significant customers include Snap-on Tools, Northern Telecom, Boeing, Mercedes-Benz, and Allied Signal. The company's competitive advantages are its recently expanded management team, a new Windows-based version of its client/server family of applications, and quick product implementation. Baan primarily competes against Dun & Bradstreet, SAP, Systems Software Associates, Marcam, PeopleSoft, Oracle, and Computer Associates. Additional challenges and risks include the highly competitive nature of the information management software industry, the need to release and improve new products frequently, currency fluctuations (most of the company's business is conducted in foreign currency), and the company's limited profitability of the last four years. Baan is unique in offering enterprise resource planning software that is easily configurable and has multinational capabilities.

215

Other

Baan was founded in the Netherlands in 1978 to provide financial and administrative consulting services. In 1982 the company expanded its business by introducing its first UNIX-based application software. Baan's IPO was completed in May 1995. The company acquired Probe Software Sciences, a Montreal software developer, in the same year. Founders Jan and Paul Baan are still active in the management of the company. CFO and managing director of operations David Cairns was formerly CFO of Uniface and of Marcam.

KEY FACTS

Year Established:	1978
Employees:	1,160
Fiscal Year End:	December
Revenues FY '94:	$122.9m
Revenues FY '95:	$163.4m (estimate)
EPS '94:	$0.03
EPS '95:	$0.30
Shares Outstanding:	37.7m
Five-Year Growth Rate:	40%

BAY NETWORKS

Product Description

Bay Networks designs and markets a comprehensive line of networking products and services, including high-speed routers, wide-area network access devices, local-area network switches, intelligent hubs, and sophisticated network management software that provides design and configuration solutions. The company offers products for customers building or enhancing their network systems, from small local-area networks to large enterprise-wide information infrastructures. Bay Networks is one of the "Big Four" internetworking companies; it has a comprehensive product line that spans various technologies and standards, including Ethernet, FDDI, Frame Relay, Token Ring, and ATM. Bay Networks owns about 17% of the router market and about 23% of the intelligent hub market. The company sells through 1,000 resellers worldwide and 1,200 direct-sales personnel.

Address:	4401 Great America Parkway
	Santa Clara, CA 95054
Telephone:	408/988-2400
Fax:	408/988-5525
E-mail:	info@baynetworks.com
Web site:	http://www.baynetworks.com
Industry:	Communications
Sector:	Computer Networking
CEO:	Andrew Ludwick
CFO:	William Ruehle
Stock Exchange:	NASDAQ
Stock Symbol:	BNET

Market Strategy/Positioning

The company's mission is to provide solutions that address customer needs for switched internetworks while extending the life of existing network investments. Bay Networks has strategic relationships with Apple, AT&T, Efficient Networks, GTE, Hewlett-Packard, IBM, Intel, Microsoft, Network General, Novell, Oracle, Sprint, StrataCom, Sun Microsystems, and WilTel. Significant customers include many of the *Fortune* 1000 companies. The company's competitive advantage is its comprehensive product line, with product strength in emerging hub, router, and switch internetworking markets. Bay Networks has also made several key acquisitions to fill gaps in its product line, including Coral Network and Centillion Networks. Bay Networks primarily competes against Cisco, 3Com, and Cabletron Systems. Additional challenges and risks include increased competition in the internetworking market with recent consolidation in the industry, and the challenge of bringing quality products to market in a timely manner.

Other

Bay Networks was formed in October 1994, following the merger of Synoptics and Wellfleet Communications—one of the largest mergers in the data networking industry. The merger created a company with over $1 billion in sales. The company also announced its plans to buy Xylogics for about $300 million in stock in September of 1995. Chairman Paul Severino co-founded Wellfleet in

KEY FACTS

Year Established:	1994
Employees:	3,200
Fiscal Year End:	June
Revenues FY '94:	$1.1b
Revenues FY '95:	$1.3b
EPS '94:	$1.06
EPS '95:	$1.55
Shares Outstanding:	122.6m
Five-Year Growth Rate:	26%

BAY NETWORKS

1986. Before Wellfleet, he founded Interlan, where he was president until 1985, when the company was acquired by Micom. He also co-founded Data Translation and held management positions at DEC and Prime Computer. CEO and president Andy Ludwick co-founded Synoptics. Before Synoptics, he was with Xerox for 15 years in a variety of line positions in marketing, market planning, and sales operations. Executive vice president and chief technical officer Ronald Schmidt also co-founded Synoptics and was senior vice president since its inception in 1985. He was in research at Xerox, a section manager at Hughes Research, and a staff member at Bell Labs.

217

BBN
BOLT BERANEK & NEWMAN

Address:	150 Cambridge Park Drive
	Cambridge, MA 02140
Telephone:	617/873-2000
Fax:	617/873-5011
E-mail:	info@bbn.com
Web site:	http://www.bbn.com
Industry:	Entertainment & Information
Sector:	Information Highway Services
CEO:	George H. Conrades
CFO:	Ralph A. Goldwasser
Stock Exchange:	NYSE
Stock Symbol:	BBN

Product Description

Bolt Beranek & Newman's major markets include Internet services, advanced technology research, consulting, speech recognition, as well as networking, security, data analysis, and management software. The company is divided into four major units: BBN Planet, BBN Hark Systems, BBN Software Products, and BBN Systems & Technologies. BBN designed the first modem, designated the @ in addressing electronic mail, and built ARPAnet, the original network from which the Internet evolved. BBN Planet is the largest provider of Internet access and security services, and BBN Hark Systems is becoming a major player in the speech recognition software market.

Market Strategy/Positioning

The company's mission is to be the leading provider of internetworking technologies and services designed to help people and businesses work and learn together. BBN has strategic relationships with AT&T, Avis, Cisco, and Sun Microsystems. Significant customers include Apple, Cisco, AT&T, IBM, Paramount, Blue Cross, and Avis. The company's competitive advantages are its business-oriented reliability, its one-stop shopping, and a rich history of Internet development. BBN primarily competes against UUNET, NETCOM, and PSI.

Other

Bolt Beranek & Newman was founded in 1948 by two professors and a graduate student from MIT. It has played an obscure but crucial role in numerous important technology events. In 1969 engineers from BBN installed the first communications processor of the first modern computer network at UCLA. BBN then became a contractor on a project sponsored by the Advanced Research Projects Agency, the ARPAnet, which led to the modern Internet. Two important regional networks, NEARnet (New England) and BARRnet (Bay Area), were acquired by the company in 1993 and 1994. George Conrades became CEO in January 1994 after spending 31 years at IBM. Other BBN top executives come from Oracle, EDS, and Dun & Bradstreet. One of Mr. Conrades' first decisions was to sell its subsidiary, Lightstream, to Cisco Systems for $120 million.

KEY FACTS

Year Established:	1948
Employees:	1,700
Fiscal Year End:	June
Revenues FY '94:	$196.1m
Revenues FY '95:	$215.0m
EPS '94:	$(0.48)
EPS '95:	$(0.66)
Shares Outstanding:	17.3m
Five-Year Growth Rate:	18%

BELL ATLANTIC

Product Description

Bell Atlantic provides services in telephone operations, cellular communications, and paging services. The company operates seven telephone subsidiaries located in the East, finances and maintains large- and small-scale computers, and leases office and industrial equipment. The company announced its "ISDN Anywhere" initiative, which provides simultaneous voice, data, and video. Bell Atlantic continues to pursue growth opportunities in wired and wireless communications, information services, and the video and entertainment markets. The company is also the parent of one of the nation's largest cellular carriers, Bell Atlantic Mobile.

Address:	1717 Arch Street
	Philadelphia, PA 19103
Telephone:	215/963-6000
Fax:	215/575-0963
E-mail:	n/a
Web site:	http://www.ba.com
Industry:	Communications
Sector:	Information Highway Services
CEO:	Raymond W. Smith
CFO:	William O. Albertini
Stock Exchange:	NYSE
Stock Symbol:	BEL

Market Strategy/Positioning

The company's mission is to establish leadership positions in the new markets that will create continued growth in the swiftly changing world of telecommunications. Bell Atlantic has strategic relationships with NYNEX, Grupo Iusacell, Oracle, Pacific Telesis, AirTouch, and U S WEST. The company's competitive advantages are its being one of the largest wireless carriers in the nation, its leadership in intelligent network software, and its modern network infrastructure. Bell Atlantic primarily competes against Ameritech, AT&T, BellSouth, Cable & Wireless, EDS, GTE, MCI, MFS, NYNEX, Pacific Telesis, Southwestern Bell, Sprint, WorldCom, U S WEST, and U.S. Long Distance. Additional challenges and risks include the threat to its current position from regulatory, legislative, and technological changes.

Other

Bell Atlantic was formed in 1984 after the breakup of AT&T. Various Bell operating hubs were molded into seven regional companies. The company failed to acquire TCI in 1994; analysts felt this purchase would have ushered in the era of interactive television. Chairman Ray Smith previously held the titles of president and vice chairman. He also served as director of finance and budgets for AT&T. Mr. Smith is known as a writer, playwright, and theatrical director, but is quoted as saying, "I have no plans to quit my day job."

KEY FACTS

Year Established:	1984
Employees:	73,600
Fiscal Year End:	December
Revenues FY '94:	$13.7b
Revenues FY '95:	n/a
EPS '94:	$3.21
EPS '95:	$3.82 (estimate)
Shares Outstanding:	436.4m
Five-Year Growth Rate:	7%

BELLSOUTH

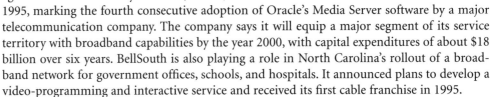

Address:	1155 Peachtree Street Northeast Atlanta, GA 30367
Telephone:	404/249-2000
Fax:	404/249-5599
E-mail:	n/a
Web site:	http://www.bls.com
Industry:	Communications
Sector:	Information Highway Services
CEO:	John Clendenin
CFO:	Earle Mauldin
Stock Exchange:	NYSE
Stock Symbol:	BLS

Product Description

BellSouth is a holding company; its subsidiaries provide services in telecommunications, information distribution, mobile communications, and other related fields. The company is conducting interactive media studies with WPP Group, Coopers & Lybrand, U S WEST, Fidelity Investments, Prudential Insurance, American Express, and the U.S. Postal Service. It announced an agreement with Oracle Systems on June 28, 1995, marking the fourth consecutive adoption of Oracle's Media Server software by a major telecommunication company. The company says it will equip a major segment of its service territory with broadband capabilities by the year 2000, with capital expenditures of about $18 billion over six years. BellSouth is also playing a role in North Carolina's rollout of a broadband network for government offices, schools, and hospitals. It announced plans to develop a video-programming and interactive service and received its first cable franchise in 1995.

Market Strategy/Positioning

BellSouth has strategic relationships with Apple Computer, IBM, Walt Disney, GTE, Ameritech, ISDN Systems, Intel, ALLTEL, RBC, Ji Tong (China), China Unicom, MCI, Oracle, Kroger, and Southwestern Bell. The company's main competitive advantage is its opportunity to benefit from entry into new business markets, such as information services, interactive communications, and cable television. BellSouth primarily competes against American Business Information, Ameritech, AT&T, BCE, Bell Atlantic, Century Telephone, Comcast, GTE, IBM, WorldCom, MCI, Motorola, Nextel, NYNEX, Pacific Telesis, SBC Communications, Sprint, Time Warner, U S WEST, and Viacom. Additional challenges and risks include successfully managing the shift from a traditional phone company to a more diversified full-service communications company, while handling increasing levels of competition.

BellSouth is unique in being the largest of the Bell operating companies.

Other

Southern Bell Telephone and Telegraph was established in 1878 as the result of an agreement between National Bell and Western Union. In 1912 the company lost its territory in Virginia and West Virginia and merged with Cumberland Telephone and Telegraph, which served Kentucky, Louisiana, Mississippi, Tennessee, and parts of Illinois and Indiana. In 1968 Southern Bell split into South Central Bell

KEY FACTS

Year Established:	1984
Employees:	95,100
Fiscal Year End:	December
Revenues FY '94:	$16.9b
Revenues FY '95:	n/a
EPS '94:	$4.35
EPS '95:	$4.45 (estimate)
Shares Outstanding:	496.3m
Five-Year Growth Rate:	7%

BELLSOUTH

(Alabama, Kentucky, Louisiana, Mississippi, and Tennessee) and Southern Bell (Florida, Georgia, North Carolina, and South Carolina); however, the companies were quickly reunited through the settlement of the AT&T antitrust case in 1984. BellSouth was the largest of the seven regional Bell operating companies to spin off. In 1986 BellSouth bought L.M. Berry, a directory publisher, and MCCA, a paging and mobile communications firm. In 1991 the company purchased 18 midwestern cellular systems from McCaw Cellular and arranged a joint venture with RAM Broadcasting to provide domestic and international wireless data network services. In 1993 BellSouth announced that it intended to invest $250 million in cable operator Prime Management. In 1994 the company received permission to provide long-distance telephone services in Chile; that same year it joined with QVC in a failed attempt to buy Paramount. BellSouth is bidding for several broadband licenses to provide personal communications services.

BERTELSMANN

Product Description

Bertelsmann is a leading media company; its core businesses include book, magazine, and music publishing, electronic media, and record labels. It operates the U.S. publishing group Bantam Doubleday Dell and owns record labels RCA, Arista, BMG Ariola (Europe), and BMG Victor (Japan). It formally combined its music, TV/film, and music production and technology operations with the formation of BMG Entertainment in 1994. In addition, the company is setting up a European online service with America Online. Bertelsmann plans to enter the Chinese market with joint venture partners in 1996.

Address:	U.S. Headquarters (BMG Entertainment) 1540 Broadway New York, NY 10036
Telephone:	212/930-4000
Fax:	212/930-4015
E-mail:	n/a
Web site:	http://www.bertelsmann.de
Industry:	Entertainment & Information
Sector:	Newspaper/Magazine Publishing
CEO:	Mark Wossner
CFO:	Siegfried Luther

Market Strategy/Positioning

Bertelsmann has a 15% stake in Multimedia Betiebsgesellschaft (MMBG), which has developed a set-top box with Seca of France, America Online, and Novell. The company also holds a substantial stake in RTL, one of Germany's largest private commercial TV channels. The company's competitive advantages are its sophisticated infrastructure for finding talent and its strategy of acquiring mid-size companies and expanding operations—as opposed to negotiating major takeovers, as many American companies have done. Bertelsmann primarily competes against Kirch Group (Munich), Nokia, Time Warner, Sony, Polygram, Walt Disney (Capital Cities/ABC), Hearst, Houghton Mifflin, Knight-Ridder, Matsushita, McGraw-Hill, News Corp., Philips, and Viacom. Additional challenges and risks include competing with Kirch Group and Nokia, whose set-top box will be used for the Berlin Cable Network, (which reaches 1.1 million homes,) and meeting consumer demands in more than 40 countries.

Other

Carl Bertelsmann founded the company in 1835. The company prospered as a religious publisher until the Nazis forced it to cease operations during WWII. In 1948 Richard Mohn, a relative by marriage, rebuilt the company and began publishing again. In 1981 Mark Wossner succeeded Mr. Mohn as CEO and began enhancing the company's presence in the U.S. In 1994 a subsidiary, T1 News Media, announced a joint venture with Novell to produce multimedia applications.

Primary VCs/Outside Financing

100% internally owned.

KEY FACTS

Year Established:	1835
Employees:	51,800
Fiscal Year End:	June
Revenues FY '94:	$10.6b
Revenues FY '95:	n/a
Date of Next Financing:	n/a
Date of Last Financing:	n/a
Size of Last Financing:	n/a
Total Capital Raised:	n/a
Post Round Valuation:	n/a
Expected IPO Date:	n/a

BHC
COMMUNICATIONS

Product Description

BHC Communications operates eight television stations—three wholly-owned and five others through its 56%-owned subsidiary, United Television. The company is a majority-owned subsidiary of Chris-Craft Industries. Six of BHC's television stations are very high frequency (VHF) stations, and the other two are ultra high frequency (UHF) stations. BHC also partnered with Viacom's subsidiary, Paramount, to create a fifth television network, United Paramount Network. UPN began broadcasting in January 1994 and plans to broadcast one hour of original children's programming on Sunday mornings. BHC currently owns 100% of UPN, with Paramount's having the option of acquiring an interest in the network equal to BHC until January 15, 1997.

Address:	767 Fifth Avenue New York, NY 10153
Telephone:	212/421-0200
Fax:	212/935-8462
E-mail:	n/a
Web site:	n/a
Industry:	Entertainment & Information
Sector:	Broadcasters & Cable Networks
CEO:	Herbert J. Siegel (Chairman and President)
Treasurer:	Laurence M. Kashdin
Stock Exchange:	AMEX
Stock Symbol:	BHC

Market Strategy/Positioning

BHC Communications reaches approximately 20% of the U.S. population, including the two largest television markets: New York and Los Angeles. One of the company's competitive advantages is its successful debut of UPN. Additional challenges and risks include facing possible changes in the rules governing cable television operators and absorbing the high startup costs of UPN.

Other

BHC Communications was organized in Delaware in 1977 under the name BHC, Inc., and changed its name to BHC Communications in 1989. The company has grown to include subsidiaries Chris-Craft Television, Pinelands, and United Television. Chairman and president Herbert Siegel has held his position since 1977 and is also chairman and president of Chris-Craft Industries.

KEY FACTS

Year Established:	1977
Employees:	1,000
Fiscal Year End:	December
Revenues FY '94:	$457.6m
Revenues FY '95:	n/a
EPS '94:	$3.71
EPS '95:	$2.00 (estimate)
Shares Outstanding:	24.9m
Five-Year Growth Rate:	n/a

223

BLOOMBERG

Address:	499 Park Avenue
	New York, NY 10022
Telephone:	212/318-2000
Fax:	212/980-4585
E-mail:	n/a
Web site:	http://www.bloomberg.com
Industry:	Entertainment & Information
Sector:	Information Services
CEO:	Michael Bloomberg
CFO:	Wolf Boehm

Product Description

Bloomberg is a global distributor of information services to the financial and investment communities. Its products include a flagship computer terminal system for information and analysis, newswire services, three periodicals, radio stations in New York and Boston, and a DirecTv channel. It has over 45,000 terminal service subscribers and is growing at a rate of over 1,000 monthly. Bloomberg has recently evolved into a more diverse company by adding a satellite TV station (Bloomberg Direct), Bloomberg News Radio, and *Bloomberg*, a monthly magazine. The company installs dishes for DirecTv wherever it has a terminal.

Market Strategy/Positioning

The company's mission is to offer financial and investment professionals all the information they need to lead their lives and run a business. Bloomberg has strategic relationships with *The New York Times* and Hughes Electronics. Significant customers include investment banks and fund managers who rely on Bloomberg's services. The company's competitive advantage is its position as the standard in the business information field, a position it has gained because of its depth of information and the number of easy-to-use services it provides to customers. Bloomberg primarily competes against Dow Jones Telerate, Knight-Ridder, and Reuters Holdings.

Other

Michael Bloomberg started his business after leaving his job as head of equity trading at Salomon Brothers. Mr. Bloomberg worked at Salomon from 1966 to 1981. While at Salomon, he worked with a group of programmers to develop debt and equity information systems he felt should be available on computer. Pushed out of Salomon in 1981, he went to Merrill Lynch with his idea for an online bond data system, which Merrill Lynch funded in exchange for 30% ownership in the company.

Primary VCs/Outside Financing

70% internally owned, Merrill Lynch owns 30%.

KEY FACTS

Year Established:	1981
Employees:	2,000
Fiscal Year End:	December
Revenues FY '94:	$600.0m
Revenues FY '95:	$700m+ (estimated)
Date of Next Financing:	n/a
Date of Last Financing:	n/a
Size of Last Financing:	n/a
Total Capital Raised:	n/a
Post Round Valuation:	n/a
Expected IPO Date:	n/a

BOSS
ENTERTAINMENT

Product Description

Boss Entertainment is the parent company of Boss Film Studios and recently-formed Boss Game Studios. Boss Film Studios is a visual effects studio with an 80,000-square-foot facility that includes computer generated image (CGI) digital technology, sound-stages, miniatures, robotic cameras, motion capture systems, and motion control photography. Its movie credits include *Alien 3, Batman Returns, Cliffhanger, Die Hard, Drop Zone, Ghostbusters, Outbreak, Poltergeist, Species, The Specialist,* and *True Lies.* The studio has produced TV ads for Ameritech, Budweiser, Chevrolet, Chrysler, Ford, KLM/Northwest, Taco Bell, and United Airlines. It also creates special venue films and ride simulations.

Address:	13335 Maxella Avenue
	Marina del Rey, CA 90292
Telephone:	310/823-0433
Fax:	310/305-8576
E-mail:	n/a
Web site:	http://www.boss.com
Industry:	Entertainment & Information
Sector:	Film & Entertainment Production
CEO:	Richard Edlund
COO:	Martin Rae

Market Strategy/Positioning

Significant customers include NHK Creative (Japan) and Gakken Publishing Company (Japan). The company's competitive advantage is the emphasis it places on the research and development of new technology. Boss Film Studios primarily competes against Industrial Light & Magic, DreamQuest, Pacific Data Images, R/GA Digital Studios, and Digital Domain. Additional challenges and risks include successfully entering the games market.

Other

Boss Film Sudios was founded in 1983 by Richard Edlund through a deal in which Mr. Edlund took over a 65mm motion picture effects facility in Marina del Rey. Boss Films Studios and its sister company, Boss Games Studios, both operate under the company Boss Entertainment. In 1993 Boss Film Studios earned dual Oscar nominations in the visual effects category for *Alien 3* and *Batman Returns*, and in 1994 *Cliffhanger* received an Academy Award nomination for visual effects. BMG Interactive Entertainment will publish and distribute Boss Games Studios' first game title in early 1996. Chairman and Founder Richard Edlund established his reputation as a filmmaker by joining Industrial Light & Magic and LucasFilm to develop the visual effects in the *Star Wars* trilogy.

Primary VCs/Outside Financing

Mr. John McCaw.

KEY FACTS

Year Established:	1983
Employees:	125
Fiscal Year End:	September
Revenues FY '94:	n/a
Revenues FY '95:	n/a
Date of Next Financing:	n/a
Date of Last Financing:	n/a
Size of Last Financing:	n/a
Total Capital Raised:	n/a
Post Round Valuation:	n/a
Expected IPO Date:	n/a

BRILLIANT MEDIA

Address:	450 Pacific Avenue First Floor San Francisco, CA 94133
Telephone:	415/434-5040
Fax:	415/777-2379
E-mail:	info@brilliantmedia.com
Web site:	http://www.brilliantmedia.com
Industry:	Entertainment & Information
Sector:	Film & Entertainment Production
CEO:	Steven L. Nelson
CFO:	n/a

Product Description

Brilliant Media is a San Francisco- and Burbank-based studio that combines the strengths of Hollywood and Silicon Valley to create interactive entertainment and information designs. It currently has three main product lines: an information access and visualization system, an interactive entertainment series for deployment as hybrid Internet/CD-ROM experiences, and CD+ music titles, including a CD featuring *Hootie & the Blowfish*. Brilliant Media created the first interactive CD-ROM featuring QuickTime video, which included hyperlinked encyclopedic background stories, a live TV-guide, and advertising. Other products include ISDN services (music shopping and animated children's video mail) and a planned interactive TV show.

Market Strategy/Positioning

The company's mission is to create innovative, high-quality interactive experiences for a global audience. Brilliant Media has strategic relationships with Warner Brothers, One Such Films, International Creative Management, Creative Artists Agency, and Real World. Brilliant Media collaborated with Peter Gabriel's company Real World to design and release *Xplora*, an award-winning multimedia title. Significant customers include Bandai, Warner Brothers, Walt Disney, Oracle, United Airlines, CNN, Kaiser Permanente, Apple, U S WEST, and Hearst New Media. The company's competitive advantages are its strong base of tools and methods, its strong industry relationships, and its successful different approach to interactive design. Brilliant Media primarily competes against Iconics, DreamWorks SKG, and Castle Rock Entertainment.

Other

Brilliant Media, founded in 1992 by CEO Steven Nelson, has been one of the pioneers in combining the interactive products of Hollywood and Silicon Valley. Mr. Nelson has created interactive products for Apple, CNN, United Airlines, and the American Film Institute. He has also served as a consultant for GTE, Home Savings of America, and the Environmental Protection Agency. Before entering interactive media, Mr. Nelson directed television and educational videos.

Primary VCs/Outside Financing

100% internally funded.

KEY FACTS

Year Established:	1992
Employees:	10
Fiscal Year End:	December
Revenues FY '94:	$0.0
Revenues FY '95:	$0.0
Date of Next Financing:	n/a
Date of Last Financing:	n/a
Size of Last Financing:	n/a
Total Capital Raised:	n/a
Post Round Valuation:	n/a
Expected IPO Date:	n/a

BROADVISION

Product Description
BroadVision's flagship product, CoMarket, offers providers of interactive services a flexible set of tools to manage customer information and consumer privacy, data collection and reporting, digital marketing programs, and order processing and payment functions. The CoMarket system is based on the COBRA standard for distributed systems. It also supports interfaces to SQL databases such as Oracle and Sybase.

Address:	333 Distel Circle
	Los Altos, CA 94022
Telephone:	415/934-3700
Fax:	415/934-3701
E-mail:	n/a
Web site:	http://www.broadvision.com
Industry:	Computers
Sector:	Enterprise & Client/Server Software
CEO:	Pehong Chen
CFO:	Randall Bolten

Market Strategy/Positioning
The company's mission is to facilitate the shift from traditional retail and catalogue sales toward new, online distribution channels, such as interactive TV, consumer online services, and the Internet. BroadVision has strategic relationships with Sybase, Logica, VeriFone, Stanford University, and Tandem Computer. The company's competitive advantages are its systems, designed from inception to support interactive applications, multiple network architectures, and appliances. Another advantage is its capability to differentiate through integration of sales, marketing, and customer account systems. BroadVision primarily competes against Oracle and U.S. Computer Services (Cable Data).

227

Other
BroadVision was founded in May 1993 by Dr. Pehong Chen. The first use of its CoMarket product in production environments is scheduled for late 1995. Chairman, president, and CEO Dr. Chen founded Gain Technology in 1989; the company was acquired by Sybase in 1992. He also served as vice president of multimedia technology at Sybase. Before founding Gain, Dr. Chen was a project manager at Olivetti Research Center.

Primary VCs/Outside Financing
Mayfield Fund, Sutter Hill Ventures, Itochu, Stanford University, and several private investors.

KEY FACTS

Year Established:	1993
Employees:	20
Fiscal Year End:	December
Revenues FY '94:	$0.0
Revenues FY '95:	$2.0m
Date of Next Financing:	June 1995
Date of Last Financing:	n/a
Size of Last Financing:	$1.7m
Total Capital Raised:	$10.3m
Post Round Valuation:	$34.0m
Expected IPO Date:	1999

BRØDERBUND
SOFTWARE

Address:	500 Redwood Boulevard
	P.O. Box 6121
	Novato, CA 94947-6121
Telephone:	415/382-4400
Fax:	415/382-4582
E-mail:	n/a
Web site:	n/a
Industry:	Entertainment & Information
Sector:	Entertainment/Education Software
CEO:	Douglas Carlston
CFO:	Michael Shannahan
Stock Exchange:	NASDAQ
Stock Symbol:	BROD

Product Description

Brøderbund Software is one of the leading software developers and publishers for the home, school, and small business markets for the Macintosh, DOS, and Windows platforms. Focusing on personal productivity and education, the company has one of the largest sales forces, selling products in over 14,000 outlets nationwide. It sells directly through schools and distributors as well as directly to software specialty retail chains, superstores, mass merchandisers, discount warehouse stores, and educational dealers.

Market Strategy/Positioning

Brøderbund has strategic relationships with Random House and eight affiliated labels, including Amtex Software, Cyan, I Motion, Inroads Interactive, Living Books (a Random House/Brøderbund company), The Logic Factory, StarWare, and Vicarious. The company's competitive advantage is its diversified product base in an extremely competitive market. Brøderbund Software primarily competes against Edmark, Davidson & Associates, The Learning Company, MECC, Humongous Entertainment, Acclaim Entertainment, and Electronic Arts. Additional challenges and risks include the consumer platform shifts to Windows, which Brøderbund views as positive.

Other

Brøderbund Software was founded by Doug and Gary Carlston in 1980 to market computer games Doug had written in his spare time. The company formed an alliance with a Japanese software house, StarCraft, and marketed a large line of home entertainment products. By the end of its third year, Brøderbund had moved from Eugene, OR to Marin County, CA and was selling millions of dollars of software. Brøderbund's plans to acquire The Learning Company fell through in late 1995. Chairman and CEO Doug Carlston served as president and director from 1980 to 1989. Director, president, and COO William McDonagh previously worked with Arthur Andersen as an auditor, joined Brøderbund in 1982 as controller, and was promoted to CFO in 1987. Current CFO Michael Shannahan previously worked at KPMG Peat Marwick.

KEY FACTS

Year Established:	1980
Employees:	470
Fiscal Year End:	December
Revenues FY '94:	$457.6m
Revenues FY '95:	$213.5m (estimate)
EPS '94:	$3.72
EPS '95:	$1.64 (estimate)
Shares Outstanding:	21.1m
Five-Year Growth Rate:	27%

C-CUBE

Product Description

C-Cube designs and markets integrated circuits that compress and decompress full-motion digital video as well as still images. The company is a leading provider of MPEG video encoders, MPEG video decoders, and JPEG compression integrated circuits.

Market Strategy/Positioning

The company's mission is to be the world leader in the delivery of digital video and image compression solutions for the computer, communications, and consumer electronics markets. C-Cube has strategic relationships with JVC and Thomson Consumer Electronics (RCA). Significant customers include Apple, Matsushita, Panasonic, Samsung, Scientific-Atlanta, and Hewlett-Packard. The company's competitive advantage is the programmable architecture of its products. C-Cube's expertise lies in its sophisticated algorithms, which produce a customizable microcode that can be adapted to meet the needs of specific applications. C-Cube primarily competes against SGS-Thomson, LSI Logic, and Philips Electronics. Additional challenges and risks include obtaining sufficient fab capacity and managing the company's rapid growth. C-Cube is unique in having a primary focus on developing the highest quality digital video and still-image compression/decompression engines in the industry. The company's competitors focus on the MPEG and JPEG markets as secondary markets; as a result, C-Cube is ahead of its competition in delivering compression technology.

Address:	1778 McCarthy Boulevard Milpitas, CA 95035
Telephone:	408/944-6300
Fax:	408/944-6314
E-mail:	scott.st.clair@c-cube.com
Web site:	n/a
Industry:	Computers
Sector:	Semiconductors
CEO:	Alex Balkanski
CFO:	Jim Burke
Stock Exchange:	NASDAQ
Stock Symbol:	CUBE

229

Other

C-Cube was founded in 1988 by Dr. Alex Balkanski and Dr. Edmund Sun. The company played a key role in defining MPEG (Moving Pictures Experts Group), the standard for digital video compression, and the JPEG (Joint Photographic Experts Group), the standard for still image compression. C-Cube introduced the first JPEG still-image processor in July 1990. Before founding C-Cube, president and CEO Dr. Alex Balkanski was founder and president of Diamond Devices. Dr. Balkanski also serves on the boards of DiviCom and Sierra Semiconductor. CFO Jim Burke previously worked at Advanced Network Solutions as COO and director. He was also the founding CFO for both Insite Peripherals and Vertex Peripherals.

KEY FACTS

Year Established:	1988
Employees:	190
Fiscal Year End:	December
Revenues FY '94:	$445.0m
Revenues FY '95:	n/a
EPS '94:	$0.30
EPS '95:	$0.76 (estimate)
Shares Outstanding:	17.2m
Five-Year Growth Rate:	30%

CABLETRON SYSTEMS

Address:	35 Industrial Way Rochester, NH 03867
Telephone:	603/332-9400
Fax:	603/337-2211
E-mail:	postmaster@ctron.com
Web site:	http://www.ctron.com
Industry:	Communications
Sector:	Computer Networking
CEO:	S. Robert Levine
CFO:	David J. Kirkpatrick
Stock Exchange:	NYSE
Stock Symbol:	CS

Product Description

Cabletron Systems develops local-area network (LAN) and enterprise network systems for Ethernet, Token Ring, FDDI, and ATM. Its products include desktop network interface cards, transmission media, bridges, repeaters, transceivers, intelligent/non-intelligent hubs, diagnostic testing equipment, and network management software. It also provides network design and installation services. With an installed base of over 63,000 customer sites, Cabletron has over 34% market share of modular ports. The company is one of the few vendors that has a direct-sales and service organization abroad.

Market Strategy/Positioning

The company's mission is to provide quality products with unmatched service and support, meeting customer requirements 24 hours a day, seven days a week. Cabletron has strategic relationships with Cisco and FORE Systems. The company's competitive advantages are being one of only four vendors to provide true virtual network switching capability and the only vendor with a network management platform. Cabletron Systems has the largest service and support organization in the industry (1,800 people). The company primarily competes against 3Com/Chipcom and Bay Networks. Additional challenges and risks include maintaining its high growth rate and delivering a unique functionality ahead of its competition.

Other

Cabletron Systems was founded by CEO Bob Levine and Chairman Craig Benson in 1983 as an Ethernet cable company and has emerged as one of the "Big Four" internetworking vendors. Craig Benson was previously with Interlan.

KEY FACTS

Year Established:	1983
Employees:	5,100
Fiscal Year End:	February
Revenues FY '94:	$598.1m
Revenues FY '95:	$810.7m
EPS '94:	$1.68
EPS '95:	$2.28
Shares Outstanding:	71.6m
Five-Year Growth Rate:	25%

230

CADENCE
DESIGN SYSTEMS

Address:	555 River Oaks Parkway
	San Jose, CA 95134
Telephone:	408/943-1234
Fax:	408/943-0513
E-mail:	n/a
Web site:	http://www.cadence.com
Industry:	Computers
Sector:	Design Automation Software
CEO:	Joseph B. Costello
CFO:	Ray Bingham
Stock Exchange:	NYSE
Stock Symbol:	CDN

Product Description

Cadence Design Systems provides electronic design automation (EDA) software and services that accelerate the process of designing electronic systems and integrated circuits (ICs). The company is aggressively building a team of consulting professionals. It holds a 26% share of the EDA market and a dominant share of the verification market. IC design is responsible for 60% of its business. Cadence announced more than 20 new products in 1995 and entered the design outsourcing business by winning a $75 million UNISYS contract.

Market Strategy/Positioning

The company's mission is to combine leading-edge technology with a complementary set of services that allow customers to improve the quality and time-to-market performance of innovative electronic products. Cadence has strategic relationships with IBM, General Motors, and several major silicon providers. Significant customers include UNISYS, Western Digital, IBM, Philips, Fujitsu, Toshiba, SGS-Thomson, Tandem Computer, Hewlett-Packard, Sun Microsystems, Cyrix, Apple, Panasonic, Motorola, Mitsubishi, Siemens, and Sony. The company's competitive advantages are its understanding of technology and the variety of services it offers. Cadence primarily competes against Integrated Silicon Systems, Viewlogic, ArcSys, Mentor Graphics, and Synopsys.

231

Other

Since its founding in 1988, Cadence Design Systems has grown steadily through mergers and acquisitions. The company focuses on helping customers achieve their business objectives. President and CEO Joe Costello formerly served as president and COO of SDA Systems. Before SDA, he was president of Electronic Speech Systems and manager of research and development at National Semiconductor.

KEY FACTS

Year Established:	1988
Employees:	2,550
Fiscal Year End:	December
Revenues FY '94:	$429.1m
Revenues FY '95:	$530.0m (estimate)
EPS '94:	$0.85
EPS '95:	$1.60 (estimate)
Shares Outstanding:	41.2m
Five-Year Growth Rate:	17%

CAPITAL CITIES/ABC

Address:	77 West 66th Street
	New York, NY 10023-6298
Telephone:	212/456-7777
Fax:	212/456-6850
E-mail:	n/a
Web site:	n/a
Industry:	Entertainment & Information
Sector:	Broadcasters & Cable Networks
CEO:	Thomas S. Murphy
CFO:	Ronald J. Doerfler
Stock Exchange:	NYSE
Stock Symbol:	CCB

Product Description

Capital Cities/ABC is composed of the ABC Television Network, eight television stations, 21 radio stations, several radio networks, seven daily newspapers, numerous business and specialized periodicals, weekly newspapers, and shopping guides. The company also holds interests in cable programming services, including ESPN, and is engaged in television program production and distribution, international broadcast/cable ventures, and multimedia activities. The company also recently formed Capital Cities/ABC Multimedia Group, which develops and manages business opportunities in new media. These include interactive TV, pay-per-view, video-on-demand, online computer applications, and location-based entertainment.

Market Strategy/Positioning

Capital Cities/ABC has strategic relationships with DreamWorks SKG, Electronic Arts, Inc.1, and Spectrum HoloByte. In May 1995 the company announced a joint venture with Spectrum Holobyte to develop interactive game software using the ABC Sports brand. The company's competitive advantage is its positioning in the broadcasting market. Capital Cities/ABC primarily competes against Advance, Bertelsmann, CBS, GE, Hearst, Knight-Ridder, News Corp., TCI, Time Warner, Times Mirror, Tribune, Turner, and Viacom.

Other

Capital Cities Communications was founded in 1954 as the Hudson Broadcasting Company, with one television and one radio station. For 13 years Capital Cities Communications operated exclusively as a broadcasting company until it entered the publishing business in 1968. American Broadcasting Companies was started in 1953, when Leonard H. Goldenson completed the merger of ABC and United Paramount Theaters, a spin-off of RCA's Blue Network. In 1986 ABC was acquired by Capital Cities Communications. Capital Cities/ABC was acquired by Walt Disney for an estimated $19 billion in August 1995. Thomas Murphy was chairman and CEO for 24 years (1966 to 1990) and resumed the title in February 1994. Mr. Murphy joined Capital Cities at its founding in 1954.

232

KEY FACTS

Year Established:	1986
Employees:	20,200
Fiscal Year End:	December
Revenues FY '94:	$6.4b
Revenues FY '95:	$6.9b (estimate)
EPS '94:	$4.42
EPS '95:	$5.15 (estimate)
Shares Outstanding:	153.9m
Five-Year Growth Rate:	13%

CASCADE COMMUNICATIONS

Address:	5 Carlisle Road
	Westford, MA 01886
Telephone:	508/692-2600
Fax:	508/692-9214
E-mail:	n/a
Web site:	n/a
Industry:	Communications
Sector:	Computer Networking
CEO:	Daniel Smith
CFO:	Paul Blondin
Stock Exchange:	NASDAQ
Stock Symbol:	CSCC

Product Description

Cascade is a global supplier of multiservice wide-area network (WAN) switching products and services that provide support for frame relay and ATM transmission technologies. The company is the price/performance leader for frame relay switches. Its products include network management systems and high-end and low-end switches for backbone networks. Cascade's multiservice switch platform provides a safe and cost-effective ATM migration path for enterprise network managers and service providers.

Market Strategy/Positioning

The company's mission is to be the leading supplier of high-performance, fully-featured, cost-effective access switching products for public and private networks. Cascade has strategic relationships with ACT Networks, Alcatel, Cisco, Hypercom Network, Motorola, Siemens, and Verilink. Significant customers include GTE Telephone, AirTouch, AT&T Wireless, Performance Systems International (PSI), BancOne, Bridge Information Systems, Dun & Bradstreet, Toshiba, Ameritech, Bell Atlantic, and U S WEST. The company's competitive advantages are its numerous technological firsts and standards-based products, and its development efforts of the multiservice WAN switch. The company primarily competes against Northern Telecom and StrataCom. Additional challenges and risks include the concentration of customers among regional Bell operating companies and sole-supplier relationships for some components.

233

Other

The company was incorporated in 1990 under the name Nexgencom, received its first round of venture capital in June 1991, and changed to its present name in August 1991. CEO Daniel Smith was formerly vice president of sales at Proteon. Executive vice president and co-founder Desh Deshpande was co-founder and vice president of engineering at Coral Network, acquired by Bay Networks.

KEY FACTS

Year Established:	1990
Employees:	160
Fiscal Year End:	December
Revenues FY '94:	$50.0m
Revenues FY '95:	n/a
EPS '94:	$0.33
EPS '95:	$0.71 (estimate)
Shares Outstanding:	27.7m
Five-Year Growth Rate:	48%

CELLNET
DATA SYSTEMS

Address:	125 Shoreway Road
	Suite 2000
	San Carlos, CA 94070
Telephone:	415/508-6000
Fax:	415/508-6900
E-mail:	rachel.silber@cellnet.com
Web site:	n/a
Industry:	Communications
Sector:	Wireless Communications
CEO:	Mick Seidl
CFO:	Paul Manca

Product Description

CellNet Data Systems provides wireless network services that link remotely located devices, such as electric-, water-, and gas meters, for data gathering and system control activities. The network can deliver up-to-the-minute usage data and other advanced services on a meter-by-meter basis.

Market Strategy/Positioning

CellNet has a strategic relationship with Kansas City Power & Light in a joint venture to provide 400,000 urban customers with service options, such as time-of-use pricing. Significant customers include Georgia Power, Northern States Power, and Pacific Gas & Electric. The company's competitive advantage is its technology, which allows for additional commercial applications, such as incorporating vending machines, office machines, traffic lights, and security systems. CellNet primarily competes against Itron. Additional challenges and risks include signing up enough utility customers, competing technologies, and uncertainty in the wireless marketplace. CellNet is unique in using an intelligent network to integrate several technologies for collecting, processing, and managing data.

234

Other

Cellnet Data Systems was founded in 1984 as Domestic Automation Corporation (DAC), which developed and manufactured a line of intelligent metering products for utilities and was discontinued in 1991. Founders Larsh Johnson and Cree Edwards formerly served at Digital Optics and General Electric Information Services. CEO Mick Seidl was chairman and CEO of Kaiser Aluminum from 1989 to 1993. Before Kaiser, he served as president of Kaiser's parent company, MAXXAM.

Primary VCs/Outside Financing

AT&T Ventures, Acorn, Hambrecht & Quist, Kleiner Perkins Caufield & Buyers, Technology Partners, and El Dorado Ventures.

KEY FACTS

Year Established:	1984
Employees:	280
Fiscal Year End:	January
Revenues FY '94:	n/a
Revenues FY '95:	n/a
Date of Next Financing:	n/a
Date of Last Financing:	February 1995
Size of Last Financing:	$6.2m
Total Capital Raised:	$85.0m
Post Round Valuation:	$125.0m
Expected IPO Date:	n/a

CENTIGRAM
COMMUNICATIONS

Address:	91 East Tasman Drive
	San Jose, CA 95134
Telephone:	408/944-0250
Fax:	408/428-3732
E-mail:	dan.spalding@centigram.com
Web site:	n/a
Industry:	Communications
Sector:	Information Highway Services
CEO:	George H. Sollman
CFO:	Anthony R. Muller
Stock Exchange:	NASDAQ
Stock Symbol:	CGRM

Product Description

Centigram Communications offers integration of voice, data, and facsimile on its adaptive information processing platform, accessible through a telephone or PC. The company is working on a unified messaging system. Centigram is one of the top five vendors in the $2.5 billion voice-processing market. The company uses its technical assistance center to provide technical software and hardware support 24 hours a day.

Market Strategy/Positioning

The company's mission is to provide products enabling information access and delivery using voice, data, and images through available terminals. Centigram has strategic relationships with Texas Instruments, Fujitsu, Text-to-Speech, and Motorola. Significant customers include Fujitsu, BellSouth, NYNEX, VoiceTel, NEC, Miltel, and Wiltel. The company's competitive advantage is its architecture, which is based on industry standard hardware and allows for cost-effective upgrades, flexibility, and technology developments by third parties. Centigram primarily competes against Octel, Boston Technologies, AVT, Activoice, Northern Telecom, and Comverse. Additional challenges and risks include assuring the timely release of innovative products.

235

Other

Centigram Communications was founded in 1977 and acquired Speechplus in 1990 to add interactive voice response and text-to-speech capabilities. President and CEO George Sollman was most recently with the Sand Hill Venture Group. Mr. Sollman has additionally worked as vice president and general manager of Shugart, as vice president of strategic planning for Xerox Memory Systems, and in various positions with Control Data, Honeywell, and MITRE. Senior vice president of operations and CFO Tony Muller formerly served as vice president of finance and CFO of the Silicon Valley Group.

KEY FACTS

Year Established:	1977
Employees:	320
Fiscal Year End:	September
Revenues FY '94:	$79.2m
Revenues FY '95:	n/a
EPS '94:	$1.19
EPS '95:	$0.04 (estimate)
Shares Outstanding:	6.5m
Five-Year Growth Rate:	21%

CHECKPOINT
SOFTWARE

Address:	U.S. Headquarters
	400 Seaport Court
	Suite 105
	Redwood City, CA 94063
Telephone:	415/562-0400
Fax:	415/562-0410
E-mail:	info@checkpoint.com
Web site:	http://www.checkpoint.com
Industry:	Computers
Sector:	Enterprise & Client/Server Software
CEO:	Gil Shwed
CEO (U.S.):	Deborah Triant

Product Description

Checkpoint Software develops and markets the leading Internet firewall product, which protects organizations against unauthorized access to their information. The software product secures all protocols, services, and applications on the Internet. The software-only solution is user-installable and has an easy-to-use graphical user interface that helps administrators develop and understand enterprise-wide security policy. The company is the leading firewall vendor, with an installed base of over 2,000 units.

Market Strategy/Positioning

The company's mission is to be the leading provider of integrated Internet security solutions, providing corporations with the highest level of network security while allowing users transparent access to the vast resources of the Internet. CheckPoint has strategic relationships with Sun Microsystems and CompuServe. Significant customers include DHL Airways, Hale & Dorr, Sun Microsystems, Time Warner, and Times Mirror. The company's competitive advantage is its patent-pending technology, which protects all protocols, applications, and services—both current and future (through a unique architectural design)—transparently and automatically. Other advantages are its position for growth on the Internet and its software, which provides management enterprise-wide security. CheckPoint primarily competes against Raptor Systems, RSA Data Security, and Trusted Information Systems.

236

Other

Checkpoint Software was founded in Israel in 1993, its first product was shipped in May 1994. Founders Gil Shwed, Marius Nacht, and Shlomo Kramer trained in the Israeli Defense Forces and later consulted for companies on security. CEO and president of U.S. operations Deborah Triant was previously vice president of marketing at Adobe, responsible for Adobe Acrobat. Before Adobe, Ms. Triant was CEO of Sitka Corporation.

Primary VCs/Outside Funding

100% internally funded.

KEY FACTS

Year Established:	1993
Employees:	30
Fiscal Year End:	December
Revenues FY '94:	$0.0
Revenues FY '95:	n/a
Date of Next Financing:	n/a
Date of Last Financing:	n/a
Size of Last Financing:	n/a
Total Capital Raised:	n/a
Post Round Valuation:	n/a
Expected IPO Date:	n/a

CIDCO

Product Description

Cidco designs, develops, and markets subscriber telephone equipment that supports the intelligent network services introduced by telephone operating companies. The company's first focus area has been Caller ID. Caller ID products connect directly to subscribers' telephone lines, receive complex network signaling, and display caller information on a liquid-crystal display. In addition, the company has developed several new products for existing and future telephone services, including a line of intelligent feature telephones. Cidco sells its products to subscribers though alliances with national and regional retailers, regional Bell operating companies, and telephone operating companies.

Address:	220 Cochrane Circle
	Morgan Hill, CA 95037
Telephone:	408/779-1162
Fax:	408/779-3106
E-mail:	n/a
Web site:	n/a
Industry:	Entertainment & Information
Sector:	Consumer Electronics
CEO:	Paul G. Locklin
CFO:	Scott C. McDonald
Stock Exchange:	NASDAQ
Stock Symbol:	CDCO

Market Strategy/Positioning

The company's mission is to be the leading provider of subscriber telephone equipment designed for use with intelligent network services. Cidco has strategic relationships with regional Bell operating companies (direct fulfillment), domestic and foreign telephone operating companies, and OEMs. Significant customers include Ameritech, AT&T, Bell Atlantic, GTE, Southern New England Telecommunications, Southwestern Bell, Sprint, U S WEST, Wal-Mart, and British Telecom. The company's competitive advantage is its control of the market—Cidco and Colonial Data Technologies together are said to have 80–90% of the market, making entry difficult for other competitors. Cidco primarily competes against Colonial Data Technologies, BellSouth Products, Southwestern Bell Freedom Phone, AT&T, Northern Telecom, Panasonic, and Sony. Additional challenges and risks include gaining adequate knowledge of requirements of the various telephone operating companies, product reliability, product design, and customer service, and support.

Other

Cidco was founded in 1988 and completed its IPO in March 1994. Since introducing its first Caller ID unit in 1989, Cidco has become a leading provider, selling more than five million units. Chairman and co-founder Robert Diamond was president of Robert Diamond Inc., an engineering consulting and manufacturers' representative firm. Paul Locklin served as president and CEO of PCI and was previously with the color and chemical division of Hercules.

KEY FACTS

Year Established:	1988
Employees:	575
Fiscal Year End:	December
Revenues FY '94:	$100.3m
Revenues FY '95:	n/a
EPS '94:	$0.88
EPS '95:	$1.46 (estimate)
Shares Outstanding:	15.0m
Five-Year Growth Rate:	37%

CIRRUS LOGIC

Address:	3100 West Warren Avenue
	Fremont, CA 94538
Telephone:	510/623-8300
Fax:	510/252-6020
E-mail:	n/a
Web site:	http://www.corp.cirrus.com
Industry:	Computers
Sector:	Semiconductors
CEO:	Michael Hackworth
CFO:	Sam Srinivasan
Stock Exchange:	NASDAQ
Stock Symbol:	CRUS

Product Description

Cirrus Logic manufactures advanced integrated circuits (ICs) for the desktop and portable computing, telecommunications, and consumer electronics markets. It provides ICs for applications such as graphics, modem and wireless communications, mass storage, audio, video, and data acquisition. Applications include multimedia graphics, video, mass storage, fax/modem, and wireless datacom. It is currently the market leader in the graphics controller/accelerator market. Cirrus is rapidly gaining share in the digital audio market and has established an early presence in the digital video market.

Market Strategy/Positioning

Cirrus has a strategic relationship with IBM in a joint manufacturing venture called MiCRUS. Significant customers include Apple, Compaq, DEC, Hewlett-Packard, AT&T Wireless, Motorola, PictureTel, Seagate, Sony, Sun Microsystems, and Toshiba. The company's competitive advantages are its breadth of product offering and a technology portfolio that allows early entry into emerging markets. Cirrus primarily competes against S3, Chips & Technologies, Adaptec, and Rockwell. An additional risk is its heavy reliance on third-party suppliers for wafer manufacturing. Cirrus is unique in being the largest semiconductor company without manufacturing facilities (fabless) and the fastest-growing semiconductor company not doing CPUs or memories.

238

Other

Cirrus Logic completed its IPO in 1989, with a secondary offering in 1994. It has made numerous acquisitions, including Pixel Semiconductor, for full-motion video; Crystal Semiconductor, for mixed-signal ICs; Acumos, for graphics controllers; and Pacific Communication Sciences, for digital wireless communications. Michael Hackworth is a founder of the company and has been president, CEO, and director since 1985. Chairman Suhas Patil, also a founder of the company, has been chairman since its inception and was vice president of research and development until March 1990. He then became executive vice president of products and technology.

KEY FACTS

Year Established:	1984
Employees:	2,500
Fiscal Year End:	March
Revenues FY '94:	$544.1m
Revenues FY '95:	$880.0m
EPS '94:	$0.67
EPS '95:	$0.97
Shares Outstanding:	60.6m
Five-Year Growth Rate:	24%

CISCO SYSTEMS

Address:	170 West Tasman Drive San Jose, CA 95134-1706
Telephone:	408/526-4000
Fax:	408/526-4100
E-mail:	info@cisco.com
Web site:	http://www.cisco.com
Industry:	Communications
Sector:	Computer Networking
CEO:	John Chambers
CFO:	Larry Carter
Stock Exchange:	NASDAQ
Stock Symbol:	CSCO

Product Description

Cisco's products include routers, bridges, workgroup systems, ATM switches, dial-up access servers, software routers, and network management software. Cisco has a strong focus on remote access and currently owns over 50% of that market's routers.

Market Strategy/Positioning

The company's mission is to be the leading global supplier of internetworking products that link computer networks together, and allow them to communicate. Cisco has strategic relationships with AT&T/NCR, Ericsson, IBM, and UNISYS (marketing partnerships), and technical alliances with Northern Telecom, Novell, Cabletron, NEC, and Compaq. Significant customers include Chevron, Motorola, Hong Kong and Shanghai Bank, and Nike. The company's competitive advantage is its list of key acquisitions, giving it one of the most comprehensive product lines in the industry and helping it leverage a commanding market share and provide one-stop shopping for networking solutions. Cisco primarily competes against Bay Networks, 3Com, FORE Systems, and Alantec. Additional challenges and risks include increasing company diversification and striving to supply solutions to all aspects of internetworking.

239

Other

Cisco was founded in December 1984 by a group of Stanford computer scientists. In 1986 Leonard Bosack and Sandra Lerner left Stanford to run the company out of their nearby home; within the same year, they had moved to an office in Menlo Park. Revenues reached $27 million by 1989 before going public in 1990. Chairman John Morgridge served as CEO from 1988 through January 1995. Before joining Cisco, Mr. Morgridge was president and COO of GRID Systems. He also spent 20 years at Honeywell, where his last position was as vice president of marketing and planning. CEO John Chambers had been executive vice president at Cisco since 1991. Before joining Cisco he was senior vice president of operations at Wang Labs.

KEY FACTS

Year Established:	1984
Employees:	3,500
Fiscal Year End:	July
Revenues FY '94:	$1.24b
Revenues FY '95:	$1.92b
EPS '94:	$1.19
EPS '95:	$1.70
Shares Outstanding:	278.9m
Five-Year Growth Rate:	32%

CKS GROUP

Address:	10443 Bandley Drive
	Cupertino, CA 95014
Telephone:	408/366-5100
Fax:	408/366-5120
E-mail:	mark@cks.com
Web site:	http://www.cks.com
Industry:	Entertainment & Information
Sector:	Information Services
CEO:	Mark Kvamme
CFO:	Carlton Baab

Product Description

The CKS Group is the parent company of CKS Partners and two new media groups, CKS Interactive, and CKS Pictures. CKS specializes in marketing communications programs and products. Recent assignments have included redesigning identities for United Airlines and Norwegian Cruise Lines and developing an ad campaign for Time Warner Interactive. The two new media groups are housed in a 22,000-square-foot state-of-the-art multimedia and broadcast production facility. CKS also produces programming, from infomercials and corporate videos to home shopping shows and interactive TV prototypes.

Market Strategy/Positioning

The company's mission is to deliver integrated marketing communications programs for its clients through the use of advanced technology and superior account service. Significant customers include Apple, National Semiconductor, McDonald's, MCI, United Airlines, Sears, NBC, and Sony. The company's competitive advantages are its creative marketing programs and products, which have been successful through the use of cutting edge technology. CKS primarily competes against Landor Associates, FCB Technology, Goodby Silverstein Cole & Weber, and Modem Media. Additional challenges and risks include its evolution from a service company to a company that provides both products and services to its clients.

240

Other

CKS Partners was formed in 1987 by former Apple executives with the premise that the diverse marketing needs of clients must be met with a full range of marketing disciplines. Mark Kvamme joined the company in 1989 and has been chairman, president, and CEO since 1991. Before CKS, Mr. Kvamme worked at Wyse Technology. Before Wyse, he was president and CEO of International Solutions, a distributor of hardware and software. Mr. Kvamme also worked at Apple from 1980 to 1984. CFO Carlton Baab has held his position since 1994 and previously co-founded and served as president and CEO of Mobilesoft.

KEY FACTS

Year Established:	1987
Employees:	185
Fiscal Year End:	November
Revenues FY '94:	$23.0m
Revenues FY '95:	$35.0m
Date of Next Financing:	n/a
Date of Last Financing:	n/a
Size of Last Financing:	n/a
Total Capital Raised:	n/a
Post Round Valuation:	n/a
Expected IPO Date:	1996

CLARIFY

Address:	2702 Orchard Parkway San Jose, CA 95134
Telephone:	408/428-2000
Fax:	408/428-0633
E-mail:	n/a
Web site:	http://www.clarify.com
Industry:	Entertainment & Information
Sector:	Online Services
CEO:	David A. Stamm
CFO:	Ray M. Fritz

Product Description

Clarify develops and markets customer service and help-desk management software designed to assist companies in increasing revenues, quality, and employee productivity. The company's products offer customizable solutions. Its software runs on PC, Macintosh, and workstation platforms with Windows, Macintosh, and Motif graphical user interfaces. The software is designed to integrate with other sales, manufacturing, and finance systems. A Clarify system can track calls, verify contracts, manage configurations, track defects, resolve problems, and generate reports.

Market Strategy/Positioning

The company's mission is to pioneer tomorrow's "virtual knowledge network" (an online, interactive world where product knowledge lets consumers use problem-solving technology to diagnose problems themselves and get answers more quickly) by creating innovative solutions that leverage the Internet and the World Wide Web. Clarify has strategic relationships with Oracle, Sybase, Microsoft, Sun Microsystems, Apple, Novell, Hewlett-Packard, NetManage, Siebel Systems, Lotus, AT&T, Aspect Telecom, and Axiom. Significant customers include Amdahl, Bay Networks, Cisco Systems, 3Com, Intel, Montgomery Securities, Motorola, Silicon Graphics, Tandem Computer, 3DO, Quantum, GE Medical Systems, Solar Turbines, and UB Networks. The company's competitive advantage is its focus on leading-edge service. Clarify is a top supplier to *Fortune* 500 companies. Clarify primarily competes against Scopus Technology, Aurum Software, and the Vantive Corporation. Additional challenges and risks include maintaining a lead in a growing and competitive market, and a lack of common interface standards—a critical requirement for the "virtual knowledge network." Clarify is unique in the diversity of technology investments.

Other

Clarify was founded by Dave Stamm, Don Smith, and Kevin Rose and is backed by a blue-chip list of inventors. Clarify shipped its first product in September of 1992; since then, the company has grown steadily, increasing its sales two- to three-fold during the past two years. Headquartered in San Jose, CA, Clarify has sales and support offices in eight major cities in the U.S. as well as operations in Europe and Japan. Founder, president, and CEO David Stamm was previously the founder and CEO

KEY FACTS

Year Established:	1990
Employees:	120
Fiscal Year End:	December
Revenues FY '94:	n/a
Revenues FY '95:	n/a
Date of Next Financing:	n/a
Date of Last Financing:	March 1994
Size of Last Financing:	$3.1m
Total Capital Raised:	$12.0m
Post Round Valuation:	n/a
Expected IPO Date:	n/a

CLARIFY

of Daisy Systems. Chairman James Patterson served as founder and CEO of Quantum. CFO Ray Fritz is a former director of finance at Synopsys.

Primary VCs/Outside Financing

Institutional Venture Partners, Matrix Partners, Menlo Ventures, New Enterprise Associates, Sigma Partners, Hooked, and Onset Computer.

CLICK 3X

Address:	16 West 22nd Street
	New York, NY 10010
Telephone:	212/627-1900
Fax:	212/627-4472
E-mail:	click3x@aol.com
Web site:	http://www.click3x.com
Industry:	Entertainment & Information
Sector:	Film & Entertainment Production
CEO:	Phil Price
CFO:	Margaret Corbett

Product Description

Click 3X is an open-architecture, software-driven video post-production studio. It specializes in the use of Discreet Logic visual effects software for digital integration of 2D and 3D graphics and video. The company has contributed to ads for the U.S. Air Force, Fruitopia, Little Caesars, and McDonald's and is pursuing opportunities to work on feature films. The company's interactive group focuses on CD-ROM development, online network design, and interactive TV. Click 3X is wholly-owned by Full Blue, and has a subsidiary, Click 3West, in San Francisco.

Market Strategy/Positioning

The company's mission is to be a leader in special effects for television and film work. Click 3x has strategic relationships with Discreet Logic, Media Circus, and BBN Planet. Significant customers include Tri-Star Columbia Pictures and all major advertising agencies, including Chiat Day, Ogilvy & Mather, Leo Burnett, and Saatchi & Saatchi. The company's competitive advantage is its open architecture, which can produce resolution independent images. Click 3X primarily competes against Pacific Data Images, Digital Domain, and R/GA Digital Studios. Additional challenges and risks include managing the vast technological changes and advancements in the industry, and coordinating the company's expansion to take advantage of those improvements. The company wants to be aggressive in new markets and gain the market share. Click 3X uses a unique combination of hardware and software to maximize efficiency. Breaking with many of the traditions of television effects work, Click 3X promotes software-driven solutions.

243

Other

Click 3X started its operations in September of 1993, with key personnel from the computer animation, design, and production/post-production areas. It was the first company on the east coast to fully utilize the "open architecture" path, using SGI Onyx supercomputers and software for high-end animation effects. President and creative director Phil Price has over 12 years of experience in high-end special effects work. Vice president of sales and executive producer John Lovelace has worked in the animation market for 10 years.

Primary VCs/Outside Financing

100% owned by Full Blue.

KEY FACTS

Year Established:	1993
Employees:	15
Fiscal Year End:	March
Revenues FY '94:	$5.2m
Revenues FY '95:	$8.0m
Date of Next Financing:	n/a
Date of Last Financing:	n/a
Size of Last Financing:	n/a
Total Capital Raised:	n/a
Post Round Valuation:	n/a
Expected IPO Date:	n/a

(COLOSSAL) PICTURES

Address:	2800 Third Street San Francisco, CA 94107
Telephone:	415/550-8772
Fax:	415/824-0389
E-mail:	marie_shell@colossal.com
Web site:	n/a
Industry:	Entertainment & Information
Sector:	Film & Entertainment Production
CEO:	Drew Takahashi
CFO:	Terry Thurlow

Product Description

(Colossal) Pictures designs and produces animated and live action effects, television commercials, broadcast graphics, special effects, music videos, interactive advertising, pilot programming for interactive TV, online interactive TV navigational systems, CD-ROM titles, and Web sites. It has 70,000 square feet of production facilities, including studios, soundstages, animation studios, and a model shop.

Market Strategy/Positioning

(Colossal) Pictures has strategic relationships with Brøderbund, Electronic Arts, and Spectrum Holobyte. Significant customers include Coca-Cola, Burger King, Pepsi, McDonald's, Hershey's, Nike, Miller Brewing, Levi Strauss, Pillsbury, Honda, Walt Disney, MTV, and Silicon Graphics. The company's competitive advantages are its very low employee turnover, and a group of animators who are multitalented and focus on a breadth of projects and techniques. The company has leveraged those creative abilities in many newly-diversified ways such as applying them to games platforms. (Colossal) Pictures primarily competes against Industrial Light & Magic, Digital Domain, Pacific Data Images, and R/GA Digital Studios. Additional challenges and risks include the current task of taking control of the content it produces by moving into other forms of production. It is pursuing alliances for access to capital, distribution, and technology.

Other

(Colossal) Pictures was started in 1976 out of Drew Takahashi's garage. The founders were formerly at Korty Films and worked with both Mr. Lucas and Mr. Coppola. Co-founders Drew Takahashi and Gary Gutierrez are both filmmakers and received degrees from both UCLA film school and the San Francisco Art Institute. Both co-founders currently direct as well as manage.

Primary VCs/Outside Financing

100% internally owned.

KEY FACTS

Year Established:	1976
Employees:	150
Fiscal Year End:	October
Revenues FY '94:	$25.0m
Revenues FY '95:	n/a
Date of Next Financing:	n/a
Date of Last Financing:	n/a
Size of Last Financing:	$0.0
Total Capital Raised:	$0.0
Post Round Valuation:	n/a
Expected IPO Date:	n/a

COM21

Product Description

Com21 focuses on the digital transmission of telephone and multimedia over existing cable, fiber-optic, and copper wire networks. It is currently developing a high-speed, transparent, digital data-overlay for the cable TV infrastructure that uses ATM. The company aims to offer hardware products which exist at both the central information storage and the users end. Its field trials commenced in late 1995.

Address:	1991 Landings Drive
	Mountain View, CA 94043
Telephone:	415/969-2100
Fax:	415/254-5883
E-mail:	info@com21.com
Web site:	http://www.com21.com
Industry:	Communications
Sector:	Computer Networking
CEO:	Michael Bowles
CFO:	David Robertson

Market Strategy/Positioning

The company's mission is to become the leader in interactive communications on a hybrid fiber-coax network. The company's competitive advantages are its multiple price/performance categories and itsencompassing network topologies. Underlying ATM technology offers scalability and ensures long-term growth. Com21 primarily competes against Hewlett-Packard, Motorola, Intel, and General Instrument, who have all announced but not yet released competitive products. Additional challenges and risks include its ability to focus on and correctly identify growth opportunities in a rapidly changing environment. Com21 wants to offer the quickest and most convenient way to provide low-cost, multimegabit online, and Internet access to 60 million cable subscribers in the U.S.

245

Other

Paul Baran, a pioneer of packet-switching technology, co-founded Com21 in 1992 with Richard Kramlich. The company first received funding June 1994 and raised a second round in September of 1994 from JAFCO. CEO and president Michael Bowles was with Hughes Aircraft for 12 years. Vice president of marketing Buck Gee was previously with Cisco and Crescendo.

Primary VCs/Outside Financing

New Enterprise Associates, Crosspoint Venture Partners, Charter Venture Capital, JAFCO, and Kleiner Perkins Caufield & Byers.

KEY FACTS

Year Established:	1992
Employees:	30
Fiscal Year End:	December
Revenues FY '94:	$0.0
Revenues FY '95:	$8–10m (estimate)
Date of Next Financing:	Q1 1996
Date of Last Financing:	May 1995
Size of Last Financing:	$7.2m
Total Capital Raised:	$11.0m
Post Round Valuation:	$27.0m
Expected IPO Date:	1997

COMBINET

Address:	333 West El Camino Real
	Suite 320
	Sunnyvale, CA 94087
Telephone:	408/522-9020
Fax:	408/732-5479
E-mail:	info@combinet.com
Web site:	http://www.combinet.com
Industry:	Communications
Sector:	Computer Networking
CEO:	Tom Williams
CFO:	Dave Newkirk

Product Description

Combinet aspires to be the standard for allowing ubiquitous, transparent local-area network (LAN) access to remote users. There is a potential market, growing over 15% annually, of 15 million telecommuters and after-hours workers. Combinet develops network management software, ISDN, and Switch 56 bridges. Its products exceed modems in performance and are priced lower than leased-line options. Combinet's products operate with Macintosh and IBM-compatible PCs, workstations, and X-terminals.

Market Strategy/Positioning

The company's mission is to be the dominant provider of digital LAN remote-access solutions for the small office/home office (SOHO) and for individual users. Combinet has strategic relationships with Ameritech, Bell Atlantic, and Pacific Bell in joint marketing agreements. Significant customers include Hewlett-Packard, the IRS, McDonald's, Price Waterhouse, Stanford University, Morgan Stanley, NTT, SGI, and Sun Microsystems. The company's competitive advantages are its recognized leadership (by Dataquest and International Data Corp.), approval in 14 countries for its product to connect directly to telephone lines, and being the only vendor to have a full family of solutions for enterprise, remote office, SOHO, and individual users. Combinet primarily competes against Shiva, Gandalf, and Ascend Communications.

Other

Combinet shipped its first products in 1991. It created the first ISDN LAN bridge router, of which 24,000 units have been distributed in 14 countries. Its management team brings experience from Micom, Novell, Netframe, and PenRil Datability. Founder, president, and CEO Tom Williams has 28 years of industry experience and previously worked at Novell as vice president of sales, as vice president of marketing at CXI, and in other positions at California Network Systems. Vice president of engineering Frank Yu has 18 years of industry experience.

Primary VCs/Outside Financing

Sierra Ventures; Menlo Ventures; Draper & Associates; Idanta Partners; Weiss, Peck & Greer; and Ameritech.

246

KEY FACTS

Year Established:	1988
Employees:	85
Fiscal Year End:	August
Revenues FY '94:	n/a
Revenues FY '95:	n/a
Date of Next Financing:	n/a
Date of Last Financing:	February 1995
Size of Last Financing:	$6.0m
Total Capital Raised:	$12.8m
Post Round Valuation:	$45.0m
Expected IPO Date:	1996

COMCAST

Address:	1500 Market Street
	Philadelphia, PA 19102
Telephone:	215/665-1700
Fax:	215/981-7532
E-mail:	n/a
Web site:	n/a
Industry:	Entertainment & Information
Sector:	Broadcasters & Cable Networks
CEO:	Brian L. Roberts
CFO:	John Alchin
Stock Exchange:	NASDAQ
Stock Symbol:	CMCSK

Product Description

Comcast is the fourth largest multiple services operator (MSO) in the U.S. It serves about 3.5 million subscribers and provides cellular service to a population of 7.4 million in 19 states, primarily in the Northeast. The company recently ordered 150,000 General Instrument converters and has also agreed to buy interactive set-top boxes from Hewlett-Packard. The company is near a video-on-demand trial in West Palm Beach. Comcast indicates that QVC is critical to its ambitions to add programming.

Market Strategy/Positioning

The company's mission is to offer customers electronic access to the information they need through wired and wireless technologies. Comcast has strategic relationships with Sprint, TCI, and Cox Communications. Comcast is poised to reach one-half of all U.S. homes and businesses through a local telephone alliance with Sprint. The company has a strong record of innovation in cellular services and marketing. Comcast primarily competes against DirecTv, Bell Atlantic, MCI, and AT&T. Additional challenges and risks include assembling a new "national local telephone company" that will combine wired and wireless technology.

247

Other

Comcast was founded as a cable company about 30 years ago, and it entered the cellular business five years ago. In September 1995 the company announced plans to build a television programming and new media business with the guidance of Richard Frank, who played a key role in the development of Walt Disney's TV business. Ralph Roberts has been chairman since 1969 and served as president from 1969 to 1989. He also serves as president and chairman of Sural Corporation, through which he is the controlling shareholder of Comcast. Brian Roberts, elected president and CEO in 1990, has been on the board of directors since 1987. Also on the board of Turner Broadcasting, QVC, Viewer's Choice, he is chairman of the National Cable Television Association. CFO John Alchin was previously a managing director with the Toronto Dominion Bank.

KEY FACTS

Year Established:	1969
Employees:	5,300
Fiscal Year End:	December
Revenues FY '94:	$1.38b
Revenues FY '95:	n/a
EPS '94:	$(0.32)
EPS '95:	$(0.50) (estimate)
Shares Outstanding:	239.4m
Five-Year Growth Rate:	25%

COMPAQ COMPUTER

Address:	P.O. Box 69200 Houston, TX 77269-2000
Telephone:	713/370-0670
Fax:	713/374-1740
E-mail:	info@compaq.com
Web site:	http://www.compaq.com
Industry:	Computers
Sector:	Desktop Computers/File Servers
CEO:	Eckhard Pfeiffer
CFO:	Daryl White
Stock Exchange:	NYSE
Stock Symbol:	CPQ

Product Description

Compaq is the world's largest PC maker and offers a wide range of personal computing products—including desktop PCs, portable computers, and tower PC systems—that store and manage data in network environments. The company plans to diversify by offering solutions for enterprise computing, data communications, multimedia, and consumer electronics.

Market Strategy/Positioning

The company's mission is to become the leading platform provider in the information technology industry, and to furnish the building blocks for personal and corporate computing. Compaq has strategic relationships with Texas Instruments, Fisher-Price, Oracle, Novell, Microsoft, Picture-Tel, AMD, KidSoft, Cisco Systems, and Books-That-Work. Significant customers include Intelligent Electronics and MicroAge. The company's competitive advantages are having the largest share of the worldwide market, value-based manufacturing, strong channel partnerships, and a global organization. Compaq primarily competes against Dell, IBM, Gateway 2000, AST Research, Packard Bell, Hewlett-Packard, Toshiba, NEC, DEC, and Apple. Additional challenges and risks include facing intense competition and anticipating demand to manufacture cost-effectively and manage component inventories effectively.

Other

Compaq was founded in 1982 by three former Texas Instruments engineers Rod Canion, Jim Harris, and Bill Murto to manufacture and sell portable IBM-compatible computers. They each invested $1,000; their first product originated as a sketch in a Houston pie shop. The company went public in 1983, the same year it came out with a portable computer (18 months before IBM). It shipped more than 53,000 portable PCs in its first year. In 1991 Eckhard Pfeiffer replaced Rod Canion as CEO. Mr. Pfeiffer has overseen a major restructuring of the company and has led its growth into becoming the world's largest PC maker.

248

KEY FACTS

Year Established:	1982
Employees:	14,400
Fiscal Year End:	December
Revenues FY '94:	$10.9b
Revenues FY '95:	$14.6b (estimate)
EPS '94:	$3.23
EPS '95:	$3.77 (estimate)
Shares Outstanding:	267.1m
Five-Year Growth Rate:	17%

COMPRESSION LABS

Address:	2860 Junction Avenue
	San Jose, CA 95134
Telephone:	408/435-3000
Fax:	408/922-5429
E-mail:	info@CLIX.com
Web site:	n/a
Industry:	Computers
Sector:	Personal Productivity Software
CEO:	John Tyson
CFO:	William Berry
Stock Exchange:	NASDAQ
Stock Symbol:	CLIX

Product Description

Compression Labs invented compressed digital video (CDV) technology. It offers two-way full-color videoconferencing that lets the user transmit video, audio, data, and graphics over a single digital channel. The company has installed over 7,000 systems worldwide. Compression Labs also has a broadcast products group, MPEG encoders, and decoders for satellite cable and telephone. The company sells spectrum-saver compressed digital broadcast for satellites and is focusing on remote education and telemedecine.

Market Strategy/Positioning

The company's mission is to make video communications an integral part of everyday life in business and in the home. Compression Labs has strategic relationships with Intel, Philips, AT&T, and MCI. Significant customers include Coca-Cola, Hewlett-Packard, National Semiconductor, Johnson & Johnson, Bell Atlantic, DirecTv, and California State Universities. The company's competitive advantage is having the highest quality video in the videoconferencing market and an easy-to-use product line. Compression Labs primarily competes against PictureTel, VTEL, Scientific-Atlanta, and General Instrument.

Other

Compression Labs was founded in 1976 to develop new technologies for facsimile and video compression. The company later shifted its focus to video compression and formed a partnership with the U.S. Air Force and Cubic Corporation. With the introduction of the first commercially successful video codec, it evolved from a research and development company to a product manufacturer. Chairman, president, and CEO John E. Tyson joined the company in 1980 as vice president of marketing and was appointed president and chairman in 1981. He has held various senior management positions at AT&T, GTE, Honeywell, General Electric, and General Motors. CFO William Berry was previously president of Optical Shields and worked at Raychem Corporation for more than 12 years. The company's chief scientist and co-founder Wen-Hsiung Chen is one of the pioneers in digital image coding. He is also a professor at SJSU and an honorary visiting professor at various universities in China.

KEY FACTS

Year Established:	1976
Employees:	600
Fiscal Year End:	December
Revenues FY '94:	$156.9m
Revenues FY '95:	n/a
EPS '94:	$0.0
EPS '95:	$0.25 (estimate)
Shares Outstanding:	14.7m
Five-Year Growth Rate:	34%

COMPUSERVE
(H&R BLOCK)

Address:	5000 Arlington Centre Boulevard
	P.O. Box 20212
	Columbus, OH 43220
Telephone:	614/457-8600
Fax:	614/457-0348
E-mail:	n/a
Web site:	http://www.compuserve.com
Industry:	Entertainment & Information
Sector:	Online Services
CEO:	Robert Massey
CFO:	Ken Marinak
Stock Exchange:	NYSE
Stock Symbol:	HRB

Product Description

CompuServe provides computer-based information and communications services to businesses and PC owners. The company charges a flat rate for unlimited access to 120 basic information services including news, sports, games, shopping, weather, and stock quotes. CompuServe also includes a shopping service with 130 merchants, support forums with 850 software and hardware companies, and over 50 newspapers online. The CompuServe Internet Division (formerly Spry) supplies Internet access to its customers. It also offers a tax preparation software that was used by more than 40,000 tax preparers in 1994. Compuserve also processes millions of Visa transactions and manages global network communications for more than 750 companies. The company gains more than 100,000 subscribers each month.

Market Strategy/Positioning

The company's mission is to develop problem-solving computer services that provide companies and individuals with reliable, cost-effective access to online services. CompuServe has strategic relationships with Fujitsu, Nissho Iwai, and CNN. Significant customers include 900 corporate customers, and 3.2 million worldwide users. The company's competitive advantages are its worldwide membership and access and being the only service that allows an Internet "browser of choice" access to over 2,000 databases. CompuServe primarily competes against America Online, Prodigy, Delphi, and Microsoft Network. CompuServe is unique in its large quantity of quality information. It is the only worldwide service with connectivity in more than 150 countries. CompuServe is also working to improve targeted services for students and women (Women's Wire).

Other

CompuServe, established as a computer time-sharing service, entered the online information industry in 1979. The CompuServe Network Services Division, formed in 1982, offers local- and wide-area networking services. It rapidly gained recognition as a major provider of telecommunications networking services, high-quality electronic mail systems, and consumer and business information services. CompuServe was bought by H&R Block in 1980. Robert Massey recently replaced Maurice Cox as CEO.

KEY FACTS

Year Established:	1969
Employees:	2,200
Fiscal Year End:	April
Revenues FY '94:	$1.2b
Revenues FY '95:	$1.4b
EPS '94:	$1.54
EPS '95:	$1.02
Shares Outstanding:	104.8m
Five-Year Growth Rate:	14%

COMPUTER
ASSOCIATES

Address:	I Computer Associates Plaza Islandia, NY II788
Telephone:	516/342-5224
Fax:	516/342-4295
E-mail:	n/a
Web site:	http://www.cai.com
Industry:	Computers
Sector:	Enterprise & Client/Server Software
CEO:	Charles B. Wang
CFO:	Peter A. Schwartz
Stock Exchange:	NYSE
Stock Symbol:	CA

Product Description

Computer Associates is the second largest independent software company worldwide, with over 300 products. The company offers integrated systems, database/systems management, business applications, and application development. Its mainframe business provides 80% of revenue, but it has diversified into mid-range and desktop computing. The company's UNIX-based Unicenter (automated data center management) has seen its strongest annual sales growth (131%). Computer Associates began shipping its CA-Clipper 5.3 Xbase application development product in August 1995.

Market Strategy/Positioning

The company's mission is to develop software that markedly improves the performance of computers and the productivity of people. Computer Associates has strategic relationships with Sun Microsystems, Hewlett-Packard, Microsoft, and UB Networks. Significant customers include Equitable Life Assurance Society and virtually all *Fortune* 500 companies. The company's competitive advantage is its installed base of nearly all of *Fortune* 500 companies; as a result, Computer Associates is focused on corporate computing needs. Computer Associates primarily competes against IBM, DEC, Hewlett-Packard, Apple, Data General, Dun & Bradstreet, Informix, Gupta, Microsoft, Oracle, Sybase, Wang, and Sun Microsystems.

251

Other

Computer Associates was founded in 1976 when Charles Wang and Russel Artzt purchased the software division of Security Data Corporation. By 1980 sales had reached $13 million, and the following year the company went public, raising $12 million. In 1981 the company acquired Capex, and in 1994 it acquired ASK Group. Co-founder, chairman, and CEO Charles Wang worked at Standard Data as a programmer before founding Computer Associates. Mr. Wang's salary for 1994 was close to $7 million. Russel Artzt, co-founder and executive vice president of research and development, wrote computer code for some of the company's first products. Before starting the company, Mr. Artzt managed software development at Standard Data.

KEY FACTS

Year Established:	1976
Employees:	6,900
Fiscal Year End:	March
Revenues FY '94:	$2.2b
Revenues FY '95:	$2.6b
EPS '94:	$2.34
EPS '95:	$2.56
Shares Outstanding:	160.1m
Five-Year Growth Rate:	20%

CONNECT

Address:	515 Ellis Street
	Mountain View, CA 94043
Telephone:	415/254-4000
Fax:	415/254-4800
E-mail:	info@connectinc.com
Web site:	http://www.connectinc.com
Industry:	Entertainment & Information
Sector:	Information Services
CEO:	Tom Kehler
CFO:	Hank Morgan

Product Description

CONNECT develops a virtual private network for real-time, one-to-one communications and purchasing transactions between corporate buyers and sellers of information technology products and services. It is both a tool vendor and an outsourcer. The company's information database includes editorial material from various International Data Group (IDG) publications, and provides evaluation information, editorial opinions, and forums for informal opinions.

Market Strategy/Positioning

The company's mission is to be the premier provider of platforms for smart and interactive online applications. CONNECT has strategic relationships with IDG and Electronic Marketplace Systems. Significant customers include Domino's Pizza, ICHIEFS, and Software AG. The company's competitive advantage is that it is the first interactive applications server to allow secure access from both standard World Wide Web browsers and custom software, via the Internet and X.25 networks. CONNECT primarily competes against NETCOM, Netscape, America Online, Prodigy, CompuServe, Advantis, and GE Information Services. Additional challenges and risks include dealing with major players in the software and telecommunications industries—such as Microsoft, IBM, MCI, and AT&T—which will play a large role in shaping the industry in the coming years.

Other

From 1987 to 1992, CONNECT operated and managed private networks for its customers. In late 1992 it began offering its customers the choice of licensing server software for use on a computer-operated network. CEO Tom Kehler was formerly chairman and CEO of IntelliCorp. Founder Michael Muller served as vice president and general manager at Apple from 1981 to 1985.

Primary VCs/Outside Financing

Quaestes Partners and Volpe Welty.

KEY FACTS

Year Established:	1987
Employees:	90
Fiscal Year End:	December
Revenues FY '94:	$10.0m
Revenues FY '95:	n/a
Date of Next Financing:	n/a
Date of Last Financing:	June 1994
Size of Last Financing:	$2.2m
Total Capital Raised:	$6.0m
Post Round Valuation:	n/a
Expected IPO Date:	1997

252

CONNER PERIPHERALS

Address:	3081 Zanker Road
	San Jose, CA 95134
Telephone:	408/456-4500
Fax:	408/456-4501
E-mail:	n/a
Web site:	http://www.conner.com
Industry:	Computers
Sector:	Storage
CEO:	Finis F. Conner
CFO:	P. Jackson Bell
Stock Exchange:	NYSE
Stock Symbol:	CNR

Product Description

In June 1992 Conner Peripherals transformed itself from a manufacturer of Winchester disk drives for PCs and workstations into a producer of total storage solutions. Based on unit volume, the company is the largest supplier of hard disk drives. Conner also offers a comprehensive line of tape drives, storage management software, and storage systems products. Conner has the largest OEM customer base in the industry.

Market Strategy/Positioning

The company's mission is to become a supplier of total storage solutions. Conner has strategic relationships with Matsushita and Quest Development. In 1994 Conner and Quest formed Arcada Software, which develops data protection and storage management software, and markets its products worldwide. Significant customers include Compaq, IBM, DEC, Toshiba, Packard Bell, Apple, Intel, Olivetti, Silicon Graphics, Sony, EDS, Ford, Fujitsu, General Electric, NASA, and Pepsi-Cola. Conner primarily competes against Cambex, DEC, Fujitsu, Hewlett-Packard, Hitachi, IBM, NEC, Komag, Quantum, Storage Technology, Toshiba, and Colorado Memory Systems. Additional challenges and risks include product delays or defects which can lead to significant market-share losses. The company is unique in reversing the usual process of designing, building, and selling products by working with customers first, to define their specific needs.

253

Other

Conner has shown steady growth since it began shipping products in 1987. In 1989, after sales topped $700 million, it became the fastest-growing manufacturing startup in U.S. business history. It also acquired Archive to bolster its position in the tape drive market. In September 1995 Seagate Technology announced its intention to acquire Conner for $1.1 million, which would create the world's largest disk-drive company. Co-founder, chairman, and CEO Finis Conner is also the co-founder of Seagate Technologies and Shugart Associates. President and COO David Mitchell previously served as president and COO of Seagate. Before joining Conner, CFO Jackson Bell held executive positions at American Airlines, Burlington Northern, and USAir.

KEY FACTS

Year Established:	1985
Employees:	9,100
Fiscal Year End:	December
Revenues FY '94:	$2.4b
Revenues FY '95:	n/a
EPS '94:	$2.10
EPS '95:	$0.98
Shares Outstanding:	52.7m
Five-Year Growth Rate:	13%

COX ENTERPRISES

Address:	1400 Lake Hearn Drive
	Atlanta, GA 30319
Telephone:	404/843-5000
Fax:	404/843-5142
E-mail:	n/a
Web site:	n/a
Industry:	Entertainment & Information
Sector:	Broadcasters & Cable Networks
CEO:	James Cox Kennedy
CFO:	John R. Dillon

Product Description

Cox Enterprises is one of the country's largest cable, newspaper, and broadcasting conglomerates. The company's subsidiaries include Cox Newspapers, publicly-held Cox Communications, Cox Broadcasting, and Manheim Auctions. Cox Communications has been conducting interactive TV tests in Omaha, NE, with IBM, Zenith, New Century Communications, and Starsight Telecast. It was the first cable system to test delivery of Prodigy. Cox is expanding its presence on the information superhighway by investing in fiber-optics and wireless communications. Cox Newspapers has created *The Interactive Studio* to bring news to customers via the Internet.

Market Strategy/Positioning

Cox has strategic relationships with Comcast, Sprint, Continental Cablevision, Times Mirror, Starsight Telecast, IBM, TCI, and New Century Network, a service set up with eight other leading newspaper publishers. The company's competitive advantage is its incorporation of new technologies in its business strategy. Cox primarily competes against Comcast, Dow Jones, Dun & Bradstreet, Hearst, Knight-Ridder, *The New York Times*, News Corp., TCI, Time Warner, Tribune, Turner Broadcasting, Viacom, Washington Post, and U S WEST. Cox Enterprises is unique as the first cable company to offer "free" cable services: in August 1995 customers in Omaha NE, were charged only the $19.95 installation fee, with no monthly fee to access local channels, public access, C-SPAN I and II, the Learning Channel, and a local sports channel.

Other

James Cox started his empire in 1898 with the purchase of the *Dayton Daily News*. The company grew through acquisitions of major newspapers, radio stations, TV stations, and Mr. Cox's successful political career. Cox was the first broadcasting company to enter the cable business. In 1995 Cox acquired Times Mirror for $2.3 billion, folding its own cable company and Times Mirror into a new company, Cox Communications. James Cox Kennedy became CEO in 1987.

Primary VCs/Outside Financing

100% internally owned.

KEY FACTS

Year Established:	1898
Employees:	31,000
Fiscal Year End:	December
Revenues FY '94:	n/a
Revenues FY '95:	n/a
Date of Next Financing:	n/a
Date of Last Financing:	n/a
Size of Last Financing:	n/a
Total Capital Raised:	n/a
Post Round Valuation:	n/a
Expected IPO Date:	n/a

254

CREATIVE TECHNOLOGY

Address:	U.S. Headquarters (Creative Labs) 1901 McCarthy Boulevard Milpitas, CA 95035
Telephone:	408/428-6600
Fax:	408/426-2394
E-mail:	n/a
Web site:	http://www. creaf.com
Industry:	Computers
Sector:	Peripherals
CEO:	W.H. Sim
CFO:	Patrick Verderico
Stock Exchange:	NASDAQ
Stock Symbol:	CREAF

Product Description

Creative Technology is a Singapore-based company that develops sound and video multimedia products for PCs and operates in the U.S. as its wholly-owned subsidiary, Creative Labs. The company sells sound boards, software drives, CD-ROM drives, and bundled applications. Its video product, Sound Blaster, lets PCs digitize, capture, and display live video or TV broadcasts in a resizable window, while multitasking. The company holds 65% of the video board market and also offers a video-conferencing product that runs over regular phone lines.

Market Strategy/Positioning

The company's mission is to be the world's leading provider of multimedia subsystems and peripherals for the PC marketplace. Creative Technology has strategic relationships with Microsoft, Intel, DEC, 3DO, Borland, Dell Computer, Gateway 2000, AST Research, IBM, Voice Processing, and is pursuing agreements with LookingGlass Technologies and Electronic Arts. The company's competitive advantages are its introduction of next-generation blaster technologies and its partnerships with leading software developers. Creative Technology primarily competes against Diamond Multimedia, U.S. Robotics, and Boca Research. Additional challenges and risks include managing the high growth of the company.

Other

Creative Technology was founded in 1981 by W.H. Sim with $10,000 startup capital. Mr. Sim was soon joined by co-founders K.W. Ng and K.S. Chay, and in 1988 the three decided to move to Silicon Valley, where Mr. Sim founded Creative Labs. The company has expanded through acquisitions, including modem company Digicom and E-mu Systems. It also has a considerable investment in 3Dlabs. Chairman and CEO Sim Wong Hoo has over 15 years of industry experience and was named Singapore's Businessman of the Year in 1992. CFO Patrick Verderico was previously CFO and vice president of finance at Cypress Semiconductor. He has also held management positions at Philips Semiconductor and National Semiconductor.

KEY FACTS

Year Established:	1983
Employees:	4,000
Fiscal Year End:	June
Revenues FY '94:	$658.0m
Revenues FY '95:	$1.2b
EPS '94:	$1.10
EPS '95:	$0.30
Shares Outstanding:	87.5m
Five-Year Growth Rate:	20%

CYAN

Product Description

Cyan develops software which creates non-linear, interactive, photo-realistic environments. Its products are designed to entertain and educate while immersing users in a computer-generated world. The company's CD-ROM *Myst* was a runaway success; it is currently developing a sequel.

Address:	10200 North Newport Highway Spokane, WA 99218
Telephone:	509/468-0807
Fax:	509/467-2209
E-mail:	cyanrobyn@aol.com
Web site:	n/a
Industry:	Entertainment & Information
Sector:	Entertainment/Education Software
CEO:	Robyn Miller
CFO:	Chris Brandkamp

Market Strategy/Positioning

The company's mission is to make games "we've always wanted to play ourselves." Cyan has strategic relationships with Brøderbund, Creative Artists Agency, Beanstock Group, Hyperion, and Sunsoft. Significant customers include Merisel, Wal-Mart, and other major software retailers and distributors. The company's competitive advantages are its installed customer base and its patience for making products highly realistic. Cyan primarily competes against Presto Studios and Trilobyte. Additional challenges and risks include the possible delay in producing titles because of the focus on realism, and the need to create challenging games that avoid "dead-end puzzles."

Other

Cyan has produced a number of hit titles. It began with *Manhole, Cosmic Osmo,* and *Spelunx.* Cyan's growth mirrors the development of its products. President Rand Miller formerly worked at Citizen's National Bank and CEO Robyn Miller was a graphic artist. CFO Chris Brandkamp has served with Lockheed Hughes and ISC.

Primary VCs/Outside Financing

Sunsoft.

KEY FACTS

Year Established:	1987
Employees:	18
Fiscal Year End:	December
Revenues FY '94:	n/a
Revenues FY '95:	n/a
Date of Next Financing:	n/a
Date of Last Financing:	n/a
Size of Last Financing:	n/a
Total Capital Raised:	n/a
Post Round Valuation:	n/a
Expected IPO Date:	n/a

CYBERCASH

Address:	2100 Reston Parkway Suite 430 Reston, VA 22091
Telephone:	703/620-4200
Fax:	703/620-4215
E-mail:	info@cybercash.com
Web site:	http://www.cybercash.com
Industry:	Entertainment & Information
Sector:	Online Services
CEO:	William Melton

Product Description

CyberCash develops payment system plans for Internet commerce. Merchants are connected to customers via the Internet and to banks by private networks. Its services work with credit and debit cards, or an electronic cash mechanism. Consumers do not need to have any prior relationship with CyberCash or a merchant to make purchases using the CyberCash Internet payment service. CyberCash lets users trace transactions.

Market Strategy/Positioning

The company's mission is to enable electronic commerce by providing a safe, convenient, and immediate payment system on the Internet. CyberCash has strategic relationships with RSA Data Security, Wells Fargo, CheckFree, Sun Microsystems, NETCOM, Frontier Technologies, Open Market, Quarterdeck, Network Computing Devices, and Trusted Information Systems. Significant customers include Wells Fargo, American Express, First National Bank of Omaha, and Virtual Vineyards. The company's competitive advantages are an independent browser and server, no additional fees for security, multiple payment instruments, and its alliances with major banks. CyberCash primarily competes against Digicash and First Virtual Corp. Additional challenges and risks include finding ways to help consumers become familiar and more comfortable with the Internet.

Other

The company was founded in 1994 to facilitate the purchase of goods and services on the Internet by providing a secure environment for transactions among consumers, merchants, and their banks, as well as between individuals. Last year Veri-Fone invested $4 million for a 10% stake in the company. Co-founder and CEO Bill Melton previously founded Real-Share, VeriFone, and Transaction Network Systems and continues to serve on the boards of both VeriFone and TNS. Co-founder and chairman Dan Lynch previously founded Interop. COO Bruce Wilson is also a founder of CyberCash and previously worked at NYNEX.

Primary VCs/Outside Financing

Internally funded and VeriFone (10% ownership).

KEY FACTS

Year Established:	1994
Employees:	25
Fiscal Year End:	December
Revenues FY '94:	$0.0
Revenues FY '95:	$0.0
Date of Next Financing:	n/a
Date of Last Financing:	September 1995
Size of Last Financing:	$12.0m
Total Capital Raised:	$17.0m
Post Round Valuation:	$40.0m
Expected IPO Date:	1996

CYBERSOURCE

Address:	1050 Chestnut Sreet Suite 200 Menlo Park, CA 94025
Telephone:	415/462-5522, 800/617-SOFT
Fax:	415/473-3066
E-mail:	pubinfo@software.net
Web site:	http://www.software.net
Industry:	Entertainment & Information
Sector:	Online Services
CEO:	William McKiernan

Product Description

CyberSource offers customers the ability to browse, purchase, and retrieve software electronically. The company has a direct-sales force that focuses on sale of products to large businesses and public sector accounts. Its Internet-based software superstore (software.net) gives customers access to over 8,200 products available for Windows, Macintosh, OS/2, and UNIX. Each product is licensed according to publisher's terms and reported monthly. Additionally, CyberSource provides asset management services to its customers.

Market Strategy/Positioning

The company's mission is to revolutionize and lead the market in electronic distribution of software, information, and other digital content. CyberSource has strategic relationships with Symantec, Farallon, FTP Software, Novell, Claris, ICL, the Software Publishers Association (SPA), NOW Software, and InterCon Systems. Significant customers include Xerox, Apple, TWA, the U.S. government, Motorola, Netscape, Yahoo!, and Silicon Graphics. The company's competitive advantages are its status as the first electronic distributor/reseller of software on the Internet, its experienced management team, its software and distribution technology, its World Wide Web server architecture, and brand awareness of its software. CyberSource primarily competes against Architext, Open Market, and Personal Library Software. Additional challenges and risks include competition, growth in bandwidth, and adding value for customers through content.

Other

Cybersource's service was launched in November 1994. The company has been aggressively pursuing customer traffic through advertisements on World Wide Web sites, including NCSA's *What's New Page*, Yahoo!, NetSurfer, and Netscape. CEO William McKiernan was the former president and COO of McAfee Associates, a developer of electronically distributed software. Mr. McKiernan also held top positions at Princeton Venture Research, IBM, and Price Waterhouse. Founder and vice president of engineering John Pettitt is a founder of several other companies, including Specialix Corp.

Primary VCs/Outside Financing

Private equity investors.

KEY FACTS

Year Established:	1994
Employees:	30
Fiscal Year End:	December
Revenues FY '94:	$0.0
Revenues FY '95:	$3.2m
Date of Next Financing:	September 1996
Date of Last Financing:	January 1995
Size of Last Financing:	$0.6m
Total Capital Raised:	$0.6m
Post Round Valuation:	$12.0m
Expected IPO Date:	n/a

DATALOGIX INTERNATIONAL

Address:	100 Summit Lake Drive Valhalla, NY 10595
Telephone:	914/747-2900
Fax:	914/747-2987
E-mail:	n/a
Web site:	n/a
Industry:	Computers
Sector:	Enterprise & Client/Server Software
CEO:	Richard Giordanella
CFO:	Rick Smith
Stock Exchange:	NASDAQ
Stock Symbol:	DLGX

Product Description

Datalogix International develops an open systems manufacturing software for international process manufacturers. The company's product line, CIMPRO (Computer Integrated Manufacturing for Process), automates and integrates a process manufacturer's business functions such as management, planning, inventory, and purchasing. Customers include food and beverage, paint, ink, chemical, and pharmaceutical companies.

Market Strategy/Positioning

The company's mission is to lead in open systems and client/server software solutions for process manufacturers. Datalogix International has strategic relationships with Oracle, Hewlett-Packard, IBM, Data General, UNISYS, Sun Microsystems, and DEC. Significant customers include Revlon, Cargill, Sara Lee, and Heinz. The company's competitive advantage is its exclusive focus on process industry with open client/server technology. Datalogix International primarily competes against SAP and MARCOM.

Other

The company, founded in 1981, pioneered the development of open systems software for managing the manufacturing and financial operations of companies. Previously known as Datalogix Formula Systems, it went public in 1995 under its current name. Its solutions are now installed in more than 30 countries. CEO Richard Giordanella was previously president and COO of Ross Systems. CFO Rick Smith was also previously at Ross Systems as CFO.

KEY FACTS

Year Established:	1981
Employees:	230
Fiscal Year End:	June
Revenues FY '94:	$24.8m
Revenues FY '95:	$43.2m
EPS '94:	$0.16
EPS '95:	$0.59
Shares Outstanding:	10.0m
Five-Year Growth Rate:	45%

DAVIDSON
& ASSOCIATES

Address:	19840 Pioneer Avenue
	Torrance, CA 90503
Telephone:	310/793-0600
Fax:	310/793-0601
E-mail:	info@davidson.com
Web site:	http://www.davd.com
Industry:	Entertainment & Information
Sector:	Entertainment/Education Software
CEO:	Robert Davidson
CFO:	Jack Allewaert
Stock Exchange:	NASDAQ
Stock Symbol:	DAVD

Product Description

Davidson & Associates develops, publishes, manufactures, and distributes educational software for K–12 home and school markets. It publishes 42 of its own titles and 34 affiliate label products. Its affiliate label program has 11 members. Its most popular products include *The Blockbuster Series* and *Kid Tools*. The company has multiple distribution channels which sell to schools through its Educational Resources subsidiary and to homes through distributors, software outlets, computer superstores, mass merchandisers, and catalogues. Its subsidiary is the largest reseller of packaged software to schools.

Market Strategy/Positioning

The company's mission is to be the leading interactive multimedia studio. Davidson has strategic relationships with Simon & Schuster, Fisher-Price, and Addison-Wesley. The company's competitive advantages are its established longevity in the marketplace and its reputation for quality products. Davidson has successfully implemented a studio strategy that outlines multiple sources of product and a heavy influence on distribution. Davidson primarily competes against Brøderbund, Edmark, MECC, and Humongous Entertainment. Additional challenges and risks include managing the growth of the company.

Other

The company, founded in 1982 by educator Dr. Jan Davidson, was the first educational software company to offer software products for the public. Before founding the company, Dr. Davidson spent 15 years as an educational instructor; she also founded Upward Bound, a non-profit educational tutorial service. Demand for the software she created at Upward Bound led to the formation of Davidson & Associates. Chairman and CEO Bob Davidson held a senior management position at The Parsons Corporation from 1978 to 1989. Jim Allewaert served as senior vice president with Green Tree Financial from 1990 to 1994 before joining Davidson. He has over 10 years of experience in public accounting with Deloitte & Touche and also held a senior management position at The Parsons Corporation.

KEY FACTS

Year Established:	1982
Employees:	600
Fiscal Year End:	December
Revenues FY '94:	$88.1m
Revenues FY '95:	$161.4m (estimate)
EPS '94:	$0.59
EPS '95:	$0.76 (estimate)
Shares Outstanding:	17.7m
Five-Year Growth Rate:	28%

DELL COMPUTER

Product Description

Dell Computer is the one of the top 5 PC vendors in the world. The company markets desktop, notebook, and server computers compatible with industry standards, all under its own name. Dell primarily markets its products and services directly to customers, which lets it better understand and respond to customer demands. The company employs a build-to-order manufacturing process that allows it to achieve rapid inventory turnover and reduces the risk of declining inventory values. The flexible manufacturing process also allows it to rapidly incorporate new technologies and components into its product offerings.

Address:	9505 Arboretum Boulevard Austin, TX 78759-7299
Telephone:	512/338-4400
Fax:	512/728-4238
E-mail:	info@dell.com
Web site:	http://www.dell.com
Industry:	Computers
Sector:	Desktop Computers/File Servers
CEO:	Michael S. Dell
CFO:	Thomas J. Meredith
Stock Exchange:	NASDAQ
Stock Symbol:	DELL

Market Strategy/Positioning

The company's mission is to provide relevant, valuable products that are tailormade for consumer's specific needs. Dell Computer has a strategic relationship with Xerox, in an agreement to sell systems in Latin America; it also has a technical support agreement with Banctec Service Corporation. The company's competitive advantages are its brand-name recognition and a direct relationship strategy with its consumers that allows it to price aggressively. Dell also carries a broader line of products than most of its competitors. Dell Computer primarily competes against Compaq, IBM, Gateway 2000, AST Research, Packard Bell, Hewlett-Packard, Toshiba, NEC, DEC, and Apple. Additional challenges and risks include intense competition and creating an operational infrastructure that meets demand consistently and cost-effectively.

261

Other

Michael Dell started the company (originally called PCs Limited) in his freshman dorm room, selling PCs directly to end-users at a discount after buying excess computers from a local retailer. The company went public in 1988 with a $34.2 million offering. Michael Dell has been chairman and CEO since he founded the company in 1984. Morton Topfer joined as vice chairman in 1994 and shares the office of CEO with Michael Dell. Before joining Dell, Mr. Topfer worked at Motorola for 23 years.

KEY FACTS

Year Established:	1984
Employees:	6,400
Fiscal Year End:	January
Revenues FY '94:	$2.9b
Revenues FY '95:	$3.5b
EPS '94:	$(-1.13)
EPS '95:	$3.36
Shares Outstanding:	45.1m
Five-Year Growth Rate:	20%

DG SYSTEMS

Address:	150 Spear Street
	Suite 1850
	San Francisco, CA 94105
Telephone:	415/546-6600
Fax:	415/546-6601
E-mail:	hank@dgsystems.com
Web site:	n/a
Industry:	Entertainment & Information
Sector:	Broadcasters & Cable Networks
CEO:	Henry Donaldson
CFO:	Tom Shanahan

Product Description

DG Systems (Digital Generation) provides high-quality, low-cost electronic distribution of digital advertising to radio stations over telephone networks. It also supplies centralized control of distribution, higher-than-CD-quality audio, and very rapid turnaround time. The company is considering entering the international radio, network radio, newswire, recorded singles, and syndicated markets. DG Systems currently has 2,000 radio stations on the system.

Market Strategy/Positioning

The company's mission is to be the electronic distribution and information system for the broadcast radio industry by linking advertisers, agencies, and production studios to radio stations via a digital multimedia network. DG Systems has strategic relationships with most major telephone companies. Significant customers include J. Walter Thompson, BBDO, Foote Cone & Belding, McCann Erickson, The Richards Group, David Cravit & Associates, Meijer Foods, Radio Shack, and Circuit City. The company's competitive advantages are speed, efficiency, and quality of its commercial delivery. DG Systems primarily competes against Digital Courier, Transmedia, and Musician Express. Additional challenges and risks include maintaining parallel growth of both platform infrastructures and distribution revenues.

Other

DG Systems was founded in 1991; since its inception it has distributed as many as 2,845 deliveries in one day and 10,324 deliveries in one week. It is one of the largest private network systems for electronic delivery of advertisements.

CEO Henry Donaldson was formerly president at Data Communications Division and has more than 27 years of experience in building telecommunications and information systems companies. Chairman Dick Harris was formerly president of Westinghouse Broadcasting Company's Group W Radio.

Primary VCs/Outside Financing

AT&T Ventures, Coral Group, Glynn Ventures, Kleiner Perkins Caufield & Byers, Mayfield Fund, and Sierra Ventures.

KEY FACTS

Year Established:	1991
Employees:	80
Fiscal Year End:	December
Revenues FY '94:	$2.4m
Revenues FY '95:	n/a
Date of Next Financing:	n/a
Date of Last Financing:	July 1995
Size of Last Financing:	$4.7m
Total Capital Raised:	$25.0m
Post Round Valuation:	$77.0m
Expected IPO Date:	1997

DIAMOND
MULTIMEDIA

Address:	2880 Junction Avenue San Jose, CA 95134-1922
Telephone:	408/325-7000
Fax:	408/325-7070
E-mail:	n/a
Web site:	http://www.diamondmm.com
Industry:	Computers
Sector:	Peripherals
CEO:	William Schroeder
CFO:	Gary B. Filler
Stock Exchange:	NASDAQ
Stock Symbol:	DIMD

Product Description

Diamond Multimedia designs, develops, manufactures, and markets multimedia add-in boards for PCs. Its products include graphics and multimedia accelerators, audio-telephony subsystems, and multimedia upgrade kits. It owns over 44% of the VRAM market and is also one of the top vendors in the DRAM and low-end VRAM peripherals market. Diamond is currently working on systems that will include 3D graphics and telecommunications applications such as fax, voicemail, modem, and duplex speakerphone.

Market Strategy/Positioning

Diamond has strategic relationships with DEC, S3, NVIDIA, Cirrus Logic, Tseng Labs, IBM, Micron, Samsung, and Weitek. Significant customers include Ingram-Micro, Merisel, Tech Data, CompUSA, Fry's Electronics, and Computer City. The company's competitive advantages are its leading position in the graphics/video arena and its strong retail presence. It is the recipient of numerous product and vendor awards. Diamond claims to offer the best graphical user interface (GUI) acceleration and video playback technology for the PC at the best value to the consumer. The company primarily competes against Creative Technologies, ATI, Number Nine Visual Technology, STB Systems, and SPEA Software. Additional challenges and risks include managing company growth and releasing new products in a highly competitive market with extremely short product cycles.

Other

Diamond Multimedia was founded in 1982 by chairman Chong-Moon Lee, who served as its president and CEO from 1982 to 1994. Diamond developed its first GUI accelerators in 1990 and expanded into multimedia in 1994. It acquired Supra Corporation, one of the top five modem manufacturers, in August 1995. Before joining Diamond, CEO Bill Schroeder was vice chairman of Conner Peripherals, president of Archive (during its integration into Conner Peripherals), and CEO of Arcada Software (a Conner entrepreneurial subsidiary); he also co-founded Priam. CFO Gary Filler formerly served as executive vice president and CFO of ASK Group.

KEY FACTS

Year Established:	1982
Employees:	350
Fiscal Year End:	December
Revenues FY '94:	$203.3m
Revenues FY '95:	$405.4m (estimate)
EPS '94:	$0.96
EPS '95:	$1.14 (estimate)
Shares Outstanding:	20.3m
Five-Year Growth Rate:	28%

DIGITAL DOMAIN

Product Description

Digital Domain develops visual effects for feature films, commercial production, CD-ROM, video games, and theme-park and location-based entertainment. The company has worked on films including *Apollo 13*, *True Lies*, and *Interview With the Vampire*, and commercials for Budweiser, Nike, and Jeep. Its New Media division is developing video games and interactive media projects.

Address:	300 Rose Avenue
	Venice, CA 90291
Telephone:	310/314-2800
Fax:	310/314-2888
E-mail:	scott@d2.com
Web site:	http://www.d2.com
Industry:	Entertainment & Information
Sector:	Film & Entertainment Production
CEO:	Scott Ross
CFO:	Steve Fredericks

Market Strategy/Positioning

The company's mission is to provide the best digital imagery and content in the world. Digital Domain has strategic relationships with IBM, Silicon Graphics, and Discreet Logic. Significant customers include 20th Century Fox, Warner Bros., MCA Universal, IBM, and AT&T. The company's competitive advantages are its in-house talent and its open architecture. Digital Domain primarily competes against Industrial Light & Magic, DreamWorks SKG, Walt Disney, (Colossal) Pictures, R/GA Digital Studios, Sony, and Pacific Data Images. Additional challenges and risks include acquiring and retaining talent. Digital Domain is unique in having one leg in technology (Silicon Valley) and one leg in creativity (Hollywood), which perfectly positions it for the digital revolution.

Other

Terminator director James Cameron, creature designer Stan Winston, and CEO Scott Ross split startup costs with IBM and founded Digital Domain to create a studio that would set the pace for visual effects and digital media. Founder James Cameron is a director, writer, and producer. Stan Winston is an eight-time Academy Award nominee and four-time Academy Award winner. CEO Scott Ross has 15 years of experience in the entertainment business and was a former senior vice president of LucasFilm and general manager of Industrial Light & Magic. Mr. Ross says, "I want Digital Domain to be to interactive TV what Aaron Spelling is to television today."

Primary VCs/Outside Financing

50% owned by IBM and 50% owned by founders Scott Ross, Jim Cameron, and Stan Winston.

KEY FACTS

Year Established:	1993
Employees:	200
Fiscal Year End:	December
Revenues FY '94:	n/a
Revenues FY '95:	n/a
Date of Next Financing:	n/a
Date of Last Financing:	n/a
Size of Last Financing:	n/a
Total Capital Raised:	n/a
Post Round Valuation:	n/a
Expected IPO Date:	n/a

DISCREET LOGIC

Address:	5505 St. Laurent Boulevard Suite 5200 Montreal, Canada H2T 1S6
Telephone:	514/272-0525
Fax:	514/272-0584
E-mail:	info@discreet.qc.ca
Web site:	http://www.discreet.qc.ca
Industry:	Entertainment & Information
Sector:	Film & Entertainment Production
CEO:	David Macrae
CFO:	Douglas Johnson
Stock Exchange:	NASDAQ
Stock Symbol:	DSLGF

Product Description

Discreet Logic develops, markets, and supports non-linear digital image-processing systems that create, edit, and compose special effects for film and video. The company's systems are used by creative professionals in production and post-production to create feature films, television programs, commercials, and video music. Its systems played key roles in *Speed*, *Forrest Gump*, *True Lies*, and *Interview with the Vampire*. The company's flagship product, Flame, sells for $595,000 per system.

Market Strategy/Positioning

Discreet Logic has a strategic relationship with Silicon Graphics. It also acquired Brughetti in 1995. Significant customers include Video Image, Industrial Light & Magic, Digital Domain, CIS/Hollywood/Paramount, and The Mill. The company's competitive advantages are its expertise in creating digital special effects within frames of video in real-time using uncompressed images. Discreet Logic primarily competes against Avid, Quantel, Kodak, Sony, Matrox, Grass Valley Group, Fast, Pinnacle, Panasonic, and Microsoft subsidiary SOFTIMAGE. Additional challenges and risks include the company's dependence on SGI—a large portion of its gross profits is generated by the sale of SGI hardware. Discreet Logic is unique in having a technology that allows creative professionals to input, create, manipulate, store, and output uncompressed visual images in a faster, easier, and more cost-effective manner.

Other

The company was founded in September 1991. Co-founder and chairman Richard Szalwinski has served as director since May 1992 and as chairman since March 1994. Before founding Discreet Logic, he held various positions at SOFTIMAGE. President and CEO David Macrae joined the company in 1994; he was previously vice president of worldwide sales and field operations at SOFTIMAGE. CFO Douglas Johnson was formerly CFO at Fusion Systems and also served as CFO, treasurer, and secretary at Excalibur Technologies. Jonathan Stone, analyst at Adam, Harkness & Hill, comments, "We expect [Discreet Logic's] new products to account for more than 30% of revenues in fiscal 1996."

KEY FACTS

Year Established:	1992
Employees:	215
Fiscal Year End:	July
Revenues FY '94:	$15.4m
Revenues FY '95:	$60.7m
EPS '94:	$0.04
EPS '95:	$0.59
Shares Outstanding:	13.9m
Five-Year Growth Rate:	50%

DIVA
COMMUNICATIONS

Address:	2150 Shattuck Avenue 5th Floor Berkeley, CA 94704
Telephone:	510/649-2900
Fax:	510/649-6099
E-mail:	info@diva.com
Web site:	n/a
Industry:	Communications
Sector:	Wireless Communications
CEO:	Amine Haoui

Product Description

DIVA Communications offers digital wireless subscriber loop systems for use as a wire alternative in newly industrialized countries. The company provides voice, data, and fax connectivity optimized for fixed applications. Its products include radio and switch controllers, mini base stations, wireless subscriber units, and network management systems.

Market Strategy/Positioning

The company's mission is to be the leader in providing newly-industrialized countries with the most cost-effective means to rapidly expand their telephone networks. DIVA has an OEM agreement with California Microwave. The company's competitive advantages include its rapid network deployment, its low cost per subscriber, its exclusive focus on the international market, and its ability to develope country-specific solutions with local switch vendors. DIVA primarily competes against Motorola, Hughes Network Systems, and Qualcomm. An additional challenge includes the lack of a domestic market for the company.

266

Other

DIVA was founded in 1993 and had its first round of financing that same year. It had a second round in 1994, and its first public demonstration of DIVA-2000 Wireless Local Loop occurred in October 1995. Its product first shipped in early 1996. Co-founder, president, and CEO Amine Haoui was formerly vice president of Teknekron Communications. Vice president and COO Wolfgang Schwarz was formerly vice president and general manager of Rolm International. Co-founder Ayman Fawaz is vice president of marketing and was previously at TCSI. Co-founder and vice president of research and development Robert Kavaler previously worked as a technical consultant in the development of digital cellular VLSI chipsets.

Primary VCs/Outside Financing

Brentwood Associates; Burr Egan, Deleage; Crosspoint Venture Partners; and Norwest Venture Capital.

KEY FACTS

Year Established:	1993
Employees:	32
Fiscal Year End:	December
Revenues FY '94:	$0.0
Revenues FY '95:	$0.0
Date of Next Financing:	n/a
Date of Last Financing:	October 1994
Size of Last Financing:	$6.3m
Total Capital Raised:	$8.3m
Post Round Valuation:	$14.8m
Expected IPO Date:	1997

DOLBY LABORATORIES

Address:	U.S. Headquarters
	100 Potrero Avenue
	San Francisco, CA 94103
Telephone:	415/558-0200
Fax:	415/863-1373
E-mail:	n/a
Web site:	http://www.dolby.com
Industry:	Entertainment & Information
Sector:	Recording Studios
CEO:	Ray Dolby
CFO:	Janet Daly

Product Description

Dolby Laboratories provides innovative audio technologies to professional recording studios, broadcasters, and filmmakers. Its technologies are used in all kinds of audio products, such as portable cassette players, high-end home theater systems, radio stations, satellite music systems, movie theaters, and professional recording studios. Dolby AC-3, its latest technology, offers high-quality, 5.1-channel surround sound in less space than is needed for just one channel on a CD.

Market Strategy/Positioning

Significant customers include BMG Classics, Digital HDTV Grand Alliance, Fox Network, and the Toshiba–Time Warner alliance. The company's competitive advantages are over 85,000 tracks worldwide being equipped with Dolby SR, its products are sold and serviced in 50 countries, and over 495 million consumer products exist with Dolby technologies. Dolby is unique in its successful sound innovation. The movie *Jurassic Park* was the seventeenth consecutive Dolby Stereo analog release to win an Academy Award for Best Achievement in Sound.

Other

American engineer and physicist Ray Dolby established Dolby Laboratories in London in 1965 with the intent of developing practical noise reduction systems to improve sound quality in a variety of professional and consumer environments. The company used this technology to start its film sound program in the 1970s. The company has recently decided to focus on digital sound. Dolby digital audio coding has been developed to enhance the entertainment experience on laserdiscs, satellite and cable TV transmissions, and future media, such as digital video disc and high-definition TV. In August 1994 Fox Network began to broadcast the entire NFL season in Dolby Sound. Founder Ray Dolby acted as president and CEO of the company from 1965 until 1983, when he became chairman. In 1995 he was awarded a Grammy Award for Lifetime Technical Achievement by the National Academy of Recording Arts and Sciences.

Primary VCs/Outside Financing

Ray Dolby.

KEY FACTS

Year Established:	1965
Employees:	300
Fiscal Year End:	September
Revenues FY '94:	$50.0m
Revenues FY '95:	n/a
Date of Next Financing:	n/a
Date of Last Financing:	n/a
Size of Last Financing:	n/a
Total Capital Raised:	n/a
Post Round Valuation:	n/a
Expected IPO Date:	n/a

DOW JONES & COMPANY

Address:	World Financial Center
	200 Liberty Street
	New York, NY 10281
Telephone:	212/416-2000
Fax:	212/416-3494
E-mail:	dpettit@dowjones.com
Web site:	http://www.djin.com;
	http://update.wsj.com
Industry:	Entertainment & Information
Sector:	Information Services
CEO:	Peter R. Kann
CFO:	Kevin J. Roche
Stock Exchange:	NYSE
Stock Symbol:	DJ

Product Description

Dow Jones & Company is one of the leading publishers of financial news and information. Its main publications are *The Wall Street Journal* and *Barron's*. It operates globally; about 40% of its business is done outside the U.S. In addition to its business publications and newspapers, the company sells online financial and business research information. One of Dow Jones' newest successes, the Dow Jones Telerate, introduced in January 1995, provides real-time financial information, decision support products, trading room systems, and transaction services. Its corporate service offers access to more than 68 database services and more than 1,800 publications. It also delivers customized clipping news and information to corporate desktops. It was put on the Internet through WAIS, a news retrieval network that allows users to search the full text of 200 magazines.

Market Strategy/Positioning

Dow Jones has strategic relationships with American City Business Journals, BellSouth, Hubbard Broadcasting, ITT, NYNEX, *AmericaEconomia* (50% ownership), Bear Island, *Asia Business News* (30% ownership), and *European Business News* (70% ownership). The company's competitive advantages are its strong reputation and its ability to provide real-time information to customers. Dow Jones primarily competes against America Online, Bloomberg, Cox, Dun & Bradstreet, *Forbes,* H&R Block, Knight-Ridder, McGraw-Hill, *The New York Times*, News Corp., Reuters, Time Warner, Tribune, and Washington Post.

Other

The company was started by Charles Dow, Edward Jones, and Charles Bergstresser, three financial reporters who left the Kiernan News Agency in 1882. Mr. Jones sold out in 1899, and in 1902 Messrs. Dow and Bergstresser sold the business to Clarence Barron. Under the leadership of Bernard Kilgore, the company branched out in many new directions and generated a circulation of 1 million by 1966. The company started same-day services in 1975. In the past few years, Dow Jones has positioned itself as one of the leading information providers on the Internet.

KEY FACTS

Year Established:	1882
Employees:	9,860
Fiscal Year End:	December
Revenues FY '94:	$2.1b
Revenues FY '95:	n/a
EPS '94:	$1.83
EPS '95:	$2.02 (estimate)
Shares Outstanding:	96.7m
Five-Year Growth Rate:	13%

DREAMWORKS
SKG

Address:	3801 Barham Boulevard
	Los Angeles, CA 90068
Telephone:	818/733-7000
Fax:	818/752-5556
E-mail:	n/a
Web site:	n/a
Industry:	Entertainment & Information
Sector:	Film & Entertainment Production
CEO:	Daniel Kaufman
CFO:	Daniel Kaufman

Product Description

DreamWorks SKG aims to be the first successfully launched major studio in 60 years. The studio will focus on five primary business sectors: film, animation, television production, music, and interactive media. Amblin Entertainment and Geffen Records have been folded into DreamWorks. The company is working on building its $50 million, fully-integrated digital movie studio. This studio will allow directors to create movie sets on the computer that would be incredibly expensive or virtually impossible to construct.

Market Strategy/Positioning

DreamWorks has strategic relationships with Capital Cities/ABC, Hasbro, Microsoft, HBO, and Silicon Graphics, which is jointly developing the digital studio at DreamWorks. The company's competitive advantages are the driving talent and strong reputations of the three partners and its solid capitalization. DreamWorks SKG primarily competes against Walt Disney, Time Warner, Viacom, Matsushita, Pixar, Turner, Cambridge Animation Systems, and Sony. Additional challenges and risks include initial large expenditures offset by little revenue for the company.

269

Other

DreamWorks SKG was conceptualized in 1994 by Steven Spielberg, Jeffrey Katzenberg, and David Geffen. The company wants to break into the elite club of entertainment companies controlling the industry. Lawyers have cleared the rights for the DreamWorks name in 108 countries, and the three partners are negotiating to buy 75 acres on the old Hughes Helicopter site in Playa del Rey, where they want to build a campus-like studio. The company plans to employ only 500 people, while a traditional studio would employ 2,000–3,000. In September 1995, the company announced a two-year first-look production deal with producers Susan Arnold and Donna Roth. In addition, DreamWorks recently hired Fox's executives Ken Solomon and Dan McDermot, as well as two senior executives from Walt Disney, Gary Krisel and Bruce Kranston. DreamWorks estimates earnings that in 2003 will be $665 million.

KEY FACTS

Year Established:	1994
Employees:	n/a
Fiscal Year End:	n/a
Revenues FY '94:	$0.0
Revenues FY '95:	$0.0
Date of Next Financing:	n/a
Date of Last Financing:	n/a
Size of Last Financing:	n/a
Total Capital Raised:	n/a
Post Round Valuation:	n/a
Expected IPO Date:	n/a

Primary VCs/Outside Financing

Mr. Spielberg, Mr. Katzenberg, and Mr. Geffen ($33.3 million each). Chemical Bank ($1 billion line of credit), Paul Allen ($500 million), and Cheil Foods & Chemicals ($300 million).

DSC
COMMUNICATIONS

Address:	1000 Coit Road
	Plano, TX 75075
Telephone:	214/519-3000
Fax:	214/519-2322
E-mail:	n/a
Web site:	n/a
Industry:	Communications
Sector:	Computer Networking
CEO:	James L. Donald
CFO:	Gerald F. Montry
Stock Exchange:	NASDAQ
Stock Symbol:	DIGI

Product Description

DSC COMMUNICATIONS designs, develops, manufactures, and markets digital switching, transmission, access, and private network system products to both local and long distance telecommunications service providers. It is currently exploring ATM access technology. It is also developing a fiber-optic cable system with General Instrument to mix video, telephone, and data services in the home.

Market Strategy/Positioning

DSC has strategic relationships with Cable & Wireless, General Instrument, Westell, General Data-Comm, Motorola, Nokia, and Northern Telecom. Significant customers include MCI, Ameritech, Motorola, Bell Atlantic, NYNEX, GTE, United Telecommunications, Alltel Supply, MCI, DDI (Japan), Sprint, and AAP Communications (Australia). The company's competitive advantages are a large installed base, strong relationships with key customers, and new product development capabilities. DSC primarily competes against AT&T, Northern Telecom, Fujitsu, Alcatel Network Systems, Tellabs, and RTEC. DSC has a strong focus on research and development. Additional challenges and risks include many foreign and domestic competitors having more extensive engineering, manufacturing, marketing, financial, and personnel resources than DSC.

Other

DSC, founded in 1976, orginally focused on the digital switching market. Its stock was first publicly traded in 1980. CEO James Donald was hired in 1981 and CFO Gerald Montry joined the company in 1986. The company entered international markets in the mid-1980s and developed a large presence in Japan. In 1990 DSC acquired Optilink, a pioneer in the next-generation digital loop carrier field. When its second biggest customer, Motorola, began diversifying away from DSC in 1991, the company immediately restructured itself to overcome that year's revenue loss of over $108 million. After downsizing and reducing inventories, the company posted positive numbers the next year.

KEY FACTS

Year Established:	1976
Employees:	5,414
Fiscal Year End:	December
Revenues FY '94:	$1.0b
Revenues FY '95:	n/a
EPS '94:	$1.39
EPS '95:	$1.80 (estimate)
Shares Outstanding:	114.2m
Five-Year Growth Rate:	24%

DUN & BRADSTREET

Address:	200 Nyala Farms Westport, CT 06880
Telephone:	203/834-4200
Fax:	203/222-4202
E-mail:	n/a
Web site:	http://www.dnb.com
Industry:	Entertainment & Information
Sector:	Information Provider
CEO:	Robert E. Weissman
CFO:	Edwin A. Bescherer Jr.
Stock Exchange:	NYSE
Stock Symbol:	DNB

Product Description

Dun & Bradstreet markets information on more than 32 million businesses in 60 countries. Its databases are complemented by investment research and portfolio management software, in-house securities database management systems, pricing information for mutual funds, and other securities operations. Its interactive data division provides online securities-related information services. The information is distributed to PCs and mainframes. All its services except its directories are available online. Divisions of Dun & Bradstreet include A.C. Nielsen, Dataquest, D&B Information Services, D&B Software, Gartner Group, IMS International, Moody's, Nielsen Media Research, and Pilot Software.

Market Strategy/Positioning

Dun & Bradstreet has a strategic relationship with Satyam Computer Services. The company's competitive advantage is supplying valuable information on many private companies which can be difficult to obtain elsewhere. Dun & Bradstreet primarily competes against American Business Information, Dow Jones, Equifax, IBM, Information Resources Inc. (IRI), McGraw-Hill, Pearson, PeopleSoft, Reuters, SGS Thomson, and TRW. Currently, a major risk includes losing accounts to competitors such as IRI.

Other

In 1933 Robert Dun's commercial credit reporting agencies merged with John Bradstreet's rival company; the name was changed to Dun & Bradstreet in 1939. The aquisition of a series of companies has made Dun & Bradstreet the largest marketing research company in the world. Chairman, president, and CEO Robert Weissman joined the company in 1979. He has been CEO since 1994, and president since 1985; he was elected chairman April 1, 1995. In 1994 he joined the company when it acquired National CSS, where he was president and CEO. Executive vice president and CFO Edwin Bescherer has held his current position since 1987 and was CFO from 1984 to 1987. He previously spent 23 years at General Electric.

KEY FACTS

Year Established:	1933
Employees:	50,000
Fiscal Year End:	December
Revenues FY '94:	$4.9b
Revenues FY '95:	n/a
EPS '94:	$3.70
EPS '95:	$3.85 (estimate)
Shares Outstanding:	170.0m
Five-Year Growth Rate:	9%

E/O NETWORKS

Product Description

E/O Networks develops, markets, and manufactures high-technology fiber-optic telecommunications systems for low-density telephone company customers. It offers telephony and video services using active electronics and fiber that require minimum maintenance. The company's revenue is generated by bringing video to areas not previously wired for cable. E/O Networks foresees the remote-area digital loops market to climb to $3 billion globally and is currently conducting field trials.

Address:	3988 Trust Way
	Hayward, CA 94545
Telephone:	510/264-3800
Fax:	510/784-1968
E-mail:	al.negrin@eonetworks.com
	emmett.smith@eonetworks.com
Web site:	n/a
Industry:	Communications
Sector:	Information Highway Equipment
CEO:	Alan Negrin
CFO:	John Sines

Market Strategy/Positioning

The company's mission is to become the leading supplier of low-density fiber-optic loop transmission systems. E/O Networks has strategic relationships with Harmonic Lightwaves, Tut Systems, Raychem, and Northern Telecom. Northern Telecom has agreed to market and distribute the company's FDS-1 Fiber Distribution System. Significant customers include Walker & Associates, Puerto Rico Telephone, and numerous small telephone companies. The company's competitive advantages are its low cost, high reliability, long range, and easy maintenance of its products. E/O Networks primarily competes against Advanced Fibre Communications. Additional challenges and risks include gaining exposure, showing consumers that its products are reliable, and facing the possibility of large telecommunications companies duplicating its technology.

Other

E/O Networks was founded in 1992 by a team of telephone professionals to meet low-density subscriber telephone company needs. Product development began in 1994. The company is in the initial stage of its trials. Before E/O Networks, Alan Negrin co-founded Optilink, a pioneer in the next generation digital loop carrier field, which was acquired by DSC in 1990. Chairman Anthony Jamroz is the former president of Telco Systems and a former vice president of sales for Northern Telecom.

Primary VCs/Outside Financing

The Sevin Rosen Funds, Vanguard, Technology Venture Investors, Sand Hill Financial, and Raychem.

KEY FACTS

Year Established:	1992
Employees:	62
Fiscal Year End:	December
Revenues FY '94:	$0.0
Revenues FY '95:	n/a
Date of Next Financing:	n/a
Date of Last Financing:	August 1995
Size of Last Financing:	$10.8m
Total Capital Raised:	$17.1m
Post Round Valuation:	$36.0m
Expected IPO Date:	1997

272

EASTMAN KODAK

Address:	343 State Street
	Rochester, NY 14650
Telephone:	716/724-4000
Fax:	716/724-0663
E-mail:	ftp.kodak.com
Web site:	http://www.kodak.com
Industry:	Entertainment & Information
Sector:	Consumer Electronics
CEO:	George M.C. Fisher
CFO:	Harry Kavetas
Stock Exchange:	NYSE
Stock Symbol:	EK

Product Description

Eastman Kodak develops, manufactures, and markets consumer and commercial imaging products. The company offers tools to digitally manipulate film and operates a post-production facility. Cineon digital film tools, unveiled in 1989, allow film to be digitized and re-recorded to film. Its Cinesite Digital Film Center offers high-volume, high-end, digital scanning services, recording services, and computer-imaging workstation tools services. Eastman Kodak uses Pixar software for retouching and automated rotoscoping. In 1992, Eastman Kodak unveiled its Photo CD system, a tool for viewing, storing, and working with images. The Photo CD format allows people to take standard 35mm film pictures and have them scanned onto Photo CD discs by a photofinisher or service bureau.

Market Strategy/Positioning

Eastman Kodak has strategic relationships with Microsoft, IBM, Apple, Sega, Hewlett-Packard, and Sprint; it acquired Qualex in 1994. The company also works with Adobe in a number of joint efforts which include Adobe's Pagemaker 6.0. Eastman Kodak primarily competes against Fuji Photo, GE, IBM, Pitney Bowes, Polaroid, Sharp, Siemens, and Xerox. Additional challenges and risks include losing market share to companies like Fuji and successfully branching out into new competitive markets.

Other

Eastman Kodak was founded by George Eastman in 1884 as The Eastman Dry Plate and Film Company, which became Kodak in 1892. The company's first products included a simple camera, a home-movie camera, a projector, and film. Kodak introduced color film in 1935 and then began producing the chemicals, plastics, and fibers used in film production. The Instamatic camera was introduced in 1963. Throughout the 1980s Kodak diversified into electronic publishing, batteries, floppy disks, and pharmaceuticals; however, the company has since sold off non-core businesses. In 1994 CEO George Fisher revealed that Kodak would focus on the digital imaging business. Mr. Fisher was previously with Motorola.

Primary VCs/Outside Financing

100% internally owned.

KEY FACTS

Year Established:	1884
Employees:	110,400
Fiscal Year End:	December
Revenues FY '94:	$14.5b
Revenues FY '95:	n/a
EPS '94:	$2.88
EPS '95:	$3.66 (estimate)
Shares Outstanding:	330.0m
Five-Year Growth Rate:	12%

EDMARK

Product Description

Edmark developes and publishes educational software and books with a focus on early childhood and special education. Edmark developed the TouchWindow accessory and other products, including *Millie's Math House* and *KidDesk,* the first menu and desk accessory software program for children. The company markets through a network of education dealers as well as through direct mail. In the past year Edmark has doubled the number of retail outlets in which it sells products. Its catalogue is distributed to more than 200,000 teachers and administrators.

Address:	6727 185th Avenue Northeast
	P.O. Box 3218
	Redmond, WA 98052
Telephone:	206/861-8200
Fax:	206/556-8998
E-mail:	amyg@edmark.com
Web site:	http://www.edmark.com
Industry:	Entertainment & Information
Sector:	Entertainment/Education Software
CEO:	Sally Narodick
CFO:	Paul Bialek
Stock Exchange:	NASDAQ
Stock Symbol:	EDMK

Market Strategy/Positioning

Edmark has strategic relationships with Harcourt, in which both companies collaborate on software development co-funded by Harcourt. The company's competitive advantages are its educational depth, richness of products, and success in finding and establishing niches early on in the industry. Edmark primarily competes against Brøderbund, The Learning Company, Walt Disney, Davidson & Associates, Knowledge Adventure, MECC, and Maxis. Additional challenges and risks include product delays and a company dependence on new products.

Other

Formed in 1970, Edmark initially focused on developing material specifically for the education market. The company later broadened its product base to include software and other educational materials targeted primarily for the special education and preschool markets. Chairman and CEO Sally Narodick has over 25 years of business experience in financial management and growth companies. Before joining Edmark, she was employed at Seafirst Bank for 14 years as corporate controller and senior vice president. Vice president of product development Donna Stranger began developing educational software in 1978 and has 20 years of experience teaching young children. She has received over 75 educational software awards. Paul Bialek is a CPA and has over 11 years of experience working on public technology companies with KPMG Peat Marwick.

KEY FACTS

Year Established:	1970
Employees:	160
Fiscal Year End:	June
Revenues FY '94:	$11.7m
Revenues FY '95:	$22.7m
EPS '94:	$(0.60)
EPS '95:	$0.48
Shares Outstanding:	3.6m
Five-Year Growth Rate:	37%

EFFICIENT NETWORKS

Address:	4201 Spring Valley Road Suite 1200 Dallas, TX 75244-3666
Telephone:	214/991-3884
Fax:	214/991-3887
E-mail:	info@efficient.com
Web site:	http://www.efficient.com
Industry:	Communications
Sector:	Computer Networking
CEO:	Mark Floyd
CFO:	Jill Manning

Product Description

Efficient Networks' products are high-performance, low-cost desktop and server ATM products. Adapters and software are differentiated by a host bus, targeted OS, and physical layer interfaces for different data rates and media types. The company is broadening its software focus through adapter drivers, local-area network (LAN) emulation, signaling software, and APIs. Its products work with a variety of platforms, including Intel-based, Power PC-board, Sun MicroSystems, DEC, SGI, and Hewlett-Packard systems. The company claims the best price/performance ratio and software capabilities.

Market Strategy/Positioning

The company's mission is to bring efficient ATM technology to the endstation (desktop PCs, servers, and workstations), with a total solution of hardware and software. Efficient Networks has strategic relationships with all major internetworking vendors, including 3Com, Cabletron Systems, Cisco Systems, and Bay Networks, to provide complete interoperability with their products. The company's competitive advantages are its own development of ASIC for segmentation and reassembly (SAR) and direct memory access (DMA) functions, software solutions for the endstation, and its interoperate with all major internetworking vendors. Efficient Networks primarily competes against FORE Systems, Interphase, and Zeitnet. Additional challenges and risks include the future acceptance of ATM technology in the market and competition from established data internetworking companies.

275

Other

Efficient Networks was founded in 1993 to bring ATM to the desktop. It received its first venture funding in July 1993 and introduced its first product in July 1994. President and CEO Mark Floyd was formerly CEO and CFO at NetWorth. Before NetWorth, he was CFO at Interphase. Mr. Floyd was also CFO and executive vice president at Scott Instruments. Chairman and founder Chase Bailey was chief scientist at Interphase and was previously involved in a number of Silicon Valley startups, including Forward Technology, Silicon Graphics, Data Stream, and JCS.

Primary VCs/Outside Financing

Crosspoint Venture Partners, El Dorado Ventures, Enterprise Partners, and Menlo Ventures.

KEY FACTS

Year Established:	1993
Employees:	55
Fiscal Year End:	June
Revenues FY '94:	n/a
Revenues FY '95:	n/a
Date of Next Financing:	n/a
Date of Last Financing:	August 1995
Size of Last Financing:	$5.0m
Total Capital Raised:	$15.5m
Post Round Valuation:	$50.0m
Expected IPO Date:	1997

ELECTRONIC ARTS

Address:	1450 Fashion Island Boulevard San Mateo, CA 94404
Telephone:	415/571-7171
Fax:	415/571-6375
E-mail:	info@ea.com
Web site:	http://www.ea.com
Industry:	Entertainment & Information
Sector:	Entertainment/Education Software
CEO:	Lawrence F. Probst, III
CFO:	E. Stanton McKee Jr.
Stock Exchange:	NASDAQ
Stock Symbol:	ERTS

Product Description

Electronic Arts develops, publishes, and distributes software for advanced entertainment systems worldwide. It is the largest interactive entertainment company in the U.S., with over 240 titles each generating over $1 million in sales and 66 titles each generating over $5 million in sales. It has a proven track record of producing products across diverse platforms and software categories. Until 32-bit set-top platforms have adequate installed bases, Electronic Arts is well-positioned to take advantage of the maturing installed base of 16-bit platforms, especially Sega's. Electronic Arts' salesforce sells directly to the retailer and has strong international distribution. The company has also released several edutainment titles under the EA*Kids label.

Market Strategy/Positioning

The company's mission is to become the world's leading interactive entertainment software company. Electronic Arts has strategic relationships with NovaLogic; a minority investment in Visual Concepts Entertainment, and relationships with Walt Disney, Capital Cities/ABC, JVC, Jane's Information Group, Sony, and 3DO. Electronic Arts has an affiliate label program with eight other U.S. software companies including Creative Wonders, Humongous Entertainment, Morgan Interactive, Motion Picture Corporation of America Interactive, Multicom Publishing, NovaLogic, Pop Rocket, and Stormfront Studios. The company's competitive advantage is its early work with software and CD-ROM, which gives it an edge over traditional computer companies. It is the best-positioned company in the industry, according to Piper Jaffray. Electronic Arts primarily competes against Acclaim Entertainment, Sega, Nintendo, Spectrum Holobyte, Maxis, Id Software, Sierra On-Line, and Microsoft. Additional challenges and risks include successfully diversifying into new markets of content such as sports and information.

Other

Electronic Arts was founded in 1982 by Trip Hawkins, who saw a huge emerging market of entertainment and game software on the horizon. By 1986 the company was the number one developer and supplier of entertainment software, and in 1989 Electronic Arts went public with a market cap of approximately $84 million. Since then, the company has expanded and opened branches in Asia, Europe, Australia, and throughout North America.

KEY FACTS

Year Established:	1982
Employees:	1,210
Fiscal Year End:	March
Revenues FY '94:	$418.3m
Revenues FY '95:	$493.4m
EPS '94:	$0.89
EPS '95:	$1.07
Shares Outstanding:	53.2m
Five-Year Growth Rate:	22%

ELECTRONIC ARTS

Founder Trip Hawkins was previously a marketing executive at Apple. Chairman, president, and CEO Lawrence Probst joined the company in 1984 as vice president of sales. He served as senior vice president of distribution from 1987 to 1990, and in December 1990 he was elected president and CEO. Before Electronic Arts, Mr. Probst was national sales manager at Activision. CFO Stan McKee has been a company executive since 1989. Before joining the company, he served as executive vice president and CFO of Digital Research where he raised over $33 million in equity.

ENTER TELEVISION

Address:	10131 Bubb Road
	Cupertino, CA 95014
Telephone:	408/366-6000
Fax:	408/366-0357
E-mail:	trudy@entertv.com
Web site:	http://www.entertv.com
Industry:	Entertainment & Information
Sector:	Online Services
CEO:	Betsy Pace
CFO:	D. Rex Golding

Product Description

Enter Television is an online entertainment service for visual and audio interaction in virtual worlds. The company's technology integrates voice compression, rendering, and distributed architecture; it is accessed through multimedia PCs connected to ordinary phone lines. It offers customers the ability to speak in real-time to other subscribers—rather than type on a keyboard—and have the ability to navigate their own computer-generated 3D personas within a true 3D environment. Enter Television plans to participate in entertainment programming tied to its platform.

Market Strategy/Positioning

The company's mission is to build a next-generation online entertainment service based on voice communication and 3D graphics, allowing subscribers to walk and talk to each other in highly realistic virtual worlds. Enter Television has a strategic relationship with MCA (Universal Interactive Studios). The company's competitive advantage is its ability to deliver voice and graphics, setting it apart from all other online subscription services. Enter Television primarily competes against Fujitsu, KA Worlds, and VR1.

Other

Enter Television was founded by Rod MacGregor and Henry Nash, two former Novell engineers, and the company is headed by Keith Schaefer. MCA may eventually obtain a 10% stake in the company. Mr. Schaefer was previously vice president of technology for Paramount Communications and president of Paramount Technology Group. Before Paramount, he was president and CEO of Simon and Schuster Technology Group and worked at NEC and Atari. CFO D. Rex Golding was previously CFO at 3DO, which he co-founded. Before 3DO, he worked at Volpe Welty and Salomon Brothers. Before Novell, Rod MacGregor founded two other software companies, IBS and Insignia Solutions.

Primary VCs/Outside Financing

AT&T; Kleiner Perkins Caufield & Byers; Merrill, Pickard, Anderson & Eyre; Mohr Davidow, New Enterprise Associates; and Wilson Sonsini Goodrich & Rosati.

KEY FACTS

Year Established:	1993
Employees:	35
Fiscal Year End:	n/a
Revenues FY '94:	n/a
Revenues FY '95:	n/a
Date of Next Financing:	n/a
Date of Last Financing:	September 1994
Size of Last Financing:	$15.7m
Total Capital Raised:	$20.0m
Post Round Valuation:	n/a
Expected IPO Date:	n/a

ERICSSON

Product Description

Ericsson develops and installs communications packages used in telephones, modems, intercom systems, radio communications, and power cable. Ericsson's equipment and other digital cellular systems can be modified for the higher radio frequencies used by personal communications services (PCS). Approximately 40% of the world's cellular phone users make calls using Ericsson cellular systems. Ericsson has also developed and manufactured defense systems such as airborne and ground-based sensing centers, and space electronics. The company's U.S. operations are located in North Carolina, Virginia, California, and New Jersey, and represent Ericsson's largest single market. In New Jersey, the company has also set up its Wireless Data & Paging Systems office which developed Mobitex, a digital two-way packet-switched architecture used in 16 countries.

Address:	U.S. Headquarters
	100 Park Avenue
	Suite 2705
	New York, NY 10017
Telephone:	212/685-4030
Fax:	212/213-0159
E-mail:	n/a
Web site:	http://www.ericsson.com
Industry:	Communications
Sector:	Wireless Communications
CEO:	Lars Ramqvist
CFO:	Carl Wilhelm Ros
Stock Exchange:	NASDAQ
Stock Symbol:	ERICY

279

Market Strategy/Positioning

Ericsson has strategic relationships with Texas Instruments, GE, RAM Mobile Data, BellSouth, and Telia AB (Sweden). Significant customers include Pacific Bell Mobile Services, Mobilios Telekomunikacijos (Lithuania), Dong Ah, Consortium of South Korea, Telebahia (Brazil), MFS Communications, Mercury Communications, and Tokyo Digital Phone. Ericsson primarily competes against Motorola, Nokia, AT&T, Siemens, and Alcatel. Additional challenges and risks include surviving the falling prices for phone-switching systems and realizing significant rate of return on research for next-generation products.

Other

Lars Magnus Ericsson started L.M. Ericsson as a telegraph equipment repair shop in 1876. The company began making telephones in 1878 and expanded overseas early in the twentieth century. Ericsson diversified into the computer and office furniture businesses in the 1980s but subsequently refocused on telephone equipment. In the early 1990s Ericsson acquired half of Orbitel Mobile Communications, a 51% interest in Fuba Telekom, and 80% voting control of Ericsson GE Mobile Communications.

KEY FACTS

Year Established:	1876
Employees:	76,200
Fiscal Year End:	December
Revenues FY '94:	$11.1b
Revenues FY '95:	n/a
EPS '94:	$0.61
EPS '95:	$0.79 (estimate)
Shares Outstanding:	794.4m
Five-Year Growth Rate:	23%

EXCALIBUR
TECHNOLOGIES

Address:	9255 Towne Center Drive
	9th Floor
	San Diego, CA 92121
Telephone:	619/625-7900
Fax:	619/625-7901
E-mail:	datkin@excalib.com
Web site:	http://www.xrs.com
Industry:	Entertainment & Information
Sector:	Online Services
CEO:	Mike Kennedy
CFO:	Jim Buchanan
Stock Exchange:	NASDAQ
Stock Symbol:	EXCA

Product Description

Excalibur Technologies offers Retrieval-Ware, which allows users to directly access the native content of digital media regardless of the data type. The company's numerous end-user applications allow users to build intelligent information retrieval solutions that provide automatic indexing and content-based retrieval of unstructured text and several multimedia types. In July 1995 Excalibur purchased ConQuest Software, which creates natural language text-management tools for access to varied information sources, including the Internet. ConQuest's products manage all aspects of the text information life-cycle for content distributors and users. Its products offer an array of search-engine options and application development tools. Its Internet solutions include seamless access to heterogeneous and geographically distributed information servers.

Market Strategy/Positioning

The company's mission is to be the leader in document imaging and multimedia information-retrieval, by providing customers with high-quality software products that offer successful solutions. Excalibur Technologies has strategic relationships with IBM, Informix, Hewlett-Packard, DEC, KPMG Peat Marwick, and Silicon Graphics. Significant customers include Ford, United Airlines, the Joint Chiefs of Staff, British Nuclear Fuels, Amgen, NYNEX, Dow Jones, and NASA. The company's competitive advantage is having the first commercially available software components that can retrieve images based on the content of the image clue. ConQuest was the first to commercialize true natural language processing. Excalibur Technologies primarily competes against Fulcrum, Dataware, Architext, and Personal Library Software. Excalibur Technologies is unique in that its product enables people to retrieve information in any form—the product adapts to the way people think, rather than making people adapt to technology.

Other

Excalibur Technologies was founded in 1980 by James Dowe III, who developed its adaptive pattern-recognition algorithms. In 1982 the company introduced the first practical applications of pattern-recognition technology. In early 1989 Excalibur released text retrieval products for DEC's VAX computers. It subsequently released a full-feature docu-

KEY FACTS

Year Established:	1980
Employees:	135
Fiscal Year End:	December
Revenues FY '94:	$11.0m
Revenues FY '95:	$16.0m (estimate)
EPS '94:	$(0.72)
EPS '95:	$(0.51) (estimate)
Shares Outstanding:	9.8m
Five-Year Growth Rate:	n/a

EXCALIBUR
TECHNOLOGIES

ment imaging application called Excalibur EFS (Electronic Filing Software). Recognizing the need to add "word meaning"–based retrieval to its content retrieval, Excalibur acquired ConQuest Software in July 1995. Founder James Dowe served as president and CEO of the company until 1984. Mr. Dowe is also vice president of Microbics Corporation, a private biotechnology company. Mike Kennedy became CEO and president of the company in 1992. He was most recently a partner in Geneva Group International. Current president Pat Condo joined Excalibur from DEC, where he was senior group manager of the document imaging and video business unit.

FIRST VIRTUAL
CORPORATION

Address:	3393 Octavius Drive
	Suite 102
	Santa Clara, CA 95054
Telephone:	408/567-7200
Fax:	408/988-7077
E-mail:	info@fvc.com
Web site:	http://www.fvcweb.com
Industry:	Communications
Sector:	Computer Networking
CEO:	Ralph Ungermann
CFO:	James Mitchell

Product Description

First Virtual Corporation focuses on developing multimedia networking technologies to run from the server to the desktop. The company develops products which utilize Asynchronous Transfer Mode (ATM) at 25-–155 megabits per second. First Virtual provides the first desktop media operating system (MOS), the first media server, and the first low-cost ATM network. Its platform, which includes a media switch and adapter card, costs $500–$800 per seat. First Virtual believes ATM to be a superior solution for multimedia and has a unique positioning within ATM because of its network management system.

Market Strategy/Positioning

The company's mission is to enable the widespread deployment of desktop multimedia applications by providing affordable ATM-based networks that will allow organizations to enrich information-sharing. First Virtual has strategic relationships with AT&T, Advanced Telecommunications Modules, Kanematsu, and Lotus (IBM). Significant customers include Reuters and Nokia. The company's competitive advantage is its software-based solution, which is designed to take advantage of ATM technology. First Virtual primarily competes against FORE Systems and Whitetree Networks. Additional challenges and risks include the speed of adoption of ATM technology.

Other

First Virtual Corporation was founded by Ungermann-Bass veterans Ralph Ungermann, Allwyn Sequeira, Jeff Leffingwell, and Marlis Rossetta. In January 1995 First Virtual became the first company to ship low-cost ATM networks for the desktop. CEO Ralph Ungermann was founder and CEO of Ungermann-Bass (acquired by Tandem Computer), which he started in 1979. Ungermann co-founded and served as COO of Zilog, an early leader in microprocessors. He also worked at Intel.

Primary VCs/Outside Financing

AT&T Ventures, Accel Partners, and internal funding.

282

KEY FACTS

Year Established:	1993
Employees:	35
Fiscal Year End:	December
Revenues FY '94:	$0.0
Revenues FY '95:	n/a
Date of Next Financing:	n/a
Date of Last Financing:	October 1994
Size of Last Financing:	$3.2m
Total Capital Raised:	$4.7m
Post Round Valuation:	n/a
Expected IPO Date:	n/a

FIRST VIRTUAL
HOLDINGS

Address:	11975 El Camino Real
	Suite 300
	San Diego, CA 92130
Telephone:	619/793-2700
Fax:	619/793-2950
E-mail:	info@fv.com, media@fv.com
Web site:	http://www.fv.com
Industry:	Entertainment & Information
Sector:	Online Services
CEO:	Lee Stein
CFO:	Kate Hopwood

Product Description

First Virtual Holdings introduced the world's first operational Internet payment system in October 1994. Its system allows anyone to buy and sell on the Internet without additional equipment or software. Buyers and sellers use a First Virtual PIN, linked to a credit card account, and is opened over a secure telephone line. The Internet system and the bank card processing system are separated by an isolated high-speed link so credit card numbers never go over the Internet.

Market Strategy/Positioning

The company's mission is to enable the largest possible global market for commerce on the Internet, by making transactions universally accessible, affordable, and safe for consumers, merchants, and banks. First Virtual Holdings has strategic relationships with Sybase, Electronic Data Systems, First USA Merchant Services, Lloyd Internetworkings, and Network Computing Devices. Significant customers include Apple, Reuters NewMedia, and National Public Radio. The company's competitive advantage is its large market share in what it hopes will be one of the fastest-growing segments on the Internet. First Virtual Holdings primarily competes against CyberCash and DigiCash. The company is unique as the first to market a service in this area.

Other

First Virtual Holdings was organized as a virtual corporation in 1994. The virtual organization was required because no two employees lived in the same area code. In less than 10 months, the company went from strictly a concept to actually introducing the world's first operational Internet payment system. The company's market potential is forecasted to reach $4 billion by 2005. Co-founder and chief scientist Nathaniel Borenstein is the author of MIME, the Internet standard for multimedia and multilingual mail messages. Co-founder and principal Marshall Rose is area director for network management on the Internet Engineering Task Force. Co-founder Einar Stefferud has been a key contributor to the development of the global Internet since 1975.

Primary VCs/Outside Financing

100% internally funded.

KEY FACTS

Year Established:	1994
Employees:	12
Fiscal Year End:	December
Revenues FY '94:	n/a
Revenues FY '95:	n/a
Date of Next Financing:	n/a
Date of Last Financing:	n/a
Size of Last Financing:	n/a
Total Capital Raised:	n/a
Post Round Valuation:	n/a
Expected IPO Date:	n/a

FLIPSIDE
COMMUNICATIONS

Product Description

Flipside Communications is a diversified media company engaged in print- and Internet-publishing and in the conference business. Flipside publishes THE RED HERRING, a monthly business magazine that focuses on the computer, communications, and entertainment industries. The company produces two international conferences: Venture Market—which brings together top private company CEOs with venture capitalists and corporate development officers—and Multimedia Market, which brings together CEOs with entertainment and publishing executives. **herring.com** is Flipside's Internet-based information and business development service. In 1996 Warner Books published *THE RED HERRING Guide to the Digital Universe*, a book written and designed by the editors of THE RED HERRING, which you are reading now.

Address:	1550 Bryant Street
	Suite 950
	San Francisco, CA 94103
Telephone:	415/865-2277
Fax:	415/865-2280
E-mail:	info@herring.com
Web site:	http://www.herring.com
Industry:	Entertainment & Information
Sector:	Newspaper/Magazine Publishing
CEO:	Anthony B. Perkins
COO:	Christopher J. Alden

Market Strategy/Positioning

The company's mission is to deliver high-level business information on the computer, communications, and entertainment industries to a worldwide audience of executives, entrepreneurs, and investors. Flipside Communications has strategic relationships with KPMG Peat Marwick, Silicon Valley Bank, Arthur Andersen, Kleiner Perkins Caufield & Byers, International Creative Management, AT&T, Apple, BBN Planet, and Warner Books. Challenges include funding growth, attracting talent, and developing a sound and profitable strategy for **herring.com**. Risks include the entry of larger, more established media companies into Flipside's market, and general downturn in the technology and entertainment financial markets.

Other

Flipside Communications is a fully-bootstrapped (i.e. no investors) Silicon Valley startup founded in early 1993 in a garage. The company has been cash-flow positive since its inception.

Primary VCs/Outside Financing

100% internally funded.

KEY FACTS

Year Established:	1993
Employees:	40
Fiscal Year End:	September
Revenues FY '94:	$1.2m
Revenues FY '95:	$3.4m
Date of Next Financing:	n/a
Date of Last Financing:	n/a
Size of Last Financing:	n/a
Total Capital Raised:	n/a
Post Round Valuation:	n/a
Expected IPO Date:	n/a

FORE SYSTEMS

Address:	174 Thorn Hill Road
	Warrendale, PA 15086
Telephone:	412/772-6600
Fax:	412/772-6500
E-mail:	info@fore.com
Web site:	http://www.fore.com
Industry:	Communications
Sector:	Computer Networking
CEO:	Eric Cooper
CFO:	Thomas Gill
Stock Exchange:	NASDAQ
Stock Symbol:	FORE

Product Description

FORE Systems designs, develops, manufactures, and sells high-performance networking products based on asynchronous transfer mode (ATM) technology. The company was first to market with complete ATM local area network (LAN) solutions, including switches, adapter cards, network management software, and other products. The company claims that its products constitute the largest installed base of ATM LAN solutions.

Market Strategy/Positioning

The company's mission is to be the worldwide leading developer and supplier of ATM local-area networking and wide-area access technology and products. FORE Systems has strategic relationships with Northern Telecom, Cabletron Systems, Sprint, ALANTEC, Tricord, LANNET, Cray Research, Optical Data Systems, and NetEdge. Significant customers include Amoco, Shell Oil, Apple, IBM, Sun Microsystems, AT&T, MCI, Sprint, NYNEX, Siemens, NTT, and Norwegian Telecom. The company's competitive advantages are having a single focus on ATM, having the largest installed base of ATM LAN products, and providing a complete end-to-end ATM solution. FORE Systems primarily competes against Cisco, Bay Networks, DEC, Newbridge Networks, and IBM. Additional challenges and risks include market acceptance of ATM and increased competition from established industry players who have made key acquisitions to offer more competitive ATM solutions.

285

Other

Founded in 1990, FORE Systems shipped its first ATM adapter for Sun workstations in October 1991 and its first ATM switch in July of 1992. FORE Systems was built largely with government research and development contracts, and insiders still own a large portion of the company. The four co-founders—chairman and CEO Eric Cooper, and vice presidents of engineering François Bitz, Onat Menzilcioglu, and Robert Sansom—were all members of the Computer Science faculty at Carnegie-Mellon University. CFO Thomas Gill has over 14 years of experience in financial management, including working at Cimflex Teknowledge and at TRW.

KEY FACTS

Year Established:	1990
Employees:	400
Fiscal Year End:	March
Revenues FY '94:	$23.6m
Revenues FY '95:	$75.7m
EPS '94:	$0.10
EPS '95:	$0.28
Shares Outstanding:	29.8m
Five-Year Growth Rate:	47%

FORTÉ SOFTWARE

Address:	1800 Harrison Street
	Oakland, CA 94612
Telephone:	510/869-3400
Fax:	510/869-2059
E-mail:	info@forte.com
Web site:	n/a
Industry:	Computers
Sector:	Enterprise & Client/Server Software
CEO:	Martin J. Sprinzen
CFO:	Rodger Weismann

Product Description

Forté Software creates application development software for enterprise-wide heterogeneous client/server networks. Forté is distinguished by its application partitioning, shared services, and business events execution. The applications possibilities include customer information systems that reference a customer's call history, financial information, and product or service status during the call; brokerage applications that analyze portfolios and alternative investments against real-time data; or health care systems that could include patient care, accounting, and medical records.

Market Strategy/Positioning

The company's mission is to address the market need for application development software that can simplify the complexities of building applications for client/server environments. Forté has strategic relationships with Apple, Data General, DEC, IBM, Mitsubishi, and Sequent. Significant customers include Abbott Labs, Corning, Medronics, and Anderson Windows. The company's competitive advantages are its easy adaptability to client/server environments, and its greater reuse of software components. Forté primarily competes against Seer, Dynasty, Uniface, and Texas Instruments. Challenges include the complexity of building client/server applications—developers must build application components on numerous systems, set up communications among them, and match applications to the levels of reliability and performance previously available.

Other

Forté Software was founded in 1991 by eight senior software professionals with experience in relational database management systems (RDBMS), development tools, object-oriented architectures, and mainframe online transaction processing. Founder and CEO Martin Sprinzen was formerly vice president of international operations of Ingres and president of NASTEC.

Primary VCs/Outside Financing

Greylock Management, Norwest Venture Capital, Sutter Hill Ventures, Trinity, Data General, Mitsubishi, Stanford University, T. Rowe Price, and Swiss Pension Fund.

KEY FACTS

Year Established:	1991
Employees:	170
Fiscal Year End:	March
Revenues FY '94:	$6.1m
Revenues FY '95:	$21.0m
Date of Next Financing:	n/a
Date of Last Financing:	February 1995
Size of Last Financing:	$13.0m
Total Capital Raised:	$28.0m
Post Round Valuation:	$117.0m
Expected IPO Date:	Summer 1996

FOUR
MEDIA COMPANY

Address:	2813 West Alameda Burbank, CA 91505
Telephone:	818/840-7000
Fax:	818/846-5197
E-mail:	n/a
Web site:	n/a
Industry:	Entertainment & Information
Sector:	Film & Entertainment Production
CEO:	Robert T. Walston
CFO:	John H. Sabin

Product Description

Four Media Company (4MC) provides diversified visual entertainment services. It offers full-service digital visual effects and a post-production facility, including digital compositioning, digital film opticals, effects systems, paint systems, and telecine. 4MC's film credits include *Blown Away, Cliffhanger, Dracula*, and *Patriot Games*. The company's other operations include duplication and standards conversion, feature mastering, film restoration and preservation, satellite services, sound operation, tape storage, and TV editing.

Market Strategy/Positioning

4MC has strategic relationships with Viacom (MTV Networks), EDS, Sony, and Snell & Wilcox. Significant customers include Paramount, Walt Disney, MCA/Universal, Warner Bros., and Fox. The company's competitive advantages are its size, geographic and product line diversity, access to capital, and an advanced technical infrastructure. 4MC primarily competes against Industrial Light & Magic, Digital Domain, Pacific Data Images, R/GA Digital Studios, and Magnet Interactive. Additional challenges include facing rapid technological advances in core businesses and maintaining control over its growing operations.

Other

Four Media Company was founded in 1993 to purchase Compact Video Group and its affiliated companies. In its first year the company focused on constructing a serial digital infrastructure to improve the company's operations. 4MC then acquired Digital Magic to expand in geographic location as well as in product lines to include digital special effects for film and television. In April 1995 the company constructed the first all-digital broadcast and post-production facility in Singapore, a $20 million capital investment. Chairman and CEO Robert Walston became chairman upon the purchase of the assets of Compact Video Group and affiliates by the Steinhardt organization in August 1993. Mr. Walston served as vice president and director of the Steinhardt Group from 1990 to 1993. President John Donlon was previously president and CEO of Compact Video Group. CFO John Sabin also worked previously at Compact Video Group as senior vice president and CFO.

KEY FACTS

Year Established:	1993
Employees:	490
Fiscal Year End:	August
Revenues FY '94:	$42.3m
Revenues FY '95:	$60.1m
Date of Next Financing:	n/a
Date of Last Financing:	August 1993
Size of Last Financing:	n/a
Total Capital Raised:	$22.4m
Post Round Valuation:	$128.0m
Expected IPO Date:	n/a

Primary VCs/Outside Financing

The Steinhardt Group.

FTP SOFTWARE

Address:	100 Brickstone Square
	Fifth Floor
	Andover, MA 01810
Telephone:	508/685-4000
Fax:	508/659-6978
E-mail:	kwharton@ftp.com
Web site:	http://www.ftp.com
Industry:	Computers
Sector:	Personal Productivity Software
CEO:	David H. Zirkle
CFO:	Robert W. Goodnow Jr.
Stock Exchange:	NASDAQ
Stock Symbol:	FTPS

Product Description

FTP Software develops internetworking software that allows PC users to access networking resources across local, enterprise-wide, and global networks. The company has positioned itself in the low-end workgroup market as well as in the high-end computer enterprise market. Its software allows service publishing on the Internet using off-the-shelf Windows applications and development tools without expertise in UNIX. The company software supports Windows and OS/2.

Market Strategy/Positioning

The company's mission is to be the primary independent supplier of TCP/IP-based products for PCs, allowing users to access heterogeneous resources across local-area, enterprise-wide, and global networks. FTP Software has strategic relationships with Control Data Corporation, Digital Communications Association, Hewlett-Packard, Unipalm, Spyglass, Intergraph, and Siemens. Significant customers include AT&T, Boeing, Citicorp, Compaq, EDS, GE, Intel, Martin Marietta, Merill Lynch, Mobil, MCI, Motorola, Texas Instruments, UNISYS, and Wal-Mart. TCP/IP-based Internet is adding networks at a rate of one every 10 minutes; 16 million protocol users are expected by 1996. FTP Software primarily competes against Novell, NetManage, Sun, Frontier, WRQL, and Wollongong. Additional challenges and risks include continuing to provide TCP/IP solutions as consumers' needs change, and anticipating market demands.

Other

FTP Software's founders include programmers involved in developing TCP/IP for the IBM PC at Massachusetts Institute of Technology in the mid-1980s. Since 1986 the company has focused on further development of TCP/IP products, including implementing TCP/IP for the PC. FTP Software went public in November 1993 and has been profitable since its inception in 1986. President and CEO David Zirkle was previously president and CEO of Racal, executive vice president of finance at Northern Telecom's Minnesota division; he also served in various capacities at Xerox.

KEY FACTS

Year Established:	1986
Employees:	490
Fiscal Year End:	December
Revenues FY '94:	$93.3m
Revenues FY '95:	n/a
EPS '94:	$0.80
EPS '95:	$1.31 (estimate)
Shares Outstanding:	24.4m
Five-Year Growth Rate:	38%

FUJITSU

Product Description

Fujitsu designs, manufactures, and markets computers, communications, and microelectronics around the world. It offers ATM products, optical transmission equipment, switching systems, teleconferencing equipment, gate arrays, and semiconductors. Fujitsu Microelectronics (a CA-based subsidiary) plans to create systems that will offer high-quality 3D graphics to the PC market. In August 1995 the company announced the development of a 42-inch-wide screen color plasma display, expected to replace the cathode ray tube and rear projection type displays as the next generation of television display devices. In September 1995 it announced the development of the world's smallest magneto-optical drive for implementation in the Macintosh Powerbook 190 and 5300 computers.

Address:	U.S. Headquarters
	3055 Orchard Drive
	San Jose, CA 95134-2022
Telephone:	408/432-1300
Fax:	408/432-1318
E-mail:	n/a
Web site:	http://www.fujitsu.com
Industry:	Computers
Sector:	Semiconductors
CEO:	Yoshio Honda
CFO:	n/a
Stock Exchange:	NASDAQ
Stock Symbol:	FJTSY (ADR)

Market Strategy/Positioning

Fujitsu has strategic relationships with Apple, Siemens, ICL (UK), TRW, Advanced Micro Devices, Sun Microsystems, Mitsui, Philips, Hewlett-Packard, CompuServe, Corporate Software, and SYNTAX. One of the company's main competitive advantages is its work in bringing 3D reality to the PC platform. Fujitsu primarily competes against Advanced Logic Research, Apple, AST, AT&T, Canon, Compaq, Conner Peripherals, Data General, DEC, Dell, Gateway 2000, Hitachi, IBM, Intel, LSI Research, Mitsubishi, Motorola, National Semiconductor, nCube, NEC, Oki, Philips, Seagate, Siemens, Silicon Graphics, Sony, Sun Microsystems, Texas Instruments, Toshiba, and UNISYS. Additional challenges and risks include its vulnerability to rises in the yen (¥), since Fujitsu exports about 15% of its products.

289

Other

Fujitsu spun off from Fuji in 1935 and became a telecommunications company. With the development of Japan's first commercial computer in 1954, the company diversified into data processing, and subsequently into semiconductor production and factory automation. Fujitsu introduced an IBM-compatible computer in 1974 and its first super-computer in 1982. In 1994 the company agreed to develop microprocessors for Sun Microsystems' line of workstations.

KEY FACTS

Year Established:	1935
Employees:	51,200
Fiscal Year End:	March
Revenues FY '94:	$32.6b
Revenues FY '95:	$36.1b
EPS '94:	$0.00
EPS '95:	n/a
Shares Outstanding:	1.817b
Five-Year Growth Rate:	n/a

GENERAL ELECTRIC

Address:	3135 Easton Turnpike Fairfield, CT 06431
Telephone:	203/373-2720
Fax:	203/373-3412
E-mail:	n/a
Web site:	http://www.ge.com http://www.nbc.com
Industry:	Communications
Sector:	Broadcasters & Cable Networks
CEO:	John F. Welch
CFO:	Dennis D. Dammerman
Stock Exchange:	NYSE
Stock Symbol:	GE

Product Description

General Electric (GE) is a technology, manufacturing, and services company that operates 12 primary businesses, from electronics to television programming (NBC) to information services. GE has 150 manufacturing plants in 31 states and 115 plants in 25 other countries. Programs broadcast on NBC are watched by viewers worldwide, among them over 60 million households in Europe and the Middle East. In September 1995 Motorola and NBC announced a 10-year multimillion-dollar agreement to develop and market financial news and information services. Also in 1995 NBC agreed to pay $1.27 billion for television rights both to the Summer Olympics in Sydney, Australia, in 2000 and to the winter games in Salt Lake City, UT, in 2002.

Market Strategy/Positioning

The company has strategic relationships with Motorola and Hitachi. GE's competitive advantages are its international exposure and its ranking first among U.S. electronics firms. Recently, it has had to cope with negative reactions related both to CEO John Welch undergoing triple bypass heart surgery, and to the delayed release of the GE90 engine resulting from its initial failure of FAA tests. General Electric primarily competes against Capital Cities/ABC (Walt Disney), CBS, General Motors, Goldman Sachs, GTE, Hitachi, Maytag, News Corp., Rolls-Royce, Time Warner, Turner Broadcasting, Westinghouse, and Whirlpool. General Electric is unique as the only Dow Jones Industrial Index company included in the original 1896 index.

Other

The Edison General Electric Company and Thomson-Houston Electric Company merged in 1892 to form General Electric. For the first two years, Thomas Edison served as director of the company. Early success was attributed to the company's development of one of the first corporate research laboratories in 1900. In the 1920s, GE, AT&T, and Westinghouse collaborated on a radio broadcasting venture, Radio Corporation of America (RCA). GE acquired RCA, including NBC, in 1986. Mr. Welch has served as chairman and CEO since 1981.

KEY FACTS

Year Established:	1892
Employees:	216,000
Fiscal Year End:	December
Revenues FY '94:	$60.1b
Revenues FY '95:	n/a
EPS '94:	$3.46
EPS '95:	$3.89 (estimate)
Shares Outstanding:	1.7b
Five-Year Growth Rate:	12%

GENERAL INSTRUMENT

Address:	181 West Madison Street
	Chicago, IL 60602
Telephone:	312/541-5000
Fax:	312/541-5039
E-mail:	n/a
Web site:	http://www.gi.com
Industry:	Communications
Sector:	Information Highway Equipment
CEO:	Daniel F. Akerson
CFO:	Charles T. Dickson
Stock Exchange:	NYSE
Stock Symbol:	GIC

Product Description

General Instrument develops technology systems and product solutions for the interactive delivery of video, voice, and data. It supplies a broad range of technologies and products required for the distribution of video programming to consumers over cable TV and satellite TV systems. General Instrument plans to develop digital entertainment terminals that will give consumers access to the broadband interactive network. Its current multimedia products include satellite encryption modules, encryption technology, and access control, and in 1996/97, interactive digital converters and high speed cable-modems will be available.

Market Strategy/Positioning

The company's mission is to be a world leader in developing technology, systems, and product solutions for the interactive delivery of video, voice, and data. General Instrument has strategic relationships with Microware Systems, DSC Communicatons, Next Level Communications, PRIMESTAR Partners, and Oracle. Significant customers include Bell Atlantic, GTE, Microsoft, Adelphia Communications, Samsung, Century Communications, Telecable, Zenith Electronics, and Motorola. The company's competitive advantage is its extensive product line, which lets the company develop new broadband technologies, anticipate and serve customer needs, and provide customers with highly integrated end-to-end systems. General Instrument primarily competes against Scientific-Atlanta. Additional challenges and risks include a high dependence on the cable TV industry and cable TV capital spending. General Instrument is unique as the only provider of end-to-end solutions to transfer any communications medium or combination of media, including video, voice, or data.

Other

General Instrument was organized in 1990 with the acquisition of General Instrument Corporation, a publicly traded company, by affiliates of private investment firm Forstmann Little. The affiliates own about 18% of the outstanding shares of the company's common stock. In 1995 the company announced its intentions to acquire Next Level Communications for approximately $75 million in stock. Chairman and CEO Daniel Akerson previously served as president and COO of MCI. CFO Charles Dickson has held various positions at MCI.

KEY FACTS

Year Established:	1967
Employees:	10,000
Fiscal Year End:	December
Revenues FY '94:	$2.0b
Revenues FY '95:	n/a
EPS '94:	$2.01
EPS '95:	$1.79 (estimate)
Shares Outstanding:	62.0m
Five-Year Growth Rate:	24%

GENSYM

Address:	125 Cambridge Park Drive
	Cambridge, MA 02140
Telephone:	617/547-2500
Fax:	617/547-1962
E-mail:	info@gensym.com
Web site:	http://www.industry.net/gensym
Industry:	Computers
Sector:	Personal Productivity Software
CEO:	Lowell Hawkinson
CFO:	Stephen Gregorio

Product Description

Gensym is a supplier of software for the development and deployment of intelligent online solutions for industrial, scientific, commercial, and government applications. With over 2,000 installations worldwide, Gensym serves 30 industrial sectors, including the discrete manufacturing, telecommunications, environmental, power, aerospace, and process industries. Gensym was selected by Loral as the artificial intelligence tools supplier for the new NASA Control Center Complex. On average its high-end systems cost $50,000.

Market Strategy/Positioning

Gensym has strategic relationships with control vendors such as Bailey, ABB, Setpoint, Foxboro, and SimSCI. Significant customers include DuPont, ABB, Lafarge Coppee, EXXON, Shell, Procter & Gamble, Chevron, BP Occidental, Mansanto, 3M, GE, and Texaco. The company's competitive advantages are a network of over 100 marketing partners, a superior product easy to use for complex applications, and a powerful rule- and model-based reasoning capability. Additional challenges and risks include serving approximately 30 industries, of which the markets and technologies tend to change at different rates.

Other

Gensym was founded in 1986 by six software industry professionals who had all worked together at Lisp Machines (LMI). As LMI was failing in its primary business, the founders left to create Gensym; five of the founders are still with the company. Before founding Gensym, CEO Lowell Hawkinson managed expert systems development at LMI and was a research associate at Massachusetts Institute of Technology working in artificial intelligence, knowledge representation, and natural languages. President Dr. Robert Moore formerly served as vice president of the Process Systems Division of LMI and co-founded Sentrol Systems.

Primary VCs/Outside Financing

Hambrecht & Quist, Jafco America Ventures, Capital Technologies, Palmer Partners, and a group of Boston-based private investors.

292

KEY FACTS

Year Established:	1986
Employees:	230
Fiscal Year End:	December
Revenues FY '94:	$20.0m
Revenues FY '95:	n/a
Date of Next Financing:	n/a
Date of Last Financing:	August 1991
Size of Last Financing:	$2.5m
Total Capital Raised:	$5.0m
Post Round Valuation:	$36.0m
Expected IPO Date:	n/a

GEOWORKS

Address:	960 Atlantic Avenue
	Alameda, CA 94501
Telephone:	510/814-1660
Fax:	510/814-4250
E-mail:	n/a
Web site:	http://www.geoworks.com
Industry:	Computers
Sector:	Personal Productivity Software
CEO:	Gordon Mayer
CFO:	Dennis Rowland
Stock Exchange:	NASDAQ
Stock Symbol:	GWRX

Product Description

Geoworks develops and publishes GEOS, a graphical, object-oriented operating system; and Ensemble, an application package for PCs and communicators. Geoworks' markets include mobile devices, smart phones, interactive TV, and information devices. The applications feature a decoupled user interface so programs can run across multiple devices without rewriting code. The applications are found in portables by Sharp, Casio, Tandy, AST, and Canon. The company also issued a patent on flexible user interface technology.

Market Strategy/Positioning

The company's mission is to establish GEOS system software as the key enabling technology of the consumer computing device markets, including mobile devices such as organizers, smart phones, and mobile companions. Geoworks has strategic relationships with Hewlett-Packard, Nokia, Novell, Toshiba, Brother, Canon, Casio, IBM, CompuServe, Motorola, America Online, and Intuit. The company's competitive advantages are its compact and efficient products and its platform offering with low-resource requirements for low-cost devices. Geoworks primarily competes against Apple Newton Intelligence and General Magic. The company is unique in its patented flexible user interface, which allows OEMs to define a unique look and feel to help differentiate devices for specific market segments.

293

Other

Geoworks was founded in 1983 by Brian Dougherty to develop software that would allow everyone to enjoy the benefits of computing. In 1986 it launched GEOS, and in 1987 it began development of GEOS for the IBM-compatible PC and other emerging consumer computing devices. In 1994 Hewlett-Packard and Novell took equity positions in the company; it also completed its IPO. Before founding Geoworks, Chairman Brian Dougherty was a founder, director, and vice president of engineering at Imagic, a startup video game company. He also worked at Mattel, where he contributed to the design of the Intellivision computer game console. President and CEO Gordon Mayer was president and CEO at InfoChip before Geoworks; he also held positions at Proxim and Adept Technology.

KEY FACTS

Year Established:	1983
Employees:	120
Fiscal Year End:	March
Revenues FY '94:	$3.9m
Revenues FY '95:	$4.0m
EPS '94:	$(1.59)
EPS '95:	$(1.12)
Shares Outstanding:	11.3m
Five-Year Growth Rate:	20%

GLOBAL VILLAGE
COMMUNICATION

Address:	1144 East Arques Avenue Sunnyvale, CA 94086
Telephone:	408/523-1000
Fax:	408/523-2407
E-mail:	n/a
Web site:	http://www.globalvillage.com
Industry:	Computers
Sector:	Peripherals
CEO:	Neil Selvin
CFO:	James M. Walker
Stock Exchange:	NASDAQ
Stock Symbol:	GVIL

Product Description

Global Village supplies integrated communications products and services for PC users. It supplies fax/modem systems for the Macintosh platform, and its Teleport family of products was named "Best Communications Product of the Year" by *MacUser* in 1995. The Teleport is the only Apple Desktop Bus (ADB) modem that plugs directly into the ADB connector of the Macintosh. Its Powerport modem is designed to connect the Powerbook to an office network over phone lines. The company currently has a Macintosh, a PC, and an Internet division.

Market Strategy/Positioning

Global Village has strategic relationships with PC vendors such as Apple, IBM, Packard Bell, and Gateway 2000; and with hardware manufacturers, including Zoom, Megahertz, Toshiba, and Hewlett-Packard. Significant customers include Bill Graham Presents, Creative Artists Agency, and Chiat Day Advertising. It has four million customers worldwide. The company's competitive advantages are its integrated communications capabilities that work independently, a broad product and service lineup that encompasses Internet services and communications software, and network communications solutions. Global Village primarily competes against Datastorm Technologies, NETCOM, PSI, Hayes, and Cheyenne. Additional challenges and risks include anticipating consumers' wants and needs and successfully integrating them into user-friendly products and services. Global Village is unique in targeting small- to medium-sized businesses, a fast-growing market largely ignored in the past.

Other

Global Village Communication was founded in 1989 to bring easy, electronic communication to the mass market. The company's name is derived from the concept of an intimate world united by vast networks of communications systems. Since its inception the company has captured almost 70% of the Macintosh fax/modem market. CEO Neil Selvin came to Global Village from Apple, where he most recently served as director of marketing for the PowerBook product family. CFO James Walker has more than 20 years of financial experience. He held senior management positions at Fujitsu America, Compression Labs, and Consolidated Video Systems.

KEY FACTS

Year Established:	1989
Employees:	80
Fiscal Year End:	March
Revenues FY '94:	$46.7m
Revenues FY '95:	$79.9m
EPS '94:	$0.37
EPS '95:	$(0.53)
Shares Outstanding:	14.8m
Five-Year Growth Rate:	30%

GOLDSTAR
(LG GROUP)

Address:	U.S. Headquarters 1000 Sylvan Avenue Englewood Cliffs, NJ 07632
Telephone:	201/816-2000
Fax:	201/816-0636
E-mail:	n/a
Web site:	n/a
Industry:	Computers
Sector:	Semiconductors
CEO:	Sung Jae Kap
CFO:	Yeo Seong-Koo
Stock Exchange:	Korea Exchange
Stock Symbol:	n/a

Product Description

The LG Group is Korea's third-largest conglomerate, after Samsung and Hyundai. Its principal businesses include consumer electronics, fiber-optic cable, and semiconductor production. Goldstar is the LG Group's successful semiconductor subsidiary. The company is shifting into high-definition television (HDTV) and thin-film transistor liquid crystal displays (LCDs) for laptop computers. In May 1995 LG Electronics released a new VCR with StarSight Telecast's technology that creates an on-screen programming guide and information service.

Market Strategy/Positioning

Goldstar has strategic relationships with Samsung, AT&T, Hitachi, NEC, Siemens, and the Vietnamese government. Significant customers include the South Korean government, J.C. Penney, and Sears. The company's competitive advantages are its size and progressive technology. The LG Group primarily competes against GE, Hewlett-Packard, Hitachi, IBM, Intel, Matsushita, Motorola, Philips, Sony, Texas Instruments, and Toshiba. In July 1995 the LG Group arranged to buy the last U.S. television producer, Zenith. Although the brand name Zenith will continue, the TVs will be manufactured outside the U.S.

295

Other

Goldstar was established in 1958 by Koo In-Hwoi, who founded Lucky Chemical Company in 1947. In the 1960s Goldstar became the first company in Korea to manufacture early electronic appliances, including fans, radios, refrigerators, TVs, washing machines, air conditioners, elevators, and escalators. In the late 1970s Goldstar expanded into the semiconductor business, and in 1982 the company established a TV factory in Alabama. It bought 5% of Zenith in 1991 and signed a patent-sharing agreement with Samsung in 1992. The company changed its name to the LG Group in 1994.

KEY FACTS

Year Established:	1958
Employees:	12,300
Fiscal Year End:	December
Revenues FY '94:	n/a
Revenues FY '95:	n/a
EPS '94:	n/a
EPS '95:	n/a
Shares Outstanding:	n/a
Five-Year Growth Rate:	n/a

GRAND JUNCTION NETWORKS

Address:	47281 Bayside Parkway
	Fremont, CA 94538
Telephone:	510/252-0726
Fax:	510/252-0915
E-mail:	info@grandjunction.com
Web site:	http://www.grandjunction.com
Industry:	Communications
Sector:	Computer Networking
CEO:	Howard Charney
CFO:	Marcel Gani

Product Description

Grand Junction Networks develops high-performance Ethernet solutions for congested and new local-area networks (LANs). Its switches include connection to other switches and servers using fast Ethernet. Grand Junction recently introduced stackable and full duplex products, and also offers fast Ethernet adapters and repeaters. The company was first-to-market with fast Ethernet capabilities.

Market Strategy/Positioning

The company's mission is to be a leading provider of high-speed connections for desktop PCs. Significant customers include AT&T, Sun Microsystems, Intel, Northern Telecom, Salomon Brothers, Networth, Farallon Computing, *USA Today*, and the U.S. government. The company's competitive advantages are custom silicon and channel diversity. Grand Junction primarily competes against 3Com and Cisco Systems. Additional challenges and risks include managing the company's explosive growth.

Other

Founded in 1992, Grand Junction Networks was the first-to-market (9/93) with 100BaseT products. It also leads in 100BaseT fast Ethernet standardization process. Before Grand Junction, president and CEO Howard Charney co-founded 3Com. He spent nine years at 3Com, where he served as vice president of engineering, manufacturing, networks systems, hardware products, and operations. Vice president of sales John Celii was formerly president of Convergent Dealership Systems, the first CFO of 3Com, where he managed 3Com's IPO in 1984. Before 3Com Mr. Celii was at Hewlett-Packard for 20 years. In 1995 Cisco Systems announced its intentions to buy Grand Junction.

Primary VCs/Outside Financing

Merril Pickard Anderson & Eyre, Technology Venture Investors, Sutter Hill Ventures, Matrix Partners, and Stanford University.

296

KEY FACTS

Year Established:	1992
Employees:	80
Fiscal Year End:	December
Revenues FY '94:	$6.2m
Revenues FY '95:	$11.4m (six months ending June 1995)
Date of Next Financing:	n/a
Date of Last Financing:	October 1993
Size of Last Financing:	$8.5m
Total Capital Raised:	$16.5m
Post Round Valuation:	$39.4m
Expected IPO Date:	n/a

GT INTERACTIVE SOFTWARE

Address:	16 East 40th Street New York, NY 10016
Telephone:	212/726-6500
Fax:	212/726-6520
E-mail:	n/a
Web site:	http://www.gtinteractive.com
Industry:	Entertainment & Information
Sector:	Entertainment/Education Software
CEO:	Ron Chaimowitz
CFO:	Maria Haggerty

Product Description

Through alliances with major software publishers, GT Interactive Software merchandises, markets, and distributes software titles for computer and gaming platforms via mass merchandisers and specialty retail chains. It is the publisher of hit titles such as *Doom* and *Doom II: Hell on Earth.* The publishing arm of GT Interactive has formed strategic relationships with several development groups to publish and distribute high-quality interactive multimedia titles.

Market Strategy/Positioning

GT Interactive Software has strategic relationships with Id Software, Microsoft, Intuit, Brøderbund, Davidson Associates, Maxis, LucasArts, Sierra On-Line, Interplay, Williams Entertainment, Big Tuna New Media, Zombie Virtual Reality Entertainment, and White Wolf. Significant customers include Wal-Mart, Caldor, and Phar-Mor. The company's competitive advantage is its strong mass merchant program. The company's distribution program services mass merchants such as Wal-Mart on a direct basis, selling directly to almost every major software retailer. Its distribution reaches music stores, toy stores, warehouse clubs, electronics chains, and discount drug stores. It also works with these chains and the publishers to develop and implement promotions supported by advertising, publicity, and special product displays. GT Interactive primarily competes against Electronic Arts (distribution of software) and other game developers.

Other

GT Interactive Software was formed in February 1993 by GoodTimes Home Video and established as an independent company in January 1995. Co-founder and CEO Ron Chaimowitz was previously vice president of GoodTimes Home Video, where he was responsible for sales, marketing, product acquisitions, and new business development. He was recruited by GoodTimes in 1987 as assistant to the president; six months later he was named executive vice president of sales and marketing. Before GoodTimes, he was employed at CBS Records for 13 years. The company will most likely go public in 1996.

Primary VCs/Outside Financing

100% Internally owned.

KEY FACTS

Year Established:	1993
Employees:	n/a
Fiscal Year End:	n/a
Revenues FY '94:	n/a
Revenues FY '95:	n/a
Date of Next Financing:	n/a
Date of Last Financing:	n/a
Size of Last Financing:	n/a
Total Capital Raised:	n/a
Post Round Valuation:	n/a
Expected IPO Date:	1996

GENERAL TELEPHONE AND ELECTRONICS

298

Address:	One Stamford Forum Stamford, CT 06904
Telephone:	203/965-2000
Fax:	203/965-2277
E-mail:	Tony.hamilton@hq.gte.Com.
Web site:	http//www.gte.com
Industry:	Entertainment & Information
Sector:	Online Services
CEO:	Charles R. Lee
CFO:	J. Michael Kelly (SVP Finance)
Stock Exchange:	NYSE
Stock Symbol:	GTE

Product Description

GTE is the largest U.S.-based local telephone company and the second largest cellular service provider. The company's services include government and defense communications systems and equipment, satellite and aircraft-passenger telecommunications, and directories and telecommunications-based information systems. GTE Telephone Operations plans to enter markets in on-demand movies, interactive games, education, shopping, banking, travel, investment, and video telephone services. GTE Interactive Media will expand GTE's presence in the interactive entertainment market. It has launched a line of interactive games that can be played on multiple platforms and across GTE's planned video network. The company is developing ATM technologies for rollout in metropolitan areas, and aims to eliminate the difference between local-area networks and wide-area networks. GTE has built desktop videoconferencing for the military that will be adapted to the consumer market. Other future goals include refining data mining, which will utilize advanced math to look for hidden relationships and assist in predicting problems, and developing a product that identifies which cellular customers are likely to discontinue service.

Market Strategy/Positioning

GTE has strategic relationships with Walt Disney, Ameritech, BellSouth, SBC Communications, Nintendo, Compania de Telefonos del Interior, Magnavox, China United Telecommunications, Valores Industriales, and Grupo Financiero Bancomer. Significant customers include Medicare, National Electronic Information Corporation, and Cincinnati Bell. The company's competitive advantages are its research facility, GTE Laboratories, and a strong international presence. GTE primarily competes against AirTouch, Ameritech, AT&T, BCE, Bell Atlantic, BellSouth, Dun & Bradstreet, Ericsson, MCI, Motorola, NYNEX, Pacific Telesis, SBC Communications, Sprint, and U S WEST. Additional challenges and risks include competitive pricing pressure, successful integration of Contel Cellular (acquired in 1995) into the corporation, and maintaining leadership as new competitors enter the marketplace. GTE is unique as the largest U.S. local telephone company, the second largest cellular service provider, and the fourth largest publicly-held telecommunications company.

KEY FACTS

Year Established:	1926
Employees:	117,400
Fiscal Year End:	December
Revenues FY '94:	$19.9b
Revenues FY '95:	n/a
EPS '94:	$2.55
EPS '95:	$2.56 (estimate)
Shares Outstanding:	970.0m
Five-Year Growth Rate:	8%

GTE
GENERAL TELEPHONE AND ELECTRONICS

Other

GTE was founded by two former staff members of the Wisconsin Railroad Commission, John O'Connell and Sigurd Odegard, who created Associated Telephone Utilities in 1926 in order to buy a Long Beach, CA telephone company. During the Depression, Associated Telephone declared bankruptcy and became General Telephone in 1935. Following the 1959 purchase of Sylvania, an electronics company, General Telephone changed its name to General Telephone and Electronics. GTE subsequently expanded by purchasing telephone companies in Florida, the Southwest, and Hawaii. In 1981 North American Philips purchased GTE's U.S. consumer electronics business; in 1982 the company established GTE Mobilnet as a provider of cellular telephone service. The 1991 merger with Contel Corporation established GTE as the largest U.S. local telephone company and the second largest cellular service provider. GTE plans to focus on several initiatives, such as enhancing the value of its wireline voice business, accelerating wireless development, expanding data services, pursuing international opportunities, and entering video services. On May 12, 1995 GTE bought back the outstanding shares on Contel Cellular. Chairman and CEO Chuck Lee joined GTE in 1983 as senior vice president of finance. Kent Foster, who has been with GTE for 25 years, was named president of telephone operations in 1989 and vice chairman in 1993.

299

[HEARST]
CORPORATION

Address:	959 Eighth Avenue New York, NY 10019
Telephone:	212/649-2000
Fax:	212/765-3528
E-mail:	n/a
Web site:	http://mmnewsstand.com
Industry:	Entertainment & Information
Sector:	Information Provider
CEO:	Frank A. Bennack Jr.
CFO:	Victor F. Ganzi

Product Description

The Hearst Corporation is one of the largest diversified communication companies, with major stakes in newspapers, magazines, books, and broadcasting. It is the largest publisher of monthly magazines in the U.S. Hearst owns approximately 17 newspapers, 14 magazines (including *Esquire*, *Smart Money*, and *Cosmopolitan*), 12 broadcasting/TV stations, and three major publishing companies as well as other entertainment, software, and real estate companies. With its New Media and Technology Group, Hearst has quickly become a presence on the information superhighway. The Hearst New Media and Technology Center was built in April 1995, and Hearst joined with eight of the largest U.S. newspaper publishers to form New Century Network (NCN), an alliance which creates a network of online newspaper services. The company is currently working on growing its multimedia business, exemplified by its new CD-ROM products. The Multimedia Newsstand, launched in January of 1995, started off with fewer than 250 magazines and currently has over 500 on the Web site. Other Web sites for Hearst include: *Esquire* (http://www.esquire2b.com), The Gate—*San Francisco Chronicle* and *San Francisco Examiner* (http://sfgate.com), *Houston Chronicle* (http://www.chron.com), *Popular Mechanics* (http://popularmechanics.com), and WCVB-TV Boston (http://www.wcvb.com).

Market Strategy/Positioning

The Hearst Corporation has strategic relationships with Dow Jones, Capital Cities/ABC (jointly formed Hearst/ABC Video Series: HAVS), Viacom, NBC, and Continental Cablevision. In November 1990 Hearst purchased a 20% interest in ESPN, and in 1995 the company purchased a 29% interest in Kidsoft. Its new media division has entered into a partnership in Canada to deploy an interactive TV system called UBI. In April 1995 the company, along with Knight-Ridder, Times Mirror, Adobe Systems, and TCI , acquired an 11% interest in Netscape. The company's competitive advantage is its ability to compete in almost any industry it desires because of a sound reputation and a large cash flow. The Hearst Corporation primarily competes against Advance, Enquirer/Star Group, Bertelsmann, Capital Cities/ABC (Walt Disney), CBS, Chronicle Publishing, Cox, Gannett, McGraw Hill, MediaNews, *The New York Times*, News Corp., *Reader's Digest*, E.W. Scripps, Time Warner, Times Mirror, Tribune, Viacom, and Washington Post.

KEY FACTS

Year Established:	1887
Employees:	16,000
Fiscal Year End:	December
Revenues FY '94:	$2.5b
Revenues FY '95:	n/a
Date of Next Financing:	n/a
Date of Last Financing:	n/a
Size of Last Financing:	n/a
Total Capital Raised:	n/a
Post Round Valuation:	n/a
Expected IPO Date:	n/a

HEARST CORPORATION

Other

The Hearst Corporation was born in 1887 when William Randolph Hearst became the editor of the *San Francisco Examiner*, which his father had won in a gambling debt. He brought great success to the paper as a result of his sensationalist writing style and acquired the *New York Morning Journal* in 1895. For the next 30 years the company branched out into magazines (1903), film (1913), and radio (1928). In 1951 control of the company fell to outsiders when Hearst died but was regained by the family in 1974. In 1994 after considering the sale of two of its book-publishing units, Hearst decided to keep them for multimedia growth opportunities. Former FCC chairman Alfred Sikes, hired in 1993 to head the New Media and Technology Group, is quickly moving Hearst into the information superhighway.

Primary VCs/Outside Financing

100% internally funded.

301

HEWLETT-PACKARD

Address:	3000 Hanover Street
	Palo Alto, CA 94304-1185
Telephone:	415/857-1501
Fax:	415/857-7299
E-mail:	webmaster@hp.com
Web site:	http://www.hp.com
Industry:	Computers
Sector:	Enterprise Computers
CEO:	Lewis E. Platt
CFO:	Robert P. Wayman
Stock Exchange:	NYSE
Stock Symbol:	HWP

Product Description

Hewlett-Packard is a leading global manufacturer of computing, communications, and measurement products and services. Its computing products, which account for 78% of revenues, include UNIX-based client/server systems, PCs, client/server software, peripheral products (printers, scanners, networking equipment, etc.), palmtop computers, and hand-held calculators. Other product lines are test and measurement equipment (11% of revenues), medical electronic equipment (5% of revenues), analytical instrumentation (3% of revenues), and electronic components such as microwave semiconductors (3% of revenues).

Market Strategy/Positioning

The company's mission is to create information products that accelerate the advancement of knowledge. Hewlett-Packard has strategic relationships with Versatest (semiconductor test equipment), Calan (cable TV test and monitoring systems), Intel, Nokia (mobile telephones and digital telecommunications), and equity participation with Apple and IBM in Taligent. Significant customers include many of the *Fortune* 1000 corporations, leading academic institutions and research laboratories, and the U.S. government. The company's competitive advantages are its substantial R&D resources, committed to identifying multidisciplinary product opportunities. Hewlett-Packard primarily competes against Xerox, QMS, Tektronix, and Apple in the peripherals segment; DEC, IBM, Silicon Graphics, and Sun Microsystems in the computer systems segment; and Conner Peripherals, Acuson, Beckman, AMD, Analog Devices, National Semiconductor, Texas Instruments, VLSI, Fluke, Network General, and Teradyne in other segments. Additional challenges and risks include meeting customer demand while keeping costs acceptable, and surviving the financial condition of distribution channels.

302

Other

In 1939 David Packard and William Hewlett started the company with $538 in a garage. Their first product was an audio oscillator which they sold to Walt Disney Studios for sound effect development for the movie classic *Fantasia*. Hewlett-Packard was incorporated in 1947; its first public stock offering was in 1957. John Young succeeded founder William Hewlett as president in 1977 and became CEO in 1978. Lewis Platt became CEO and president in 1992 and was named chairman in 1993, succeeding David Packard.

KEY FACTS

Year Established:	1939
Employees:	98,600
Fiscal Year End:	October
Revenues FY '94:	$25.0b
Revenues FY '95:	n/a
EPS '94:	$3.06
EPS '95:	$4.42 (estimate)
Shares Outstanding:	511.5m
Five-Year Growth Rate:	16%

HUGHES
ELECTRONICS

Product Description

Hughes Electronics is divided into four operating divisions: Defense Electronics (missile, electro-optical, and radar systems), Automotive Electronics (powertrain and air bag electronics), Commercial Technologies (air traffic control, database, and large-screen projector systems), and Telecommunications and Space (satellites and communications networks). The company is currently working on a digital satellite TV network (DirecTv) and a data, video, and voice communications satellite system (Spaceway). It also plans to begin person-to-person videoconferencing services over high-speed satellite links by 1997.

Address:	7200 Hughes Terrace
	PO Box 80028
	Los Angeles, CA 90080-0028
Telephone:	310/568-7200
Fax:	310/568-6390
E-mail:	n/a
Web site:	n/a
Industry:	Communications
Sector:	Information Highway Services
CEO:	C. Michael Armstrong
CFO:	Charles H. Noski
Stock Exchange:	NYSE
Stock Symbol:	GMH

Market Strategy/Positioning

The company's mission is to further the application of advanced electronic systems and components for customers' needs and to lead in the design, manufacturing, marketing, and servicing of high technology electronic systems and products for global defense, telecommunications, space, and automotive industries. Hughes Electronics has strategic relationships with Olivetti, CAE-Link, and Inmarsat-P. Significant customers include Viacom's Paramount, Disney, CNN (programming), General Motors, and the U.S. government. The company primarily competes against Allied Signal, Boeing, British Aerospace, Cooper Industries, Cox, Hercules, Hubbard Broadcasting, Lockheed, Loral, McDonnell Douglas, Motorola, Northrop Grumman, Orbital Sciences, Raytheon, Rockwell, Siemens, TCI, Textron, SGS Thomson, and Time Warner. Additional challenges and risks include facing a decline in defense budgets, managing in extremely competitive pricing environment, and "steering a course that generates innovation with sufficient financial return to support the technology investment that brings future value." Hughes Electronics is unique in having designed the world's most-purchased satellite model to date. As of July 1995 orders for the HS 601 model totaled 56.

KEY FACTS

Other

Founded in 1932, Hughes Aircraft began as a manufacturer of experimental airplanes for test pilot Howard Hughes. The company moved into defense electronics and benefited from the U.S. military expansion during the Korean War. Several milestones were achieved by the company in the 1960s. In 1960 the first beam of coherent laser light was produced, the first communications satellite was put

Year Established:	1932
Employees:	80,000
Fiscal Year End:	December
Revenues FY '94:	$14.1b
Revenues FY '95:	n/a
EPS '94:	$6.41
EPS '95:	$7.00 (estimate)
Shares Outstanding:	754.0m
Five-Year Growth Rate:	8%

HUGHES
ELECTRONICS

into geosynchronous orbit in 1963, and in 1966 the Hughes-manufactured *Surveyor* landed on the moon. General Motors purchased the company in 1985 in an effort to increase GM's technological savvy. Delco Electronics was merged with Hughes Aircraft to form GM Hughes Electronics. Hughes Aircraft won a $114 million suit against the U.S. government regarding satellite technology patents in 1994. In 1995 Hughes Electronics dropped the "GM" from its name, but not from its side. C. Michael Armstrong joined Hughes in 1992 to lead a management team that has focused on diversifying the company into businesses compatible with defense electronics. Mr. Armstrong was formerly senior vice president and chairman of the board of IBM World Trade Corporation.

HUMONGOUS
ENTERTAINMENT

Address:	16932 Woodinville-Redmond Road NE Suite 204 Woodinville, WA 98072
Telephone:	206/487-1079
Fax:	206/486-9494
E-mail:	shellyd@humongous.com
Web site:	n/a
Industry:	Entertainment & Information
Sector:	Entertainment/Education Software
CEO:	Shelly Day
CFO:	n/a

Product Description

Humongous Entertainment develops interactive children's software on CD-ROM for PCs and the 3DO multiplayer. Its main product is the *Junior Adventure* series, in which the stories unfold through the user's actions. By pointing and clicking, the user discovers clues, solves puzzles, and collects information. The interaction which includes speech, music, and hand-drawn art, features proprietary characters *Putt-Putt*, *Fatty Bear*, and *Freddi Fish*.

Market Strategy/Positioning

Humongous Entertainment has strategic relationships with Electronic Arts and Random House. The company's competitive advantages are its hand-drawn animation, proprietary technology, original characters, low production costs, and the company's short development and production cycle. Humongous Entertainment primarily competes against Edmark, Brøderbund, Davidson & Associates, and Living Books. Additional challenges and risks include staying on the cutting edge of interactive entertainment.

Other

The inspiration for Humongous Entertainment came from co-founders Shelly Day and Ron Gilbert, professional creators and producers of high-quality and imaginative multimedia entertainment. They researched the children's software market and determined there were no comparable high-quality animated entertainment products available for young children. In March 1992 they established Humongous. Shelly Day, previously employed at LucasFilm, Accolade, Electronic Arts, and Aurora Systems, has an extensive background in project management and game design. Ron Gilbert, co-founder and creative director, was also previously employed at LucasFilm for eight years and has been designing and writing games and interactive stories for over 10 years.

Primary VCs/Outside Financing

Hummer Winblad Ventures and Random House.

305

KEY FACTS

Year Established:	1992
Employees:	50
Fiscal Year End:	March
Revenues FY '94:	$5.0m
Revenues FY '95:	n/a
Date of Next Financing:	n/a
Date of Last Financing:	n/a
Size of Last Financing:	n/a
Total Capital Raised:	n/a
Post Round Valuation:	n/a
Expected IPO Date:	n/a

IBM

Address:	One Old Orchard Road Armonk, NY 10504
Telephone:	914/765-1900
Fax:	914/765-4190
E-mail:	n/a
Web site:	http://www.ibm.com
Industry:	Computers
Sector:	Enterprise Computers
CEO:	Louis V. Gerstner, Jr.
CFO:	G. Richard Thoman
Stock Exchange:	NYSE
Stock Symbol:	IBM

Product Description

IBM is involved in all aspects of the computer industry, including networking, client/server systems, PCs, and software development. It recently entered the multimedia database market through a combination of already-announced products integrated and packaged for specific vertical markets. The company is aimed at storing, managing, and retrieving text, video, and digitized images over a network. It also has an easy-to-use tool for creating desktop multimedia screen presentations with voice, music, animation, still images, and text. IBM sells a local-area network (LAN) video access product controlled by a remote. IBM provides services from consulting to outsourcing.

Market Strategy/Positioning

The company's mission is to lead in the creation, development, and manufacture of the industry's most advanced information technologies, including computer systems, software, networking systems, and microelectronics. IBM wants to translate these advanced technologies into value for its customers worldwide through its sales and professional services units in North America, Europe, Middle East, Africa, Asia Pacific, and Latin America. IBM has strategic relationships with Siemens, Toshiba, Apple, Motorola, and Sears. The company's competitive advantage is top-to-bottom, multinational, one-stop shopping for technology, experience, and name recognition. IBM competes against AMD, Apple, Arthur Andersen, ADT, AT&T, Canon, Compaq, Computer Associates, Conner Peripherals, Cray Research, Cyrix, Data General, DEC, Dell, Fuji, Gateway 2000, General Motors, H&R Block, Hewlett-Packard, Hitachi, Intel, Matsushita, Microsoft, NEC, Oracle, Packard Bell, Siemens, Silicon Graphics, Sun Microsystems, Toshiba, and UNISYS. Additional challenges and risks include improving its IBM Global Network, providing value to customers in new models of computing, combatting weak sales in some European countries, including England, France, Germany, and Italy, and improving margins and growth which are still below those of the industry. IBM is unique in its ability to provide customers with anything they need.

Other

In 1914 Thomas J. Watson took control of the Computing-Tabulating-Recording Company and marketed its punch card tabulator to the U.S. government during WWI. The company's revenues

306

KEY FACTS

Year Established:	1914
Employees:	219,000
Fiscal Year End:	December
Revenues FY '94:	$64.1b
Revenues FY '95:	n/a
EPS '94:	$5.02
EPS '95:	$9.85 (estimate)
Shares Outstanding:	580.7m
Five-Year Growth Rate:	12%

IBM

tripled by 1920. Operations were expanded abroad into Europe, Latin America, and the Far East, and in 1924 Mr. Watson changed the company's name to International Business Machines. By 1940 IBM had become the largest producer of office machinery in the U.S. IBM released its first computer, the 701, in 1952 and the first compatible family of computers, System/360, in 1964. IBM also developed the FORTRAN programming language (1957) and floppy disk storage (1971). The IBM PC (1981) led to the development of entire new PC-related industries. Throughout the late 1980s and early 1990s, increased competition on all fronts forced IBM to downsize and restructure. In 1994 the company agreed to produce computer chips designed by Cyrix. In 1995 IBM initiated an aggressive takeover of Lotus. Louis Gerstner was formerly chairman of the board and CEO of RJR Nabisco Holdings from 1989 to 1993 when he was elected CEO of IBM. Mr. Gerstner also served as president of American Express Company from 1985 to 1989 and as chairman and CEO of American Express Travel Related Services from 1983 to 1989. CFO Richard Thoman previously held the positions of executive vice president–finance and CFO of Chrysler Corporation from 1979 to 1993.

ID
SOFTWARE

Product Description

Id Software is a game producer focused on 3D representation and shooting elements; its top titles include *Wolfenstein*, *Doom*, *Doom II*, *Heretic*, and *Quake*. The first stages of *Doom* were distributed free via the Internet, with the rest available for $40. The company is currently developing three titles and targeting price points below $70. Id Software is currently available for DOS, Sega, and Atari Jaguar. It plans to develop for Macintosh, Windows, OS/2, 3DO, PSX, and Nintendo.

Address:	18601 LBJ Freeway
	Suite 615
	Mesquite, TX 75150
Telephone:	214/613-3589
Fax:	214/686-9288
E-mail:	jayw@idsoftware.com
Web site:	http://www.idsoftware.com
Industry:	Entertainment & Information
Sector:	Entertainment/Education Software
CEO:	Jay Wilbur
CFO:	Jay Wilbur

Market Strategy/Positioning

Id Software has strategic relationships with Universal Pictures and GT Interactive Software. Significant customers include all major retailers through GT Interactive. Approximately 20 million copies of *Doom* have been sold worldwide. The company's competitive advantage is its philosophy of creating a new way to market computer games. The "try before you buy" strategy freely releases a portion of a game to the public through online services and the Internet. Id Software primarily competes against Acclaim, Electronic Arts, Brøderbund, Sony, Nintendo, and Davidson & Associates. Additional challenges and risks include focusing on improving the multiplayer capabilities of its games. Id Software believes that improved multiplayer technology will be the next true revolution in 3D interactive games.

Other

The company began in 1990 when John Carmack, John Romero, Tom Hall, and Adrian Carmack created the first game in the Commander Keen series, *Invasion of the Vorticons*. The three founders left their jobs and officially began Id Software on February 1, 1991. All four previously worked with Softdisk Publishing. CEO Jay Wilbur also previously worked at Softdisk.

Primary VCs/Outside Financing

100% internally funded.

KEY FACTS

Year Established:	1991
Employees:	13
Fiscal Year End:	December
Revenues FY '94:	$12.0m
Revenues FY '95:	$25.0m
Date of Next Financing:	n/a
Date of Last Financing:	n/a
Size of Last Financing:	n/a
Total Capital Raised:	n/a
Post Round Valuation:	n/a
Expected IPO Date:	n/a

ILLUSTRA INFORMATION TECHNOLOGIES

Address:	1111 Broadway
	Suite 2000
	Oakland, CA 94706
Telephone:	510/652-8000
Fax:	510/869-6388
E-mail:	info@illustra.com
Web site:	http://www.illustra.com
Industry:	Computers
Sector:	Enterprise & Client/Server Software
CEO:	Dick Williams
CFO:	Paul Siedschlag

Product Description

Illustra Information Technologies develops and supplies object-relational database software designed to manage video, audio, 2D and 3D spatial data, text, and numbers. Its modules snap into the server and manage specific types of data locally or over the World Wide Web. Illustra focuses on areas including financial services, multimedia, media distribution, government, and earth sciences. In August 1995 the company introduced a suite of development tools enabling users to create applications that integrate spreadsheets, images, and text with or without knowledge of programming languages. The pricing for the new tools ranges from $99 to $700 per user.

Market Strategy/Positioning

The company's mission is to be the leading worldwide supplier of media asset management systems and tools for applications in multimedia and entertainment, digital media distribution, and financial services. Illustra has strategic relationships with Silicon Graphics, Sun Microsystems, Intel, Nichimen, America Online, Fujitsu, PLS, and Avid Technology. Significant customers include Sun Microsystems, Tandem Corporation, Hewlett-Packard, ELECTROGIG, Fujitsu, Lehman Brothers, Merrill Lynch, and Morgan Stanley. The company's competitive advantages are its reputation as the first true multimedia base, an extensible database and unique access methods which extend in any direction, and a modular implementation. Illustra primarily competes against UniSQL. Additional challenges and risks include maintaining market focus and managing growth as the market need for object-relational database management systems increases.

Other

Illustra Information Technologies, founded in August 1992, represents the commercialization of the University of California's seven-year breakthrough POSTGRES database research project, developed under the direction of Dr. Michael Stonebraker at the University of California. Illustra shipped its first production release of its database system in August 1993. The company claims the Illustra Server is the world's first object-relational database management system. CEO Dick Williams was a vice president at IBM for 22 years; he left in December 1986 to become CEO of Digital Research. He turned the company around twice before a merg-

KEY FACTS

Year Established:	1992
Employees:	135
Fiscal Year End:	June
Revenues FY '94:	n/a
Revenues FY '95:	n/a
Date of Next Financing:	n/a
Date of Last Financing:	April 1995
Size of Last Financing:	$7.0m
Total Capital Raised:	$21.0m
Post Round Valuation:	n/a
Expected IPO Date:	1997

ILLUSTRA INFORMATION
TECHNOLOGIES

er with Novell in 1991, and then became executive vice president of worldwide sales and general manager of Desktop Systems Group. Mr. Williams retired in 1992 and joined Illustra in December of 1993.

Primary VCs/Outside Financing

Morgenthaler Ventures, Accel Partners, Oak Investment Partners, Sequoia Capital, and Trinity Ventures. Outside financing also from Roger Sipple (founder of Informix), Harvey Jones (founder and chairman of Synopsys), Dr. Michael Stonebraker (co-founder of Illustra), Gary Morgenthaler, and Dick Williams.

INDIVIDUAL

Address:	8 New England Executive Park West Burlington, MA 01803
Telephone:	617/273-6000
Fax:	617-273-6060
E-mail:	info@individual.com
Web site:	http://www.newspage.com
Industry:	Entertainment & Information
Sector:	Information Services
CEO:	Yosi Amram
CFO:	Bruce Glabe

Product Description

Individual develops online news and information database services, based on software licensed from Cornell University, called SMART. It scans more than 200 news sources, collects stories suited to each customer's profile, and then creates a customized report using desktop publishing technology. Its principal product, *First!*, is distributed daily to subscribers via fax, e-mail, or the Internet and World Wide Web. Its interactive news site, News-Page, filters over 15,000 stories from hundreds of news sources every night. Clients use Individual's products to track competitors, identify opportunities in sales, and stay on top of major trends affecting their particular market interests.

Market Strategy/Positioning

The company's mission is to spread knowledge by intelligently connecting electronic publishers and knowledge workers. Individual has strategic relationships with Folio, Apple, AT&T, Knight-Ridder, Gartner Group, Lotus, Motorola, and PRODIGY. Significant customers include most *Fortune* 500 companies. The company's competitive advantages are its timely information and attractive pricing. Individual primarily competes against Desktop Data and Sandpoint. Additional challenges and risks include creating innovative ideas to set the company apart in a very competitive market.

311

Other

Individual was founded in 1989 to connect electronic publishers and knowledge workers. The company is a founding member of the OCPS Committee. Individual subsidizes much of the costs of its successful NewsPage with targeted vendor sponsorships. CEO Yosi Amram was previously CEO at Rational Software and also worked at Aegis Fund, a high-tech venture capital firm in Boston. Before Individual, CFO Bruce Glabe was president of communications at BBN. Vice president of engineering Jacques Bouvard was most recently director of advanced systems technology at Honeywell Bull. Steve Case of America Online and Patrick Tierney of Knight-Ridder are on its board.

Primary VCs/Outside Financing

Aegis Fund, American Capital, Burr Egan Deleage & Co., Grace Ventures, Kleiner Perkins Caufield & Byers, VC Fund of New England, and Knight-Ridder.

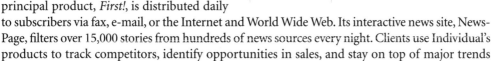

KEY FACTS

Year Established:	1989
Employees:	125
Fiscal Year End:	December
Revenues FY '94:	n/a
Revenues FY '95:	n/a
Date of Next Financing:	n/a
Date of Last Financing:	September 1993
Size of Last Financing:	$3.0m
Total Capital Raised:	$11.9m
Post Round Valuation:	$30.0m
Expected IPO Date:	n/a

INDUSTRIAL
LIGHT & MAGIC

Address:	P.O. Box 2459
	San Rafael, CA 94912
Telephone:	415/258-2000
Fax:	415/721-3540
E-mail:	n/a
Web site:	n/a
Industry:	Entertainment & Information
Sector:	Film & Entertainment Production
CEO:	Jim Morris (President)
CFO:	n/a

Product Description

Industrial Light & Magic develops cutting-edge visual effects serving the motion picture, commercial production, and theme park industries. ILM has produced visual effects for approximately 100 feature films, including *Forrest Gump, Jurassic Park, E.T.,* and the *Star Wars* trilogy. ILM has pioneered the development of motion control cameras, optical compositioning, and other advances in effects technology.

Market Strategy/Positioning

Industrial Light & Magic has strategic relationships with Silicon Graphics, SOFTIMAGE, Alias, Pixar, and Discreet Logic. Significant customers include Amblin Entertainment, Paramount, Universal, Warner Bros., and Tri-Star. The company's competitive advantage is its strong reputation as the pioneer of digital film production. The company has 14 years of experience and is the largest proprietary software company for computer graphics imagery. ILM focuses on more "high-end" projects because of the competition in digital work. Industrial Light & Magic primarily competes against Boss Films, Dream Quest, PDI, R/GA Digital Studios, and Digital Domain. Additional challenges and risks include getting projects that advance the industry as a whole.

Other

Industrial Light & Magic was created by George Lucas to supply himself as well as other directors and producers with the best visual effects possible. Since the 1980s, ILM has been the leader in using computer graphics and digital imaging in films and in developing breakthrough software techniques like morphing, enveloping, and film input scanning. ILM is part of the parent company Lucas Digital, which also runs Skywalker Sound. There are three Lucas companies: Lucas Digital, LucasArts Entertainment, and LucasFilm Ltd. The management consists of filmmakers and computer graphics professionals.

Primary VCs/Outside Financing

Owned by Lucas Digital, Ltd.

KEY FACTS

Year Established:	1975
Employees:	500
Fiscal Year End:	March
Revenues FY '94:	n/a
Revenues FY '95:	n/a
Date of Next Financing:	n/a
Date of Last Financing:	n/a
Size of Last Financing:	n/a
Total Capital Raised:	n/a
Post Round Valuation:	n/a
Expected IPO Date:	n/a

INFORMIX

Product Description

Informix products include distributed relational database management systems (RDBMS), application development tools for creating client/server production applications, and connectivity software that allows information to be shared transparently between PCs and mainframes within the corporate computing environment. Its product takes advantage of massively parallel and loosely coupled multiprocessor systems, which enables users to perform complex "what-if" queries on large databases. Informix also takes advantage of the trend toward combining databases into large data warehouses and transitioning the UNIX database management systems market into a 3-tier system (i.e. operating system, database, and application).

Address:	4100 Bohannon Drive Menlo Park, CA 94028
Telephone:	415/926-6300
Fax:	415/926-6593
E-mail:	info@informix.com
Web site:	http://www.informix.com
Industry:	Computers
Sector:	Enterprise & Client/Server Software
CEO:	Phillip E. White
CFO:	Howard H. Graham
Stock Exchange:	NASDAQ
Stock Symbol:	IFMX

Market Strategy/Positioning

The company's mission is to provide, through partnerships worldwide, the best technology and services to develop enterprise-wide data management applications for open systems. Informix has strategic relationships with SAP, PeopleSoft, Hewlett-Packard, IBM, and Sun Microsystems. Significant customers include Holiday Inn, AT&T, MCI, the U.K.'s Royal Air Force, GTE, Kuwait Petroleum, and Sears. The company's competitive advantages are its leading-edge parallel database technology and its strong strategic relationships. Informix primarily competes against Oracle, Sybase, Computer Associates, and Microsoft. Additional challenges and risks include continuing to provide leading edge solutions and increasing market share in a highly combative market.

313

Other

Informix was started in 1980 by Roger Sipple, a medical student who left his studies after he developed Hodgkin's disease. The company grew quickly and went public in 1986. Mr. Sipple hired Phillip White in 1989 after the company merged with Innovative Software, and Mr. Sipple left to start Visigenic in 1992. In recent years the company has increased its share of the RDBMS market at the expense of rival Sybase. CEO Phillip White was previously president of Wyse Technology and vice president of sales and marketing at Altos Computer Systems. Mr. White also spent 15 years at IBM in various sales and marketing positions.

KEY FACTS

Year Established:	1980
Employees:	2,700
Fiscal Year End:	December
Revenues FY '94:	$468.7m
Revenues FY '95:	$699.2m (estimate)
EPS '94:	$0.51
EPS '95:	$0.71 (estimate)
Shares Outstanding:	138.2m
Five-Year Growth Rate:	30%

INSOFT

Address:	Executive Park West 1
	Suite 307
	4718 Old Gettysburg Road
	Mechanicsburg, PA 17055
Telephone:	717/730-9501
Fax:	717/730-9504
E-mail:	info@insoft.com
Web site:	http://www.insoft.com
Industry:	Communications
Sector:	Information Highway Services
CEO:	Daniel Harple Jr.
CFO:	Scott Mumma

Product Description

InSoft is a worldwide provider of communications software and development tools, desktop conferencing, and distributed digital video solutions for UNIX and Windows systems. The company's products, which enable transparent digital convergence, are based on its open software architecture, Digital Video Everywhere (DVE). Its television application provides "CNN to the desktop." The company recently announced an open application development architecture for third-party and corporate developers.

Market Strategy/Positioning

The company's mission is to make DVE software architecture the worldwide desktop standard. InSoft has strategic relationships with AT&T, BellSouth, DEC, Hewlett-Packard, IBM, Newbridge, and Sprint. Significant customers include GE, Eastman Kodak, Sprint, the Department of Defense, Hughes Aircraft, Lehman Brothers, Bear Stearns, and NYNet. The company's competitive advantage is that it remains the only provider to address the heterogeneous enterprise desktop computer environment with multiplatform, fully interoperable solutions. InSoft primarily competes against Compression Labs, PictureTel, Sun Microsystems, and VTEL. Additional challenges and risks include taking products into mainstream deployment. Additionally, the influx of larger companies into nascent markets like collaborative computing and desktop conferencing makes it necessary for quality products to be introduced quickly.

Other

InSoft was formed in 1991 and has grown consistently. Sun Microsystems originally supported InSoft's software but then released its own videoconferencing applications. InSoft obtained backing from Hewlett-Packard and successfully attracted additional workstation producers. Co-founder, chairman, and CEO Daniel Harple held senior management positions with Raytheon, Naval Underwater Systems Center, Ingersoll-Rand, and AMP. Co-founder Richard Pizzaro is the company's lead software engineer and founded his own software consulting firm.

Primary VCs/Outside Financing

Edison Venture Fund, Fostin Capital, Now Enterprise Associates, Loyalhanna, and Patricof Ventures.

KEY FACTS

Year Established:	1991
Employees:	65
Fiscal Year End:	December
Revenues FY '94:	n/a
Revenues FY '95:	n/a
Date of Next Financing:	n/a
Date of Last Financing:	October 1994
Size of Last Financing:	$5.0m
Total Capital Raised:	n/a
Post Round Valuation:	$23.0m
Expected IPO Date:	1996

INTEL

Product Description

Intel designs, develops, manufactures, and markets advanced microcomputer components such as integrated circuits and microprocessors. Intel supplies the PC industry with chips, boards, systems, and software. Its microprocessor chips are also called central processing units (CPUs), the "brains" of a computer. Approximately 75% of all personal computers in use are based on Intel microprocessors.

Address:	2200 Mission College Boulevard Santa Clara, CA 95052
Telephone:	408/765-8080
Fax:	408/765-1402
E-mail:	n/a
Web site:	http://www.intel.com
Industry:	Computers
Sector:	Semiconductors
CEO:	Andrew Grove
CFO:	Andy Bryant
Stock Exchange:	NASDAQ
Stock Symbol:	INTC

Market Strategy/Positioning

Intel has strategic relationships with Oracle, AT&T Network Systems, Hybrid Networks, Tivoli, and Bay Networks. Significant customers include primarily IBM. The company's competitive advantage is its position as the largest semiconductor supplier in the world. Intel primarily competes against Apple, Motorola, IBM (PowerPC), and AMD. Additional challenges and risks include business conditions and growth in the personal computer industry, competitive factors such as rival chip architectures, imitators of the company's key microprocessors, price pressures, and ongoing litigation involving Intel's intellectual property.

315

Other

Intel was established in 1968 to realize the potential of large-scale integration (LSI) technology for silicon-based chips. The company initially supplied semiconductor memory for large computers and later began to develop the microprocessor designs that revolutionized the electronics industry. In 1971 Intel introduced the first microprocessor. IBM chose Intel's 8088 chip for its PC in 1981. Founders Robert Noyce, Gordon Moore, and CEO Andrew Grove were formerly Ph.D. engineers at Fairchild Semiconductor. When Intel was formed in 1968, Mr. Noyce and Mr. Grove focused on long-range planning, while Mr. Moore handled manufacturing. Robert Noyce became the company's first CEO and was succeeded by Mr. Grove in 1979.

KEY FACTS

Year Established:	1968
Employees:	32,600
Fiscal Year End:	December
Revenues FY '94:	$11.5b
Revenues FY '95:	n/a
EPS '94:	$2.62
EPS '95:	$4.20 (estimate)
Shares Outstanding:	828.2m
Five-Year Growth Rate:	18%

INTERPLAY
PRODUCTIONS

Address:	17922 Fitch Avenue
	Irvine, CA 92714
Telephone:	714/553-6655
Fax:	714/553-1406
E-mail:	info@interplay.com
Web site:	http://www.interplay.com
Industry:	Entertainment & Information
Sector:	Entertainment/Education Software
CEO:	Brian Fargo
CFO:	Steven "Chuck" Camps

Product Description

Interplay Productions is a publisher of entertainment and educational software and video games. It publishes titles for IBM, Macintosh, Amiga, 3DO, and other leading console game platforms. Its MacPlay division is devoted to producing educational programs solely for the Macintosh consumer. The company's Virtual Reality Sports division develops and publishes realistic sports software for both game console systems and PCs.

Market Strategy/Positioning

The company's mission is to remain one of the leading innovative software publishers, producing high-quality interactive entertainment titles while staying on the forefront of emerging multimedia technologies. Interplay has strategic relationships with I-MOTION, Mission Studios, Informative Graphics, Real World Entertainment, Great Wave, and Griffen Fathom. Significant customers include NeoStar, CompUSA, Toys'R'Us, Wal-Mart, Electronic Boutique, and Target. The company's competitive advantage is its being divisionalized by platform and by genre to ensure focus on strategic objectives. Interplay Productions primarily competes against Acclaim Entertainment, Electronic Arts, Davidson & Associates, Humongous Entertainment, MECC, Edmark, Maxis, Sony, Nintendo, and Id Software.

Other

Founded in 1983, Interplay Productions developed into an affiliate publisher in 1987 and emerged as an independent publisher in 1991. Interplay launched MacPlay, a division that creates Macintosh products, in early 1993 and the VR Sports division, which produces realistic sports software, in 1995. Interplay had its first acquisition in 1995 with its purchase of Shiny Entertainment, makers of the video game *Earthworm Jim*. CEO Brian Fargo founded the company in 1983 and has been programming game software since 1979. CFO/COO Chuck Camps previously managed all financial operations at Pratt Industries and also worked as a senior manager at Arthur Andersen.

Primary VCs/Outside Financing

Internally owned, with MCA holding a minority interest.

KEY FACTS

Year Established:	1983
Employees:	320
Fiscal Year End:	March
Revenues FY '94:	$80.0m
Revenues FY '95:	$110.0m
Date of Next Financing:	n/a
Date of Last Financing:	n/a
Size of Last Financing:	n/a
Total Capital Raised:	n/a
Post Round Valuation:	n/a
Expected IPO Date:	n/a

INTUIT

Product Description

Intuit develops, markets, and supports personal-finance, small-business-accounting, and tax-preparation software, as well as related supplies and electronic services that allow individuals and businesses to automate commonly performed financial tasks. The company claims to hold 70% of the market share across all platforms with its personal finance products, used by eight million consumers.

Address:	155 Linfield Avenue
	Menlo Park, CA 94026
Telephone:	415/322-0573
Fax:	415/329-6999
E-mail:	Bill_Campbell@Intuit.com
Web site:	n/a
Industry:	Computers
Sector:	Personal Productivity Software
CEO:	William V. Campbell
CFO:	William H. Lane, III
Stock Exchange:	NASDAQ
Stock Symbol:	INTU

Market Strategy/Positioning

The company's mission is to revolutionize how individuals, professionals, and small businesses manage their finances, by delivering innovative, automated financial solutions. Intuit has strategic relationships with Visa, American Express, Bank of Boston, Citibank, Chase Manhattan, First Chicago, First Interstate, Home Savings of America, Sanwa Bank California, Smith Barney, Union Bank, and Wells Fargo. Significant customers include individuals and small business users, who obtain the software through retailers such as Egghead, Price Costco, and Best Buy. The company's competitive advantage is its domination of the personal finance/tax software market for all key products on all platforms. Its product Quicken is market leader; Microsoft attempted to buy Intuit in its effort to enter online financial services. The October 13, 1994, merger agreement between Intuit and Microsoft was terminated by Intuit on May 20, 1995. Intuit received from Microsoft a $46 million termination payment reflected in fourth quarter earnings (July 31, 1995). Intuit primarily competes against Microsoft, Computer Associates, Deluxe, H&R Block, Mail Boxes Etc., Moore, ADP, NationsBank, Novell, NEBS, Visa, Citibank, Fidelity Investments, ValueLine, and Charles Schwab. Additional challenges and risks include the market for the company's products, which is intensely competitive and subject to rapid change, characterized by constant pressures to reduce prices, to incorporate new product features, and to accelerate the release of new products and product enhancements.

Other

In 1983 founders Scott Cook and Tom Proulx set out to make financial software so intuitive that people would succeed with it immediately. In 1984 they introduced Quicken, which has become the most successful personal finance program ever created. *Inc.* Magazine named Mr. Cook and Mr. Proulx recipients of its Entrepreneur of the Year Award in 1992. Intuit had its IPO in March 1994 and acquired ChipSoft in December of that same year. In July

KEY FACTS

Year Established:	1983
Employees:	2,320
Fiscal Year End:	July
Revenues FY '94:	$223.4m
Revenues FY '95:	$396.8m
EPS '94:	$(5.45)
EPS '95:	$(1.18)
Shares Outstanding:	21.5m
Five-Year Growth Rate:	34%

INTUIT

1994 Intuit acquired National Payment Clearinghouse and in August 1994 purchased Parsons Technology. Additionally, the company partnered with 19 leading financial institutions to provide financial services. Chairman Scott Cook spent three years at Procter & Gamble and four years at Bain & Co. In 1983 he decided to apply his brand management expertise to create personal financial software. CEO Bill Campbell was formerly executive vice president of Apple's marketing organization, president of Claris, and president of GO.

ITRON

Product Description

Itron is a full-service supplier of data acquisition and wireless communications products for meter reading and related data management needs of electric, gas, and water utility companies. The company offers products for automatic meter reading, distribution automation, and demand-side management applications.

Address:	2818 North Sullivan Road
	Spokane, WA 99216
Telephone:	509/924-9900
Fax:	509/891-3355
E-mail:	billw@qmail.itron.com
Web site:	http://www.itron.com
Industry:	Communications
Sector:	Wireless Communications
CEO:	John Humphreys
CFO:	Larry A. Panattoni (acting)
Stock Exchange:	NASDAQ
Stock Symbol:	ITRI

Market Strategy/Positioning

The company's mission is to be the leading provider of superior system solutions that combine data acquisitions and communication technologies to meet the changing needs of utility companies worldwide. Itron has a strategic relationship with Scientific-Atlanta. Significant customers include Duke Power, Georgia Power, Midwest Gas, Northeast Utilities, Pacific Gas & Electric, and PECO Energy. The company's competitive advantage is its pioneered efforts in automated meter reading systems; Itron is said to hold about 60% of that market. Itron primarily competes against Cellnet Data Systems. An additional challenge for the company is reconciling higher spending on development without a parallel gain in earnings.

319

Other

Itron was incorporated in 1977 to develop a portable computer system for utility industry on-site billing. In 1983 the company developed an electronic data capture system built around the DataCap H. Its DOS-based hand-helds were added in 1992 through the acquisition of Husky Computers. CEO John Humphreys was formerly president of Datachecker Systems, a subsidiary of National Semiconductor. Acting CFO Larry Panattoni joined Itron in 1990 as vice president of manufacturing. Previously, Mr. Panattoni spent 21 years at National Semiconductor.

KEY FACTS

Year Established:	1977
Employees:	750
Fiscal Year End:	December
Revenues FY '94:	$120.7m
Revenues FY '95:	n/a
EPS '94:	$0.67
EPS '95:	$0.80 (estimate)
Shares Outstanding:	12.1m
Five-Year Growth Rate:	25%

Product Description

IUMA (Internet Underground Music Archive) is the first and largest high-fidelity Internet music archive. Using a visual interface, users browse through music on IUMA's Web site as they would in record stores, by genre, band, or artist, as well as by release date, artists' location, and record label. Listeners may purchase tapes and CDs, post public reviews of bands, and e-mail the bands directly. The company's Web site receives 300,000 "hits" a day.

Address:	303 Potrero Street
	Suite 7A
	Santa Cruz, CA 95060
Telephone:	408/426-4862
Fax:	408/426-5918
E-mail:	asavara@iuma.com
Web site:	http://www.iuma.com
Industry:	Entertainment & Information
Sector:	Online Services
CEO:	Brandee Selck
CFO:	Jeff Patterson

Market Strategy/Positioning

The company's mission is to allow the music maker to have as close to a one-to-one relationship with the music listener as possible. IUMA has a strategic relationship with Silicon Graphics. Significant customers include major music labels and music magazines. IUMA offers more than 600 independent, unsigned artists online to an estimated 30 million people. The company's competitive advantages are its technology, creativity, and established link to the artists who form its base audience. IUMA Consulting is an additional branch of the company. IUMA primarily competes against startup service providers Organic Online and On Ramp. Additional challenges include actively participating in the restructuring of the music industry.

Other

The release of IUMA 2.0 established the company as the leader in how to present content. The company hopes this release will mark its transition into a standard-setting company. Founders Rob Lord and Jeff Patterson were computer science students at UC Santa Cruz and have been in discussions with venture capitalists over the past year.

KEY FACTS

Year Established:	1993
Employees:	25
Fiscal Year End:	December
Revenues FY '94:	$0.0
Revenues FY '95:	$0.0
Date of Next Financing:	n/a
Date of Last Financing:	n/a
Size of Last Financing:	n/a
Total Capital Raised:	n/a
Post Round Valuation:	n/a
Expected IPO Date:	n/a

KLA INSTRUMENTS

Product Description

KLA Instruments is a leading supplier of inspection systems to improve chip yields. It pioneered the wafer inspection (56% of sales) and reticle inspection equipment (12% of sales) markets, and maintains an estimated 85% worldwide market share. The company's growth is driven by a new system that enables real-time data acquisition during the manufacturing process. KLA also supplies wafer probers (12% of sales) and metrology systems (12% of sales).

Address:	160 Rio Robles
	San Jose, CA 95134
Telephone:	408/434-4200
Fax:	215/659-7588
E-mail:	n/a
Web site:	http://hrweb.kla.com
Industry:	Computers
Sector:	Semiconductor Equipment
CEO:	Kenneth Levy
CFO:	Robert J. Boehlke
Stock Exchange:	NASDAQ
Stock Symbol:	KLAC

Market Strategy/Positioning

KLA Instruments has a strategic relationship with Tokyo Electron. The company's competitive advantages are its sales to virtually all the world's semiconductor manufacturers, and a worldwide organization of over 50 applications engineers who serve as yield management consultants to KLA's customers. KLA Instruments primarily competes against Tencor.

Other

Kenneth Levy co-founded KLA Instruments in 1975, serving as president, CEO, and director of the company until 1991, when he became chairman. Since 1993 Mr. Levy has served as a director of Ultratech Stepper and as a director of Network Peripherals. CFO Robert Boehlke joined KLA in 1983 as vice president and general manager of the RAPID Division. He was elected COO in 1989 and CFO in 1990.

 321

KEY FACTS

Year Established:	1976
Employees:	1,300
Fiscal Year End:	June
Revenues FY '94:	$243.8m
Revenues FY '95:	$442.4m
EPS '94:	$1.35
EPS '95:	$2.38
Shares Outstanding:	23.34m
Five-Year Growth Rate:	26%

KNIGHT-RIDDER

Address:	One Herald Plaza
	Miami, FL 33132-1693
Telephone:	305/376-3800
Fax:	305/376-3876
E-mail:	n/a
Web site:	http://www.dialog.com
Industry:	Entertainment & Information
Sector:	Information Provider
CEO:	Anthony Ridder
CFO:	Ross Jones
Stock Exchange:	NYSE
Stock Symbol:	KRI

Product Description

Knight-Ridder is a newspaper publishing and information services company. It publishes 29 daily newspapers which reach 100 million people in 135 countries. It offers access to summaries of more than 100,000 journals and the complete text from over 3,000 publications. Its financial information service has 28,000 subscribers, and accesses 40 international exchanges and 10-year historical price data. It recently established a new media center primarily for its Internet activities. The center also offers software integration, installation, training, and advertising applications for all its newspapers.

Market Strategy/Positioning

Knight-Ridder has strategic relationships with Bell Atlantic, Tribune, America Online, Andrews, and McMeel. It acquired stake in Netscape and has minority interests in Individual, Newspapers First, Personal Library Software, *Seattle Times*, Southeast Paper Manufacturing, TKR Cable, and U.S. Order. The company's competitive advantages are its strong alliances and profitable investments. Knight-Ridder primarily competes against Advance, American Business Information, Bloomberg, Dow Jones, Dun & Bradstreet, Gannet, Hearst, Information America, McGraw-Hill, *The New York Times*, Reed Elsevier, Reuters, SGS Thomson, Tribune, and Washington Post.

Other

Knight Newspapers began in 1903 with the *Akron Beacon Journal*, and Ridder publications began in 1892 with a German paper, the *Staats-Zeitung*. Knight-Ridder was formed in 1974 after the merger of Knight Newspapers and Ridder Publications. During the 1970s and '80s the company entered television, radio, and book publishing. In 1992 Knight-Ridder and Tribune teamed up to provide business news electronically. It also recently purchased Lesher, a chain of California newspapers, for $360 million. Anthony Ridder was appointed chairman and CEO July 21, 1995. He had been president of the company since 1989 and was president of the newspaper division from 1986 to 1989. He also served as publisher of the *San Jose Mercury News* from 1977 to 1986. CFO Ross Jones has held his position since 1993 and was previously vice president and treasurer of Reader's Digest Association.

KEY FACTS

Year Established:	1974
Employees:	20,000
Fiscal Year End:	December
Revenues FY '94:	$2.65b
Revenues FY '95:	n/a
EPS '94:	$3.15
EPS '95:	$3.49 (estimate)
Shares Outstanding:	55.0m
Five-Year Growth Rate:	11%

KNOWLEDGE ADVENTURE

Address:	4502 Dyer Street
	La Crescenta, CA 91214
Telephone:	818/542-4200
Fax:	818/542-4205
E-mail:	info@adventure.com
Web site:	http://www.adventure.com
Industry:	Entertainment & Information
Sector:	Entertainment/Education Software
CEO:	Bill Gross
CFO:	Frank Greico

Product Description

Knowledge Adventure develops and markets educational multimedia applications with proprietary movie technology, an interactive reference engine, a hypertext linking engine, and compression technology. Its products include an adventure series, reference titles, children's creativity products, and curriculum/skills products. The company's staff is made up of former reporters, producers, TV writers, computer engineers, and physicists.

Market Strategy/Positioning

The company's mission is to challenge the boundaries of electronic exploration by delivering products that foster a highly interactive, multisensory learning experience. Knowledge Adventure has strategic relationships with Steven Spielberg, Random House, and Marvel Entertainment Group. Significant customers include retailers such as Ingram, Merisel, Egghead, and CompUSA. The company's competitive advantages are its proprietary compression technology, its interactive movie technologies, and its strong distribution. Knowledge Adventure primarily competes against 3DO, Accolade, Brøderbund, The Learning Company, Davidson & Associates, Edmark, Humongous Entertainment, Walt Disney, Time Warner, Sierra On-Line, MECC, Maxis, Interplay Productions, and Electronic Arts. Additional challenges and risks include continually producing compelling educational software in a competitive market.

323

Other

Knowledge Adventure was founded in 1991 by Bill Gross. In June 1994 it announced an agreement with film director Steven Spielberg to produce educational multimedia software, and in August of 1994 an alliance with Random House was announced. Before founding Knowledge Adventure, CEO Bill Gross was employed at Lotus Development, where he developed a variety of products, including HAL and Magellan. President Ruth Olte was formerly president and COO at Discovery Networks, which manages and operates *The Discovery Channel* and *The Learning Channel*. Frank Greico was previously at Baker & Taylor Software as CFO.

Primary VCs/Outside Financing

Mohr Davidow, AT&T Ventures, Mayfield Fund, Software Ventures, Integral Capital Partners, Stanford University, Mr. Steven Spielberg, Viacom, Mr. Michael Dell, and Random House.

KEY FACTS

Year Established:	1991
Employees:	150
Fiscal Year End:	March
Revenues FY '94:	$35.0m
Revenues FY '95:	n/a
Date of Next Financing:	n/a
Date of Last Financing:	June 1992
Size of Last Financing:	$1.5m
Total Capital Raised:	$2.5m
Post Round Valuation:	n/a
Expected IPO Date:	n/a

RESEARCH

Address:	4650 Cushing Parkway
	Fremont, CA 94538
Telephone:	510/572-0200
Fax:	510/572-1560
E-mail:	n/a
Web site:	n/a
Industry:	Computers
Sector:	Semiconductor Equipment
CEO:	Roger Emerick
CFO:	Henk Evenhuis
Stock Exchange:	NASDAQ
Stock Symbol:	LRCX

Product Description

Lam Research manufactures etch and chemical vapor deposition (CVD) equipment for the worldwide semiconductor industry. The company is the fourth largest equipment provider globally and the biggest supplier in the dry etch market, with an estimated 34% market share. Its advanced transformer-coupled plasma products, crucial to achieve requirements for next-generation microprocessors, now account for one-third of bookings. The company's new products, its chemical vapor deposition system and its flat panel display etch equipment, are scheduled to ship in 1996.

Market Strategy/Positioning

The company's mission is to offer thin film process solutions. Lam Research has strategic relationships with U.S. Display Consortium, DuPont, and Air Products. Significant customers include all major semiconductor manufacturers. The company's competitive advantages are its etch and chemical vapor deposition equipment, which covers a broad range of chip production requirements, from the simplest chips to advanced sub-micron memory chips. Lam Research primarily competes against Applied Materials, Hitachi, Tokyo Electronics, and Novellus. Additional challenges and risks include managing market fluctuations and achieving a global presence. Lam Research is unique in that its patented transformer-coupled plasma source can produce very uniform etch results with challenging high-density design structures.

Other

Founded in 1980, Lam Research was the first recipient of the IBM Technology Product Division's Customer Satisfaction Award in 1993. Chairman and CEO Roger Emerick joined Lam in 1982. Previously, he served as senior vice president of both Optical Specialties and Cobilt (a division of Computervision). Senior vice president and CFO Henk Evenhuis was formerly vice president of finance and administration at Corvus Systems. Before Corvus, he held executive positions at Trimedia, Ferix, and Benson.

324

KEY FACTS

Year Established:	1980
Employees:	3,700
Fiscal Year End:	June
Revenues FY '94:	$493.7m
Revenues FY '95:	$810.6m
EPS '94:	$1.55
EPS '95:	$2.86
Shares Outstanding:	27.3m
Five-Year Growth Rate:	25%

LEGATO SYSTEMS

Address:	3145 Porter Drive
	Palo Alto, CA 94304
Telephone:	415/812-6000
Fax:	415/812-6032
E-mail:	n/a
Web site:	http://www.legato.com
Industry:	Computers
Sector:	Enterprise & Client/Server Software
CEO:	Louis Cole
CFO:	Gary Thompson
Stock Exchange:	NASDAQ
Stock Symbol:	LGTO

Product Description

Legato Systems develops and markets network storage management software for heterogeneous client/server computing environments. Server and desktop computer platforms include DOS, NetWare, OS/2, UNIX, Windows, and Windows NT. The storage management server can operate on NetWare and on UNIX from numerous vendors. The company licenses its source code to leading computer systems and software developers; it also has a private label reseller agreement with SunSoft.

Market Strategy/Positioning

The company's mission is to create an integrated set of solutions centered around storage management that enhance and simplify network computing as a whole. Legato Systems has strategic relationships with Data General, ICL, Hewlett-Packard, Silicon Graphics, Siemens, UNISYS, and Sun Microsystems. Significant customers include Boeing, Ericsson, Lehman Brothers, Oracle, Shell Oil, 3Com, UPS, the U.S. Navy, and Xerox. The company's competitive advantage is its technical leadership in network storage management because of its heterogeneity, scalability, performance, and ease-of-use. Legato Systems primarily competes against Cheyenne, Seagate, Symantec, and Aracada on the NetWare platform; against Peripheral Devices, Software Moghuls, EMC2, and Spectra Logic on the Solaris/SunOS platform; and against IBM on the AIX platform. Additional challenges and risks include the company's dependence on one product and reliance on resellers, as well as rapid technological change and competition from new entrants.

325

Other

Legato Systems was incorporated in 1989; its first product was a network file server. In late 1992 the company decided to phase out its hardware products and focus on its network storage management software. Before Legato, CEO Louis Cole was executive vice president at Novell and president of CXI, acquired by Novell in 1987. CFO Gary Thompson was previously at Novell as vice president of finance and information systems. He also worked at CXI and Arthur Andersen for 10 years.

KEY FACTS

Year Established:	1989
Employees:	130
Fiscal Year End:	December
Revenues FY '94:	$16.4m
Revenues FY '95:	$26.9m (estimate)
EPS '94:	$0.27
EPS '95:	$0.60 (estimate)
Shares Outstanding:	2.05m
Five-Year Growth Rate:	35%

LOOKINGGLASS
TECHNOLOGIES

Address:	100 Cambridge Park Drive
	Cambridge, MA 02140
Telephone:	617/441-6333
Fax:	617/441-3946
E-mail:	n/a
Web site:	http://www.vie.com/lgt
Industry:	Entertainment & Information
Sector:	Entertainment/Education Software
CEO:	Paul Neurath
CFO:	Jeff Kalowski

Product Description

LookingGlass Technologies develops entertainment and simulation software for PC and video game systems. It is focused on creating processor-intensive, real-time 3D and virtual reality software. Its first title published in-house is a flight simulator that allows "pilots" to capture the sensation of flying. The simulator uses a physics system that lets it model the air around the plane, increasing flight accuracy as users soar over photorealistic images of terrain such as Alaska, Maine, and France. Its titles have been reviewed as the closest a game developer has come to offering virtual reality on a PC.

Market Strategy/Positioning

The company's mission is to forge a new medium. Its craft, a synthesis of art and technology, allows consumers to shape new worlds to explore. LookingGlass Technologies has a strategic relationship with Viacom New Media to develop several entertainment titles on multiple platforms. Significant customers include Sega, Electronics Arts, Origin Systems, and Access. The company's competitive advantage is its expertise and experience with 3D technologies. LookingGlass Technologies primarily competes against Id Software, Acclaim Entertainment, Sega, Magic Edge, Nintendo, Fightertown, and Electronic Arts. Additional challenges and risks include the constant change of video game platforms and consumer tastes in what games they want to play. LookingGlass Technologies is unique as one of the first gaming companies to release fully localized versions of its products simultaneously in the U.S. and in Europe.

Other

The company was founded in 1992 through a merger of Blue Sky Productions and Lerner Research. President and CEO Paul Neurath began his career as the developer of a 3D space combat game published by Sir-Tech. Mr. Neurath then worked for two years as a consultant with Origin and in 1990 founded Blue Sky Productions, a developer of entertainment titles. Ned Lerner, founder of Lerner Research, developed the ground-breaking *Chuck Yeager's Flight Trainer*.

Primary VCs/Outside Financing

Matrix Partners and Institutional Venture Partners.

KEY FACTS

Year Established:	1992
Employees:	70
Fiscal Year End:	March
Revenues FY '94:	n/a
Revenues FY '95:	n/a
Date of Next Financing:	n/a
Date of Last Financing:	August 1995
Size of Last Financing:	n/a
Total Capital Raised:	$3.8m
Post Round Valuation:	n/a
Expected IPO Date:	1997/1998

LSI LOGIC

Address:	1551 McCarthy Boulevard Milpitas, CA 95035
Telephone:	408/433-8000
Fax:	408/433-7715
E-mail:	info@lsil.com
Web site:	http://www.lsil.com
Industry:	Computers
Sector:	Semiconductors
CEO:	Wilfred J. Corrigan
CFO:	Albert A. Pimentel
Stock Exchange:	NYSE
Stock Symbol:	LSI

Product Description

LSI Logic designs and manufactures application-specific integrated circuits (ASICs) that allows system-level integration: the process of integrating complex electronic systems on a single chip. The company focuses on high-margin ASICs for vertical markets such as telecommunications, networking, workstations, digital video, file servers, and multimedia. Its products include 32-bit RISC microprocessors, single-chip ATM modules and Ethernet solutions, and video compression chips. The company's system-on-a-chip approach reduces costs and time-to-market for its clients. LSI Logic owns two manufacturing facilities and recently started construction on a third in Oregon.

Market Strategy/Positioning

LSI Logic has strategic relationships with Sony, Hewlett-Packard, Cisco, Sun Microsystems, and Silicon Graphics. Significant customers include Alcaltel, AT&T, Compaq, DEC, IBM, Intel, Matsushita, Newbridge Networks, and Siemens. The company's competitive advantages are its ASIC methodology with leading-edge deep sub-micron process technology, high-level system design expertise, manufacturing abilities, proprietary product libraries, and computer-aided design tools. LSI Logic primarily competes against Fujitsu, Toshiba, NEC, AT&T, Motorola, Texas Instruments, and VLSI Technology. Additional challenges and risks include competition from diversified electronics companies, and the ability to migrate expertise to new process technologies and manufacture these designs in a cost-effective manner.

327

Other

LSI Logic was founded in 1980 during the high-capacity surplus in the semiconductor industry. LSI designed chips manufactured elsewhere; recently the company has de-emphasized the chip business and refocused on designing high complexity ASIC for industry leaders in several vertical markets. CEO Wilfred Corrigan is a founder and one of the pioneers of the semiconductor industry. He began at Motorola and headed the transistor department. Mr. Corrigan then moved to Fairchild where he became president and chief executive officer.

KEY FACTS

Year Established:	1980
Employees:	3,750
Fiscal Year End:	December
Revenues FY '94:	$901.8m
Revenues FY '95:	n/a
EPS '94:	$0.98
EPS '95:	$1.64 (estimate)
Shares Outstanding:	121.4m
Five-Year Growth Rate:	23%

LUCASARTS
ENTERTAINMENT

Product Description

LucasArts Entertainment develops and publishes interactive entertainment software and educational multimedia software. It incorporates cinematic elements in storytelling, characters, and settings. The company has a proprietary interactive sound system, and it publishes on multiple platforms, including CD-ROM, PCs, and video game consoles. Its titles include *Star Wars* and *Indiana Jones* derivatives, as well as *Sam & Max* and *Full Throttle*. Its products retail for $20–$55.

Address:	P.O. Box 10307
	San Rafael, CA 94912
Telephone:	415/472-3400
Fax:	415/444-8240
E-mail:	n/a
Web site:	http://www.lucasarts.com
Industry:	Entertainment & Information
Sector:	Entertainment/Education Software
CEO:	Jack Sorensen
CFO:	n/a

Market Strategy/Positioning

LucasArts has strategic relationships with Apple, The National Geographic Society, Visa, and The National Audubon Society. Significant customers include Nintendo, Sony, Sega, and 3DO. The company's competitive advantages are its name recognition, built-in familiarity for its titles on the market (S*tarWars*), and a creative workforce. LucasArts holds the second largest market share for computer entertainment software companies. LucasArts Entertainment primarily competes against Sierra On-Line, Brøderbund, Maxis, Edmark, Davidson & Associates, Acclaim Entertainment, and Electronic Arts. Additional challenges and risks include further developing this branch of the business to succeed in the competitive industry of entertainment and education software.

328

Other

LucasArts was founded in 1982 by George Lucas to provide an interactive branch to his vision of a state-of-the-art entertainment company. LucasArts is continually on the cutting edge of visual effects, 3D animation, live-action video, and interactive digital sound. George Lucas is a strong believer in the education process for children and has focused this branch of his business on creating innovative educational games for kids.

Primary VCs/Outside Financing

100% internally funded.

KEY FACTS

Year Established:	1982
Employees:	160
Fiscal Year End:	March
Revenues FY '94:	n/a
Revenues FY '95:	n/a
Date of Next Financing:	n/a
Date of Last Financing:	n/a
Size of Last Financing:	n/a
Total Capital Raised:	n/a
Post Round Valuation:	n/a
Expected IPO Date:	n/a

MACROMEDIA

Address:	600 Townsend Street
	Suite 310W
	San Francisco, CA 94103
Telephone:	415/252-2000
Fax:	415/626-0554
E-mail:	macropr@macromedia.com
Web site:	http://www.macromedia.com
Industry:	Computers
Sector:	Personal Productivity Software
CEO:	John (Bud) Colligan
CFO:	Richard B. Wood
Stock Exchange:	NASDAQ
Stock Symbol:	MACR

Product Description

Macromedia develops multimedia authoring tools for the Windows and Macintosh platforms and sells digital arts software. Macromedia's products, which allow multiplatform development, have been used in creating more than 60% of all Macintosh multimedia titles. Macromedia offers a paint program, special-effects graphics, frame-by-frame animation, two channels of sound, and scripting language. It also has 3D tools, sound edit software, and easy-to-use business and education presentation software. The company's products include Macromedia Director, Macromedia Freehand, Authorware, and MacroModel.

Market Strategy/Positioning

The company's mission is to be the leading provider of multimedia and digital arts tools and services that enable creative, business, and learning professionals to revolutionize the way people learn and communicate. Macromedia has strategic relationships with Netscape, Organic Online, and Silicon Graphics to expand its presence in the Internet market. Significant customers include American Airlines, Hewlett-Packard, Procter & Gamble, 3M, Nike, Ernst & Young, Levis, the U.S. Department of Defense, the CIA, and NASA. One of the company's competitive advantages is its Digital Design Studio, through which Macromedia enables business and learning professionals to integrate various media elements into interactive presentations, commercial CD-ROM titles, educational curriculum, corporate training materials, informational kiosks, and printed graphics. Macromedia primarily competes against Asymetrix, Apple, Adobe, and Autodesk. Additional challenges and risks include remaining ahead of the segmented competition from companies with strong products for either Windows or Macintosh. Macromedia is the only company with a cross-platform line of products for multimedia and digital art development. Macromedia offers the only off-the-shelf tools that support cross-platform authoring and playback on Windows and Macintosh PCs. As the market expands, Macromedia will add support for other important multimedia platforms.

KEY FACTS

Year Established:	1992
Employees:	270
Fiscal Year End:	March
Revenues FY '94:	$29.9m
Revenues FY '95:	$48.4m
EPS '94:	$0.29
EPS '95:	$0.48
Shares Outstanding:	15.5m
Five-Year Growth Rate:	30%

Other

Macromedia was formed in April 1992 through the merger of Authorware and MacroMind/Paracomp. Authorware began operations in 1987. MacroMind, founded in 1984, merged with Paracomp in 1991 to

MACROMEDIA

form MacroMind/Paracomp. Macromedia grew from a vision that computers would have a strong impact on the art of communication. The company extended its vision further by acquiring Altsys, developer of Freehand, in January 1995. President and CEO John Colligan was previously president and CEO at Authorware before the merger. Before Authorware, he held various senior positions at Apple and was instrumental in launching the Macintosh in 1983. CFO Richard Wood was CFO, vice president of operations, and secretary of MacroMind from July 1990 until the formation of Macromedia. Before that, he was CFO at Altos Computer Systems.

330

MAGIC EDGE

Address:	1245 Spacepark Way Mountain View, CA 94043
Telephone:	415/254-5500
Fax:	415/965-2703
E-mail:	n/a
Web site:	n/a
Industry:	Entertainment & Information
Sector:	Entertainment/Education Software
CEO:	Michael P. Chan
CFO:	Amir Ameri

Product Description

Magic Edge designs, equips, and licenses high-quality, technology-based entertainment centers. The company has developed a proprietary, full-motion simulation capsule that features advanced graphics and fully interactive software. In addition, Magic Edge has developed theme simulation centers, called Magic Edge Centers, that provide a full entertainment experience by incorporating networked capsules, theatrical effects, and restaurant facilities.

Market Strategy/Positioning

The company's mission is to become the leading designer and premier provider of motion capsules and software to interactive simulation centers and theme parks worldwide. Magic Edge has strategic relationships with Namco Cybertainment, Village Nine Leisure, Silicon Graphics, Paradigm Simulations, and Parker Hannifin. The company's competitive advantages are a high-quality simulation experience and two patents that provide claim coverage for various aspects of the capsules. It has centers in California, Japan, and Australia. Magic Edge primarily competes against Fightertown, Virtual World Entertainment, Virtuality, Iwerks, and Sega. Additional challenges and risks include reducing product costs, raising sufficient capital, gaining market acceptance, and reducing dependence on high-quality software. Magic Edge is unique in producing texture-mapped graphics for its simulation rides.

Other

Established in 1990, Magic Edge built its first capsule in 1992 and opened its first centers in Tokyo and Mountain View in July and August of 1994, respectively. CEO Michael Chan has over twenty years experience in marketing, sales, and business development. Amir Ameri has over 15 years of experience in finance and investments with Occidental Petroleum, Castle & Cooke, IBC, and Pako International.

Primary VCs/Outside Financing

Namco Cybertainment and NAL.

KEY FACTS

Year Established:	1990
Employees:	35
Fiscal Year End:	December
Revenues FY '94:	$3.9m
Revenues FY '95:	$4.5m
Date of Next Financing:	1996
Date of Last Financing:	1995
Size of Last Financing:	$10.0m
Total Capital Raised:	$2.4m
Post Round Valuation:	$20.0m
Expected IPO Date:	Q1 1997

MAGNET
INTERACTIVE STUDIOS

Address:	3255 Grace Street NW
	Washington, DC 20007
Telephone:	202/625-IIII
Fax:	202/625-1352
E-mail:	webmaster@magnet.com
Web site:	http://www.magnet.com
Industry:	Entertainment & Information
Sector:	Film & Entertainment Production
CEO:	Basel Dalloul
CFO:	Greg Johnson (CTO)

Product Description

Magnet Interactive develops applications for various multimedia platforms as well as for online and broadband network platforms. Its production teams use a number of authoring tools to create and publish multimedia programs. Magnet creates filmed content in resolutions ranging from cinematic 35mm to low-resolution cinepak QuickTime movies. It also creates high-end animation and special effects using a variety of software on Silicon Graphics workstations and Macintosh stations. It offers services including storyboard, video, interface, and graphic design, as well as 2D print and pre-press packaging, movie digitization, image and video compressing, animation, rendering, and morphing.

Market Strategy/Positioning

The company's mission is to be the premier interactive multimedia development studio by creating revolutionary products for corporate markets. Magnet Interactive has strategic relationships with Alias, Apple, IBM, Kaleida Labs, Macromedia, SOFTIMAGE, 3DO, and Silicon Graphics. Significant customers include NYNEX, Nations Fund, Dow Jones, Peace Corps, KPMG Peat Marwick, Wells Fargo, and L.L. Bean. The company's competitive advantages are its diverse management background and the company's ability to invest in state-of-the-art technology to provide its employees with the latest tools. Magnet Interactive primarily competes against Industrial Light & Magic, R/GA Digital Studios, PDI, Digital Domain, and (Colossal) Pictures.

Other

Magnet Interactive was founded in 1989 as a progressive print and 3D design firm, but as it saw the potential in multimedia, the company became dedicated to becoming a full-service interactive development studio. Co-founder and CEO Basel Dalloul has extensive background in international business and electronic media. Chief technical director and senior creative director Greg Johnson has 13 years of experience in the design industry and studied design at top international schools including Parsons School of Design in Italy and the Corcoran School of Art in Washington, DC.

Primary VCs/Outside Financing

100% owned by Millennium Group.

KEY FACTS

Year Established:	1989
Employees:	210
Fiscal Year End:	December
Revenues FY '94:	n/a
Revenues FY '95:	n/a
Date of Next Financing:	n/a
Date of Last Financing:	n/a
Size of Last Financing:	n/a
Total Capital Raised:	n/a
Post Round Valuation:	n/a
Expected IPO Date:	n/a

MATSUSHITA

Product Description

Matsushita manufactures electronic products for home, industrial, and commercial uses. Its principal product categories include video equipment, audio equipment, home appliances, communication and industrial equipment, electronic components, and entertainment. The company's products are marketed worldwide under the brand names National, Panasonic, Technics, and Quasar; it also owns MCA Universal Studios.

Address:	U.S. Headquarters
	One Panasonic Way
	Secaucus, NJ 07094
Telephone:	201/348-7000
Fax:	201/348-7579
E-mail:	n/a
Web site:	http://www.mei.co.jp
Industry:	Entertainment & Information
Sector:	Consumer Electronics
CEO:	Yoichi Morishita (President)
CFO:	Motoi Matsuda
Stock Exchange:	NYSE
Stock Symbol:	MC

Market Strategy/Positioning

Matsushita has strategic relationships with 3DO, General Magic, Siemens, and Sears. Matsushita is also engaged in many different joint research projects with Carnegie-Mellon University, Massachusetts Institute of Technology, Stanford University, the University of California at Berkeley, Tokyo University, Kyoto University, Osaka University, and the Japanese Ministry of International Trade and Industry. The company's competitive advantage is its leading role in producing consumer electronics around the world. Matsushita primarily competes against Sony, Compaq, Fujitsu, IBM, 3M, Motorola, NEC, News Corp., Oki, Philips, Samsung, Sanyo, and Sharp. Additional challenges and risks include effectively steering its giant consumer electronics corporation onto the faster-paced tracks of the multimedia industry.

333

Other

In 1918 Konosuke Matsushita founded Matsushita Electric Industrial as a small producer of affordable home electronic products. The company opened its first American sales office in New York City in 1959, and the Panasonic brand name for lightweight transistor radios was introduced in 1961. In 1974 the company established Quasar as a TV manufacturing operation in Illinois. Matsushita has since expanded to include 17 factories and nine research and development labs. The company moved into the entertainment business through its acquisition of MCA in 1990; however, in June 1995 Matsushita sold an 80% interest in MCA to Seagram, leaving the Matsushita with 20% ownership of MCA. Yoichi Morishita joined Matsushita Electric in 1957. In the early 1990s Mr. Morishita served as head of the living business group and executive vice president before becoming president of the company in 1993.

KEY FACTS

Year Established:	1918
Employees:	254,100
Fiscal Year End:	March
Revenues FY '94:	$64.3b
Revenues FY '95:	$70.0b
EPS '94:	$1.14
EPS '95:	$4.14
Shares Outstanding:	2.1b
Five-Year Growth Rate:	10%

MAXIS

Address:	2121 North California Boulevard Suite 600 Walnut Creek, CA 94596-3572
Telephone:	510/933-5630
Fax:	510/927-3530
E-mail:	info@maxis.com
Web site:	www.maxis.com
Industry:	Entertainment & Information
Sector:	Entertainment/Education Software
CEO:	Jeff Braun
CFO:	Fred Gerson
Stock Exchange:	NASDAQ
Stock Symbol:	MXIS

Product Description

Maxis develops, publishes, and distributes entertainment, home creativity, and children's software focused on user creativity and experimentation. Maxis products use innovative simulations that enhance learning through visualization, experimentation, and creativity. Maxis is recognized for its successful *Sim* family of products. The average user is over 25. Its titles are developed for Windows, Macintosh, and CD-ROM, and retail for $25–$45.

Market Strategy/Positioning

The company's mission is to put the power of exploration, learning, and creativity into the hands and minds of its customers. Maxis has strategic relationships with Compaq, IBM, Microsoft, America Online, CompuServe, and many affiliate partners for which Maxis distributes the software. Significant customers include Ingram Micro, ABCO, TechData, Egghead, Best Buy, NeoStar, and Electronics Boutique. The company's competitive advantages are the strength and sophistication of its consumer marketing approach and its profitability record—it has been profitable since it was founded. Maxis primarily competes against Sierra On-Line, Humongous Entertainment, Id Software, LucasArts, Brøderbund, The Learning Company, Electronic Arts, and Acclaim Entertainment. Additional challenges and risks include competing for shelf space, managing development schedules, and moving beyond its dependence on *Sim* products.

Other

Founded in 1987, Maxis completed its IPO in April 1995. Co-founder and CEO Jeffrey Braun has served as CEO since 1993, before which he was president of the company. Mr. Braun has over 13 years of experience in the software industry. CFO Fred Gerson joined the company in November 1994. Before this move, he was CFO at Farallon Computing and CFO at Structural Research and Analysis. Co-founder and chief designer Will Wright is a self-taught Macintosh programmer. President Sam Poole was previously at Disney Software.

KEY FACTS

Year Established:	1987
Employees:	155
Fiscal Year End:	March
Revenues FY '94:	$23.3m
Revenues FY '95:	$38.1m
EPS '94:	$0.24
EPS '95:	$0.37
Shares Outstanding:	9.8m
Five-Year Growth Rate:	28%

MCCLATCHY NEWSPAPERS

Address:	2100 Q Street
	P.O. Box 15779
	Sacramento, CA 95852-0779
Telephone:	916/321-1000
Fax:	916/321-1964
E-mail:	n/a
Web site:	http://www.nando.net
Industry:	Entertainment & Information
Sector:	Information Provider
CEO:	Erwin Potts
CFO:	James P. Smith
Stock Exchange:	NYSE
Stock Symbol:	MNI

Product Description

McClatchy Newspapers publishes 12 daily and eight community newspapers, including *The Sacramento Bee, The Fresno Bee, The Anchorage Daily News,* and the *Tri-City Herald,* which are distributed primarily in the western coastal states and in South Carolina. The company is a supporter of Partners Affiliated for Exploring Technology (PAFET), a consortium McClatchy and five other newspaper companies formed to analyze and exchange information. It has also established The Newspaper Network, a domestic venture that allows advertisers to participate in multiple markets with one order and one bill. Other new services include Legi-Tech, McClatchy's online service, and Legi-Fax, a fax-on-demand service.

Market Strategy/Positioning

McClatchy Newspapers has a strategic relationship with Pondera. The company's competitive advantage is that its seven daily newspapers all have the largest circulation in their respective markets. Challenges and risks include managing newsprint costs, venturing into new media, and increasing its circulation during a period in which 20 of the country's 25 largest newspapers are experiencing circulation losses. McClatchy Newspapers is unique as the only major information and advertisement supplier in the local communities.

Other

In 1857 James McClatchy helped found *The Sacramento Bee.* Two others, *The Fresno Bee* and *Modesto Bee,* were added in the 1920s. Four other dailies were acquired, including *The Anchorage Daily News, The News Tribune* (Tacoma), *The Tri-City Herald,* and *The Herald* (Rock Hill). In August 1995 the company acquired The News and Observer Publishing Company, which publishes *The Raleigh News and Observer* newspaper, seven other publications, and the NandO.net online service. Erwin Potts has served as CEO since 1989 and has previously held the titles of COO, executive vice president, and vice president. Mr. Potts has been a director of McClatchy since 1976 and also serves on the board of The News and Observer Publishing Company.

KEY FACTS

Year Established:	1857
Employees:	6,250
Fiscal Year End:	December
Revenues FY '94:	$471.4m
Revenues FY '95:	n/a
EPS '94:	$1.58
EPS '95:	$1.40 (estimate)
Shares Outstanding:	29.9m
Five-Year Growth Rate:	12%

MCI
COMMUNICATIONS

Address:	1801 Pennsylvania Avenue Northwest Washington, DC 20006
Telephone:	202/872-1600
Fax:	202/887-3140
E-mail:	n/a
Web site:	http://www2.pcy.mci.net
Industry:	Communications
Sector:	Information Highway Services
CEO:	Bert C. Roberts Jr.
CFO:	Douglas L. Maine
Stock Exchange:	NASDAQ
Stock Symbol:	MCIC

Product Description

MCI Communications offers an array of services including long distance, local access, paging, wireless, Internet software and access, information services, business software, and global telecommunications services. After accepting $4.3 billion from British Telecom for 20% of its stock, MCI rolled out "network MCI." Network MCI will integrate MCI's high-speed fiber-optical communications network. It also took a 45% stake in a joint venture with Grupo Financiero Banamex-Accival to provide competitive domestic telecommunications services in Mexico (a $450 million investment). In August 1995 MCI announced a new technology, Tri-Color Wave Division Multiplexing (Tri-CWDM), which allows the company to increase the capacity of its network by 50% without adding fiber-optic lines.

Market Strategy/Positioning

MCI has strategic relationships with AVANTEL, British Telecom, Grupo Financiero Banamex-Accival, Stentor, GTE Mobilnet, BellSouth, NewPar (joint venture between AirTouch and Cellular Communications), News Corp., and First Union. The company's competitive advantages are its position as the second largest long distance provider in the U.S., and its high growth in voice and data traffic in major metropolitan areas. MCI primarily competes against Ameritech, AT&T, Bell Atlantic, BellSouth, Cable & Wireless, Century Telephone, GTE, NYNEX, Pacific Telesis, PictureTel, Southwestern Bell, Sprint, U S WEST, and U.S. Long Distance. Additional challenges and risks include remaining successful in an intense long-distance telecommunications market, with primary competition coming from substantially larger AT&T, and managing deregulation.

Other

In 1966 the FCC ruled that MCI Communications was qualified to compete against AT&T's monopoly. MCI has continued to provide services that compete directly with AT&T and has expanded into new divisions. In 1987 it was awarded a contract to improve Internet data transfer speed. By 1991 MCI's nationwide network was completely digital. In 1993 British Telecom purchased 20% of MCI and formed a joint venture to market communications services globally. Bert Roberts was named chairman in 1992 and CEO in 1991. He served as president and COO from 1985 to 1992.

KEY FACTS

Year Established:	1966
Employees:	40,700
Fiscal Year End:	December
Revenues FY '94:	$13.3b
Revenues FY '95:	n/a
EPS '94:	$1.33
EPS '95:	$1.55 (estimate)
Shares Outstanding:	541.0m
Five-Year Growth Rate:	12%

MECC

Address:	6160 Summit Drive North Minneapolis, MN 55430-4003
Telephone:	612/569-1500
Fax:	612/569-1551
E-mail:	investor_relations@mecc.com
Web site:	http://www.mecc.com
Industry:	Entertainment & Information
Sector:	Entertainment/Education Software
CEO:	Dale LaFrenz
CFO:	Donald Anderson
Stock Exchange:	NASDAQ
Stock Symbol:	MECC

Product Description

MECC (Minnesota Education Computing Corporation) develops, publishes, and distributes educational software for the home and school. The company's main products target children ages 5 to 18. MECC's products are developed for Macintosh, Windows, MS-DOS, Apple II, and CD-ROM. Its products are available in retail stores nationwide or can be ordered directly through MECC.

Market Strategy/Positioning

The company's mission is to maintain and enhance a well-established position in the school educational software market. MECC has strategic relationships with Houghton Mifflin and additional alliances with firms in Japan and Europe. The company's competitive advantages are its recognition in the school market and its presence there for over 20 years. MECC primarily competes against Edmark, Brøderbund, The Learning Company, Maxis, Knowledge Adventure, Davidson & Associates, Sanctuary Woods, and Humongous Entertainment.

Other

MECC was founded in 1973 as a state organization to provide computer services to the Minnesota education community. Co-founder, president, and CEO Dale LaFrenz sold the company because of reluctancy from the state's legislature to fund MECC's expansion. North America Fund II bought a majority position in the company in 1991. Since 1990 MECC has invested over $22.0 million in product development and released over 65 IBM- and Macintosh-compatible products. The company went public in 1994 and completed a secondary offering in 1995.

KEY FACTS

Year Established:	1973
Employees:	210
Fiscal Year End:	March
Revenues FY '94:	$4.0m
Revenues FY '95:	$28.0m
EPS '94:	$0.25
EPS '95:	$0.46
Shares Outstanding:	8.42m
Five-Year Growth Rate:	n/a

MENTOR GRAPHICS

Address:	8005 Southwest Boeckman Road Wilsonville, OR 97070-7777
Telephone:	503/685-8000 and 800/547-3000
Fax:	503/685-1204
E-mail:	mgc_info@mentorg.com
Web site:	www.mentorg.com
Industry:	Computers
Sector:	Design Automation Software
CEO:	Walden C. Rhines
CFO:	R. Douglas Norby
Stock Exchange:	NASDAQ
Stock Symbol:	MENT

Product Description

Mentor Graphics manufactures and markets integrated circuits and electronic design automation (EDA) software. The company intends to automate the entire design process, from initial design and analysis to final testing and documentation. Its software assists in the design of a broad range of products across several markets, including supercomputers, automotive electronics, missile guidance, signal processors, PCs, microprocessors, and telecommunications switching. Its new products include a simulator as well as synthesis offerings.

Market Strategy/Positioning

The company's mission is to be the leading provider of the tools, integration, and process technologies—including consistent libraries and parts models—as well as the services essential for successfully managing design data and processes. Mentor Graphics has strategic relationships with Sun Microsystems and Hewlett-Packard. Significant customers include Advanced Micro Devices, Allied Signal, Motorola, and Texas Instruments. The company's competitive advantages are its EDA software and professional design services, which support customers' complete design environments. Mentor Graphics primarily competes against Cadence, Synopsys, and Viewlogic. An additional challenge includes installing entire systems, both hardware and software, on a single piece of silicon. Mentor Graphics is unique in developing a "Systems on Silicon" (SOS) initiative that extends current ASIC and cell-based integrated circuit paradigms to the system level.

Other

Founded in 1981, the company focuses on leading advancements in electronic design automation. Mentor established its Professional Services Division in 1987 to assist in increasing productivity while reducing costs. In 1994 Mentor acquired ANACAD, a German-based developer of software for the mixed-signal integrated circuit market. In 1995 the company purchased Axiom Dalerer Skandinavien, the largest supplier of vendor-independent symbol library and generation technology. President and CEO Wally Rhines formerly served as executive vice president of Texas Instruments' Semiconductors Group. Senior vice president and CFO Douglas Norby was previously president and CEO of Pharmetrix and president and COO of LucasFilm.

338

KEY FACTS

Year Established:	1981
Employees:	2,100
Fiscal Year End:	December
Revenues FY '94:	$345.6m
Revenues FY '95:	n/a
EPS '94:	$0.50
EPS '95:	$0.83 (estimate)
Shares Outstanding:	49.5m
Five-Year Growth Rate:	16%

MICRON TECHNOLOGY

Product Description

Micron Technology designs, manufactures, and markets semiconductor memory components primarily for use in various computer applications. Its products include dynamic random access memories (DRAMs), static RAMs (SRAMs), specialty DRAMs, and specialty SRAMs. DRAMs and specialty DRAMs have accounted for over 70% of the company's revenues. Micron's SRAM family focuses on the high-performance sector of the market and accounts for about 8% of revenues. Its board-level products and PCs account for the remaining portion of revenues.

Address:	8000 Federal Way
	P.O. Box 6
	Boise, ID 83707-0006
Telephone:	208/368-4000
Fax:	208/368-4435
E-mail:	invrel@vax.micron.com
Web site:	http://www.micron.com
Industry:	Computers
Sector:	Semiconductors
CEO:	Joseph Parkinson
CFO:	Reid Langrill
Stock Exchange:	NYSE
Stock Symbol:	MU

Market Strategy/Positioning

The company's mission is to become world-class in developing advantages for its customers. Micron has strategic relationships with several third parties in the form of cross-license agreements in return for royalty payments. Significant customers include major manufacturers of PCs, workstations, and other computer systems. Compaq accounted for 11% of Micron's sales in 1994. The company's competitive advantages are its numerous technology and process patents, and its position as one of the lowest-cost producers in the industry. Micron primarily competes against Fujitsu, Goldstar, Hitachi, Hyundai Electronics, Mitsubishi Electric, Motorola, NEC, Samsung Semiconductor, Texas Instruments, and Toshiba. Additional challenges and risks include the ability to migrate successfully to 16-megabyte DRAMs while keeping costs down, the ability to successfully transition to larger wafer sizes, and the risk of massive overcapacity if the personal computer industry experiences a slowdown.

339

Other

Micron Technology was founded in 1978 as a semiconductor design consulting firm. It is a holding company for the following subsidiaries: Micron Electronics, Micron Construction, Micron Display Technology, Micron Communications, Micron Quantumm Devices, Micron Europe Limited, Micron Semiconductor (Germany), and Micron Semiconductor Asia Pacific. It acquired the Zeos line of personal computers in 1994. Co-founder Joseph Parkinson served as president from 1980 to 1986, when he was named chairman and CEO.

KEY FACTS

Year Established:	1978
Employees:	7,900
Fiscal Year End:	August
Revenues FY '94:	$1.63b
Revenues FY '95:	$2.9b
EPS '94:	$1.92
EPS '95:	$3.94
Shares Outstanding:	206.0m
Five-Year Growth Rate:	25%

MICROSOFT

Product Description

Microsoft is the world's largest developer of software for personal computers. The Microsoft juggernaut represents a broad array of products that provide access to ideas, information, entertainment, and tools. The company develops operating system software, desktop and business applications, home and entertainment software, development tools, and hardware accessories that provide leading-edge technology. Microsoft has aggressively entered the multimedia and online markets. The company's Advanced Technology Group focuses on applying software to mobile computing, voice recognition, interactive TV, and video-on-demand technology. Current projects include its OLE technology, which allows the creation of documents consisting of multiple sources of information, and of different applications. Microsoft is also working on a new system that offers an advanced object-oriented environment based on Windows NT, and will make creating, accessing, manipulating, organizing, and sharing information easier for computer users. Microsoft's new online service Microsoft Network (MSN) allows Windows 95 users to connect to the Internet. Microsoft and the Paramount Television group announced an agreement last year to showcase exclusive online content for *Star Trek* and *Entertainment Tonight* properties on MSN. MSN is also exploring online multiplayer gaming, full-motion video clips, animation, live interviews, and online shopping.

Address:	One Microsoft Way
	Redmond, WA 98052-6399
Telephone:	206/882-8080
Fax:	206/883-8101
E-mail:	billg@microsoft.com
Web site:	http://www.microsoft.com
Industry:	Computers
Sector:	Personal Productivity Software
CEO:	William H. Gates, III
CFO:	Michael W. Brown
Stock Exchange:	NASDAQ
Stock Symbol:	MSFT

Market Strategy/Positioning

The company's mission is to place a computer on every desk and in every home. Microsoft has strategic relationships with MasterCard, Simon & Schuster, Sonic Images, Avid Technology, and UUNET. Microsoft recently acquired SOFTIMAGE, Imageware Research, Altamire Software, and RenderMorphics. Significant customers include tens of millions of PC users and 400 hardware manufactures who pre-install Windows on their systems. The company's competitive advantage is being the world's leading software provider. Microsoft products are recognized around the world by the Microsoft brand name. Microsoft primarily competes against Apple, ASK Computer, AT&T, Borland, Brøderbund, Computer Associates, Davidson & Associates, Electronic Arts, Gupta, IBM, Intuit, Netscape, NeXT, Nintendo, Novell, Oracle, Pearson, Sybase, Symantec, and Tribune. Additional challenges and risks include main-

340

KEY FACTS

Year Established:	1975
Employees:	17,100
Fiscal Year End:	June
Revenues FY '94:	$4.7b
Revenues FY '95:	$5.9b
EPS '94:	$1.87
EPS '95:	$2.32
Shares Outstanding:	588.0m
Five-Year Growth Rate:	23%

MICROSOFT

taining market share and releasing quality products in a timely fashion. Microsoft is unique in setting standards around which other hardware and software providers develop products. Its installed base for its Windows operating system stands at more than 60 million units worldwide.

Other

In January 1975 Bill Gates and Paul Allen sold BASIC to MITS, maker of the Altair 8800 (and their first customer). In November 1984 Microsoft Corporation was formed; it then moved to Bellevue, WA. Microsoft announced Windows, an extension to the MS-DOS operating system in November 1983. In 1993 the company became the largest company in the computer industry based on market value. Co-founders Bill Gates and Paul Allen developed BASIC, the first computer language program for a PC.

MICROUNITY
SYSTEMS

Address:	255 Caspian Drive
	Sunnyvale, CA 94089
Telephone:	408/734-8100
Fax:	408/734-8136
E-mail:	n/a
Web site:	n/a
Industry:	Computers
Sector:	Semiconductors
CEO:	John Moussouris
CFO:	n/a

Product Description

MicroUnity Systems develops, manufactures, and markets ultra-high bandwidth digital systems as general-purpose platforms for digital media communications. It claims to be working on a media processor chip with 100 times the bandwidth ability of current microprocessors, at comparable costs. The functions performed would include audio, video, compression, encryption, and communication protocols. MicroUnity has completed the construction of a $50 million, 0.5 micron BiCMOS manufacturing facility in Silicon Valley, and has secured 20 device-level, process-packaging, and CAD patents, with 30 more pending.

Market Strategy/Positioning

The company's mission is to satisfy the appetite for bandwidth—the pragmatic measure of a user's intensity of experience—in high-volume digital media and communications applications. The company's competitive advantage is its patented technology. MicroUnity does not compete against anyone presently but could face competition from companies like Motorola and Intel. Additional challenges and risks include MicroUnity being a development-stage company. Many industry experts are skeptical of the company's ambitious claims.

342

Other

MicroUnity Systems was founded in 1988 with initial financial backing from William Randolph Hearst III. Its development team includes Curtis Abbot, former chief programmer for LucasFilm; Al Matthews, inventor of the 386 chip process at Intel; and Jack Holloway, video chip designer at AT&T. CEO John Moussouris co-founded MIPS before joining the company.

Primary VCs/Outside Financing

The company would not disclose its backers, but they are rumored to include Microsoft, U S WEST, TCI, Hewlett-Packard, and Mr. William Randolph Hearst III.

KEY FACTS

Year Established:	1988
Employees:	170
Fiscal Year End:	December
Revenues FY '94:	n/a
Revenues FY '95:	n/a
Date of Next Financing:	n/a
Date of Last Financing:	n/a
Size of Last Financing:	n/a
Total Capital Raised:	n/a
Post Round Valuation:	n/a
Expected IPO Date:	n/a

MINERVA SYSTEMS

Address:	2933 Bunker Hill Lane Suite 202 Santa Clara, CA 95054
Telephone:	408/970-1780
Fax:	408/982-9877
E-mail:	info@minervasys.com
Web site:	http://www.zynet.co.uk
Industry:	Entertainment & Information
Sector:	Film & Entertainment Production
CEO:	Mauro Bonomi
CFO:	John Doerner

Product Description

Minerva Systems develops a system for digital video processing and encoding that converts film and video to MPEG compliance. Its system has a real-time encoding platform, a Mac-based host, and application software; it also enables color correction, filtering, and noise reduction. The company's MPEG encoding system was the first to offer a human-assisted approach to the video-compression process. Minerva sells to the film production, post-production, TV, cable, and phone markets.

Market Strategy/Positioning

The company's mission is to develop and market the highest quality MPEG digital video publishing workstations. Minerva has strategic relationships with Avid Technology, Optimage/Philips, and Sonic Solutions. Significant customers include Bell Atlantic, TCI, Microsoft, Oracle, and Laser Pacific. The company's competitive advantage is its leadership position in the high-end MPEG encoding market resulting from the company's unique application software and propietary video pre-processing algorithms. Minerva has pioneered human-assisted encoding video pre-processing techniques, which yield the highest quality compressed video for publishing on CD-ROMs or for distribution over digital video networks. Minerva primarily competes against FutureTel, OptiVision, and Optibase. Additional challenges and risks include developing a strong resale channel to enter the mid-range market.

343

Other

Minerva Systems was founded in December of 1992 by CEO Mauro Bonomi. Mr. Bonomi was formerly vice president of marketing with C-Cube. James Swartz, general partner at Accel Partners, became director of Minerva in January 1995. CFO John Doerner was formerly vice president of marketing at Communications Intelligence and CFO at Agilis. The company's core team includes professionals from Radius, Adobe Systems, Digital F/X, and C-Cube.

Primary VCs/Outside Financing

Accel Partners; Merrill, Pickard, Anderson & Eyre; U.S. Venture Partners; and Eastman Kodak's Aperture Fund.

KEY FACTS

Year Established:	1992
Employees:	50
Fiscal Year End:	December
Revenues FY '94:	$3.0m
Revenues FY '95:	n/a
Date of Next Financing:	n/a
Date of Last Financing:	December 1994
Size of Last Financing:	$5.0m
Total Capital Raised:	$7.5m
Post Round Valuation:	n/a
Expected IPO Date:	n/a

MNI
INTERACTIVE

Product Description

MNI Interactive develops interactive services for entertainment product purchases. Its flagship product offers subscribers a personalized, interactive music previewing and purchasing service using phones, CD-ROMs, and online services. Its product also offers overnight delivery, descriptive information, and personalized messaging on particular performers. The company is considering concert-related offerings.

Address:	501 Second Street Suite 350 San Francisco, CA 94107
Telephone:	415/904-6222
Fax:	415/777-2851
E-mail:	musicnet@mni.com
Web site:	http://www.mni.com
Industry:	Entertainment & Information
Sector:	Online Services
CEO:	John Atcheson
CFO:	Frank Mattson

Market Strategy/Positioning

The company's mission is to provide personalized and entertaining home shopping services. MNI Interactive has strategic relationships with *Rolling Stone* (co-marketing) and distribution agreements with Ingram Periodicals and Ameritech. The company's competitive advantage is its navigation system, which guides consumers through media product choices to make purchase decisions. MNI Interactive primarily competes against MusicLine, Music Marketing Access, Music Marketing Network, Touch Tunes, CD Now!, and Noteworthy Music. Additional challenges and risks include the entertainment industry's being in a state of flux and new players aligning themselves as competition. MNI is unique in having a world-class interface-design team and superior data-linking capabilities.

Other

President and CEO John Atcheson founded the company in 1990 to provide a fun and easy way to learn about and buy new music. Mr. Atcheson combined his interests in music, computers, and multimedia to create an interactive music previewing and shopping service that addresses a real need and uses technology to make it better. Mr. Atcheson formerly served as vice president of sales and marketing at Digidesign as well as multimedia marketing consultant for Apple and Macromedia. Chairman Timothy Mott is a co-founder of Electronic Arts and the former chairman and CEO of Macromedia. CEO Frank Mattson formerly served as vice president of distribution and strategic planning at Ingram Entertainment.

Primary VCs/Outside Financing

Kleiner Perkins Caufield & Byers, The Mayfield Fund, and Ameritech.

KEY FACTS

Year Established:	1990
Employees:	25
Fiscal Year End:	December
Revenues FY '94:	n/a
Revenues FY '95:	n/a
Date of Next Financing:	n/a
Date of Last Financing:	March 1995
Size of Last Financing:	$5.0m
Total Capital Raised:	n/a
Post Round Valuation:	n/a
Expected IPO Date:	n/a

MOTOROLA

Product Description

Motorola is a provider of wireless communications, semiconductors, and electronic systems and services. Its markets include computers; cellular, two-way radio, paging, and data communications; and personal communications, automotive, defense, and space electronics. Its New Enterprises group evaluates projects in emerging worldwide high-technology markets. As the prime contractor for the IRIDIUM project, the company will assist in the design, production, and launch of a networked infrastructure of 66 low-level satellites. This system offers the ability to place and receive calls from anywhere on earth to subscribers with hand-held phones. Motorola won a silicon carbide contract, for its high-temperature electronics market, from AARP, in conjunction with Cree Research, Honeywell, and GE. Motorola is developing holographic reflective material to improve the image quality of liquid crystal displays (LCDs) used in hand-helds and portables. It also has handwriting recognition technology for interactive TV through its Lexicus division. A joint effort with In Focus Systems will produce integrated circuits that will deliver video speeds to passive matrix LCDs. Motorola also has an interactive TV network alliance with Amatic.

Address:	1303 East Algonquin Road Schaumburg, IL 60196
Telephone:	708/576-5000
Fax:	708/576-8003
E-mail:	n/a
Web site:	http://www.mot.com
Industry:	Computers
Sector:	Semiconductors
CEO:	Gary Tooker
CFO:	Carl Koenemann
Stock Exchange:	NYSE
Stock Symbol:	MOT

345

Market Strategy/Positioning

The company's mission is "Total Customer Satisfaction." Motorola has strategic relationships with IBM, Apple, and Toshiba. The company's competitive advantages are its position as the largest producer of mobile and portable cellular phones, as the fourth largest semiconductor producer, and as the leader in developing the wireless data industry. Motorola primarily competes against AMD, Analog Devices, Apple, AT&T, Cirrus Logic, Cyrix, DEC, Ericsson, Fujitsu, Hewlett-Packard, IBM, Intel, Matsushita, National Semiconductor, NEC, Nokia, Oki, Philips, Siemens, Silicon Graphics, Texas Instruments, Toshiba, and U.S. Robotics. Additional challenges and risks include producing products at a Six Sigma (99.9997% defect-free) standard while reducing cycle time. Motorola feels it is the best-positioned company for the wireless revolution.

Other

Motorola was founded in 1928 as Galvin Manufacturing by Paul Galvin. Mr. Galvin's first product was known as the "battery eliminator," a device that allows radios to run on a household current. In the 1930s it produced car radios under the Motorola

KEY FACTS

Year Established:	1928
Employees:	132,000
Fiscal Year End:	December
Revenues FY '94:	$22.2b
Revenues FY '95:	$27.5b (estimate)
EPS '94:	$2.66
EPS '95:	$3.26 (estimate)
Shares Outstanding:	589.8m
Five-Year Growth Rate:	18%

MOTOROLA

brand name. The company then adopted Motorola as its name in 1947. During the 1940s the company also opened a research laboratory and entered into government work. In the 1960s Motorola moved away from consumer electronics to focus upon the commercial, industrial, and government areas. By 1990 it was one of the world's largest cellular telephone suppliers. Vice chairman and CEO Gary Tooker joined Motorola's semiconductor division in 1962. He held numerous positions in product and corporate management before being named CEO in 1993. President and COO Christopher Galvin, grandson of founder Paul Galvin, joined the company in 1973 and was named vice president of Tegal, a subsidiary of Motorola, in 1984. He was elected president in 1993.

MULTIGEN

Address:	550 South Winchester Boulevard Suite 500 San Jose, CA 95128
Telephone:	408/261-4100
Fax:	408/261-4101
E-mail:	multigen!ginny@uunet.UU.NET
Web site:	http://www.sbwinc.com/multigen
Industry:	Entertainment & Information
Sector:	Entertainment/Education Software
CEO:	Joseph Fantuzzi
CFO:	Kevin J. Rains

Product Description

MultiGen develops graphical-modeling tools used to create scenes for interactive, 3D, real-time computer simulations. Its software operates on a simulation interchange database format. MultiGen's tools can be used to create military, commercial, location-based entertainment, gaming, and virtual reality simulations. Its options let users create and edit textures and sound as well as generate terrain. MultiGen, currently Silicon Graphics–based, is migrating to PCs.

Market Strategy/Positioning

The company's mission is to be a leader in developing real-time 3D modeling tools for use in simulations and emerging entertainment markets. MultiGen has strategic relationships with Silicon Graphics, Nintendo, Alias Research, Gemini Technology, Paradigm Simulation, and MaK Technologies. Significant customers include Boeing, Ford Motor Company, NASA, Volvo, Walt Disney, Magic Edge, Time Warner, and Xatrix Entertainment. The company's competitive advantages are its visual scene modeler, real-time 3D optimization, and new integrated 3D scene content technology. In addition, the company has virtually no employee turnover and maintains profitability. MultiGen primarily competes against Coryphaeus Software in visual simulation and WAVEFRONT/Activation in entertainment.

347

Other

MultiGen historically concentrated on simulation tools used on high-end computing platforms, and on the specialized hardware used for military and commercial flight simulation. More recently, the company has taken advantage of opportunities in emerging markets such as entertainment, virtual reality, and computer-aided design. Founder and chief technical officer Dennis Yeo previously worked at NASA and left to form Software Systems, the predecessor to MultiGen. CEO Joseph Fantuzzi was vice president of marketing at Macromedia and vice president of Autodesk's Multimedia Division. He joined MultiGen in May 1995. CFO Kevin Rains was previously CFO and co-founder of MultiVideo and vice president of finance and CFO at The Complete PC.

Primary VCs/Outside Financing

RAF Ventures, and Safeguard Scientifics, which owns 31%.

KEY FACTS

Year Established:	1986
Employees:	50
Fiscal Year End:	December
Revenues FY '94:	n/a
Revenues FY '95:	n/a
Date of Next Financing:	n/a
Date of Last Financing:	February 1995
Size of Last Financing:	n/a
Total Capital Raised:	n/a
Post Round Valuation:	n/a
Expected IPO Date:	n/a

MYSOFTWARE

Address:	2197 East Bayshore Road
	Palo Alto, CA 94303
Telephone:	415/473-3600
Fax:	415/325-0873
E-mail:	n/a
Web site:	n/a
Industry:	Computers
Sector:	Personal Productivity Software
CEO:	David P. Mans
CFO:	David P. Mans
Stock Exchange:	NASDAQ
Stock Symbol:	MYSW

Product Description

MySoftware develops task-specific sales and marketing software for small businesses. Its four core product categories are brochures, mailing, labeling, and invoicing/estimates, and its products are sold in over 7,000 stores throughout the U.S.

Market Strategy/Positioning

MySoftware has strategic relationships with Avery, BeaverPrints, Paper Direct, and Moore. Significant customers include CompUSA, Office Depot, and Best Buy. The company's competitive advantage is its strategy of focusing on leading the markets in its four core product categories. This strategy enables the company to understand its market and to develop more effective solutions to customers' problems. MySoftware primarily competes against Avery, Intuit, NEBS, SoftKey, Adobe, Microsoft, and Novell. Additional challenges and risks include operating and competing in an emerging market and facing uncertain market acceptance. As the software industry changes, existing software companies could broaden their product lines to compete with MySoftware's products.

Other

MySoftware was founded in 1986 and released its first core product, MyMailList, in September 1987. Subsequently, MyLabelDesigner was introduced in March 1988, followed by MyInvoices in December 1990, MyAdvanced Invoices & Estimates in August 1993, and MyBrochures in April 1994. The company went public in June 1995. President, CEO, and CFO David Mans joined the company in 1988. Previously, he was vice president of Power Projects at International Power Technologies and vice president at Qume Corporation. Co-founder and chairman James Willenborg was managing general partner of Crosspoint Venture Partners and co-founded Inmac.

348

KEY FACTS

Year Established:	1986
Employees:	50
Fiscal Year End:	December
Revenues FY '94:	$9.2m
Revenues FY '95:	$14.2m (estimate)
EPS '94:	$0.26
EPS '95:	$0.51 (estimate)
Shares Outstanding:	3.7m
Five-Year Growth Rate:	33%

NASHOBA NETWORKS

Address:	9 Goldsmith Street
	Littleton, MA 01460
Telephone:	508/486-3200
Fax:	508/486-0990
E-mail:	info@nashoba.com
Web site:	http://www.harpell.com/nashoba
Industry:	Communications
Sector:	Computer Networking
CEO:	Nick Grewal
CFO:	n/a

Product Description

Nashoba Networks develops switching products to enhance token ring and FDDI networks without leaping to foreign technologies. The company anticipates 500,000 ports on switched token ring networks by 1998. FDDI, while smaller, generates more revenue per port. The company unveiled its first product, Concord, in March 1995 as the industry's first token ring packet switch.

Market Strategy/Positioning

The company's mission is to develop and manufacture high-performance, low-cost network switching products that address the need for increased bandwidth, while preserving existing infrastructure migration to ATM technology. Nashoba Networks has strategic relationships with Cabletron Systems and Fibronics. Significant customers include Bolt Baranek & Newman, UB Networks, and IDEAssociates. The company's competitive advantages are its full support for token ring protocols, its imbedded RMON support, and its low prices. Nashoba primarily competes against Centillion/Bay Networks, Madge, and IBM. Additional challenges and risks include reducing the cost of existing products and adding FDDI and ATM uplink connections.

349

Other

Nashoba Networks, formerly NeTREAND, was founded in 1993 by industry veteran Nick Grewal to deliver turnkey networking services to local-area network, wide-area network, and internetworking vendors. President and CEO Nick Grewal previously worked as senior vice president at CrossComm, a leading router in the IBM networking market. He also worked at Proteon, where he was instrumental in taking the company public. Vice president of sales Sean Walsh has 12 years of experience in the market and was previously with Synernetics, acquired by 3Com. Vice president of marketing Bob Rosenbaum has 15 years of experience with startup companies and previously co-founded Windata, one of the pioneers in the wireless market. He was also vice president of marketing at Amnet and co-founded Xyplex.

KEY FACTS

Year Established:	1993
Employees:	20
Fiscal Year End:	n/a
Revenues FY '94:	n/a
Revenues FY '95:	n/a
Date of Next Financing:	n/a
Date of Last Financing:	n/a
Size of Last Financing:	n/a
Total Capital Raised:	n/a
Post Round Valuation:	n/a
Expected IPO Date:	n/a

NATIONAL SEMICONDUCTOR

350

Address:	2900 Semiconductor Drive P.O. Box 58090 Santa Clara, CA 95052
Telephone:	408-721-5000
Fax:	408/721-3238
E-mail:	n/a
Web site:	http://www.nsc.com
Industry:	Computers
Sector:	Semiconductors
CEO:	Dr. Gilbert Amelio
CFO:	Donald MacLeod
Stock Exchange:	NYSE
Stock Symbol:	NSM

Product Description

National Semiconductor focuses on areas in the communications, analog-intensive, personal-systems, and consumer markets. The company develops, designs, and markets semiconductor technologies for moving and shaping information.

Market Strategy/Positioning

The company's mission is to excel in serving its chosen markets by delivering semiconductor-intensive products and services of the highest quality and value. National Semiconductor has strategic relationships with Kyocera, MEMC, NEC, Sharp, Siltec, Toshiba, and Varian. The company also received $8 million in funding last year from the Advanced Research Project Agency (ARPA) for the development of advanced embedded substrate technologies. Significant customers include Acer, AT&T, Apple, Cabletron, Compaq, Ericsson, Goldstar, Hewlett-Packard, IBM, Intel, Motorola, Nokia, Philips, Samsung, Siemens, and 3Com. The company's competitive advantages are a high competency in analog and mixed-signal technologies and its movement into the wireless silicon market, estimated to grow to $30 billion by the year 2000. National Semiconductor primarily competes against Analog Devices, Linear Technology, Maxim, Motorola, and SGS-Thomson.

Other

National Semiconductor was founded in 1959 as a supplier of circuits for the military. The company became a broad-based supplier of semiconductors while specializing in analog technology. In 1987 the company acquired Fairchild Semiconductor. CEO and president Gil Amelio has held his position since 1991 and was appointed chairman in 1995. He was previously president of Rockwell Communications Systems and a general manager of Fairchild Camera and Instrument. There are 16 patents that Mr. Amelio holds alone or jointly. CFO and executive vice president Donald Macleod joined the company in 1978 and has held his current position since 1991. He has worked in the company's offices in England, Scotland, Germany, and the U.S.

KEY FACTS

Year Established:	1959
Employees:	22,400
Fiscal Year End:	May
Revenues FY '94:	$2.3b
Revenues FY '95:	$2.4b
EPS '94:	$1.87
EPS '95:	$1.92
Shares Outstanding:	n/a
Five-Year Growth Rate:	n/a

Product Description

NEC is a global supplier of computers, telecommunications, and other electronic products. Japan's largest supplier of PCs, it has agreed to sell IBM-compatible PC servers in Japan. The company established NEC Interchannel in October 1995 to focus on multimedia software development. The new company develops specialized multimedia software for complex computers and communications applications. 8% of the company's revenue is devoted to research and development.

Address:	U.S. Headquarters
	8 Old Sod Farm Road
	Melville, NY 11747-3112
Telephone:	516/753-7000
Fax:	516/753-7041
E-mail:	n/a
Web site:	http://www.nec.co.jp
Industry:	Computers
Sector:	Semiconductors
CEO:	Hisashi Kaneko
CFO:	Yoshihiro Suzuki
Stock Exchange:	NASDAQ
Stock Symbol:	NIPNY (ADR)

Market Strategy/Positioning

NEC has strategic relationships with Groupe Bull, Packard Bell, AT&T, Silicon Graphics, Samsung, Oracle, Tandem Computer, and Radish. The company's competitive advantages are its strength in monitors and its well-balanced research and development expenditures. NEC primarily competes against Apple, IBM, Compaq, AT&T, Dell, Ericsson, Fujitsu, Hewlett-Packard, Honeywell, Intel, Machines Bull (France), Microsoft, Motorola, Nokia, Oki, Philips, Siemens, Silicon Graphics, Texas Instruments, and Toshiba. Additional challenges and risks include preventing rivals IBM, Apple, and Compaq from taking its market share. NEC is unique in being among the top 10 companies in all three of its markets: computers, telecommunications, and semiconductors.

351

Other

Nippon Electric Company was founded in 1899 in a joint venture between a group of Japanese investors and Western Electric. The company initially imported telephone equipment and eventually manufactured and supplied equipment to Japan's Communications Ministry. Throughout the 1950s and 1960s NEC's sales consisted of business with NTT, international sales, home appliances, and computers. The company collaborated with the Japanese government to develop VLSI chips in the 1970s and produced the first 4-megabit DRAM chip in 1986. It plans to build an $800 million DRAM chip plant in Scotland. President Hisashi Kaneko was formerly the head of NEC's American operations.

KEY FACTS

Year Established:	1899
Employees:	147,900
Fiscal Year End:	March
Revenues FY '94:	$35.1b
Revenues FY '95:	$43.0b (estimate)
EPS '94:	$0.26
EPS '95:	n/a
Shares Outstanding:	308.0m
Five-Year Growth Rate:	4%

NETCOM

Address:	3031 Tisch Way
	San Jose, CA 95128
Telephone:	408/983-5950, 800/353-6600
Fax:	408/556-3153
E-mail:	info@netcom.com
	jslone@ix.netcom.com
Web site:	www.netcom.com
Industry:	Entertainment & Information
Sector:	Online Services
CEO:	David W. Garrison
CFO:	Warren J. Kaplan
Stock Exchange:	Nasdaq
Stock Symbol:	NETC

Product Description

NETCOM is a provider of Internet connection services. The company offers subscribers a complete Internet access solution comprised of front-end software, high-quality access service and 24-hour customer support. Subscribers receive access to a full range of Internet applications, including e-mail, World Wide Web sites, USENET news groups, and database information. It supplies a Windows-based graphical user interface for navigation.

Market Strategy/Positioning

The company's mission is to be the leading provider of Internet service. NETCOM has strategic relationships with Sun Microsystems, Silicon Graphics, Auto-Graphics, NEC, Artisoft, Global Village, and Sybex. Significant customers include Fry's Electronics, CompUSA, Micro City, Radio Shack, Software City, and Incredible Universe. The company's competitive advantage is its providing direct Internet access via an owned and operated network. NETCOM was first-to-market with an integrated solution comprising access, transport, and communications protocol, as well as tools and applications. NETCOM primarily competes against Spyglass, Performance Systems International, Bolt Beranek & Newman, UUNET, America Online, CompuServe, Prodigy, Delphi, GEnie, AT&T, MCI, Sprint, Pacific Bell, Microsoft, News Corp., and Netscape. Additional challenges and risks include facing competitive entry in the market for Internet access services. The company relies on other companies, particularly WilTel, to provide data communications transmission via leased telephone lines. NETCOM is unique as the first Internet service provider to go public and the first to offer individuals value-pricing through a flat rate. NETCOM was selected by *PC World* as winner of the 1995 Best Internet Access Provider World Class Award.

Other

NETCOM was founded in 1988 by Robert Reiger, who began charging his night school students to access the Internet. The company went public in December 1994. From 1994 to 1995, NETCOM's subscriber base doubled to 150,000. Mr. Reiger was previously an information services engineer for Lockheed. David Garrison, formerly of Skytel, took over as president in 1995.

KEY FACTS

Year Established:	1988
Employees:	300
Fiscal Year End:	December
Revenues FY '94:	$16.3m
Revenues FY '95:	$42.5m
EPS '94:	n/a
EPS '95:	$(0.99) (estimate)
Shares Outstanding:	6.76m
Five-Year Growth Rate:	150%

352

NETEDGE SYSTEMS

Address:	P.O. Box 14993
	Research Triangle Park, NC 27709
Telephone:	919/991-9000, 800/638-3343
Fax:	919/991-9060
E-mail:	n/a
Web site:	http://www.netedge.com
Industry:	Communications
Sector:	Computer Networking
CEO:	Albert Bender
CFO:	Lee Palles

Product Description

NetEdge Systems develops an asynchronous transfer mode (ATM) edge router that integrates local-area networks (LANs) into virtual enterprise networks. This integration allows Ethernet, token ring, or FDDI LAN devices located anywhere in the enterprise to participate in secured workgroup teams with ATM-attached servers and hosts. The company believes the first ATM market opportunity will be in data networking services provided by telecommunication companies, as ATM allows the telcos to integrate voice and data over a common transmission system.

Market Strategy/Positioning

The company's mission is to provide high-performance, low-cost ATM access to legacy LANs for LAN backbone applications and telecommunication data services. NetEdge has strategic relationships with FORE Systems (NetEdge is integrated in FORE's product line) and MFS Datanet. NetEdge also has a technology licensing relationship with Stratacom. The company's competitive advantages are its successful focus on LAN to ATM connectivity and providing solutions optimized for ATM. NetEdge primarily competes against 3Com, Cisco, and Bay Networks.

353

Other

NetEdge Systems was formerly the internetworking division of FiberCom. It was established as a separate company in December 1993 to focus on the commercial internetworking market. In 1982 CEO Dr. Albert Bender also founded FiberCom, where he led the product development effort for NetEdge's flagship product, and spearheaded FiberCom's effort to implement an FDDI bridge/router for the new Boeing 777 commercial aircraft.

Primary VCs/Outside Financing

Merril, Pickard, Anderson & Eyre; and TA Associates.

KEY FACTS

Year Established:	1993
Employees:	115
Fiscal Year End:	December
Revenues FY '94:	$6.6m
Revenues FY '95:	$20.0m
Date of Next Financing:	n/a
Date of Last Financing:	August 1995
Size of Last Financing:	$1.0m
Total Capital Raised:	$19.0m
Post Round Valuation:	n/a
Expected IPO Date:	n/a

NETMANAGE

Address:	10725 North DeAnza Boulevard Cupertino, CA 95014
Telephone:	408/973-7171
Fax:	408/257-6405
E-mail:	donna@netmanage.com
Web site:	http://www.netmanage.com
Industry:	Computers
Sector:	Personal Productivity Software
CEO:	Zvi Alon
CFO:	Walt Amaral
Stock Exchange:	NASDAQ
Stock Symbol:	NETM

Product Description

NetManage develops, markets, and supports an integrated set of TCP/IP internetworking connectivity applications and development tools for Windows. The company's products emphasize functionality, ease-of-use and easy installation, as well as the ability to efficiently manage computer resources. The applications include local and remote connectivity, e-mail, file and printer sharing, Internet access, and network communications and utilities.

Market Strategy/Positioning

The company's mission is to provide PC users with a complete global connectivity desktop that connects them to other users, data, and applications. NetManage has strategic relationships with Network Computing Devices, 3Com, IBM, and SynOptics. Significant customers include AC Nielsen, AT&T, Bank of America, GE, Hewlett-Packard, Honeywell, MIT, Merck, Motorola, Pepsi-Cola, Sony, the U.S. Army, WilTel, World Bank, and Xerox. The company's competitive advantages are its positioning that capitalizes on the growing importance of Windows-based desktop computing, and the emergence of TCP/IP as the most widely used open Internetworking protocol. NetManage primarily competes against FTP Software, IBM, Microsoft, Novell, and Sun Microsystems. Additional challenges and risks include developing new products on a timely and cost-effective basis, and responding to emerging industry standards and other technological changes.

Other

Founded in 1990, NetManage has been profitable since the second half of 1991. It currently has over 6,000 customers. NetManage recently acquired Arabesque Software for $6 million. Founder and president Zvi Alon was formerly president of Halley Systems and served as manager of standard product lines at Sytek. CFO Walt Amaral joined NetManage in April 1995. He was formerly senior vice president and CFO of Maxtor Corporation for three years. Before working at Maxtor, Mr. Amaral worked for 15 years with Intel in various financial and marketing positions.

KEY FACTS

Year Established:	1990
Employees:	85
Fiscal Year End:	December
Revenues FY '94:	$61.6m
Revenues FY '95:	n/a
EPS '94:	$0.41
EPS '95:	$0.98
Shares Outstanding:	39.7m
Five-Year Growth Rate:	50%

354

NETSCAPE

Address:	501 East Middlefield Road
	Mountain View, CA 94043
Telephone:	415/254-1900
Fax:	415/528-4124
E-mail:	info@netscape.com
Web site:	http://home.netscape.com
Industry:	Communications
Sector:	Online Services
CEO:	James Barksdale
CFO:	Peter Currie
Stock Exchange:	NASDAQ
Stock Symbol:	NSCP

Product Description

Netscape offers a full line of open software that enables electronic commerce and secure information exchange on the Internet and private TCP/IP-based networks. Its software line includes three families of products: client software, server software, and Internet applications. The products deliver secure communications, advanced performance, and point-and-click simplicity to companies and individuals who want to create or access information services on the Internet or on private TCP/IP networks. Netscape also offers a modem-compatible graphical user interface navigator or browser.

Market Strategy/Positioning

The company's mission is to lead the business of enabling information exchange and commerce over networks. Netscape has strategic relationships with Novell, Silicon Graphics, Yahoo!, MCI, Bank of America, First Data, and Sun Microsystems. Significant customers include Delphi, Bank of America, and Novell. The company's competitive advantage is that it is the first to ship a server side product. Netscape primarily competes against Spyglass, Open Market, Process Software, Quarterdeck, America Online, AT&T, California Software, CompuServe, Delphi, Microsoft, NET-COM, NetManage, PRODIGY, and UUNET. Additional challenges and risks include intense competition to control the browser market. The company that achieves early dominance in this market has the opportunity to set standards for this key component of doing business online.

Other

Twenty-three-year-old Marc Andreessen was instrumental in writing Mosaic, Internet software developed at the University of Illinois. In 1994 Mr. Andreessen joined James Clark to start Mosaic Communications. The University of Illinois pressured Mosaic to change its name and in November 1994 the company became Netscape, but was not required to seek a license to market Mosaic. Netscape's IPO in August 1995 was one of the most successful offerings in the history of Wall Street. Co-founder and chairman James Clark started Silicon Graphics and was an associate professor at Stanford. Co-founder and vice president of technology Marc Andreessen created Mosaic at the University of Illinois. President James Barksdale formerly headed AT&T Wireless Services and was COO of McCaw Cellular.

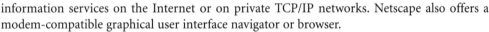

KEY FACTS

Year Established:	1994
Employees:	250
Fiscal Year End:	December
Revenues FY '94:	$0.7m
Revenues FY '95:	n/a
EPS '94:	$(0.25)
EPS '95:	n/a
Shares Outstanding:	5.0m
Five-Year Growth Rate:	n/a

NEWBRIDGE
NETWORKS

Address:	North and South American Headquarters 593 Herndon Parkway Herndon, VA 22070
Telephone:	703/834-3600
Fax:	703/471-7080
E-mail:	webmaster@newbridge.com
Web site:	www.newbridge.com
Industry:	Communications
Sector:	Computer Networking
CEO:	Terence Matthews
CFO:	Peter D. Charbonneau
Stock Exchange:	NYSE
Stock Symbol:	NN

Product Description

Newbridge Networks is a Canadian company that creates and markets solutions for wide- and local-area networks (WANs and LANs) under the name MainStreet. Its multimedia standards-based networking products have global LAN and WAN applications. Its systems are used by telcos to provide virtual business networks as an outsourced managed network service. Its products include digital overlay networks, intelligent networks, circuit switching, and packet switching. It recently created a desktop LAN ATM division. 13% of the company's revenues is dedicated to research and development.

Market Strategy/Positioning

Newbridge Networks has strategic relationships with Hewlett-Packard, AT&T, MCI, CrossKeys Systems, Advanced Computer Communications, TimeStep, and West End. Significant customers include Deutsche Telekom, Pacific Bell, Alcatel, AT&T, Siemens, NYNEX, Bloomberg, MCI, U S WEST, and Telecom Argentina. The company's competitive advantages are the effectiveness of its products in public, private, or hybrid networks, and its systems, designed to build seamless networks based upon a relational database that allows flexible service. Newbridge Networks primarily competes against GDC, AT&T, Fore Systems, Stratacom, Cascade, Northern Telecom, Timeplex, and NET. Additional challenges and risks include maintaining a market share lead in the multiplexor sector, and remaining the second largest supplier of frame relay switches.

Other

CEO Terence Matthews founded the Newbridge Networks in 1986 to design an open networking system that could be used on all major telephone systems throughout the world. Newbridge first secured multinational companies as customers and then expanded to included telephone companies.

356

KEY FACTS

Year Established:	1986
Employees:	2,960
Fiscal Year End:	April
Revenues FY '94:	$416.6m
Revenues FY '95:	$578.8m
EPS '94:	$1.50
EPS '95:	$1.67
Shares Outstanding:	81.5m
Five-Year Growth Rate:	31%

NEWS CORP.

Address:	U.S. Headquarters (News America Holdings) 1211 Avenue of the Americas New York, NY 10036
Telephone:	212/852-7000
Fax:	212/852-7145
E-mail:	n/a
Web site:	www.foxnetwork.com
Industry:	Entertainment & Information
Sector:	Broadcasters & Cable Networks
CEO:	Keith Rupert Murdoch
CFO:	David F. DeVoe
Stock Exchange:	NYSE
Stock Symbol:	NWS

Product Description

The News Corporation is the world's largest publisher of newspapers, magazines, and books. Its publications account for approximately 55% of the company's business. It owns 20th Century Fox, Fox Broadcasting, British Sky Broadcasting (BSkyB), Hong Kong's Star Television, and Delphi. News Corp. is also creating a strong presence on the Internet through Delphi, newspaper online serivces, News Datacom (encryption technologies for pay TV), ETAK (digital mapping), and a Fox Network Web site.

Market Strategy/Positioning

The company's mission is to be the preeminent supplier of first-class creative and editorial product to readers and viewers around the world. News Corp. has strategic relationships with Turner, Foxtel, Savoy Pictures, and MCI. News Corp. and MCI announced in August 1995 that they would launch new, Internet-based online services, including a guide to the Internet, games, online space for children, and specialized programming. The venture will encompass all online and interactive operations of both MCI and News Corp. The company's competitive advantage is its expanding market share in other mediums such as television and the Internet. News Corp. primarily competes against Advance Publications, America Online, Bertelsmann, CBS, Cox, Dow Jones, Gannett, GE, H&R Block, Hearst, Knight-Ridder, Matushita, McGraw-Hill, *The New York Times*, Pearson, PRODIGY, Sony, Time Warner, Times Mirror, Turner Broadcasting, Viacom, and Walt Disney.

Other

News Corp. was started in 1952 when Rupert Murdoch inherited two Australian newspapers. 20th Century Fox was purchased in 1985, and the next year the company began buying TV stations from Metromedia that would eventually become Fox Broadcasting. In 1993 News Corp. acquired a minority stake in Star Television, which let it broadcast over six channels to audiences in Asia. CFO David DeVoe has served as deputy finance director, and before working at News Corp. was the CFO of XCOR International, a manufacturing company.

KEY FACTS

Year Established:	1952
Employees:	25,900
Fiscal Year End:	June
Revenues FY '94:	$8.0b
Revenues FY '95:	n/a
EPS '94:	$2.04
EPS '95:	n/a
Shares Outstanding:	494.0m
Five-Year Growth Rate:	16%

NEXGEN

Product Description

NexGen's product is a microprocessor compatible with Intel's Pentium processor that is designed to maintain binary compatibility with the large installed base of software and peripherals designed for PCs. Future implementations will increase operating frequencies and reduce die size. NexGen plans to introduce next-generation products concurrently with Intel's P6 and next-generation processors. Its target markets are PC, OEMs, and PC motherboard manufacturers.

Address:	1623 Buckeye Drive
	Milpitas, CA 95035
Telephone:	408/435-0202
Fax:	408/526-9192
E-mail:	webmaster@nexgen.com
Web-site:	http://www.nexgen.com
Industry:	Computers
Sector:	Semiconductors
CEO:	S. Atiq Raza
CFO:	Anthony Chan
Stock Exchange:	NASDAQ
Stock Symbol:	NXGN

Market Strategy/Positioning

The company's mission is to achieve leadership in x86 high-performance processors for mainstream PC users. NexGen has strategic relationships with IBM for microprocessors, VLSI and Samsung for PCI chipsets, and Fujitsu for VL chipsets. Significant customers include Compaq, Alaris, DigiCom, Fountain, Aquarius, and Actebis. The company's competitive advantages are proprietary high-performance systems logic chipsets, and its innovative architecture that combines aspects of RISC architecture with the industry standard PC instruction set. NexGen was Intel's first competitor in the x86 market, and the company established key strategic alliances early on. NexGen primarily competes against Intel, AMD, and Cyrix. Additional challenges include capturing explosive growth.

358

Other

The company was founded in 1986 and spent its first two years gaining an understanding of the x86 standard instruction set behavior. In 1988 NexGen started to independently create superscalar, high-performance x86 products. It initially received $100 million from investors and had its IPO in May 1995. Atiq Raza is chairman, president, CEO, treasurer, and secretary. He has been with the company since 1988 and was previously vice president of Technology Centers at VLSI. Vice president and CFO Anthony Chan has more than 20 years of industry experience in finance for startup companies. He previously served as CFO at Cygnus Therapeutic and as controller at LSI Logic.

KEY FACTS

Year Established:	1986
Employees:	140
Fiscal Year End:	June
Revenues FY '94:	$0.0
Revenues FY '95:	$20.8m
EPS '94:	n/a
EPS '95:	$(1.21)
Shares Outstanding:	29.6m
Five-Year Growth Rate:	30%

NEXT COMPUTER

Address:	900 Chesapeake Drive
	Redwood City, CA 94063
Telephone:	415/366-0900
Fax:	415/780-3914
E-mail:	kindle_diguisto@next.com
Web site:	http://www.next.com
Industry:	Computers
Sector:	Enterprise & Client/Server Software
CEO:	Steven Jobs
CFO:	Dominique Trempont

Product Description

NeXT Computer develops and markets OpenStep, the first volume object standard for developing cross-platform object-oriented applications. The product is used primarily by financial service companies, the entertainment industry, and government services industries to simplify and speed the process of developing distributed client/server software. NeXT has announced implementations of OpenStep for several desktop and server operating systems, including Sun's Solaris, DEC's UNIX, and Microsoft's Windows 95 and Windows NT. In addition, NeXT has developed WebObjects, a software program for building object-oriented applications for use on the World Wide Web.

Market Strategy/Positioning

The company's mission is to be the leading provider of object technology for desktop and server operating systems. NeXT Computer has strategic relationships with Sun, Hewlett-Packard, DEC, and Bell Atlantic. Significant customers include Chrysler Financial, AT&T, Helsinki Telephone, U S WEST, MCI, Telecom Australia, NTT, and NASA. NeXT Computer primarily competes against Microsoft and Novell. Additional challenges and risks include providing versions of OpenStep that are compatible with the many different operating systems for desktop and servers computers. NeXT Computer is unique as one of the first companies to create an enterprise-wide object-oriented development and delivery solution.

359

Other

Steven Jobs and five senior managers from Apple Computer founded NeXT Computer in 1985. In September 1989 the company introduced the NeXT Computer and NEXTSTEP Release 1.0. During that year, Canon invested in the company. In May 1993 NeXT began shipping NEXSTEP Release 3.1 and NEXTSTEP Developer for Intel and Motorola processors. OpenStep was introduced in 1994 and WebObjects in 1995. Chairman and CEO Steven Jobs also co-founded Apple Computer and co-designed the Apple II computer. CFO Dominique Trempont previously worked in Raychem's Electronics Group.

Primary VCs/Outside Financing

Canon and Sun Microsystems.

KEY FACTS

Year Established:	1985
Employees:	300
Fiscal Year End:	December
Revenues FY '94:	$50.0m
Revenues FY '95:	n/a
Date of Next Financing:	n/a
Date of Last Financing:	n/a
Size of Last Financing:	n/a
Total Capital Raised:	n/a
Post Round Valuation:	n/a
Expected IPO Date:	n/a

NINTENDO

Product Description

Nintendo is the largest video game company in the world. In the U.S. at least 40% of homes owns a Nintendo system. The Super Nintendo Entertainment System is a 16-bit cartridge-based system that costs $100–$150. Nintendo announced a project with Silicon Graphics in 1993 to create a 64-bit machine featuring real-time 3D worlds and high-resolution video. This system was scheduled to be available in fall 1995 for fewer than $250.

Address:	U.S. Headquarters
	4820 150th Avenue Northeast
	Redmond, WA 98052-9733
Telephone:	206/882-2040
Fax:	206/882-3585
E-mail:	n/a
Web site:	www.nintendo.com
Industry:	Entertainment & Information
Sector:	Entertainment/Education Software
CEO:	Minoru Arakawa
CFO:	Bruce Holdren
Stock Exchange:	NASDAQ
Stock Symbol:	NTDOY (ADR)

Market Strategy/Positioning

Nintendo has strategic relationships with Silicon Graphics, Rare, WMS Industries, DMA Design, Alias, Software Creations, Reflection Technology, Virgin Atlantic, China Air, Sheraton, Best Western, and GameTek. Significant customers include 190 game developers and licensees in the U.S. alone. The company's competitive advantage is its position as the largest manufacturer and marketer of video games. Nintendo primarily competes against 3DO, 7th Level, LucasArts Entertainment, NEC, Matsushita, Philips, Sega, Sony, Virgin Interactive, Walt Disney, Acclaim, Activision, Atari, Maxis, Electronic Arts, and Id Software. Nintendo is unique in having developed a new proprietary chip, a result of RISC technology, which enables the fastest cartridge-based video game play.

Other

The company, founded in 1889 as the Marufuku Company, originally designed Japanese card games. In 1907 it began producing Western playing cards, and it became the Nintendo Playing Card Company in 1951. Nintendo expanded into video games and arcade games in the 1970s and established its U.S. subsidiary in 1980. Its first hit was *Donkey Kong*, which was followed up by another success, *Super Mario Bros.* Other products that increased Nintendo's market share were the Nintendo Entertainment System (1986), Game Boy (1989), and the Super NES (1991). In 1994 it became the first hardware and software video-game company to introduce a new product online. The founding Yamauchi family dominates the company in both the U.S. and Japan, owning 11% of Nintendo.

KEY FACTS

Year Established:	1889
Employees:	570
Fiscal Year End:	March
Revenues FY '94:	$4.7b
Revenues FY '95:	n/a
EPS '94:	$0.45
EPS '95:	n/a
Shares Outstanding:	142.0m
Five-Year Growth Rate:	9%

NOKIA

Product Description

Telecommunications-related businesses account for 70% of Nokia's operations. The company manufactures cellular phones, sold in approximately 100 countries. The company is also involved in digital communications, GSM/DCS cellular networks, advanced cable products, and consumer and industrial electronics.

Market Strategy/Positioning

Nokia has strategic relationships with NYNEX CableComms England, Telecom Finland, ADC, E-Plus, Ericsson, and Hewlett-Packard. Significant customers include Omnitel Pronto (Italy), City of Beijing, and the Kirch Group (Germany). The company's competitive advantage is its position as the largest European manufacturer of mobile phones. Nokia was also the first company to manufacture a family of phones compatible with every digital standard in the world. Nokia primarily competes against AT&T, Ericsson, Fujitsu, GE, GTE, Matsushita, Motorola, NEC, Philips, Siemens, Sony, and Toshiba. Additional challenges include attaining its goal of becoming the leading player in the Philippines' mobile phone industry. Nokia is unique as the first Finnish company listed on the New York Stock Exchange (July 1994).

Other

Nokia was established by combining three Finnish companies: Nokia (forest industry), Finnish Rubber Works, and Finnish Cable Works. Throughout the 1980s Nokia focused on the telecommunications and consumer electronics markets. In 1982 the company designed and installed the first European digital telephone system in Finland. In 1988 through the purchase of Ericsson's Data Division, Nokia created the largest information technology group in Scandinavia, Nokia Data. The division was subsequently sold to ICL in 1991 when Nokia bought a U.K. mobile phone producer, Technophone.

Address:	U.S. Headquarters (Nokia Mobile Phones) 2300 Tall Pines Drive P.O. Box 2930 Largo, FL 34649
Telephone:	813/536-5553
Fax:	813/530-7245
E-mail:	n/a
Web site:	http://www.nokia.com
Industry:	Communications
Sector:	Wireless
CEO:	Jorma Ollila
CFO:	Olli-Pekka Kallasvuo
Stock Exchange:	NYSE
Stock Symbol:	NOK Pr

361

KEY FACTS

Year Established:	1966
Employees:	31,000
Fiscal Year End:	December
Revenues FY '94:	$6.3b
Revenues FY '95:	n/a
EPS '94:	$2.31
EPS '95:	$5.39 (estimate)
Shares Outstanding:	10.5m
Five-Year Growth Rate:	n/a

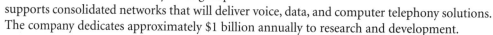

NORTHERN
TELECOM

Product Description

Northern Telecom (Nortel) develops, manufactures, installs, and services fully digital telecommunications systems. It offers enabling technologies for residential, enterprise, community, carrier, and wireless industries. Nortel has four network businesses to assist customers globally: Broadband Networks, Enterprise Networks, Switching Networks, and Wireless Networks. Additionally, its Multimedia Communication Systems group supports consolidated networks that will deliver voice, data, and computer telephony solutions. The company dedicates approximately $1 billion annually to research and development.

Address:	2221 Lakeside Boulevard Richardson, TX 75082
Telephone:	214/684-1000
Fax:	214/684-3733
E-mail:	n/a
Web site:	http://www.nortel.com
Industry:	Communications
Sector:	Information Highway Equipment
CEO:	Jean C. Monty
CFO:	Peter W. Curie
Stock Exchange:	NYSE
Stock Symbol:	NT

Market Strategy/Positioning

The company's mission is to deliver market leadership through customer satisfaction and product excellence. Northern Telecom has strategic relationships with Daimler-Benz, Lagardere Group, and E/O Networks. Nortel agreed to market and support the FDS-1 Fiber Distribution System from E/O Networks in September 1995. The company's competitive advantage is its installed base—Nortel has sold, or has on order, over 125 million ports of fully digital switching systems, more than any other company. Northern Telecom primarily competes against Alcatel, AT&T, Australian Telecom, Bellcore, Canadian Pacific, Deutsche Telekom, Ericsson, France Télécom, Fujitsu, GTE, Hitachi, Motorola, NEC, Oki, Siemens, Toshiba, and Unitel Communications. Additional challenges and risks include managing the push into international markets.

Other

Northern Telecom was founded in 1895 as the Northern Electric and Manufacturing Company. Northern Electric and Imperial Wire & Cable formed the Northern Electric Company in 1914. In an effort to increase research and development, Bell Canada and Northern Electric established Northern Electric Laboratories in 1958. Bell Canada began selling off Northern Electric stock in 1973. In 1976 the company changed its name to Northern Telecom and helped introduce digital technology to the telecommunications industry. Currently, it has more than 110 million digital lines in use in 90 countries. BCE, a management holding company, owns 52% of Northern Telecom.

KEY FACTS

Year Established:	1895
Employees:	60,000
Fiscal Year End:	December
Revenues FY '94:	$8.96b
Revenues FY '95:	n/a
EPS '94:	$1.60
EPS '95:	$1.93 (estimate)
Shares Outstanding:	251.0m
Five-Year Growth Rate:	15%

NOTABLE
TECHNOLOGIES

Address:	411 108th Avenue Northeast
	Suite 1000
	Bellevue, WA 98004
Telephone:	206/455-4040
Fax:	206/455-4440
E-mail:	n/a
Web site:	http://www.airnote.net
Industry:	Computers
Sector:	Wireless Communications
CEO:	Stephen Wood
CFO:	Cynthia Gissler

Product Description

Notable Technologies provides wireless data communications services, from information to hardware and software. Its first product is a financial information service that delivers customized stock quotes and news to customers via a paging system. The company also offers a service that allows paging from phone, computer, e-mail, and the Internet. The company also offers a World Wide Web site that allows people to page subscribers instantly.

Market Strategy/Positioning

The company's mission is to offer applications and services that offers customers the information they need. Notable Technologies has strategic relationships with Paging Network (PageNet), SkyTel, AT&T Wireless, National Dispatch Center, Sharp Electronics, and Telescan. Significant customers include private investors, institutional investors, analysts, and portfolio managers. The company's competitive advantage is its expertise in PC hardware and software and in the wireless industry. Notable Technologies primarily competes against Data Broadcasting, America Online, PRODIGY, and CompuServe. Additional risks include not being aligned with any single communications network and the fact that Notable may be too early with its technology. There is also the risk of competition from established companies who may enter wireless markets.

363

Other

Notable Technologies developed end-user applications running on GO's PenPoint operating system. In 1994 the company received venture funding and shifted its focus to the wireless market. The company estimates its current customer-base at 100 million paging service users, 30 million cellular phone users, and five million people equipped with personal digital assistants. CEO Stephen Wood was formerly vice president of information broadcasting at McCaw Development, and he began his career at Microsoft. CFO Cynthia Gissler served as controller of Bananafish Software.

Primary VCs/Outside Financing

Kleiner Perkins Caufield & Byers, the Sevin Rosen Funds, Olivetti Venture Funds, Integral Capital Partners, and AT&T Wireless.

KEY FACTS

Year Established:	1991
Employees:	35
Fiscal Year End:	December
Revenues FY '94:	n/a
Revenues FY '95:	n/a
Date of Next Financing:	n/a
Date of Last Financing:	November 1994
Size of Last Financing:	$5.0m
Total Capital Raised:	$10.0m
Post Round Valuation:	n/a
Expected IPO Date:	n/a

NOVELL

Product Description

Novell is a vendor of network operating systems software that integrates desktop computers, servers, and minicomputer or mainframe hosts on local-area networks (LANs). The company's products provide a distributed infrastructure, network services, advanced network access, and network applications. In 1994 the company broke into the desktop applications market with the acquisition of Quattro Pro and WordPerfect, making it the second-largest PC-software company after Microsoft. The acquisition of UNIX system labs in 1993 was aimed at Novell's entering the enterprise networking software market. Novell now offers client/server products that support standards to integrate DOS, OS/2, Macintosh, and UNIX desktop computers with IBM, DEC, and other UNIX hosts.

Address:	1555 North Technology Way Orem, UT 84057
Telephone:	801/429-7000
Fax:	801/429-5555
E-mail:	info@novell.com
Web site:	http://www.novell.com
Industry:	Computers
Sector:	Enterprise & Client/Server Software
CEO:	Robert Frankenberg
CFO:	James R. Tolonen
Stock Exchange:	NASDAQ
Stock Symbol:	NOVL

Market Strategy/Positioning

By teaming up with the world's best content, systems, communications, and solution providers, Novell constantly redefines networking. Novell has strategic relationships with Onward Technologies, AT&T, Wall Data, Pioneer, Canon, Fujitsu, NEC, Sony, Toshiba, Softbank, Intel, and Xerox. Significant customers include most major corporations that use PC-based LANs. The company's competitive advantages are its dominant market share in the PC networking software market and a large installed base of Novell users, which gives it critical mass to take on Microsoft in several markets at once. Novell primarily competes against Microsoft in the desktop application market, and with IBM, Banyan Systems, Computer Associates, Cheyenne Software, Proteon, and Wang in the networking software business.

Other

Novell was founded in 1980; in 1981 Safeguard Scientifics bought 55% of the company. In 1983 turnaround specialist Raymond Noorda was brought in to create a new Novell. After going public in 1985, Novell began acquiring companies to enhance its product line, and in 1994 it acquired both WordPerfect and Borland's QuattroPro and transferred its database products to Btrieve (a company in which Novell has a 15% stake). Raymond Noorda invested $125,000 of his own money to boost Novell in 1983. Chairman, president, and CEO Robert Frankenberg succeeded Ray Noorda in 1994 and was formerly at Hewlett-Packard.

364

KEY FACTS

Year Established:	1980
Employees:	8,460
Fiscal Year End:	October
Revenues FY '94:	$2.0b
Revenues FY '95:	$2.18b (estimate)
EPS '94:	$0.57
EPS '95:	$1.07 (estimate)
Shares Outstanding:	368.6m
Five-Year Growth Rate:	18%

NTT
NIPPON TELEGRAPH AND TELEPHONE

Product Description

Nippon Telegraph and Telephone is the largest supplier of telecommunications services in Japan, offering telephone, cellular telephone, leased circuit, data communication facilities, digital data exchange, pocket pagers, and other services, as well as leasing and purchase plans for terminal equipment. Its new Multimedia Business Development division will manage opportunities for new media communications as NTT forges ahead in multimedia and interactive communications.

Address:	U.S. Headquarters
	800 El Camino Real West
	Suite 103
	Mountain View, CA 94040
Telephone:	415/940-1414
Fax:	415/940-1375
E-mail:	n/a
Web site:	http://www.ntt.jp
Industry:	Communications
Sector:	Information Highway Services
CEO:	Masashi Kojima
CFO:	n/a
Stock Exchange:	NYSE
Stock Symbol:	NTT (ADR)

365

Market Strategy/Positioning

The company's mission is to provide high-quality telecommunications services, and to conduct research and development activities that will support the network of the 21st century. The company plans to emphasize overseas activities. NTT has strategic relationships with General Magic, AT&T, Motorola, Ericsson, Microsoft, Silicon Graphics, and Nextel. Significant customers include Toyota, Honda, Mitsubishi, and Sony. The company's competitive advantage is that the Japanese market lacks the cable penetration the U.S. market has. As a monopoly player, NTT has initiated a Japan-wide plan to deliver narrow-band ISDN for Internet access and videoconferencing. NTT primarily competes against AT&T, Cable & Wireless, Daini-Denden, Japan Telecom, Nippon Idou Tshshin, Teleway Japan, Tokyo Digital Phone, and Tu-ka Cellular Tokyo. Additional challenges and risks include overcoming regulatory hurdles and managing any opportunities deregulation offers. NTT is unique as a service, not a manufacturing, company. As a result, NTT is not tied to a plant and can pick and choose among vendors. It also has access to one of the largest basic research labs in the world.

Other

NTT began telephone services in Tokyo and Yokohama in 1890. Established in 1952, NTT Public Corporation began a public fax service in 1981 and a videotex network in 1984. In 1985 telecommunications were deregulated in Japan and NTT became a publicly-owned corporation. NTT chose Motorola, AT&T, and Ericsson to create a digital mobile phone network in 1990. The company began projects in interactive cable TV and e-mail in 1993 and formed alliances with several U.S. companies. NTT began trading on the New York and the London stock exchanges in 1994.

KEY FACTS

Year Established:	1890
Employees:	200,000
Fiscal Year End:	March
Revenues FY '94:	n/a
Revenues FY '95:	n/a
EPS '94:	$0.21
EPS '95:	n/a
Shares Outstanding:	15.6m
Five-Year Growth Rate:	29%

NVIDIA

Product Description

NVIDIA develops VLSI and software acceleration technology. The company's multimedia accelerator offers a wide range of advanced multimedia functions, including real-time photorealistic 3D graphics, full-motion video, video-based special effects, and high-fidelity audio. NVIDIA's flagship product is a single chip that provides coherent multimedia architecture. Its products enhance the quality and speed of multimedia applications and enable the conversion of high-end Sega and arcade software to CD-ROMs for Pentium-based PCs.

Address:	1226 Tiros Way
	Sunnyvale, CA 94086
Telephone:	408/720-6100
Fax:	408/720-6111
E-mail:	n/a
Web site:	http://www.nvidia.com
Industry:	Computers
Sector:	Semiconductors
CEO:	Jen-Hsun Huang
CFO:	Marshall Smith

Market Strategy/Positioning

The company's mission is to transform the PC into the ultimate multimedia machine. NVIDIA has a strategic relationship with Sega, which is porting Saturn titles exclusively to NVIDIA chips on PCs and CD-ROMs. It also is involved in a manufacturing agreement with SGS-Thomson. Significant customers include Sega and Diamond Multimedia. The company's competitive advantages include having the only product with necessary components for multimedia content (video, audio, and direct input devices) in Windows 95, and a graphics engine that delivers the most aggressive Windows acceleration performance. NVIDIA primarily competes against Cirrus, S3, 3Dfx, and Rendition. Additional challenges and risks include educating the market on 3D and developing applications to make the best use of available technology.

Other

NVIDIA was founded in 1993 with backing from several venture capital firms. It developed and filed 20 patents for its proprietary architecture. Within one year, the company created a complex, million-transistor chip, which became its primary product. Co-founder, president, and CEO Jen-Hsun Huang has worked in the semiconductor industry for 12 years. He formerly served as director and general manager of LSI Logic's Coreware division and held positions at Advanced Micro Devices. Chris Malachowsky, vice president of engineering and co-founder, worked for Sun Microsystems and holds 22 patents. Co-founder and chief technical officer Curtis Priem hails from Sun Microsystems and Vermont Microsystems and holds 27 patents.

Primary VCs/Outside Financing

Sequoia Capital, Sutter Hill Ventures, Itochu, and Jafco America Ventures.

KEY FACTS

Year Established:	1993
Employees:	55
Fiscal Year End:	December
Revenues FY '94:	$0.0
Revenues FY '95:	$10.0m
Date of Next Financing:	n/a
Date of Last Financing:	July 1995
Size of Last Financing:	$5.0m
Total Capital Raised:	$12.0m
Post Round Valuation:	$140.0m
Expected IPO Date:	Early 1997

NYNEX

Product Description

NYNEX provides telecommunications, cable television, information systems, video entertainment, directory publishing, and business services. It filed with the FCC in August 1994 to offer video dial-tone services in Eastern Massachusetts and Rhode Island, now being tested in New York City. The company is committed to FLAG, a $1 billion project to lay undersea fiber-optic cable from the U.K. to Japan. Other projects include the creation of Tele-TV, a new company that will provide digital broadcast and interactive channels giving consumers information, entertainment, and communications services.

Address:	1113 Westchester Avenue White Plains, NY 10604
Telephone:	914/644-6400
Fax:	914/644-7649
E-mail:	n/a
Web site:	http://www.niyp.com
Industry:	Communications
Sector:	Information Highway Services
CEO:	Ivan G. Seidenberg
CFO:	Alan Z. Senter
Stock Exchange:	NYSE
Stock Symbol:	NYN

Market Strategy/Positioning

The company's mission is to be a world-class leader in helping people communicate using information networks and services. NYNEX has strategic relationships with Viacom, Citibank, Philips, Bell Atlantic, Creative Artists Agency, AirTouch, U S WEST, Philips, Dow Jones, TelecomAsia, Nokia, Telecom Holdings, Dallah Al Baraka Group, Marubeni, and Gulf Investors. The company's competitive advantage is its investment of $2.3 billion in network improvements and expansion. NYNEX primarily competes against American Business Information, Ameritech, AT&T, Bell Atlantic, BellSouth, Cable & Wireless, GTE, MCI, Nextel, Pacific Telesis, Southwestern Bell, Sprint, Teleport, U S WEST, and U.S. Long Distance. Upon divestiture from AT&T in 1984, the company received the most antiquated network of the seven regional Bell operating companies (RBOCs). NYNEX is unique in being the first RBOC to offer video dial-tone—a service that allows users to view movies and programs whenever they want to on a trial basis.

367

Other

NYNEX's two divisions, New York Telephone and New England Telephone, began as branches of AT&T. In 1984 the RBOCs were split as part of the AT&T antitrust settlement. In 1993 NYNEX bought $1.2 billion of Viacom stock to back Viacom's bid for Paramount and now owns 5% of Viacom. The following year, NYNEX, Bell Atlantic, U S WEST, and AirTouch began a wireless partnership. NYNEX invested more than $150 million in research and development in 1994.

KEY FACTS

Year Established:	1984
Employees:	76,200
Fiscal Year End:	December
Revenues FY '94:	$13.3b
Revenues FY '95:	n/a
EPS '94:	$1.89
EPS '95:	$3.14 (estimate)
Shares Outstanding:	418.8m
Five-Year Growth Rate:	6%

OBJECT DESIGN INC. (ODI)

Address:	25 Mall Road
	6th Floor
	Burlington, MA 01803-4194
Telephone:	617/674-5000
Fax:	617/674-5252
E-mail:	info@odi.com
Web site:	http://www.odi.com
Industry:	Computers
Sector:	Enterprise & Client/Server Software
CEO:	Gerald Bay
CFO:	Stanley Miller

Product Description

Object Design is a developer of object-oriented databases that store, distribute, and manage all forms of data in a client/server environment. The company has a leading 35% market share in one of the fastest growing segments of the software market. The company's primary product is a distributed heterogeneous database designed to manage text and numerical data as well as multimedia audio, video, graphics, and documents. The company's target markets are business re-engineering, computer-aided design, computer-aided publishing, computer-aided software engineering, mapping and geographic information systems, financial and scientific modeling, and increasingly advanced office automation applications.

Market Strategy/Positioning

Object Design has strategic relationships with IBM, Sun Microsystems, SunSoft, Hewlett-Packard, DEC, Cadence, and AT&T. Significant customers include Bellcore, six of the regional Bell operating companies (RBOCs), Zuken, Ericsson, SunSoft, Computervision, Ameritech, Intel, Martin Marietta, NEC, Texas Instruments, Price Waterhouse, Boeing, and Ford. The company's competitive advantages are its leading market share, strong strategic partnerships, and technological leadership. ODI primarily competes against Versant, ONTOS, Sevio, ADB, and Objectivity. Additional challenges and risks include acceptance of technology in the marketplace and the threat of competition from established relational database vendors.

Other

Chairman Thomas Atwood founded Object Design in 1988 with funding from a prestigious group of investors. Mr. Atwood also founded Ontologic. The company introduced its first product in 1990 and received equity investment from IBM in 1993. CEO Kenneth Marshall was former vice president at Oracle and headed East coast operations.

Primary VCs/Outside Financing

Aeneas, Orien Ventures, The Vista Group, Aperture, Silverado, Brentwood Associates, Zuken (Japan), Harvard Management, New Enterprise Associates, Philips, Silverado, Eastman Kodak, AT&T, IBM, Intel, and Olivetti.

KEY FACTS

Year Established:	1988
Employees:	240
Fiscal Year End:	December
Revenues FY '94:	$30.0m
Revenues FY '95:	$35.0m
Date of Next Financing:	n/a
Date of Last Financing:	March 1994
Size of Last Financing:	$7.0m
Total Capital Raised:	$38.2m
Post Round Valuation:	$150.0m
Expected IPO Date:	n/a

OBJECTIVE SYSTEMS

Address:	865 Tahoe Boulevard
	Suite 203
	Incline Village, CA 89451
Telephone:	702/832-1930
Fax:	702/832-1935
E-mail:	dickvento@osi.com
Web site:	http://www.osi.com
Industry:	Communications
Sector:	Information Highway Services
CEO:	Thomas Johnson/Dick Vento
CFO:	Gay Hirahara

Product Description

Objective Systems develops software frameworks that deliver operational support systems solutions to a range of telecommunication companies, including inter-exchange carriers, cellular providers, and independents. It also provides software for interactive TV. The company's flagship product collects and filters data from standard and non-standard equipment. Its main features include network and service management, data collection, service activation, test management, AIN service management, and electronic bonding. OSI's rapid programmerless implementation provides clients with speed-to-market benefits. All its products are based on UNIX platforms.

Market Strategy/Positioning

The company's mission is to provide deployment of operations support systems to public and private network services providers by using open, object-oriented software systems. Objective Systems has strategic relationships with Hewlett-Packard, Amdahl, Logica, Loral, Tandem, Tellabs, Stratacom, Andersen Consulting, DSC, Ericsson, and Siemens. Significant customers include all inter-exchange and local exchange carriers, 60% of the U.S. cellular market, major telecom manufacturers, cable TV, and international carriers. The company's competitive advantages are its ability to help clients reduce time to market for new services (Frame Relay) from 30 months to four months, and its programmerless interfacing implementation. Objective Systems primarily competes against in-house programmers using Platform products, e.g. Hewlett-Packard's OpenView, and IBM NetView 6000. Additional challenges and risks include recruiting and training adequate support staff to meet its market requirements.

Other

The company was founded in 1989 by Tom Johnson and Dick Vento. OSI is their third telecomunications software venture. They initially developed their first product, NetExpert, as a tool-kit for the telecommunications companies. After leaving CSC's time-sharing division in 1981, Co-CEOs Mr. Johnson and Mr. Vento formed several call management companies, including TelAccount and TelWatch.

KEY FACTS

Year Established:	1989
Employees:	175
Fiscal Year End:	n/a
Revenues FY '94:	$19.0m
Revenues FY '95:	$40.0m
Date of Next Financing:	n/a
Date of Last Financing:	n/a
Size of Last Financing:	n/a
Total Capital Raised:	n/a
Post Round Valuation:	$300.0m
Expected IPO Date:	Q1 1996

ONSALE

Address:	1953 Landings Drive
	Mountain View, CA 94043
Telephone:	415/428-0600
Fax:	415/428-0163
E-mail:	info@onsale.com
Web site:	http://www.onsale.com
Industry:	Entertainment & Information
Sector:	Online Services
CEO:	Jerry Kaplan
CFO:	n/a

Product Description

ONSALE is an interactive retail service on the Internet's World Wide Web that aims to add fun and adventure to the online shopping experience. ONSALE is designed to appeal to the Internet's current primary audience: high-income males in technical professions, with an average household income of $65,000. ONSALE's current inventory includes computers and electronics, special wine collections, vintage and collectible watches, sports memorabilia, rock and roll memorabilia, and vacation packages. The selling formats include standard auctions, Dutch auctions, and markdowns.

Market Strategy/Positioning

The company's competitive advantages are its one-of-a-kind service that focuses on entertainment and the excitement aspect of online interactive retail shopping. ONSALE primarily competes against numerous online sites that offer retail services, including the Web sites of major retail companies. ONSALE also competes with other shopping Web sites such as Internet Shopping Network, and all the major commercial online services (America Online, etc.) Additional challenges and risks include the need to attract users to its site and provide them with a satisfying experience to ensure repeat business, and to keep an inventory of goods and services offered that is interesting and exciting enough to attract visitors.

Other

ONSALE was founded by CEO Jerry Kaplan and chief technical officer Alan Fisher in 1994. Its service was launched in May 1995 to simulate the excitement and entertainment of bidding at an auction and hunting for bargains. CEO Jerry Kaplan was chairman and co-founder of GO, which developed a pen-based operating system. Before GO Mr. Kaplan was principal technologist at Lotus where he co-authored Agenda, the first personal information management software. He also founded Teknowledge in 1981. Chief technical officer Alan Fisher was previously a project manager at Teknowledge and a technical staff member at AT&T Bell Labs.

Primary VCs/Outside Financing

Internally funded and private individual investors.

KEY FACTS

Year Established:	1994
Employees:	n/a
Fiscal Year End:	n/a
Revenues FY '94:	n/a
Revenues FY '95:	n/a
Date of Next Financing:	n/a
Date of Last Financing:	n/a
Size of Last Financing:	n/a
Total Capital Raised:	n/a
Post Round Valuation:	n/a
Expected IPO Date:	n/a

OPEN MARKET

Product Description

Open Market develops and markets software, services, and custom solutions for electronic commerce over the Internet and eventually for other media. The company has rights to Massachusetts Institute of Technology security, search, and agent technology. It offers an Internet storefront creation tool, services for merchants, and a buyer environment. Open Market offers solutions for both small companies and global businesses.

Address:	245 First Street Cambridge, MA 02142
Telephone:	617/621-9500
Fax:	617/621-1703
E-mail:	info@openmarket.com
Web site:	http://www.openmarket.com
Industry:	Entertainment & Information
Sector:	Online Services
CEO:	Shikhar Ghosh
CFO:	Reggie Sommer

Market Strategy/Positioning

The company's mission is to offer merchants a complete electronic infrastructure to establish and manage a business on the Internet. Open Market has strategic relationships with Tandem Computer, BancOne, RoweCom, First Union, LEXIS-NEXIS, and the Copyright Clearance Center. Significant customers include Time Warner, Condé Nast, Tribune Company, and Ipswitch. The company's competitive advantages are its strong technology infrastructure and its concentration on the server; it does not offer a browser. Open Market primarily competes against Netscape and Microsoft. Additional challenges and risks include facilitating acceptance of the Internet from the public and making consumers feel comfortable. Open Market is unique in applying both advanced technology and a business perspective to the expansion of business into an electronic marketplace.

Other

Founded in 1994, Open Market quickly announced affiliations with several companies. It linked up with Time Warner, First Union, LEXIS-NEXIS, and several other companies in 1995, and is beginning its effort to enable commerce on the Internet. It is also part of the WWW Consortium. Open Market was co-founded by Shikhar Ghosh and David Gifford. CEO Mr. Ghosh was previously CEO of Appex before selling it to EDS. Chief scientific officer David Gifford is a professor and head of the Programming Systems Research Group at Massachusetts Institute of Technology. Mr. Gifford also serves as a policy advisor to agencies involved in the National Information Infrastructure.

Primary VCs/Outside Financing

Greylock Management and Gulrez Arshad.

KEY FACTS

Year Established:	1994
Employees:	80
Fiscal Year End:	n/a
Revenues FY '94:	n/a
Revenues FY '95:	$5.0m
Date of Next Financing:	n/a
Date of Last Financing:	June 1994
Size of Last Financing:	$1.8m
Total Capital Raised:	n/a
Post Round Valuation:	n/a
Expected IPO Date:	n/a

ORACLE
SYSTEMS

Address:	500 Oracle Parkway
	Redwood City, CA 94065
Telephone:	415/506-7000
Fax:	415/506-7200
E-mail:	info@oracle.com
Web site:	http://www.oracle.com
Industry:	Computers
Sector:	Enterprise & Client/Server Software
CEO:	Larry Ellison
CFO:	Jeffrey Henley
Stock Exchange:	NASDAQ
Stock Symbol:	ORCL

Product Description

Oracle Systems is the world's largest independent vendor of database software; it has an integrated family of portable software that includes relational database management system (RDBMS), applications development, office automation, end-user accounting, and manufacturing applications that run in client/server environments. UNIX and desktop system platforms account for more than 80% of its revenues. Oracle is the leader in the UNIX RDBMS market, with an estimated 40% market share. Its pre-packaged applications include solutions for human resources, finance and accounting, manufacturing, and project control. In recent years, revenues from consulting and applications have been growing much more rapidly than revenues from database licenses. Its consulting revenues make it the fourth largest consulting firm in the world. Oracle is also active in the new media market with a variety of software products, including a media server and tools, for interactive television and video-on-demand applications. Oracle's software runs on everything from personal digital assistants, set-top devices, PCs, workstations, minicomputers, mainframes, and massively parallel computers.

Market Strategy/Positioning

Oracle Systems has strategic relationships with IBM and Apple in a joint marketing effort for development tools, and with 50 leading set-top device vendors to speed the delivery of interactive TV. Significant customers include U.S. EPA, the IRS, Ciba-Geigy, Eli Lily, Johnson & Johnson, McDonald's, Walgreens, BMW, Sony, Bechtel, Chevron, Shell, AT&T, Motorola, NTT, Hertz, Fidelity, and Chemical Bank. The company's competitive advantages are its breadth of product, technology leadership across its products, leading market share in the RDBMS market, and strength in a number of high-growth areas such as applications, data-warehousing, new media applications, and parallel databases. Oracle Systems primarily competes against Informix, Sybase (Powersoft), Computer Associates (Ingres), Progress, Gupta, IBM, PeopleSoft, Dun & Bradstreet, Business Objects, Baan, and SAP. Additional challenges and risks include the possible erosion of profit margins for enterprise software, timely development of new products, and the ability to staff for rapid growth, particularly in the application-consulting area.

372

KEY FACTS

Year Established:	1977
Employees:	16,100
Fiscal Year End:	May
Revenues FY '94:	$2.0b
Revenues FY '95:	$3.0b
EPS '94:	$0.64
EPS '95:	$1.00
Shares Outstanding:	431.2m
Five-Year Growth Rate:	33%

Other

Larry Ellison founded Oracle Systems in 1977 and introduced the first commercially available DBMS in 1979. In 1992 Oracle released Version 7 of the RDBMS, developed to support large numbers of users and higher rates of transaction processing. In 1994 Oracle's revenues climbed over $2 billion. Larry Ellison has been president and CEO of the company since 1977. Before founding Oracle, he was vice president of systems development at Omex, a manufacturer of laser recording devices for image-processing. Mr. Ellison also held various technical positions at Ampex and Amdahl. CFO Jeff Henley worked previously as executive vice president and CFO at Pacific Holding Company and also as director of finance at Memorex in its large storage division.

PACIFIC DATA IMAGES (PDI)

Address:	1111 Karlstad Drive
	Sunnyvale, CA 94089
Telephone:	408/745-6755
Fax:	408/745-6746
E-mail:	crosendahl@pdi.com
Web site:	http://www.pdi.com
Industry:	Entertainment & Information
Sector:	Film & Entertainment Production
CEO:	Carl Rosendahl
CFO:	Richard Chuang

Product Description

Pacific Data Images (PDI) provides animation and special effects for feature films, television programs, and interactive products. Its services range from conceptualization and design to all aspects of production. PDI is also developing original content for feature film, TV, and interactive projects. Films credits include *Batman Forever*, *True Lies*, *Natural Born Killers*, *Terminator 2*, and *Start Trek VI*. Commercial credits include works for AT&T, British Airways, Coca-Cola, Federal Express, Jaguar, Levi's, Pacific Bell, Pepsi-Cola, Sony, and Xerox. All current work is done in the Sunnyvale studio, which is online with its Burbank office.

Market Strategy/Positioning

The company's mission is to be a leader in high-end digital animation and effects for the entertainment industry. PDI has strategic relationships with Marks Communications and Silicon Graphics. Its significant customers include Warner Bros., 20th Century Fox, Universal Pictures, Hollywood Pictures, CarolCo, Leo Burnett, J. Walter Thompson, Lintas, Chiat Day, Young & Rubicam, Ogilvy & Mather, TNT, and ESPN. The company's competitive advantages are its proprietary software for high-end projects, its character animation group, and its directing and design talent. PDI primarily competes against Industrial Light & Magic, Digital Domain, Rhythm & Hues, and Pixar. Additional challenges and risks include moving from a service provider to a content developer.

374

Other

Pacific Data Images was founded in 1980 by Carl Rosendahl and originally produced broadcast graphics. Mr. Rosendahl was joined in 1982 by his two partners, Richard Chuang and Glenn Entis. In 1985 PDI expanded into advertising and commercials, and in 1990 it branched into feature film effects. In addition, it now produces original animated films. Carl Rosendahl started PDI in 1980 to combine his interest in filmmaking and computer graphics. Other management comes from R/GA Digital Studios, Xaos Tools, and SOFTIMAGE.

Primary VCs/Outside Financing

100% internally funded.

KEY FACTS

Year Established:	1980
Employees:	85
Fiscal Year End:	n/a
Revenues FY '94:	$10–15.0m
Revenues FY '95:	$15–20.0m
Date of Next Financing:	n/a
Date of Last Financing:	n/a
Size of Last Financing:	n/a
Total Capital Raised:	n/a
Post Round Valuation:	n/a
Expected IPO Date:	n/a

PACIFIC
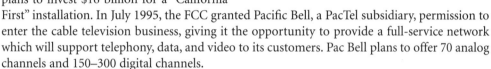
TELESIS GROUP

Address:	130 Kearny Street San Francisco, CA 94108
Telephone:	415/394-3000
Fax:	415/362-2913
E-mail:	webmaster@pactel.com
Web site:	http://www.pactel.com
Industry:	Communications
Sector:	Information Highway Services
CEO:	Philip J. Quigley
CFO:	William E. Downing
Stock Exchange:	NYSE
Stock Symbol:	PAC

Product Description

The Pacific Telesis Group (PacTel) provides communications and information services in California and Nevada and is the smallest of the seven regional Bell operating companies (RBOCs). The company plans to expand into interactive TV in its territory. PacTel united with Hewlett-Packard and AT&T for an actual introduction of video-on-demand services. It predicts 100,000 subscribers and plans to invest $16 billion for a "California First" installation. In July 1995, the FCC granted Pacific Bell, a PacTel subsidiary, permission to enter the cable television business, giving it the opportunity to provide a full-service network which will support telephony, data, and video to its customers. Pac Bell plans to offer 70 analog channels and 150–300 digital channels.

Market Strategy/Positioning

The company's mission is to provide high-quality, competitively-priced voice, data, video, and wireless communications services that enhance customers' work, learning, and leisure. PacTel has strategic relationships with Hewlett-Packard, AT&T, Sony, and Ascend Communications. The company's competitive advantage is its deployment of digital technology, allowing consumers to take advantage of the voice, data, and video capabilities of ISDN. PacTel primarily competes against American Business Information, Ameritech, AT&T, Bell Atlantic, BellSouth, Cable & Wireless, RR Donnelley, GTE, MCI, NYNEX, Southwestern Bell, Sprint, TCI, U S WEST, U.S. Long Distance, and Viacom. Additional challenges include becoming the first company to bring the benefits of the convergence of telecommunications, television, and computers to California, and entering two new markets: personal communications service (PCS) and consumer video services.

375

Other

After divesting from AT&T in 1984, Pacific Bell was placed into parent Pacific Telesis Group. With the 1986 purchase of Communications Industries, PacTel became a key competitor in cellular radio and paging. The company formed CalREN, a program to stimulate the development of new applications for high-speed data communications. In 1993 the company bought a 51% stake in NordicTel Holdings, a Swedish cellular service provider. In 1994 PacTel spun off AirTouch, its wireless communications unit. That same year, the company

KEY FACTS

Year Established:	1984
Employees:	51,600
Fiscal Year End:	December
Revenues FY '94:	$9.2b
Revenues FY '95:	n/a
EPS '94:	$2.37
EPS '95:	$2.52 (estimate)
Shares Outstanding:	423.0m
Five-Year Growth Rate:	4%

PACIFIC
TELESIS GROUP

joined Sony in a plan to bring movies to theaters over fiber-optic cable. Chairman, president, and CEO Phil Quigley was formerly president and CEO of Pacific Bell, executive president and COO of PacTel, and CEO of PacTel Personal Communications. Executive vice president, CFO, and treasurer Bill Downing has held various executive finance positions at Pacific Bell, PacTel, and AT&T.

PARAMETRIC TECHNOLOGY

Product Description

Parametric Technology develops and markets an integrated family of mechanical design automation software products. The company supplies CAD/CAM/CAE software to 6,200 companies throughout the world for mechanical design, manufacturing, and product data management. It emphasizes technological leadership, aggressive pricing, hardware independence, worldwide distribution, and customer support in its business strategy.

Address:	128 Technology Drive
	Waltham, MA 02154
Telephone:	617/398-5000
Fax:	617/398-6000
E-mail:	n/a
Web site:	http://www.ptc.com
Industry:	Computers
Sector:	Design Automation Software
CEO:	Stephen C. Walske
CFO:	Mark J. Gallagher
Stock Exchange:	NASDAQ
Stock Symbol:	PMTC

Market Strategy/Positioning

The company's mission is to be the dominant vendor in the mechanical design automation industry. Significant customers include Ford, Whirlpool, Lockheed Martin, Caterpillar, Motorola, AlliedSignal, Texas Instruments, Hughes Aircraft, John Deere, J.I. Case, Toyota, Volkswagen, AT&T, AMP, Siemens, Westinghouse, Sony, NEC, Hitachi, United Technologies, and Seiko Epson. Parametric's competitive advantages are having the industry's largest direct-sales force, hardware independence, ease-of-use; and delivering two major releases of software every year. Parametric Technology primarily competes against Computervision, IBM, EDS/Unigraphics, Autodesk, SDRC, and Intergraph. Additional challenges and risks include managing its growth and acquisition strategy.

377

Other

Founded in 1985, Parametric Technology began its first product shipments in 1988 and went public in December of 1989. Both *Business Week* and *Forbes* ranked Parametric among America's most valuable companies (based upon market value) in 1994. The company also announced several management transitions and formed a new Office of the Chairman in 1994. The company acquired the conceptual design and rendering system, a division of Evans & Sutherland Computer. As of August 1995, it had plans to acquire Rasna. Chairman and CEO Stephen Walske, previously president and CEO of Multiplications Software was instrumental in the company's merger with Computer Corporation of America. President and COO Richard Harrison has served as Parametric's vice president of sales and distribution since 1987.

KEY FACTS

Year Established:	1985
Employees:	1,700
Fiscal Year End:	September
Revenues FY '94:	$244.2m
Revenues FY '95:	n/a
EPS '94:	$1.14
EPS '95:	$1.53 (estimate)
Shares Outstanding:	61.9m
Five-Year Growth Rate:	29%

PARCPLACE SYSTEMS

Address:	999 East Arques Avenue
	Sunnyvale, CA 94086-4593
Telephone:	408/481-9090, 800/759-7272
Fax:	408/481-9095
E-mail:	snichols@parcplace.com
Web site:	http://www.parcplace.com
Industry:	Computers
Sector:	Enterprise & Client/Server Software
CEO:	William P. Lyons
CFO:	Carolyn V. Aver
Stock Exchange:	NASDAQ
Stock Symbol:	PARQ

Product Description

ParcPlace creates object-oriented application development environment solutions for software developers to create group-wide applications. It is the creator of ParcPlace SmallTalk, the first object-oriented programming language. Its flagship product, VisualWorks, is an object-oriented cross-platform ADE, which incorporates data access capability, SmallTalk as a scripting language, binary portability across 11 platforms, and a reusable application framework. The company also has a graphical user interface builder for UNIX C++ application development.

Market Strategy/Positioning

The company's mission is to be the object partner of choice for enterprise development. ParcPlace Systems has strategic relationships with AMS, Hewlett-Packard, Object Design, IBM, Gemini Consulting, Sun Microsystems, DEC, Andersen Consulting, EDS, Oracle, Sybase, and Mercury Interactive. Significant customers include Texas Instruments, American Airlines, Sprint, Northern Telecom, BellSouth, Federal Express, Dun & Bradstreet, and Chrysler. The company's competitive advantages are its SmallTalk language and its focus on the needs of enterprise-wide developers. ParcPlace Systems primarily competes against IBM and NeXT Computer; smaller competitors include Powersoft, Gupta, KnowledgeWare, Digitalk, Neuron Data, XVT, and Visix. Additional challenges and risks include significantly improving programmer productivity and developing platform portability for applications. ParcPlace Systems is unique in developing VisualWorks, the only SmallTalk application development tool available on over 12 platforms.

Other

In the 1970s researchers at Xerox's PARC invented SmallTalk, the first true object-oriented programming language. This technology became the model for the Macintosh and Windows user interfaces. ParcPlace's founders, part of the Xerox PARC efforts, formed the company to commercialize their object-oriented technology. ParcPlace and Digitalk signed a merger agreement in 1995. Chairman Adele Goldberg spent 14 years as a researcher and lab manager at Xerox PARC. President and CEO Bill Lyons was formerly chairman and CEO of Ashton-Tate Corporation, which merged with Borland.

KEY FACTS

Year Established:	1988
Employees:	140
Fiscal Year End:	March
Revenues FY '94:	$26.5m
Revenues FY '95:	$39.1m
EPS '94:	$0.30
EPS '95:	$0.39
Shares Outstanding:	8.4m
Five-Year Growth Rate:	40%

378

PEOPLESOFT

Address:	4440 Rosewood Drive
	Pleasanton, CA 94588-3031
Telephone:	510/225-3000
Fax:	510/225-3100
E-mail:	n/a
Web site:	http://www.peoplesoft.com
Industry:	Computers
Sector:	Enterprise & Client/Server Software
CEO:	David Duffield
CFO:	Ronald Codd
Stock Exchange:	NASDAQ
Stock Symbol:	PSFT

Product Description

PeopleSoft develops client/server software applications, including human resources product distribution, and corporate finance packages. The company was first-to-market with a pure client/server solution for the human resources market. PeopleSoft's target customer is the medium-to-large organization with over 1,000 employees that wants to upgrade from legacy systems.

Market Strategy/Positioning

The company's mission is to provide client/server applications that empower individuals to make informed decisions in large or complex organizations with dynamic, rapidly changing requirements. PeopleSoft has strategic relationships with DEC, IBM, Sequent, Andersen Consulting, Deloitte & Touche, Ernst & Young, Price Waterhouse, AT&T, Hewlett-Packard, IBM, Informix, Sybase, Oracle, Sun Microsystems, Microsoft, and Novell. Significant customers include over 700 companies worldwide, including AT&T, Coca-Cola, Dow Chemical, and The Gap. The company's competitive advantages are its client/server architecture, fast implementation, scalability and flexibility, and lower cost of operation. PeopleSoft primarily competes against SAP, Oracle, Sybase, PLATINUM, and Dun & Bradstreet. Additional challenges and risks include increased competition from established database players such as Oracle, margin erosion for enterprise software products, the ability to manage growth, and the ability to maintain a high level of customer service.

379

Other

CEO Dave Duffield, inspired by his idea that networks would make PCs more powerful, left Integral Systems in 1987 to start PeopleSoft. PeopleSoft went public in November of 1992 and revenues for the company have doubled every year for the past five years. Mr. Duffield founded the company with senior vice president Ken Morris. Mr. Duffield owns about 35% of the company.

KEY FACTS

Year Established:	1987
Employees:	1,000
Fiscal Year End:	December
Revenues FY '94:	$112.9m
Revenues FY '95:	$215.0m (estimate)
EPS '94:	$0.56
EPS '95:	$0.89 (estimate)
Shares Outstanding:	24.2m
Five-Year Growth Rate:	44%

PERFORMANCE
SYSTEMS INTERNATIONAL

Address:	510 Huntmar Park Drive
	Herndon, VA 22070
Telephone:	703/904-4100
Fax:	703/904-1207
E-mail:	investor_relations@psi.com
Web site:	http://www.psi.net
Industry:	Entertainment & Information
Sector:	Online Services
CEO:	William L. Schrader
CFO:	Daniel P. Cunningham
Stock Exchange:	NASDAQ
Stock Symbol:	PSIX

Product Description

Performance Systems International (PSI) is a provider of Internet access and services. The company plans to offer a graphical user interface (GUI) to increase the convenience of its products for less computer-savvy consumers. The GUI will be used with its national online service, which features locally-oriented content in addition to global Internet access. This product allows use of e-mail, newsgroups, bulletin boards, and directory services. PSI claims to provide access to 35% of the U.S. Internet users. Its public data network is a combination of hardware, software, and communication facilities.

Market Strategy/Positioning

The company's mission is to be the leading full-service provider of Internet access to organizations and individuals in the U.S. and around the globe. PSI has strategic relationships with Ascend, Cascade, NetManage, Dell, Compaq, Motorola, and International Design Group. Significant customers include over 4,000 organizations and 19,000 individual customers, including Bell Atlantic, GTE Mobilnet, HBO, *The Boston Globe*, Apple, UNISYS, Shell, NYSE, Wells Fargo, and Montgomery Securities. The company's competitive advantages are its 105 points of presence in the U.S. and Japan. PSI primarily competes against NETCOM, UUNET, Bolt Beranik & Newman, AT&T, MCI, Sprint, Delphi, GEnie, Prodigy, CompuServe, America Online, Microsoft, and IBM. PSI is unique in having an online service based on a fixed monthly rate, rather than the typical hourly fee charged by most service providers.

Other

The company was founded in 1989 and began operations in 1990 as a developer of Internet access tools for organizations. It started with 40 customers on its new network, and had nearly 5,000 by the end of 1993. In an effort to reach more individuals, the company acquired Pipeline, a GUI-based Internet service provider, in February 1995. Bill Schrader is a co-founder and has been chairman, president, and CEO since the company's creation. Before PSI, Mr. Schrader was co-founder and CEO of NYSERNet, and co-founded the Cornell Theory Center. Co-founder and senior vice president Martin Schoffstall also co-founded NYSERNet, was an instructor at Renssalaer Polytechnic, and worked as systems engineer for Internet protocols at BBN.

KEY FACTS

Year Established:	1989
Employees:	140
Fiscal Year End:	December
Revenues FY '94:	$10.3m
Revenues FY '95:	n/a
EPS '94:	$(0.38)
EPS '95:	$(0.83) (estimate)
Shares Outstanding:	30.3m
Five-Year Growth Rate:	40%

380

PERSONAL LIBRARY SOFTWARE

Address:	2400 Research Boulevard Suite 350 Rockville, MD 20850
Telephone:	301/990-1155
Fax:	301/963-9738
E-mail:	matt@pls.com, info@pls.com
Web site:	http://www.pls.com
Industry:	Entertainment & Information
Sector:	Information Services
CEO:	Matthew Koll
CFO:	Andrew Rodnan

Product Description

Personal Library Software (PLS) creates intelligent text-retrieval systems, document management engines, and applications for online and CD-ROM publishing. Its forums include workgroups, enterprises, and the Internet. Its recent server software for the World Wide Web offers aggregation of distributed data, natural-language searching, and relevance ranking. PLS also plans to offer a navigational service to guide users toward the best databases for its searches.

Market Strategy/Positioning

The company's mission is to build technology that brings people and relevant information together. PLS provides the leading-edge search engine that powers major online information systems. PLS has strategic relationships with America Online, Appleton & Lange, *Congressional Quarterly*, *DataTimes*, *Financial Times*, Grolier, Hewlett-Packard, Knight-Ridder, NewsNet, Telebase, *Time*, and Wave Systems. Significant customers include Associated Press, Apple, NewsNet, Telebase, Dow Jones, Grolier, Hewlett-Packard, Knight-Ridder, Paramount, Prodigy, Time Warner, KPMG Peat Marwick, and the U.S. House of Representatives. The company's competitive advantages are its automatic dynamic intelligence, its scalability, its distributed database architecture, and a proven track record in the information retrieval business. Personal Library Software primarily competes against Architext, ConQuest, Dataware, Fulcrum, Verity, Folio, Microsoft, and Oracle. Additional risks include the many new entrants in the text-retrieval industry.

381

Other

Personal Library Software was founded in 1983 by Dr. Matthew Koll as a vehicle for implementing information management products. Its first CD-ROM title was released in 1985. PLS introduced a product with a Windows graphical user interface in 1988, licensed the engine for an online service in 1989, and began designing Internet publishing search tools in 1994. CEO Matthew Koll founded PLS as the first company dedicated to information retrieval.

Primary VCs/Outside Financing

Paul Kagan & Associates and Knight-Ridder Information.

KEY FACTS

Year Established:	1983
Employees:	65
Fiscal Year End:	n/a
Revenues FY '94:	n/a
Revenues FY '95:	n/a
Date of Next Financing:	n/a
Date of Last Financing:	July 1993
Size of Last Financing:	n/a
Total Capital Raised:	n/a
Post Round Valuation:	n/a
Expected IPO Date:	n/a

PHILIPS ELECTRONICS

Product Description

Philips Electronics is a diversified multinational company that manufactures and distributes electronic products. Its research accomplishments include developing the first system for continuous speech recognition, which directly transcribes voice to text on a computer system, and the Philips car navigation system (developed in conjunction with BMW), which uses digitized street maps produced by Navigation Technologies. The company is working on systems architecture, multimedia components, digital television, content authoring systems, and user environments, including "New Topia," a virtual electronic city implemented on a cable network combined with telephone lines.

Address:	U.S Headquarters
	100 East 42nd Street
	New York, NY 10017-5699
Telephone:	212/850-5000
Fax:	212/850-7314
E-mail:	n/a
Web site:	http://www.philips.com
Industry:	Entertainment & Information
Sector:	Consumer Electronics
CEO:	Jan D. Timmer (President)
CFO:	D.G. Eustace
Stock Exchange:	NYSE
Stock Symbol:	PHG

Market Strategy/Positioning

Philips has strategic relationships with IBM, SI Diamond Technology, United International Holdings, Joint Open Stock Company Velt (Russia), and Nintendo. The company's competitive advantage is its heavy investment in research and development. Philips primarily competes against AMD, AT&T, Bell Atlantic, Compaq, Dell, Fujitsu, Gateway 2000, GE, Hitachi, IBM, Intel, Matsushita, Motorola, NEC, Nokia, Samsung, Sanyo, Siemens, Sony, Time Warner, Toshiba, Tribune, Viacom, and Xerox. Additional challenges and risks include the possibility that despite emphasis on research and development for consumer electronics, the company may have missed its chance to capture the markets for the next wave of products, which includes interactive CD-ROMs and digital compact cassettes.

Other

Gerard Philips founded Philips in 1891 in Eindhoven, Holland, as a maker of light bulbs. During WWI, Philips expanded into glass manufacturing, X-ray, and radio tubes. The company began selling televisions and appliances in the 1950s, and it signed a technology-licensing agreement with Matsushita Electronics in 1952. In the 1960s Philips added audiocassettes, VCRs, and laserdiscs. The company became Philips Electronics in 1991, and in the same year, formed a partnership with Nintendo to develop CD-ROM video games. Philips established its TriMedia division to research and develop multifunctional digital signal processors for multimedia markets.

KEY FACTS

Year Established:	1891
Employees:	238,500
Fiscal Year End:	December
Revenues FY '94:	$35.3b
Revenues FY '95:	n/a
EPS '94:	$3.56
EPS '95:	$5.03 (estimate)
Shares Outstanding:	336.0m
Five-Year Growth Rate:	26%

PICTURETEL

Product Description

PictureTel develops, manufactures, and markets a complete line of videoconferencing solutions. These include $250 local-area network (LAN) products, $2,500 desktop systems, and high-end $50,000 group systems. Its standards-based solutions are marketed by two divisions, Group Systems and Personal Systems. By making videoconferencing as ubiquitous as the telephone, fax, and PC, PictureTel provides its customers with a truly global meeting room. The company's visual telecommunications products are for use with public and private digital networks. PictureTel holds 49% of the global videoconferencing market share with more than 20,000 installed systems and 4,000 customers. It also offers desktop products that run over LANs, and leads the market in desktop videoconferencing, according to The Gartner Group.

Address:	The Tower at Northwoods
	222 Rosewood Drive
	Danvers, MA 01923
Telephone:	508/762-5000
Fax:	508/762-5245
E-mail:	n/a
Web site:	n/a
Industry:	Communications
Sector:	Information Highway Equipment
CEO:	Dr. Norman E. Gaut
CFO:	Les B. Strauss
Stock Exchange:	NASDAQ
Stock Symbol:	PCTL

Market Strategy/Positioning

The company's mission is to provide worldwide customers with visual communications products and services that significantly enhance their productivity. PictureTel hopes to take part in "redefining the way the world meets." PictureTel has strategic relationships with Microsoft (data conferencing products), Compaq (personal conferencing products), NTT, IBM, and AT&T. It also created a telemedicine network with MCI Business Markets and United Medical Network. Significant customers include 3Com, Andersen Consulting, Bank of Boston, Bell Atlantic, Chevron, Estée Lauder, Ford, Goldman Sachs, IBM, Novell, Oracle, Reader's Digest, Shell, Stanford University, and Viacom. The company's competitive advantages are that it is the only vendor with a leading presence in both group and personal videoconferencing systems, and its ability to provide an enterprise-wide videoconferencing solution. PictureTel primarily competes against AT&T, Intel (desktop), Compression Labs, and VTEL (group videoconferencing). Additional challenges and risks include new competitors entering the market, and the fact that telecom infrastructure must improve to meet customers' needs for its products. PictureTel is unique in its singular focus on videoconferencing.

Other

PictureTel is a founding member of the Consortium for Audiographics Teleconferencing Standards (CATS), a non-profit group now known as the International Multimedia Teleconferencing Con-

KEY FACTS

Year Established:	1984
Employees:	950
Fiscal Year End:	December
Revenues FY '94:	$255.1m
Revenues FY '95:	n/a
EPS '94:	$0.29
EPS '95:	$0.76 (estimate)
Shares Outstanding:	15.6m
Five-Year Growth Rate:	28%

PICTURETEL

sortium (IMTC). The company has been awarded more than 27 patents for video technology, many of which have been incorporated into industry standards. In 1995 PictureTel ranked among *Fortune* magazine's 100 fastest-growing companies for its third consecutive year. It also controls 50% of the worldwide market (30,000 systems). Chairman, president, and CEO Norman Gaut has served on the company's board since PictureTel was founded and he has held his current position since 1986.

PIXAR

Address:	1001 West Cutting
	Point Richmond, CA 94804
Telephone:	510/236-4000
Fax:	510/236-0388
E-mail:	info@pixar.com
Web site:	http://www.pixar.com
Industry:	Entertainment & Information
Sector:	Film & Entertainment Production
CEO:	Steven P. Jobs
CFO:	Lawrence B. Levy

Product Description

Pixar is a digital animation studio that through a unique blend of art and technology creates next-generation animated feature films, CD-ROM titles, television commercials, and other animated products. It adds three-dimensional animation, and the company's first movie, *Toy Story*, released by Walt Disney, is the first fully computer-animated feature film.

Market Strategy/Positioning

Pixar has a strategic relationship with Walt Disney that dates back to 1987. Pixar and Walt Disney, in a joint technical venture, developed CAPS, the Academy Award–winning 2D computer animation production system. CAPS was used to animate scenes in *The Little Mermaid, Beauty & the Beast, Aladdin,* and *The Lion King.* Significant customers include all major advertising companies. The company's competitive advantages are its strong and experienced management team and its creative talent. Pixar primarily competes against Digital Domain, R/GA Digital Studios, Industrial Light & Magic, and PDI.

Other

Pixar was formed in 1979 as the computer division of LucasFilm. Dr. Ed Catmull, president of Pixar, was recruited by George Lucas while Dr. Catmull was working at the New York Institute of Technology. In 1986 Pixar was acquired by Steven Jobs, and was incorporated as an independent company. Pixar has received 12 Academy Awards, including an Oscar in 1988 for *Tin Toy*, chosen as the year's best animated short film. Dr. Catmull has been awarded the Coons Award, the highest award in computer graphics, for lifetime achievements. Steven Jobs is also co-founder, chairman, and CEO of NeXT Computer. Before founding NeXT, Mr. Jobs co-founded and was chairman of Apple Computer. CFO Lawrence Levy was previously a founder, vice chairman, and CFO of Electronics for Imaging, a company that provides hardware and software products for the digital color imaging market.

Primary VCs/Outside Financing

Steven Jobs.

KEY FACTS

Year Established:	1986
Employees:	150
Fiscal Year End:	n/a
Revenues FY '94:	n/a
Revenues FY '95:	n/a
Date of Next Financing:	n/a
Date of Last Financing:	n/a
Size of Last Financing:	n/a
Total Capital Raised:	n/a
Post Round Valuation:	n/a
Expected IPO Date:	November 1995

PLATINUM
TECHNOLOGY

Address:	1815 South Meyers Road
	Oakbrook Terrace, IL 60181-5241
Telephone:	800/442-6861 and 708/620-5000
Fax:	708/691-0718
E-mail:	info@platinum.com
Web site:	n/a
Industry:	Computers
Sector:	Enterprise & Client/Server Software
CEO:	Andrew "Flip" Filipowksi
CFO:	Michael Cullinane
Stock Exchange:	NASDAQ
Stock Symbol:	PLAT

Product Description

PLATINUM Technology makes tools for managing information stored and distributed among various relational databases. The software works with mainframes, midrange-UNIX-based, and client/server systems. PLATINUM was built on an IBM-installed base, but now has Sybase and Oracle products. PLATINUM has internally developed software bridges between mainframe and non-mainframe systems. The company pursues a multitiered sales strategy.

Market Strategy/Positioning

The company's mission is to be the world's leading open-enterprise management company with products that address virtually all information technology issues encountered by large corporations. PLATINUM Technology has strategic relationships with Oracle, Sybase, Informix, and IBM. Significant customers include AT&T, Baxter, BMW, Dun & Bradstreet, Federal Reserve Bank, IBM, Kraft, Sony, and United Airlines. The company's competitive advantage is its large research and development budget to develop "best-of-breed" products, then integrated into a comprehensive open enterprise management solution. PLATINUM Technology primarily competes against BMC Software, Computer Associates, and CompuWare. Additional challenges and risks include integrating all its products into a centralized management system.

Other

PLATINUM Technology was founded in April 1987 and has recently shifted its focus from the IBM DB2 market to the client/server market. PLATINUM has pursued an acquisition strategy to offer many integrated solutions for its customers. The company went public in April 1991 with one of the most successful IPOs of the year. Founder and CEO Andrew Filipowski was founder and CEO of DBMS and also held executive management positions at Cullinet Software. CFO Michael Cullinane joined the company in March 1988. He became a director of PLATINUM in 1991 and previously worked at DBMS as CFO and vice president of corporate operations.

KEY FACTS

Year Established:	1987
Employees:	385
Fiscal Year End:	December
Revenues FY '94:	$95.8m
Revenues FY '95:	$250.0m
EPS '94:	$(0.13)
EPS '95:	$0.92
Shares Outstanding:	24.3m
Five Year Growth Rate:	28%

Product Description

Play develops and sells video tools for PCs. Its first product, *Snappy*, is a still-image digitizer which can take video input from a VCR, camcorder, TV, or any video source, and capture true-color (24-bit) digital still images. *Snappy* will snap onto any PC (portables included) and can instantly incorporate a video snapshot into a slideshow presentation. The software lets the user preview the incoming video in a small window that can be updated several times per second. Play's other main product, *Trinity*, is a complete desktop video production system for PCs. It includes a 10-inch input switcher, dual digital video effects engines, a paint system, animation system, audio mixer, and a video editor. The system sells for $5,995; combined with a Pentium PC, it claims to replace the functionality of a $150,000 video-production studio.

Address:	2890 Kilgore Road
	Rancho Cordorva, CA 95670-6133
Telephone:	916/851-0800
Fax:	916/851-0801
E-mail:	comments@play.com
Web site:	http://www.play.com
Industry:	Computers
Sector:	Peripherals
CEO:	Mike Moore (Chairman)
	Paul Montgomery (President)
CFO:	Ed Moran

Market Strategy/Positioning

Play has strategic relationships with Intel, Microsoft, and Minolta. Significant customers include Computer City, CompUSA, Good Guys, Best Buy, and Ingram. The company's competitive advantages are its initial product development, its VLSI chip technology, and its high-quality still-image capturing ability. Play primarily competes against high-end post-production houses but has also created its own niche in video imaging. Additional challenges and risks include managing the company's growth.

Other

Play was founded by a 1994 merger between a group of senior managers and research and development staff from Video Toaster-maker NewTek, Amiga software leader Digital Creations, and video hardware developer Progressive Image Technologies. All founding partners have worked in desktop video industry for over 10 years. Paul Montgomery co-founded NewTek and brought over 12 top people from the company. John Botteri previously founded Digital Creations, and Mike Moore previously founded Progressive Image Technologies, which has been creating hardware for PCs since 1978.

Primary VCs/Outside Financing

100% internally owned.

KEY FACTS

Year Established:	1994
Employees:	65
Fiscal Year End:	n/a
Revenues FY '94:	$0.0
Revenues FY '95:	n/a
Date of Next Financing:	n/a
Date of Last Financing:	n/a
Size of Last Financing:	n/a
Total Capital Raised:	n/a
Post Round Valuation:	n/a
Expected IPO Date:	n/a

QUALCOMM

Address:	6455 Lusk Boulevard
	San Diego, CA 92121-2779
Telephone:	619/587-1121
Fax:	619/658-2100
E-mail:	mfoerster@qualcomm.com
Web site:	http://www.qualcomm.com
Industry:	Communications
Sector:	Wireless Communications
CEO:	Irwin M. Jacobs
CFO:	Anthony Thornley
Stock Exchange:	NASDAQ
Stock Symbol:	QCOM

Product Description

Qualcomm develops a digital cellular telephone communications system using its Code Division Multiple Access (CDMA) technology, which improves voice quality and increases capacity 10–20 times over the FM analog cellular system. Most of Qualcomm's total revenue comes from its Omni TRACS system, which offers two-way mobile satellite communications and tracking services to transportation companies in North America. In January 1995 the FCC authorized the low-earth orbit plan Globalstar, a joint venture between Qualcomm and Loral Aerospace Corporation. Globalstar is a satellite-based, cellular-like voice and data service for mobile or fixed applications.

Market Strategy/Positioning

Qualcomm has strategic relationships with Loral, AT&T, and Motorola, and a 51% ownership with Sony in QPE Manufacturing. Significant customers include 11 of the top 14 U.S. cellular carriers, Sprint, Samsung, Crete Carriers, and Tyson Foods. It has also licensed its CDMA technology to AT&T and Motorola. The company's competitive advantages are that it holds the most patents on CDMA and that it will receive royalties for the use of the technology. Qualcomm primarily competes against Ericsson and Nokia for CDMA, Rockwell and Hiway Master for tracking services, and Motorola's IRIDIUM and TRW's Oddessey for low-earth orbit service.

Other

Qualcomm was established in 1985 to develop and sell advanced digital wireless communications systems. In 1988 the company introduced the OmniTRACS two-way messaging and tracking system, and later developed the digital wireless system based on its CDMA technology. In 1994 Qualcomm, Loral Corporation, and several other companies formed the joint venture to design, construct, and operate Globalstar. CEO and founder Irwin Jacobs has served as Qualcomm's CEO since 1985. Before founding Qualcomm, he was executive vice president and a director of the telecommunications company M/A-COM, Inc. CFO Anthony Thornley joined Qualcomm as vice president and CFO in 1994. Previously, he held various financial and information systems management positions for 16 years at Northern Telecom.

KEY FACTS

Year Established:	1985
Employees:	1,900
Fiscal Year End:	September
Revenues FY '94:	$271.6m
Revenues FY '95:	$386.2m (estimate)
EPS '94:	$0.28
EPS '95:	$0.52 (estimate)
Shares Outstanding:	52.1m
Five-Year Growth Rate:	42%

388

QUANTUM

Product Description

Quantum is a worldwide independent supplier of disk drives. The company develops mass storage products, including high-performance 5.25-inch, 3.5-inch, and 2.5-inch disk drives, solid state drives, thin film heads, PCMCIA-based flash memory cards, and backup tape drives. Quantum is focused on providing storage solutions for several markets, including entry-level to high-end desktop PCs, notebook and sub-notebook systems, workstations, servers, minicomputers, and hand-held and palmtop systems.

Address:	500 McCarthy Boulevard
	Milpitas, CA 95035
Telephone:	408/894-4000
Fax:	408/894-3218
E-mail:	bfagansm@qntm.com
Web site:	www.quantum.com
Industry:	Computers
Sector:	Storage
CEO:	William J. Miller
CFO:	Joseph T. Rodgers
Stock Exchange:	NASDAQ
Stock Symbol:	QNTM

Market Strategy/Positioning

The company's mission is to be the world's leading supplier of mass storage products. Quantum has strategic relationships with DEC, Silicon Storage Technology, and Matsushita-Kotobuki Electronics. Significant customers include Apple, Compaq, DEC, Dell, Hewlett-Packard, Fujitsu, NEC, Siemens, UNISYS, V-Tech, and Goldstar. The company's competitive advantages are its strong technology portfolio, which holds more than 73 patents, and its quadrupled market share in the past five years. Quantum primarily competes against Seagate, Western Digital, Conner, IBM, Micropolis, and Maxtor. Additional challenges and risks include meeting storage demands of new media, such as downloading images and video from the Internet and video-on-demand, and areal density doubling every 18 months.

Other

Founded in 1980, Quantum has held the market share lead in disk drive volume since January 1993. In 1992 Quantum sales topped $1 billion, and in 1994 it shipped its 25 millionth disk drive. More recently, it acquired a majority share of Rocky Mountain Magnetics, allowing the company to increase areal density (the number of data bits per square inch available for recording) and to enhance drive performance. CEO Bill Miller joined Quantum in 1992 and was named chairman in 1993. Before working at Quantum, Mr. Miller served as executive vice president and president of information services of Contol Data and as president and CEO of Imprimis Technology, then a subsidiary of Control Data. CFO Joseph Rodgers joined Quantum in 1980. Mr. Rodgers previously held executive positions in finance at Braegen, Plantronics, and Consolidated Video Systems.

KEY FACTS

Year Established:	1980
Employees:	9,000
Fiscal Year End:	March
Revenues FY '94:	$2.1b
Revenues FY '95:	$3.4b
EPS '94:	$0.06
EPS '95:	$1.72
Shares Outstanding:	46.2m
Five-Year Growth Rate:	17%

389

R/GA
DIGITAL STUDIOS

Address:	350 West 39th Street
	New York, NY 10018
Telephone:	212/239-6767
Fax:	212/947-3769
E-mail:	n/a
Web site:	http://www.rga.com
Industry:	Entertainment & Information
Sector:	Film & Entertainment Production
CEO:	Robert Greenberg
CFO:	Phyllis Ginestra

Product Description

R/GA Digital Studios is a special effects company that works on broadcast commercials, feature films, and interactive multimedia. Credits include *Demolition Man*, *In the Line of Fire*, and *Mortal Kombat*. It has also done ads for Miller, Nike, Pizza Hut, and Shell. The company will continue to do visual-effects work for feature films, but last year announced a shift in focus to digital production for content-driven and interactive advertising projects, online interface design, and World Wide Web sites. The company is actually made up of six companies: R/Greenberg Associates, Savoy Commercials, R/GA Print, Michael Schrom and Co., R/GA Interactive, and R/GA Pictures.

Market Strategy/Positioning

R/GA Digital Studios has strategic relationships with Microsoft, Silicon Graphics, and Philips. Significant customers include BBDO, Chiat Day, DDB Needham, Saatchi & Saatchi, Young & Rubicam. The company's competitive advantages are its bicoastal presence and its extensive equipment to facilitate its creative possibilities. R/GA Digital Studios primarily competes against Digital Domain, Industrial Light & Magic, Four Media Company, Pixar, and Pacific Data Images. Additional challenges and risks include its recent mission to establish the Transparent Studio, a "production company without walls," which will allow artists at different locations to harness the creative and technical abilities of both R/GA's studios.

Other

R/GA began in 1977 in the founders' NY apartment with an animation stand brought through the window. R/GA now has 600,000 square feet between its New York and Hollywood locations. By the mid 1980s the company had established the first component D-1 digital video suite on the East coast and combined this technology with film and computer-generated imaging techniques. R/GA expanded to Hollywood in 1992 and formed an interactive multimedia division to handle the company's new demand for content. Founder and CEO Robert Greenberg has presided over the company since its inception.

Primary VCs/Outside Financing

100% internally funded.

KEY FACTS

Year Established:	1977
Employees:	250
Fiscal Year End:	December
Revenues FY '94:	n/a
Revenues FY '95:	$25.0m (estimate)
Date of Next Financing:	n/a
Date of Last Financing:	n/a
Size of Last Financing:	n/a
Total Capital Raised:	n/a
Post Round Valuation:	n/a
Expected IPO Date:	n/a

RADIOMAIL

Address:	2600 Campus Drive
	San Mateo, CA 94403
Telephone:	415/286-7800
Fax:	415/286-7805
E-mail:	info@radiomail.net
Web site:	http://www.radiomail.net
Industry:	Communications
Sector:	Wireless Communications
CEO:	Bruce Walter
CFO:	Alan Beringsmith

Product Description

RadioMail provides two-way wireless communications and information services, including e-mail, global fax service, news headlines, and stock quotes on demand. The company's services combine e-mail's two-way communication with paging's guaranteed delivery.

Market Strategy/Positioning

The company's mission is to be the world's leading provider of global personal wireless messaging services. RadioMail has strategic relationships with ARDIS, Ericsson, GE Mobile Communications, Motorola, RAM Mobile Data, Wireless Telecom, QuoteCom, ConnectSoft, Comtex, and Qualcomm. Significant customers include Chevron, Pacific Gas & Electric, CMP Publications, and BankAmerica. The company's competitive advantages are being first-to-market, operating on third-generation technology, and offering services that operate on all leading platforms, including Windows, DOS, Macintosh, and H-P Palmtops. RadioMail primarily competes against Wyndmail, Destineer, and PersonaLink. Additional challenges and risks include controlling the relatively high initial cost for consumers of RadioMail equipment.

Other

In 1988 founder Geoffrey Goodfellow left Stanford Research Institute (SRI) to form Anterior Technology, which introduced the first service allowing e-mail to be sent from the Internet to pagers and subsequently, to the cc:Mail gateway service. Anterior changed its name to RadioMail Corporation in 1992 and introduced the RadioMail two-way wireless e-mail service on the RAM Mobile Data network. Chairman and chief technical officer Geoffrey Goodfellow founded RadioMail after spending 12 years as senior researcher and principal investigator of computer security and networking for the Computer Science Laboratory at SRI International. CEO Bruce Walter joined RadioMail in October 1994 from Coactive Computing. Before Coactive, Mr. Walter was president and CEO of GRiD Systems, a subsidiary of Tandy. CFO Alan Beringsmith was formerly coordinator of corporate planning and assistant treasurer for Pacific Gas & Electric Company, and vice president of corporate development and treasurer of PG&E Enterprises.

KEY FACTS

Year Established:	1988
Employees:	35
Fiscal Year End:	December
Revenues FY '94:	n/a
Revenues FY '95:	n/a
Date of Next Financing:	n/a
Date of Last Financing:	April 1993
Size of Last Financing:	$3.0m
Total Capital Raised:	n/a
Post Round Valuation:	n/a
Expected IPO Date:	n/a

Primary VCs/Outside Financing

Motorola.

RAM
MOBILE DATA

Address:	10 Woodbridge Center Drive Suite 950 New Jersey, NJ 07095
Telephone:	908/602-5500
Fax:	800/763-1110
E-mail:	customer services@ram.co.uk
Web site:	http://www.ram.co.uk
Industry:	Communications
Sector:	Wireless Communications
CEO:	William Lenahan
CFO:	Ken Mory

Product Description

RAM Mobile Data provides two-way nationwide wireless data communications services that cover over 90% of the U.S. urban business population. It ties together servers, information services, and mobile and fixed terminals, covering 10–30 channels in most urban areas. RAM's uses include e-mail, brokerage, field sales, and dispatch services. RAM's networks are based on MOBITEX technology. The company plans to roll out 500 base stations in the coming five years.

Market Strategy/Positioning

RAM has strategic relationships with Oracle, IBM/Lotus, and Ericsson. Significant customers include GE Consumer Service, UNISYS, British Airways, BASF, Conrail, Hobart, and Boston Edison. RAM mainly competes against Motorola. The company's competitive advantage is its service, based on international wireless data standards. Additional challenges and risks include increasing penetration, creating a unified infrastructure for billing and accounting, and increasing its distribution capability.

Other

RAM Mobile Data was started in 1988 by RAM Broadcasting Corporation. BellSouth invested $300 million to acquire a 49% stake in 1992. William Lenahan has been CEO since November 1994. He was previously president and general manager at Omaha-based Inacom. Before Inacom, Mr. Lenahan was president and CEO of Sears Business Centers and Sears Office Centers; he has also held executive positions at Bell Atlantic's Compushop, United Telecom's Amerisource, and IBM.

Primary VCs/Outside Financing

RAM Broadcasting Corporation (51%) and Bell-South (49%).

KEY FACTS

Year Established:	1989
Employees:	400
Fiscal Year End:	n/a
Revenues FY '94:	n/a
Revenues FY '95:	n/a
Date of Next Financing:	n/a
Date of Last Financing:	n/a
Size of Last Financing:	n/a
Total Capital Raised:	n/a
Post Round Valuation:	n/a
Expected IPO Date:	n/a

392

REAL WORLD

Address:	Mill Lane
	Box Wilshire SN 149 PL
	United Kingdom
Telephone:	441-225-743-188
Fax:	441-225-744-370
E-mail:	n/a
Web site:	n/a
Industry:	Entertainment & Information
Sector:	Entertainment/Education Software
CEO:	David Stephen
CFO:	Mike Large (COO)

Product Description

Real World is the umbrella name for Peter Gabriel's business ventures, namely Real World Records and Real World Studios. Other operations of the company include: Real World Productions, which produces in-house videos; Real World Trading, the merchandising arm that sells T-shirts, jackets, records, etc.; directing WOMAD (World of Music, Arts and Dance festival series); and publishing *The Box*, a magazine that focuses on art, technology, and the environment. The company also produces multimedia CD-ROM titles, namely *Xplora*, through Real World Multimedia.

Market Strategy/Positioning

Real World has strategic relationships with Brilliant Media and Virgin Records, the company's main distributor. The company's competitive advantages are its focus on quality creative product, and its access to talent across the entertainment board. Real World primarily competes against all major record labels, Acclaim Entertainment, Electronic Arts, LucasArts, and Maxis. Additional challenges and risks include managing the diffused distribution channels for software and record companies, competing against the big entertainment conglomerates, and keeping a global appeal for Real World's products.

393

Other

Real World began in 1986 as a recording studio and has since branched out into numerous other areas of business. CEO David Stephen was brought in by Peter Gabriel brought in CEO David Stephen to run the company. Before Real World, Mr. Stephen worked at Columbia/Tri-Star Pictures in Los Angeles and Sega in London. COO Mike Large worked for the SSL and the BBC designing recording studios before coming to the company.

KEY FACTS

Year Established:	1982
Employees:	90
Fiscal Year End:	April
Revenues FY '94:	n/a
Revenues FY '95:	n/a
Date of Next Financing:	n/a
Date of Last Financing:	n/a
Size of Last Financing:	n/a
Total Capital Raised:	n/a
Post Round Valuation:	n/a
Expected IPO Date:	n/a

RED
BRICK SYSTEMS

Address:	485 Alberto Way
	Los Gatos, CA 95032
Telephone:	408/399-3200
Fax:	408/399-3277
E-mail:	info@redbrick.com
Web site:	http://www.redbrick.com
Industry:	Computers
Sector:	Enterprise & Client/Server Software
CEO:	Christopher Erickson
CFO:	Robert Hausmann

Product Description

Red Brick Systems develops relational data-base products and services for data warehouse applications. Its systems are designed for decision support and business management as opposed to transaction processing and record keeping. Red Brick components include server-access through server query language, connectivity software for desktop computers, and administrative utilities.

Market Strategy/Positioning

The company's mission is to be the leading provider of relational database products and services for data warehouse applications for decision support. Red Brick has strategic relationships with AT&T, DEC, Hewlett-Packard, IBM, Sequent, and Sun Microsytsems. Significant customers include General Mills, 3M, Hewlett-Packard, Mobil Oil, BellSouth, Southern Pacific Transportation Company, and Tufts Association Health Plan. The company's competitive advantages are designing and optimizing products for data warehousing applications and achieving 10 times the performance of traditional RDBMS. Red Brick primarily competes against Oracle, Sybase, and IBM.

Other

Red Brick Systems started as a consulting firm specializing in the design of high-performance decision support systems. It then developed a core set of technologies which became the basis of a specialized Relational Database Management Systems designed for large-scale, query-intensive application environments. Red Brick experienced revenue growth of over 200% in 1995. CEO Chris Erickson was formerly president of Tandem Telecommunications. CFO Richard Hausmann was former director of finance at Cadence Design Systems and CFO at Centura.

Primary VCs/Outside Financing

Advent International, Asset Managment, Menlo Ventures, Hambrecht & Quist, Shea, and Stanford University.

394

KEY FACTS

Year Established:	1986
Employees:	70
Fiscal Year End:	n/a
Revenues FY '94:	n/a
Revenues FY '95:	n/a
Date of Next Financing:	late 1995
Date of Last Financing:	November 1994
Size of Last Financing:	$6.4m
Total Capital Raised:	$14.8m
Post Round Valuation:	$19.0m
Expected IPO Date:	n/a

REMEDY

Product Description

Remedy develops client/server help-desk software for tracking and resolving support requests and problems in PC and UNIX computing environments. The product's adaptability and scalability allow it to be tailored to many other business processes. In addition to help-desk applications, the company provides templates for other applications, including asset management, defect tracking, and recruiting management. Remedy sells through a direct-sales force as well as VARs, integrators, and OEMs.

Address:	1505 Salado Drive
	Mountain View, CA 94043
Telephone:	415/903-5200
Fax:	415/905-9001
E-mail:	sales@remedy.com
	marketing@remedy.com
Web site:	http://www.remedy.com
Industry:	Computers
Sector:	Enterprise & Client/Server Software
CEO:	Larry Garlik
CFO:	George de Urieste
Stock Exchange:	NASDAQ
Stock Symbol:	RMDY

Market Strategy/Positioning

The company's mission is to build the most adaptable applications for support and business processes. Remedy has strategic relationships with AT&T, Sun Microsystems, Hewlett-Packard, IBM, Silicon Graphics, and Motorola. Significant customers include AT&T, Motorola, Bell-Northern, Ford, Hewlett Packard, and PG&E. The company's competitive advantage is its high-growth business model and an adaptable product able to meet numerous business needs. Remedy primarily competes against third-party professional service organizations that develop custom software, and MIS departments of potential customers that develop custom software. Competition from established client/server software companies is likely to intensify; a few private companies such as Scopus Technology also offer competitive products. Additional challenges and risks include developing new applications to take advantage of existing technology.

395

Other

Founded in 1990, Remedy shipped its first product in December 1991 and was profitable by the first quarter of 1992. The company went public in March 1995. Co-founder and vice president of marketing David Mahler was formerly product marketing manager at Hewlett-Packard. Co-founder and CEO Larry Garlick was formerly vice president of distributed systems at Sun Microsystems and was also previously at Xerox.

KEY FACTS

Year Established:	1990
Employees:	180
Fiscal Year End:	December
Revenues FY '94:	$19.8m
Revenues FY '95:	n/a
EPS '94:	$0.43
EPS '95:	$0.63
Shares Outstanding:	8.1m
Five-Year Growth Rate:	43%

RENDITION

Product Description

Rendition develops single-chip graphics controllers and system software for 3D rendering, Windows acceleration, and the digital video playback market. The company's first product was Verite, a single-chip 3D graphics engine and digital video accelerator for the PC. Its technology concentrates on texture mapping, true color, and high pixel throughput. The company also plans to sell to OEM customers in the add-in board and computer systems segments.

Address:	1675 North Shoreline Boulevard
	Mountain View, CA 94043-1366
Telephone:	415/335-5900
Fax:	415/335-5999
E-mail:	mike@rendition.com.
	laura@rendition.com
Web site:	http://www.rendition.com
Industry:	Computers
Sector:	Semiconductors
CEO:	Michael Boich
CFO:	Laura Perrone

Market Strategy/Positioning

The company's mission is to deliver 3D graphics of unprecedented quality and performance to the PC entertainment market. The company's competitive advantages are its focus on the PC entertainment market and its technical expertise in 3D rendering. Rendition's strength lies in its close relationships with content developers. Rendition primarily competes against 3Dfx, 3Dlabs, Cirrus Logic, S3, NVIDIA, and Trident. Additional challenges include encouraging the development of content that exploits capabilities of Rendition devices, and meeting OEM needs.

Other

The company was founded in 1993 with the goal of delivering high quality, low-cost 3D graphics solutions for PCs. Founder and CEO Michael Boich was a member of the original Macintosh team and was co-founder and CEO of Radius. Co-founder James Peterson was formerly vice president of engineering at Bipolar Integrated Technology and a chip designer at Intel.

Primary VCs/Outside Financing

InterWest Partners, Matrix Partners, Enterprise Partners, and Unterberg & Harris.

396

KEY FACTS

Year Established:	1993
Employees:	25
Fiscal Year End:	December
Revenues FY '94:	n/a
Revenues FY '95:	n/a
Date of Next Financing:	n/a
Date of Last Financing:	September 1995
Size of Last Financing:	$7.4m
Total Capital Raised:	$12.6m
Post Round Valuation:	n/a
Expected IPO Date:	n/a

REUTERS
HOLDINGS

Product Description

Reuters Holdings provides textual and photo news to virtually all newspaper and online services, including AOL, CompuServe, Prodigy, Apple, and Delphi. The company currently delivers news in 20 languages. The company also provides online financial information to Wall Street, including real-time quotes and 1,800 international periodicals. It launched a foreign exchange matching service which allows users to exchange currency anonymously and to access the best bids automatically. Reuters offers an online, registered stock broker/dealer services in international equities markets. It also owns an online service, through the acquisition of Reality, that competes with Intuit's Quicken. Reuters' Money Network for DOS/Windows is an online personal investing service for individual investors. It also has third-party deals with major Wall Street brokers and has plans for personal digital assistant products and interactive TV with Intel and Comcast. In July 1995 Reuters New Media agreed to supply the Reuters Online News Service to Yahoo! for one year.

Address:	U.S. Headquarters
	1700 Broadway
	New York, NY 10019
Telephone:	212/603-3300
Fax:	212/247-0346
E-mail:	n/a
Web site:	n/a
Industry:	Entertainment & Information
Sector:	Information Services
CEO:	Peter J.D. Job
CFO:	Robert O. Rowley
Stock Exchange:	NASDAQ
Stock Symbol:	RTRSY

Market Strategy/Positioning

Reuters has strategic relationships with Hewlett-Packard, Microsoft, NCR, Yahoo!, DEC, ABC Radio Networks, and Multex Systems. Reuters also has an online education joint venture with TCI, called Ingenius, which develops interactive multimedia delivered daily to schools' PCs over cable TV. The company's competitive advantages are its depth of editorial coverage, a global reach of communications network and customer support, and the largest TV news gathering network of any news organization. Last year Reuters introduced the first bilingual database online to customers. Reuters primarily competes against ADP, Associated Press, Bloomberg, Dow Jones/Telerate, Dun & Bradstreet, GE, CompuServe, Knight-Ridder, NASDAQ, *The New York Times*, NYSE, Tribune, Turner, and United Press International.

Other

Reuters Holdings was founded in England by Paul Julius Reuters, a German immigrant. After sending its first telegraphic transmission of stock quotations between London and Paris, general and financial news became an integral part of the Reuters service. In 1964 the company launched the first international computerized information retrieval system. CEO Peter Job has been with Reuters since 1963, when he joined as a graduate trainee journalist. He

KEY FACTS

Year Established:	1850
Employees:	14,000
Fiscal Year End:	December
Revenues FY '94:	$3.6b
Revenues FY '95:	n/a
EPS '94:	$2.12
EPS '95:	$2.50 (estimate)
Shares Outstanding:	267.2m
Five-Year Growth Rate:	15%

REUTERS
HOLDINGS

CEO Peter Job has been with Reuters since 1963, when he joined as a graduate trainee journal-ist. He served in various countries as a correspondent, was appointed managing director of Reuters Asia in 1988, joined the board of directors in 1989, and was appointed managing direc-tor and CEO in March 1991. CFO Robert Rowley joined Reuters in 1978 as assistant financial manager. He has served in various managerial positions at the company and was appointed a director and CFO in 1990.

RHYTHM & HUES STUDIOS

Address:	5404 Jandy Place
	Los Angeles, CA 90066
Telephone:	310/448-7500
Fax:	310/448-7600
E-mail:	Suze@Rhythm.com
Web site:	http://www.rhythm.com
Industry:	Entertainment & Information
Sector:	Film & Entertainment Production
CEO:	John Hughes
CFO:	Ron Hein

Product Description

Rhythm & Hues Studios develops high-quality live action, animation, and visual effects for commercials, feature films, theme-park rides, and music videos. It is involved in both traditional and computer-generated film-making, and about 50% of its work is digital. The company has won Clio awards six years in a row. Rhythm & Hues does more commercial work than any other studio in the country. Of the company's digital work, 50% is special venue work, 25% film work, and 25% commercials. Rhythm & Hues is responsible for creating the successful Coca-Cola Bears.

Market Strategy/Positioning

Rhythm & Hues has strategic relationships with RX and Silicon Graphics. Significant customers include Walt Disney, IBM, Paramount, Coca-Cola, MCA, Universal, Warner Bros., DDB Needham, Young & Rubicam, and J. Walter Thompson. The company's competitive advantages are its creative employees and a strong employee philosophy. Rhythm & Hues employees are encouraged to not be workaholics; it has no overtime—only "comp" time. The company has an education fund for employees and prefers that they use it for non-job-related subjects. Rhythm & Hues Studios primarily competes against Digital Domain, Pacific Data Images, R/GA Digital Studios, and Industrial Light & Magic. Additional challenges and risks include new techniques and constant new competition. Rhythm & Hues Studios is unique as one of the few companies that can scan at 4K resolution.

Other

Since its inception in 1987, Rhythm & Hues has had a massive explosion of opportunity and has continually capitalized on this opportunity to position itself where it is presently. The founders, John Hughes, Pauline Ts'o, Charles Gibson, and Keith Goldfarb, came from Robert Abel & Associates; all previously worked as animators. Other top management came from Universal Studios, Digital Productions, ILM, and Digital Domain.

Primary VCs/Outside Financing

100% internally funded by the four founders.

KEY FACTS

Year Established:	1987
Employees:	170
Fiscal Year End:	December
Revenues FY '94:	$20.0m
Revenues FY '95:	n/a
Date of Next Financing:	n/a
Date of Last Financing:	n/a
Size of Last Financing:	n/a
Total Capital Raised:	n/a
Post Round Valuation:	n/a
Expected IPO Date:	n/a

RSA
DATA SECURITY

Address:	100 Marine Parkway
	Suite 500
	Redwood City, CA 94065-1031
Telephone:	415/595-8782
Fax:	415/595-1873
E-mail:	info@rsa.com
Web site:	http://www.rsa.com
Industry:	Entertainment & Information
Sector:	Online Services
CEO:	James Bidzos
CFO:	Kathy Conrow

Product Description

RSA Data Security is a data encryption and authentication technology company. Its services include security reviews, development assistance, end-user applications, software development kits, algorithm optimizations, literature searches, and cryptographic consulting. Its flagship method encrypts and decodes through public and private key algorithms, specific to each party in a transaction. It has products for e-mail, messaging, and software development. RSA primarily sells to developers and seeks standard status for basic crypto technologies.

Market Strategy/Positioning

The company's mission is to perform basic research in cryptography and mathematics and sell software and developers' tool kits for encryption, authentication, and data security applications. RSA Data Security has strategic relationships with Apple, Netscape, CyberCash, Dun & Bradstreet, GE Information Services, Intel, National Semiconductor, Sun Microsystems, Hewlett-Packard, DEC, and Novell. Significant customers include Apple, Banker's Trust, Digital Delivery, Enterprise Integration Technologies, Funk Software, General Magic, Microsoft, Netscape, Motorola, NASA, Visa, MasterCard, the Department of Defense, Hewlett-Packard, Northern Telecom, and Oracle. The company's competitive advantage is that it does not gouge on pricing. RSA primarily competes against Bellcore, IBM, and Viacrypt. Additional challenges and risks include its patent expiring in five years, and other companies' competition.

Other

The public key cryptosystem was invented in 1977 by three Massachusetts Institute of Technology professors—Dr. Ronald Rivest, Dr. Adi Shamir, and Dr. Leonard Adleman. In 1982 they founded RSA Data Security to develop and refine privacy and authentication techniques. Mssrs. Rivest and Adleman are both still active in the company's management. VeriSign, a spinoff of RSA, markets digital ID products. CEO James Bidzos speaks frequently around the world on the applications, mathematics, and politics of public-key cryptography, and has testified before Congress several times on behalf of the U.S. computer and telecommunications industries. Mr. Bidzos has been president of RSA Data Security since 1986.

KEY FACTS

Year Established:	1982
Employees:	50
Fiscal Year End:	n/a
Revenues FY '94:	$7.0m
Revenues FY '95:	$15.0m
Date of Next Financing:	n/a
Date of Last Financing:	n/a
Size of Last Financing:	n/a
Total Capital Raised:	n/a
Post Round Valuation:	n/a
Expected IPO Date:	n/a

400

Product Description

S3 develops graphics acceleration chips for PCs. Its family of acceleration products includes multimedia-enabled graphics accelerators, a video accelerator, and peripheral chips. Through a joint agreement with IBM, S3 also offers a video processor chip which has a software MPEG decoding solution that targets multimedia applications such as online video help, pre-installed video messages, and linear video playback. It runs up to 24 frames per second. S3 will make MPEG devices optimized for the PC.

Address:	2770 San Tomas Expressway
	Santa Clara, CA 95051-0968
Telephone:	408/980-5400
Fax:	408/980-5444
E-mail:	n/a
Web site:	n/a
Industry:	Computers
Sector:	Semiconductors
CEO:	Terry N. Holdt
CFO:	George A. Hervey
Stock Exchange:	NASDAQ
Stock Symbol:	SIII

Market Strategy/Positioning

S3 has strategic relationships with Compaq, United Microelectronics (Taiwan), and Alliance Semiconductor to set up a wafer foundry plant in Taiwan. Significant customers include IBM, DEC, Dell, and AT&T. The company's competitive advantages are its expansion into mobile PC graphics, and its home PC/set-top box multimedia graphics which provide major opportunities for growth. S3 primarily competes against Cirrus Logic, Trident, AT&T Technology, and Oak Technology. Additional challenges and risks include an extremely competitive environment in the PC graphics and multimedia chip businesses.

401

Other

In June 1995 S3 and Compaq announced a joint strategy that uses S3's MPEG hardware to provide consumer PCs with advanced multimedia capabilities. The two companies planned to have TV-quality video and CD-quality audio available at affordable prices by December 1995.

KEY FACTS

Year Established:	1989
Employees:	190
Fiscal Year End:	December
Revenues FY '94:	$140.3m
Revenues FY '95:	$270.0m (estimate)
EPS '94:	$0.26
EPS '95:	$1.39 (estimate)
Shares Outstanding:	18.5m
Five-Year Growth Rate:	25%

SAP

Address:	U.S. Headquarters
	701 Lee Road
	Suite 200
	Wayne, PA 19087
Telephone:	610/725-4500
Fax:	610/725-4555
E-mail:	n/a
Web site:	http://www.sap-ag.de
Industry:	Computers
Sector:	Enterprise & Client/Server Software
CEO:	Dietmar Hopp (Chairman)
CFO:	Dieter Mattheis
Stock Exchange:	German Exchange
Stock Symbol:	SAG GR (Bloomberg)

Product Description

SAP is a leading provider of client/server business applications. It offers a library of 800 pre-defined business processes. In September 1995 new and extended versions of its financial accounting and manufacturing applications were announced. SAP's R/3 client/server suite has been installed in over 4,000 sites worldwide. "Real-time integration" links entire organizations to allow immediate response to change.

Market Strategy/Positioning

SAP has strategic relationships with the "Big Six" consulting firms, Legato, Siemens, and Computer Sciences. Significant customers include Compaq, Hewlett-Packard, Massachusetts Institute of Technology, and First National Bank of Chicago. The company's competitive advantages are its applications, which work with several database packages, whereas many of its competitors do not; and its delivery of software ahead of their release dates. SAP primarily competes against Oracle, Sybase, Informix, and Dun & Bradstreet. SAP is unique in its international strength: all applications are available in 12 languages, support multiple currencies, and automatically handle country-specific import/export, tax, and legal requirements.

Other

SAP was founded in 1972 by employees of IBM Germany. They wanted to carry out their ideas, which could not be done in a large corporation. In 1988, SAP went public, and in September 1995 the company announced an agreement to have Legato Systems provide backup and recovery services for SAP's R/3 applications.

402

KEY FACTS

Year Established:	1972
Employees:	6,400
Fiscal Year End:	December
Revenues FY '94:	$1.2b
Revenues FY '95:	n/a
EPS '94:	2.78 DM
EPS '95:	4.52 DM
Shares Outstanding:	101.0m
Five-Year Growth Rate:	n/a

SBC
COMMUNICATIONS

Address:	175 East Houston
	San Antonio, TX 78205-2233
Telephone:	210/821-4105
Fax:	210/351-2071
E-mail:	n/a
Web site:	http://www.sbc.com
Industry:	Communications
Sector:	Information Highway Services
CEO:	Edward E. Whitacre Jr.
CFO:	Donald E. Kiernan
Stock Exchange:	NYSE
Stock Symbol:	SBC

Product Description

SBC Communications (formerly Southwestern Bell Corporation) provides local telephone service to five states: Arkansas, Kansas, Missouri, Oklahoma, and Texas. New products and services include Caller ID, voice-activated dialing for residential customers, and the Advanced Intelligent Network (AIN) for business customers. The company's subsidiary, Southwestern Bell Mobile Communications, provides cellular service to markets such as Chicago; Boston; Washington, DC; Dallas; and St. Louis. In Austin SBC offers ISDN service that provides simultaneous transmission of voice, graphics, video, and data over a single phone line. The company also plans to enter the Internet access business.

Market Strategy/Positioning

SBC Communications has strategic relationships with France Télécom, Grupo Carso, Telmex (Mexico), Cox Communications (U.K.), GTE, CGE (France), VTR (Chile), TeleWest, Texas Instruments, Walt Disney, Ameritech, and BellSouth. The company's competitive advantage is its success in diversifying operations from telephone services into mobile communications. The company became the first regional Bell operating company to enter the domestic cable business by acquiring two cable properties in Washington, DC. SBC Communications primarily competes against American Business Information, Ameritech, AT&T, Bell Atlantic, BellSouth, British Telecom, Cable & Wireless, Century Telephone, Dun & Bradstreet, GTE, MCI, Metromedia, MFS Communications, Motorola, NYNEX, Pacific Telesis, Sprint, TCI, Telephone and Data Systems, and U S WEST. Additional challenges and risks include attempting to diversify too widely too quickly.

403

Other

Telephone service arrived in Southwestern Bell territory in 1878. The company joined AT&T in 1917 and then broke apart in 1984 because of the AT&T antitrust suit. It received service rights in five states, Southwestern Bell Mobile Systems, a directory advertising business, and a ⅓ share in Bell Communications Research. By 1988 SBC had put in place more ISDN lines than any other company. In 1994 SBC added to its cellular business by buying systems in New York State.

KEY FACTS

Year Established:	1984
Employees:	58,400
Fiscal Year End:	December
Revenues FY '94:	$11.6b
Revenues FY '95:	n/a
EPS '94:	$2.74
EPS '95:	$3.04 (estimate)
Shares Outstanding:	60.0m
Five-Year Growth Rate:	9%

SCIENTIFIC–ATLANTA

Address:	One Technology Parkway
	Box 105600
	South Norcross, GA 30092
Telephone:	404/903-5000
Fax:	404/903-4779
E-mail:	n/a
Web site:	n/a
Industry:	Communications
Sector:	Information Highway Equipment
CEO:	James F. McDonald
CFO:	Kenneth V. Jaeggi
Stock Exchange:	NYSE
Stock Symbol:	SFA

Product Description

Scientific-Atlanta provides broadband communications systems, cable TV electronics, satellite-based communications networks, and instrumentation for industrial, telecommunications, and government applications. It has developed a product for cable TV that stores movies digitally and distributes them as near video-on-demand.

Market Strategy/Positioning

Scientific-Atlanta has strategic relationships with Ameritech, Siemens, Broadcom, Apple, IBM, BellSouth, and Silicon Graphics. Significant customers include Pacific Telesis, TimeWarner, Sega, Oracle, U S WEST, Interactive Network, Jones Intercable, MCI, Optus Vision, Motorola, Tribune, and Cablevision. The company's competitive advantages are its marketing strategy, its engineering skills, and broad coverage by its sales personnel. Scientific-Atlanta primarily competes against General Instrument. Additional challenges and risks include competition from many companies that have greater resources and a greater number of products.

Other

Scientific-Atlanta began as a manufacturer of electronic test equipment for antennas and electronics for the cable industry. James McDonald was elected president and CEO of Scientific-Atlanta in July 1993. He was formerly a general partner of J.H. Whitney, a private investment firm. From 1989 to 1991, Mr. McDonald served as president and CEO of Prime Computer, a supplier of CAD/CAM software and computer systems. From 1984 to 1989, he was president and COO of Gould, a computer and electronics company.

KEY FACTS

Year Established:	1951
Employees:	3,700
Fiscal Year End:	June
Revenues FY '94:	$811.8m
Revenues FY '95:	$1.2b
EPS '94:	$0.44
EPS '95:	$0.83
Shares Outstanding:	76.7m
Five-Year Growth Rate:	24%

SCOPUS
TECHNOLOGY

Address:	1900 Powell Street
	Suite 900
	Emeryville, CA 94608
Telephone:	510/428-0500
Fax:	510/428-1027
E-mail:	info@scopus.com
Web site:	n/a
Industry:	Computers
Sector:	Enterprise & Client/Server Software
CEO:	Ori Sasson
CFO:	William Leetham

Product Description

Scopus Technology develops client/server-based customer information management systems. Its product family includes applications for help-desk and customer support, defect resolution, quality management, and sales cycle management. Its products work with Microsoft, Oracle, and Sybase databases, UNIX and Windows NT servers, and Macintosh, UNIX, Windows, and Windows NT clients.

Market Strategy/Positioning

The company's mission is to provide software solutions that increase productivity, product quality, and customer satisfaction. Scopus has strategic relationships with Apple, Atria Software, Hewlett-Packard, Frame Technology, IBM, Microsoft, Northern Telecom, Oracle, PLATINUM Technology, Sun Microsystems, Sybase, Tektronix, and Verity. Significant customers include Corporate Software, MicroAge, 3Com, Alcatel, AT&T, Boeing, Charles Schwab, CompuServe, Genentech, Hitachi, Intuit, Netscape, Sequent, Visa, and Wells Fargo. The company's competitive advantages are its product flexibility, its customer information management expertise, and its ability to provide global solutions. Scopus primarily competes against Aurum, Clarify, Remedy, and Vantive. Additional challenges and risks include developing and marketing software that brings enterprises closer to its customers, and delivering comprehensive support and services to guarantee technology transfer.

405

Other

Scopus introduced its first product in 1991 to help technology companies track and manage the customer support function. In 1993 the company introduced remote access and database replication capabilities for Motif, Microsoft, Macintosh, and ORACLE7. CEO Ori Sasson was a former engineering manager at Sybase and worked as a consultant for Mitsubishi Trust Bank of Japan, American Airlines, and IBM. Co-founder and vice president of engineering Dr. Bahram Nour-Omid has written more than 40 publications. Co-founders Aaron Omid and David Schwab served at Sun Microsystems and Lockheed.

KEY FACTS

Year Established:	1991
Employees:	130
Fiscal Year End:	March
Revenues FY '94:	n/a
Revenues FY '95:	n/a
Date of Next Financing:	n/a
Date of Last Financing:	May 1994
Size of Last Financing:	3.8m
Total Capital Raised:	5.2m
Post Round Valuation:	n/a
Expected IPO Date:	n/a

Primary VCs/Outside Financing

General Atlantic and Hummer Winblad Ventures.

SEAGATE
TECHNOLOGY

Address:	920 Disc Drive
	Scotts Valley, CA 95066
Telephone:	408/438-6550
Fax:	408/438-6172
E-mail:	n/a
Web site:	http://www.seagate.com
Industry:	Computers
Sector:	Storage
CEO:	Alan F. Shugart
CFO:	Donald L. Waite
Stock Exchange:	NYSE
Stock Symbol:	SEG

Product Description

Seagate Technology is a data technology company that provides data storage, management, and access products for computer and data communications systems. The company offers more than 150 rigid disk drives with form factors from 2.5 to 5.25 inches. Seagate is leveraging its core competencies to pursue applications for the components, software, and technology related to the storage, communications, and management of all forms of electronic data, including text, image, sound, video, and graphics. Seagate also markets flash memory products manufactured by SunDisk, in which Seagate has acquired a 25% interest.

Market Strategy/Positioning

The company's mission is to capitalize on market opportunities created by the shift to client/server computing environments and the development of the global information infrastructure. Seagate has strategic relationships with Areal Technology, Ceridian, Hewlett-Packard, Hitachi, Machines Bull (France), Quantum, UNISYS, and Western Digital. Significant customers include DHL, DreamWorks SKG, and IBM. The company's competitive advantage is being a leader in the disk drive storage industry and having the broadest product line. Seagate is looking for acquisition targets and intends to move into the data management software business. Seagate primarily competes against Maxtor, Micropolis, Western Digital, Canon, DEC, Fujitsu, Hewlett-Packard, Hitachi, IBM, Matsushita, NEC, Mitsubishi, Quantum, Toshiba, UNISYS, Wang, and Storage Technology.

Other

In 1979 Alan Shugart, Tom Mitchell, Douglas Mahon, and Finis Conner (of Conner Peripherals) founded Seagate Technology. Seagate pioneered the downsizing of mainframe hard disk drives for PCs. In early 1995 the company signed an agreement to acquire NetLabs. Since 1993 it has acquired Crystal Computer Services, Palindrome, Imprimis Technology, and Network Computing, and in September 1995 announced its plans to acquire Conner Peripherals, which would make it the largest disk-drive maker. Founder and CEO Alan Shugart also founded Shugart Associates, was vice president of Product Development at Memorex, and is an 18-year IBM veteran.

406

KEY FACTS

Year Established:	1979
Employees:	64,900
Fiscal Year End:	June
Revenues FY '94:	$3.50b
Revenues FY '95:	$4.54b
EPS '94:	$3.08
EPS '95:	$3.53
Shares Outstanding:	73.1m
Five-Year Growth Rate:	15%

SEGA
ENTERPRISES

Address:	U.S. Headquarters
	Sega of America
	255 Shoreline Boulevard
	Suite 200
	Redwood City, CA 94065
Telephone:	415/508-2800
Fax:	415/802-3063
E-mail:	webmaster@sega.com
Web site:	http://www.segaoa.com
Industry:	Entertainment & Information
Sector:	Entertainment/Education Software
CEO:	Tom Kalinske (Sega of America)
CFO:	Shinobu Toyota
Stock Exchange:	NASDAQ
Stock Symbol:	SEGNY

Product Description

Sega Enterprises develops consumer products, including video game systems, toys, portable video games, and also operates amusement centers. The Sega Saturn game system was introduced in May 1995 and Sega of America manufactures 85% of all Sega software. Sega also has a virtual ride system in place at the Luxor Hotel in Las Vegas developed by Motion Picture, Douglas Trumbull, and Kleiser-Walzcak Construction. It plans to build 50 Japanese theme parks and 50 U.S. theme parks on 1–5–acre lots over the next several years, each costing between $10 million and $50 million, and is seeking partners to help defray the costs.

Market Strategy/Positioning

The company's mission is to lead the interactive entertainment industry in offering the most immersive video-gaming experience for all segments of the market. Sega has strategic relationships with Intel, MGM, Time Warner, and TCI. The company's competitive advantages are its proven in-house game development expertise and its thriving arcade business. It has an estimated 55% market share in the U.S. arcade business. Sega Enterprises primarily competes against Sony, Nintendo, Magic Edge, Fightertown, Acclaim Entertainment, and Electronic Arts. Additional challenges and risks include staying on top of market demand.

Other

Sega Enterprises was founded in Japan in 1951 as Rosen Enterprises. Founder Dave Rosen began importing coin-operated games into Japan in 1957. The company became Sega in 1965 and developed its first video game, *Periscope*, in the late 1960s. Sega of America, the company's U.S. subsidiary, was established in 1986 to market video game products, one of the fastest growing markets in the mid 1980s. In 1994 Sega, Time Warner, and TCI created their own cable channel which offers many game titles to Sega Genesis owners. Sega's 32-bit system was expected to arrive in late 1995. When Tom Kalinske joined Sega in 1990 as CEO, he decided to target a slightly older users crowd than that of Nintendo's, and Sega quickly became one of the most popular brands to appeal to young adults.

KEY FACTS

Year Established:	1965
Employees:	3,760
Fiscal Year End:	March
Revenues FY '94:	$3.9b
Revenues FY '95:	$3.7b
EPS '94:	$0.57
EPS '95:	n/a
Shares Outstanding:	402.0m
Five-Year Growth Rate:	n/a

SGS-THOMSON

Product Description

SGS-Thomson is an independent semi-conductor company that creates a broad range of integrated circuits (ICs) and other devices with microelectronic applications. It is the largest supplier of analog ICs, mixed-signal ICs, power ICs, dedicated telecommunications ICs, and dedicated analog automotive ICs. The company's New Ventures Group markets x86 microprocessors designed by Cyrix. The company has used its broad intellectual property portfolio to enter into cross-licensing agreements with other large semiconductor manufacturers.

Address:	U.S. Headquarters
	SGS-Thomson Microelectronics
	1310 Electronic Drive
	Carollton, TX 75006
Telephone:	214/466-6000
Fax:	214/466-7196
E-mail:	n/a
Web site:	http://www.inmos.com
Industry:	Computers
Sector:	Semiconductors
CEO:	Pasquale Pistorio
CFO:	Maurizio Ghirga
Stock Exchange:	NYSE
Stock Symbol:	STM

Market Strategy/Positioning

SGS-Thomson has strategic relationships with Alcatel, Seagate Technology, Shenzhen Electronics Group, Cadence Design, Mitsubishi, Philips, and Northern Telecom. The company's competitive advantages are its linear and mixed signal ICs, EPROMs, smart power, dedicated telecom, analog automotive devices, chips for smart cards, and gains in market share. SGS-Thomson primarily competes against AMD, Hitachi, Intel, Motorola, National Semiconductor, NEC, Philips, Samsung, Siemens, Texas Instruments, and Toshiba. Additional challenges and risks include the semiconductor industry's highly cyclical and extremely competitive nature. SGS-Thomson is unique in being the second largest chip maker in Europe, after Philips.

Other

French state-owned Thomson-CSF and SGS Microelectronica, an Italian state-controlled telephone company, formed SGS-Thomson. It acquired Inmos, a British semiconductor company, and Microwave Semiconductor in 1989. In 1993 the company purchased Tag Semiconductors from Raytheon. President and CEO Pasquale Pistorio formerly worked at Motorola.

408

KEY FACTS

Year Established:	1987
Employees:	n/a
Fiscal Year End:	December
Revenues FY '94:	$2.6b
Revenues FY '95:	$3.3b (estimate)
EPS '94:	$3.04
EPS '95:	$3.60 (estimate)
Shares Outstanding:	128.0m
Five-Year Growth Rate:	n/a

SHIVA

Address:	Northwest Park
	63 Third Avenue
	Burlington, MA 01803
Telephone:	617/270-8300
Fax:	617/270-8599
E-mail:	info@shiva.com
Web site:	http://www.shiva.com
Industry:	Communications
Sector:	Computer Networking
CEO:	Frank A. Ingari
CFO:	Cynthia M. Deysher
Stock Exchange:	NASDAQ
Stock Symbol:	SHVA

Product Description

Shiva's products provide transparent remote connectivity to enterprise networks. One product line provides enterprise-wide remote access, while another provides remote access for workgroups. Its products include server hardware and software, client software, and network management software.

Market Strategy/Positioning

Shiva has strategic relationships with IBM, Hewlett-Packard, Nortel, and Microsoft. Significant customers include American Airlines, ARCO, GE, Phillip Morris, Northern Telecom, Grand Metropolitan, and the Shanghai Stock Exchange. The company's competitive advantages are its high-quality performance and ease-of-use of all products, as well as its strong partnership ties with other companies. Shiva primarily competes against 3Com, Ascend Communications, Cisco Systems, Combinet, Microcom, Telebit, and Xylogics. Additional challenges and risks include managing its growth as well as maximizing and capitalizing on all opportunities in the market.

409

Other

Shiva was founded in 1985 by chairman Daniel Schwinn and Frank Slaughter to pioneer technologies for the dial-in remote access market for the Macintosh and PC environments. President and CEO Frank Ingari joined the company in September 1993. Mr. Ingari previously held numerous senior management positions at high-technology companies. He was vice president of marketing at Lotus Development, chairman and CEO of ONTOS, and senior vice president of marketing at Atex. CFO Cynthia Deysher came to Shiva from Bytex, where she also held a CFO position. Before working at Bytex, she was director of finance and operations, systems marketing, and development at Prime Computer.

KEY FACTS

Year Established:	1985
Employees:	175
Fiscal Year End:	December
Revenues FY '94:	$41.5m
Revenues FY '95:	n/a
EPS '94:	$0.27
EPS '95:	$0.65
Shares Outstanding:	10.1m
Five-Year Growth Rate:	50%

SIEBEL SYSTEMS

Address:	4005 Bohannon Drive
	Menlo Park, CA 94025
Telephone:	415/329-6500
Fax:	415/329-9511
E-mail:	73221,3553@compuserve.com
Web site:	http://www.siebel.com
Industry:	Computers
Sector:	Enterprise & Client/Server Software
CEO:	Thomas Siebel
CFO:	Wayne Snyder

Product Description

Siebel Systems develops high-end sales-force automation software for multinational corporations that employ multitiered distribution strategies. Designed for mobile computing, with support for laptop and pen-based computers, the system is groupware-enabled for team selling, allowing sales teams to collaborate on sales opportunities. Its Windows-based client/server software is highly scalable and can support very large data stores and large numbers of concurrent users.

Market Strategy/Positioning

The company's mission is to develop comprehensive sales information systems for large organizations that employ multiple distribution systems. Siebel Systems has strategic relationships with Microsoft, Andersen Consulting, KPMG Peat Marwick, Adobe, Oracle, Aspect Telecommunications, and Clarify. Significant customers include Cisco and Times Mirror. The company's competitive advantages are its strong products, an expansive market, experienced management, and powerful strategic partnerships. Siebel Systems primarily competes against Salesoft, Trilogy, and Scopus. Additional challenges and risks include managing a fragmented segment with numerous players and offering sales-force automation software solutions in its various forms.

Other

CEO Tom Siebel founded the company in July 1993 with his own funds to create a sales-force automation solution that would take advantage of new remote access technology and client/server architecture. From 1991 to 1992 Mr. Siebel was CEO of Gain Technology, which was sold to Sybase in 1992. Prior to that he held several executive management positions at Oracle.

Primary VCs/Outside Financing

Hambrecht & Quist and other private investors.

410

KEY FACTS

Year Established:	1993
Employees:	30
Fiscal Year End:	December
Revenues FY '94:	n/a
Revenues FY '95:	n/a
Date of Next Financing:	n/a
Date of Last Financing:	March 1995
Size of Last Financing:	1.0m
Total Capital Raised:	1.0m
Post Round Valuation:	n/a
Expected IPO Date:	n/a

SIEMENS

Address:	U.S. Headquarters
	1301 Avenue of the Americas
	New York, NY 10019-6055
Telephone:	212/258-4000
Fax:	212/767-0580
E-mail:	webmaster@siemens.de
Web site:	http://www.siemens.de
Industry:	Computers
Sector:	Semiconductors
CEO:	Heinrich von Pierer
CFO:	Karl-Hermann Baumann
Stock Exchange:	NASDAQ
Stock Symbol:	SMAWY

Product Description

Siemens is one of the largest electrical engineering and electronics companies in the world. It operates in over 120 countries and is involved in industrial electronics, energy, telecommunications, information systems, transportation, healthcare, components, and lighting. It also works on image and video database management, image processing and analysis, and imaging hardware and architecture. In conjunction with IBM and Toshiba, the company has prototyped a 256 megabit DRAM chip, which is at least 13% smaller and has an access time nearly twice as fast as other chips.

Market Strategy/Positioning

The company's mission is to be the top company in the field of electrical and electronic engineering and to set the pace for technological progress. Siemens has strategic relationships with Robert Bosch (Bosch-Siemens Hausgerate, Munich), GPT Holdings, Corning, Matsushita, China National Posts, Telecommunications Industry, IBM, Toshiba, Apple, Scientific-Atlanta, and Sun Microsystems. The company's competitive advantages are its commitment to research and development and its exceptional financial strength. Siemens primarily competes against Amdahl, AT&T, DEC, Eastman Kodak, Ericsson, Fujitsu, GE, Hewlett-Packard, IBM, Intel, ITT, Motorola, NEC, Nokia, Northern Telecom, Philips, Rolls-Royce, Samsung, Sanyo, Sharp, Toshiba, and Westinghouse. Additional challenges and risks include managing its high labor costs particularly in Germany, facing increasing competition worldwide, and compensating for currency translation. Siemens is unique for a company its size in placing a high value on training apprentice programs.

411

Other

Siemans was founded in 1847 by Werner von Siemens. Its first major project linked Berlin and Frankfurt with the first long-distance telegraph system in Europe in 1848. Other early accomplishments include Europe's first electric power transmission system, the world's first electrified railway, and one of the first elevators. In the 1950s Siemens began developing silicates for semiconductors and data processing equipment. In 1989 Siemens purchased ROLM Systems from IBM. Heinrich von Pierer replaced Karlheinz Kaske as CEO in 1992.

KEY FACTS

Year Established:	1847
Employees:	382,000
Fiscal Year End:	September
Revenues FY '94:	$51.3b
Revenues FY '95:	n/a
EPS '94:	$3.64
EPS '95:	$4.58 (estimate)
Shares Outstanding:	56.0m
Five-Year Growth Rate:	15%

SIERRA ON-LINE

Product Description

Sierra On-Line publishes and develops entertainment and education software. Its software is compatible with PCs, Macintosh, Sega CD, and 3DO systems. It has been developing CD-ROM titles for four years, a lead-time over the competition that gave the company an estimated leading 12% market share in the industry. Sierra On-Line has important proprietary development tools, some of which are patented, covering speech animation and synchronization, and object-oriented tools. The company primarily focuses on sports, fantasy role playing, and adventure titles.

Address:	3380 146th Place, Southeast
	Suite 300
	Bellevue, WA 98007
Telephone:	206/649-9800
Fax:	206/641-7617
E-mail:	n/a
Web site:	http://www.sierra.com
Industry:	Entertainment & Information
Sector:	Entertainment/Education Software
CEO:	Kenneth Williams
CFO:	Michael Brochu
Stock Exchange:	NASDAQ
Stock Symbol:	SIER

Market Strategy/Positioning

Sierra On-Line has strategic relationships with Pioneer Electronic of Tokyo, Impressions, Print Artist, and Pixell Lite Group. It also acquired Green Thumb Software in July 1995. Sierra On-Line primarily competes against Brøderbund, Electronic Arts, Acclaim Entertainment, Id Software, Maxis, Nintendo, Sega, and Sony. Sierra On-Line is unique as the largest in-house developer of entertainment and educational software in the industry.

Other

The company was founded in 1979, initially as On-Line Systems, by Ken and Roberta Williams at their kitchen table. They designed the first text adventure game with graphics, *Mystery House*, and during the early 1980s produced some of the best-selling game series in the industry. Since going public in 1989, Sierra On-Line has acquired Dynamix, Bright Star Technologies, Coktel Vision, and Green Thumb, and has opened international offices in Japan and England. CEO Kenneth Williams previously worked at Informatics, Warner Bros., and Bekins. CFO Michael Brochu joined Sierra On-Line in July 1994. He previously worked at El Paso Natural Gas and at Burlington Environmental.

KEY FACTS

Year Established:	1979
Employees:	600
Fiscal Year End:	March
Revenues FY '94:	$62.7m
Revenues FY '95:	$83.4m
EPS '94:	$(0.60)
EPS '95:	$0.73
Shares Outstanding:	16.6m
Five-Year Growth Rate:	28%

SILICON GRAPHICS

Product Description

Silicon Graphics designs and produces visual processing workstations and computer systems that incorporate 3D graphics, digital media, and multiprocessing supercomputing technologies. Its workstation products are used to simulate, analyze, develop, and display 3D objects and phenomena. In 1994 the company formed Silicon Studio, a wholly-owned subsidiary created to offer applications development for the emerging interactive digital media markets. Silicon Studio will work with third-party developers, content creators, and distributors to extend its role in media authoring markets, including film, video, publishing, interactive TV, and location-based entertainment.

Address:	2011 North Shoreline Boulevard Mountain View, CA 94043-1389
Telephone:	415/960-1980
Fax:	415/969-6289
E-mail:	n/a
Web site:	http://www.sgi.com
Industry:	Computers
Sector:	Desktop Computers/File Servers
CEO:	Edward McCracken
CFO:	Stanley J. Meresman
Stock Exchange:	NYSE
Stock Symbol:	SGI

Market Strategy/Positioning

Silicon Graphics has strategic relationships with Time Warner, Nintendo, Walt Disney, Dream-Works SKG, AT&T, and NTT. The company's competitive advantage is its ability to rapidly develop highly differentiated and technologically complex products. Silicon Graphics primarily competes against DEC, Hewlett-Packard, IBM, Sun-Microsystems, Cray Research, Intel, and Motorola. An additional challenge includes avoiding delays in new product introduction. The company depends on continued funding from its semiconductor partners in order to further the development and encourage broad acceptance of its MIPS RISC microprocessor architecture. Silicon Graphics is unique in pioneering visual computing and currently holds approximately 50% of the market.

413

Other

Professor James Clark founded Silicon Graphics in 1982 in order to develop and market 3D computer graphics technology. The first 3D terminal (IRIS 1000) and IRIS Graphics library were released in 1983, followed by the first workstation in 1984. The company protected its 3D technology for six years until it licensed its IRIS Graphics Library to IBM in 1988. Silicon Graphics was first company to use the RISC chips developed by MIPS Computer Systems, and in 1991 the company introduced the IRIS Indigo as the first RISC-based PC. Founder James Clark was formerly a professor at Stanford University. CEO Edward McCracken joined Silicon Graphics in 1984 from Hewlett-Packard.

KEY FACTS

Year Established:	1982
Employees:	3,700
Fiscal Year End:	June
Revenues FY '94:	$1.5b
Revenues FY '95:	$2.2b
EPS '94:	$0.92
EPS '95:	$1.31
Shares Outstanding:	158.6m
Five-Year Growth Rate:	27%

SONY

Product Description

Sony is a consumer electronics conglomerate. Its major subsidiaries include Sony
Electronics, Sony's Wireless Communications Company, Sony Computer Entertainment, Sony Music, and Sony Pictures,
which manages Columbia Pictures and Tri-
Star. Columbia is the number two studio,
with an estimated 11.2% market share. Tri-
Star has the ninth biggest box office take,
with a 6.3% market share. Tri-Star wants to
release 35 pictures in 1995, up from 25 in
1994. Currently the company is remaking *Godzilla*, which may be the biggest special-effects
movie in history. Sony also operates Sony Imageworks, a digital studio, and Sony Imagesoft, an
entertainment software producer. It has developed 30 CD-ROM multimedia titles and has taken
advantage of content like *Wheel of Fortune, Jeopardy*, and *Johnny Mnemonic*. It is also involved
in a joint venture to produce music CD-ROMs. Sony's video game unit made its debut in September 1995 with over 20 titles. In September 1995, Sony's Wireless Communications Company announced it would distribute the first two-way paging system, developed by SkyTel. Also in
September 1995 Sony Electronics introduced two Digital Handycam camcorders that offer digital picture and sound and digital editing and dubbing. Sony also announced in 1995 that it would
use C-Cube's system decoder for its new line of VideoCD players.

Address:	U.S. Headquarters
	9 West 57th Street
	New York, NY 10019-2791
Telephone:	212/833-6800
Fax:	212/833-6923
E-mail:	n/a
Web site:	http://www.sony.com
Industry:	Entertainment & Information
Sector:	Consumer Electronics
CEO:	Norio Ohga
CFO:	Tsunao Hashimoto
Stock Exchange:	NYSE
Stock Symbol:	SNE

Market Strategy/Positioning

The company's mission is to be the best at bringing advanced technology together with the
needs of the user, and to develop revolutionary products that enhance the quality of life and
create new markets. Sony has strategic relationships with AT&T, Sega, Oracle, Microsoft, Graphix
Zone, Farcast, SkyTel, C-Cube, and Midway Manufacturing. The company's competitive advantages are that it produces both content and the hard-
ware on which to experience it, and that it is
reducing its reliance on imports from Sony factories in Japan (the proportion of U.S.-made Sony
products jumped 40% in 1994). Sony primarily
competes against AT&T, Bertelsmann, Canon,
DreamWorks SKG, Fujitsu, Hitachi, LG Group, Matsushita, Motorola, NEC, News Corp., Nokia, Philips,
Walt Disney, and all major entertainment software
companies. Additional challenges and risks include
avoiding past film disasters, like *North* (which cost
$40 million to produce and took in $20 million), *I'll
Do Anything* (costing another $40 million and yield-

KEY FACTS

Year Established:	1946
Employees:	130,000
Fiscal Year End:	March
Revenues FY '94:	$35.1b
Revenues FY '95:	$41.1b
EPS '94:	$0.41
EPS '95:	$(7.00)
Shares Outstanding:	373.7m
Five-Year Growth Rate:	12%

ing only $6.6 million), *Wolf*, and *Last Action Hero*. Sony is unique as the first Japanese corporation to establish a non-profit, philanthropic organization in the U.S. (1972), and to initiate a corporation-wide environmental action plan.

Other

In 1946 Akio Morita, Masaru Ibuka, and Tamon Maeda founded Tokyo Telecommunications Engineering, which produced Japan's first tape recorder in 1950. The company changed its name to Sony in 1958 and manufactured the first transistor TV a year later. The Walkman, introduced in 1979, became an instant success. Sony acquired CBS Records from CBS in 1988 and Columbia Pictures from Coca-Cola in 1989. On April 1, 1995, CEO Norio Ohga became Sony's chairman of the board.

SPRINT

Address:	2330 Shawnee Mission Parkway
	Westwood, KS 66205
Telephone:	913/624-3000
Fax:	913/624-3281
E-mail:	n/a
Web site:	http://www.sprint.com
Industry:	Communications
Sector:	Information Highway Services
CEO:	William T. Esrey
CFO:	Arthur B. Krause
Stock Exchange:	NYSE
Stock Symbol:	FON

Product Description

Sprint provides global voice, video, data, and videoconferencing telecommunications services and related products. The company has a presence in all three national telecom markets: long distance, local, and cellular (as the result of its merger with Centel). Sprint controls one of the world's largest data networks. It operates local telephone service in 19 states and intends to become more active abroad, taking advantage of the global trend of deregulation in the telecommunications industry. Sprint is also scouting for a wireless communications ally.

Market Strategy/Positioning

The company's mission is to be a world-class telecommunications company. Sprint has strategic relationships with Motorola, France Télécom, Deutsche Telekom, TCI, Comcast, and Cox Cable. Significant customers include GE, Western Union, Johnson & Johnson, Apple, Hewlett-Packard, and the U.S. government. The company's competitive advantages are that it operates the only 100% digital fiber-optic long distance network in the U.S. and that it was the first to install ATM broadband switching technology. Sprint primarily competes against Ameritech, AT&T, Bell Atlantic, BellSouth, Cable & Wireless, RR Donnelley, Dun & Bradstreet, GTE, MCI, NYNEX, Pacific Telesis, Southwestern Bell, Telephone and Data Systems, U S WEST, and U.S. Long Distance. Additional challenges include providing advanced voice, video, and data services as part of an integrated group of local, long distance, wireless, and international services. Sprint is unique as the first to offer ATM service and the first to announce a national synchronous optical network (SONET).

Other

In 1899 Jacob and Cleyson Brown received a franchise for one of the first non-Bell telephone companies in the West. In 1971 then-president Paul Henson named the company United Telecommunications. In 1985 United bought 50% of GTE's long distance provider, GTE Sprint. United purchased the remaining portion from GTE in 1992 and renamed the company Sprint. Sprint received access to Bell Communications Research in 1993. William Esrey joined Sprint in 1980 as executive vice president of corporate planning; he was named CEO in 1985 and chairman in 1990.

KEY FACTS

Year Established:	1899
Employees:	50,000
Fiscal Year End:	December
Revenues FY '94:	$12.7b
Revenues FY '95:	n/a
EPS '94:	$2.53
EPS '95:	$2.67 (estimate)
Shares Outstanding:	348.6m
Five-Year Growth Rate:	11%

SPYGLASS

Product Description

Spyglass markets commercial versions of Mosaic access- and navigation-software for the Internet. It is available for Macintosh, Windows, and UNIX platforms. Spyglass is upgrading the Mosaic Web browser with digital audio support, improved text and image formatting, and security. It recently announced a new version designed for electronic commerce.

Market Strategy/Positioning

The company's mission is to be the leading provider of World Wide Web technologies, enabling organizations to offer products and services that facilitate electronic publishing, commerce, and collaboration on the Internet. Spyglass has strategic relationships with University of Illinois (license for commercialized versions of Mosaic), Microsoft, SPRY (CompuServe), Performance Systems International, DEC, Ventana Media, Firefox, and FTP Software. Significant customers include AT&T, IBM, Microsoft, NEC, Ventana Communications, Ipswitch, Corel, and Quarterdeck. The company's competitive advantage is its ability to offer flexible World Wide Web technologies that its clients can customize for end-users. Spyglass primarily competes against Netscape, PRODIGY, NETCOM, NetManage, Frontier Technologies, and IBM. Additional challenges and risks include the fast progression of Internet services and products and the ability to develop and market World Wide Web technologies.

Other

Spyglass began operations in February 1990, and until 1994 focused most of of its resources on data visualization products it sold to the scientific market. In May 1994 after entering into an agreement with the University of Illinois, the company began to develop, distribute, and sublicense commerical products based on the Mosaic browser. CEO Doug Colbeth previously served at Stardent. Co-founder and Chief Technical Officer Timothy Krauskopf was a developer at NCSA Telnet.

Address:	Naperville Corporate Center
	1230 East Diehl Road
	Suite 304
	Naperville, IL 60563
Telephone:	708/505-1010
Fax:	708/505-4944
E-mail:	n/a
Web site:	http://www.spyglass.com
Industry:	Entertainment & Information
Sector:	Online Services
CEO:	Douglas Colbeth
CFO:	Thomas S. Lewicki
Stock Exchange:	NASDAQ
Stock Symbol:	SPYG

417

KEY FACTS

Year Established:	1990
Employees:	55
Fiscal Year End:	September
Revenues FY '94:	$3.6m
Revenues FY '95:	n/a
EPS '94:	$0.08
EPS '95:	n/a
Shares Outstanding:	5.0m
Five-Year Growth Rate:	n/a

STARSIGHT
TELECAST

Address:	39650 Liberty Street
	3rd Floor
	Fremont, CA 94538
Telephone:	510/657-9900
Fax:	510/657-5022
E-mail:	info@starsight.com
Web site:	n/a
Industry:	Entertainment & Information
Sector:	Information Highway Services
CEO:	Larry Wangberg
CFO:	Marty Henkel
Stock Exchange:	NASDAQ
Stock Symbol:	SGHT

Product Description

StarSight Telecast develops StarSight, a highly patented on-screen guide for interactive TV, which offers one-touch VCR recording. The company holds three broad patents that cover one-touch VCR recording and other on-screen guide functions. Viewers using StarSight can select desired programs by titles or specific categories and create customized channels for themselves. StarSight is a primary directory tool for consumers using Viacom's 77-channel system.

Market Strategy/Positioning

The company's mission is to be the leading developer of an interactive on-screen TV programming guide with one-button VCR recording. StarSight has strategic relationships with Viacom, Cox Communications, Tribune, and Providence Journal. In May 1995 the following companies signed licensing agreements with StarSight: Zenith, Goldstar, Mitsubishi, Philips, Samsung, SGS-Thomson, Sony, Matsushita, Daewoo, Sharp, and Toshiba. It also has an agreement with Bell Atlantic, which has the right to distribute StarSight to homes. The company's competitive advantage is its strong relationships with some of the top companies in the telecommunications and entertainment areas. StarSight Telecast primarily competes against *TV Guide*, Prevue Networks, United Video, VideoGuide, and Gemstar. Additional risks include StarSight's ambiguous market status and its susceptibility to lawsuits.

Other

StarSight Telecast, founded in 1986, has spent thousands of hours developing, researching, and testing technology for which it received groundbreaking patents. The company went public in July 1993 and today covers 97% of households in the U.S. via the Public Broadcast System. Larry Wangberg was elected CEO and president in February 1995. Previously, he was president and CEO of Times Mirror Cable and also served as senior vice president of Times Mirror. CFO Marty Henkel became a director of the company in July 1992. He was previously vice president of operations and CFO of Phylon Communications and a division head at Apple.

418

KEY FACTS

Year Established:	1986
Employees:	105
Fiscal Year End:	March
Revenues FY '94:	$70.0m
Revenues FY '95:	n/a
EPS '94:	$(0.55)
EPS '95:	$(1.95)
Shares Outstanding:	20.9m
Five-Year Growth Rate:	n/a

STORMFRONT STUDIOS

Address:	4000 Civic Center Drive Suite 450 San Rafael, CA 94903
Telephone:	415/479-2800
Fax:	415/750-2880
E-mail:	n/a
Web site:	n/a
Industry:	Entertainment & Information
Sector:	Entertainment/Education Software
CEO:	Donald L. Daglow
CFO:	Pat Killingsworth (acting)

Product Description

Stormfront Studios develops entertainment and edutainment products for the multimedia, video game, and interactive network markets. The company utilizes high-quality visual and audio technology to improve interactive game-play and story-telling. Its products are designed for use on every major platform.

Market Strategy/Positioning

The company's mission is to develop and publish the highest-quality entertainment and edutainment software for home computers and online networks. Significant customers include Electronic Arts, Microsoft, Sony, Viacom, and America Online. The company's competitive advantages are its engines for interactive sports and storytelling, which allow development of such high-profile titles as *Star Trek*. Stormfront was cited by the *San Francisco Business Times* as one of the "top twenty" growth companies in the Bay Area in both 1993 and 1994. Stormfront Studios primarily competes against Acclaim Entertainment, Brøderbund, The Learning Company, Electronic Arts, Maxis, LucasArts, LookingGlass Technologies, Sculptured Software, Kesmai, Accolade Entertainment, and Davidson & Associates. Additional challenges and risks include the rising cost of software development and publishing as trends move toward bigger projects, and managing the production of 32-bit games without becoming too exposed. Stormfront Studios is unique in developing the first interactive graphic adventure game for America Online and the first online e-mail game that links players across the country.

419

Other

Stormfront Studios was founded in 1988 as Beyond Software. Every game released since 1991 has been ranked in the top 10. In May 1995 the release of *Tony La Russa Baseball 3* marked its first self-published title. Founder, president, and CEO Don Daglow previously held various management positions at Brøderbund, Electronic Arts, and Mattel. Co-founder David Bunnet serves as vice president and executive art director and has worked in film animation and illustration at Paramount Studios and Industrial Light & Magic.

Primary VCs/Outside Financing

100% internally funded.

KEY FACTS

Year Established:	1988
Employees:	60
Fiscal Year End:	December
Revenues FY '94:	$2.1m
Revenues FY '95:	$6.0m
Date of Next Financing:	n/a
Date of Last Financing:	n/a
Size of Last Financing:	n/a
Total Capital Raised:	n/a
Post Round Valuation:	n/a
Expected IPO Date:	n/a

SUN MICROSYSTEMS

Address:	2550 Garcia Avenue
	Mountain View, CA 94043-1100
Telephone:	415/960-1300
Fax:	415/336-0555
E-mail:	info@sun.com
Web site:	http://www.sun.com
Industry:	Computers
Sector:	Desktop Computers/File Servers
CEO:	Scott McNealy
CFO:	Michael Lehman
Stock Exchange:	NASDAQ
Stock Symbol:	SUNW

Product Description

Sun Microsystems is a leading supplier of enterprise computing products that feature workstations and servers. Its products include RISC-based workstations and servers that run the UNIX operating systems, and a variety of related hardware and software products. "The Network is the Computer" has long been Sun's slogan, and its servers are ideally suited for enabling enterprise-wide networks. It is estimated that nearly 70% of all the backbone servers on the Internet are Sun servers. Sun's hottest new creation is its object-oriented programming language, Java. HotJava is Sun's World Wide Web browser that showcases the capabilities of Java language such as its real-time multimedia functions.

Market Strategy/Positioning

The company's mission is to be the leading provider of open technologies for distributed computing. Sun has strategic relationships with Fujitsu, Texas Instruments, Cray Research, IBM, and NeXT Computer. Significant customers include engineering and technical companies involved in software development, financial brokerage houses, educational institutions, and government agencies. The company's competitive advantage is its leading market share in the UNIX workstation market with the largest installed base, and technological leadership in client/server computing. Sun primarily competes against Hewlett-Packard, IBM, DEC, and Silicon Graphics. Additional challenges and risks include responding to threats from PC-based client/server environments, delivering superior price/performance that compares favorably to PC-based solutions, and increasing penetration into the enterprise computing market.

Other

Sun was founded in 1982 to take advantage of the market potential for workstations that share data using the UNIX operating system. The company has since expanded into the commercial and corporate marketplace. Recently, Sun has benefited from the explosive growth on the Internet since Sun's computer systems are ideal servers for the Internet. Scott McNealy is a co-founder, and has been CEO since December 1984. He was also vice president of operations 1982 to 1984.

420

KEY FACTS

Year Established:	1982
Employees:	13,000
Fiscal Year End:	June
Revenues FY '94:	$4.7b
Revenues FY '95:	$5.9b
EPS '94:	$2.04
EPS '95:	$3.58
Shares Outstanding:	95.6m
Five-Year Growth Rate:	16%

SYNOPSYS

Address:	700 East Middlefield Road Mountain View, CA 94043
Telephone:	415/962-5000
Fax:	415/965-8637
E-mail:	paula@synopsys.com designinfo@synopsys.com
Web site:	http://www.synopsys.com
Industry:	Computers
Sector:	Design Automation Software
CEO:	Aart J. de Geus
CFO:	A. Brooke Seawell
Stock Exchange:	NASDAQ
Stock Symbol:	SNPS

Product Description

Synopsys offers high-level design automation (HLDA) solutions, including logic and behavioral synthesis; simulation; DSP design; and design re-use tools, as well as software modelers, hardware modelers, and the CBA architecture and tool set for the design of integrated circuits and electronic systems. Its markets include the semiconductor, communications, consumer electronics, and aerospace industries.

Market Strategy/Positioning

The company's mission is to continually innovate the way in which electronic design is done, and to deliver new methodologies, tools, and services that maximize the productivity of its customers. Synopsys has strategic relationships with Intel and other leading semiconductor and electronic design automation (EDA) vendors throughout the world. Significant customers include Actel, Altera, AT&T, Fujitsu, Hitachi, IBM, LSI Logic, Motorola, National Semiconductor, NEC, Texas Instruments, Toshiba, and Xilinx. The company's competitive advantages are its growth rate, which has outpaced the overall EDA market growth for the last six years because of the company's focus on high-level design. Synopsys primarily competes against Cadence Design, Mentor Graphics, and Viewlogic. Additional challenges and risks include executing the integration of Silicon Architects. Synopsys is unique as the market share leader in computer-aided engineering (CAE), according to Dataquest. Synopsys intends to bring its customers 10 times more productivity every six years.

421

Other

Synopsys was founded in 1986 by a group of six engineers from GE's Microelectronics Center to productize the logic synthesis technology they had developed. Synopsys then began to acquire or merge with a number of smaller companies. In the last three years the company has expanded its product line of high-level design tools and added leading-edge technology to meet a broader segment of the market. Synopsys acquired Silicon Architects in May 1995. CEO and co-founder Aart de Geus was manager of the advanced computer-aided engineering group at GE. Chairman Harvey Jones was previously with Merrill, Pickard, Anderson & Eyre, and was CEO and co-founder of Daisy Systems.

KEY FACTS

Year Established:	1986
Employees:	1,200
Fiscal Year End:	September
Revenues FY '94:	$196.0m
Revenues FY '95:	n/a
EPS '94:	$0.84
EPS '95:	$1.79 (estimate)
Shares Outstanding:	18.4m
Five-Year Growth Rate:	31%

TAIWAN
SEMICONDUCTOR

Product Description

Taiwan Semiconductor provides wafer processing, mask-making service; wafer probing service/assembly; and a final testing, ASIC service. The company produces untested wafers, probed and tested wafers, or final packaged and tested parts. The company is the largest and fastest-growing semiconductor foundry in the world, and currently dedicates 60% of every revenue dollar to capital expansion to keep pace with the worldwide demand for manufacturing capacity.

Address:	U.S. Headquarters
	1740 Technology Drive
	Suite 660
	San Jose, CA 95110
Telephone:	408/437-8762
Fax:	408/441-7713
E-mail:	n/a
Web site:	n/a
Industry:	Computers
Sector:	Semiconductors
CEO:	Donald Brooks
CFO:	Tsung-Lin Tseng
Stock Exchange:	Taiwan Exchange
Stock Symbol:	n/a

422

Market Strategy/Positioning

The company's mission is to be a dedicated foundry that produces no standard products of its own, but rather provides complete manufacturing services to its customers. Taiwan Semiconductor has strategic relationships with Philips and ITRI. Significant customers include most major U.S. "fabless" semiconductor design houses, companies that do not have the facilities to produce products. The company's competitive advantage is that it does not compete with its customers, since it produces no standard products. The company leads in the migration to advanced processes and will offer 0.35 micron processes in its latest facility. Taiwan Semiconductor primarily competes against Chartered Semiconductor (Singapore), the only other pure foundry that does not produce its own standard products. Additional challenges and risks include adapting to new process technologies and being vulnerable to swings in global-capacity supply and demand.

Other

Taiwan Semiconductor was founded in 1987 as a consortium between Philips and independent investors. Chairman Morris Chang was formerly president and COO of General Instrument and a senior vice president at Texas Instruments. President and CEO Donald Brooks ran Fairchild Semiconductor and headed up the MOS division of Texas Instruments.

KEY FACTS

Year Established:	1987
Employees:	2,600
Fiscal Year End:	n/a
Revenues FY '94:	$744.0m
Revenues FY '95:	n/a
EPS '94:	n/a
EPS '95:	n/a
Shares Outstanding:	n/a
Five-Year Growth Rate:	n/a

TCI
TELE-COMMUNICATIONS INC.

Address:	Terrace Tower II
	5619 DTC Parkway
	Englewood, CO 80111-3000
Telephone:	303/267-5500
Fax:	303/779-1228
E-mail:	n/a
Web site:	n/a
Industry:	Communications
Sector:	Information Highway Services
CEO:	John C. Malone
CFO:	Bernard Schotters
Stock Exchange:	NASDAQ
Stock Symbol:	TCOMA

Product Description

TCI is the nation's largest cable TV operator. TCI has five regional divisions supported by 35 state offices and more than 500 system offices, which together own about 260,000 miles of coaxial and fiber-optic cable and optical fiber in the U.S. The company also operates cable systems or provides cable programming in nine foreign countries. TCI deploys digital compression technology to allow it to offer up to 500 channels and new interactive services. The four main groups of the company consist of TCI Communications, Liberty Media, Tele-Communications International, and TCI Technology Ventures. In 1994 the company also opened its National Digital Television Center (NDTC) in Denver.

Market Strategy/Positioning

TCI has strategic relationships with Microsoft, Time Warner, Comcast, Viacom, US WEST, Turner, AT&T, and an acquired interest in Netscape. TCI and Kleiner Perkins Caufield & Byers entered into a joint venture in 1995 to form @Home, an Internet service company. Significant customers include 10.2 million customers in the U.S. TCI primarily competes against Advance Publications, Bell Atlantic, Cablevision, Walt Disney/Capital Cities/ABC, CBS, Comcast, Continental Cablevision, Cox, GE, Hearst, News Corp., Time Warner, and Viacom. TCI is unique in establishing its NDTC, the first of its kind. The NDTC is a multifunctional facility that provides digital video production, post-production, and satellite distribution services.

423

Other

In 1956 rancher Bob Magness and his wife sold their cattle to build a cable system in the Texas Panhandle. They had 3,000 customers by the second year, moved their partnership to Denver in 1965, and established TCI in 1968. When the cable industry was deregulated in 1984, TCI began aggressively acquiring other cable operators. TCI has made substantial investments in Turner Broadcasting, Discovery Channel, and Black Entertainment Television. TCI conducted unsuccessful merger discussions in late 1993 with Bell Atlantic. Dr. John Malone, Ph.D., has been president and CEO since 1973. He worked previously at General Instrument, McKinsey & Company, and Bell Telephone Labs/AT&T.

KEY FACTS

Year Established:	1968
Employees:	22,000
Fiscal Year End:	December
Revenues FY '94:	$4.9b
Revenues FY '95:	n/a
EPS '94:	$0.09
EPS '95:	$(0.01) (estimate)
Shares Outstanding:	450.0m
Five-Year Growth Rate:	12%

TELEDESIC

Address:	5220 Carillon Point
	Kirkland, WA 98033
Telephone:	206/803-1400
Fax:	206/803-1404
E-mail:	n/a
Web site:	n/a
Industry:	Communications
Sector:	Information Highway Services
CEO:	Russell Daggatt
CFO:	n/a

Product Description

Teledesic plans to construct a global network of 840 low-earth orbit satellites by 2001. Its goal is to build an interactive broadband network that covers rural areas and developing countries that don't currently have extensive wired infrastructures. Its customers will be local telephone exchanges and telecom authorities. A relatively low orbit enables broadband interactivity by eliminating the signal delays inherent to higher orbits. Teledesic is in a development phase—it is looking for financing, seeking regulatory approval, and obtaining technology partners. If it succeeds, it will be the most massive space project in history, costing over $9 billion. Teledesic aims to launch more satellites in only a few years than have been launched in the rest of space history. The FCC recently allotted a portion of the wireless spectrum to Teledesic, which it will share with wireless cable TV operators and Hughes Aircraft.

Market Strategy/Positioning

Teledesic aims to be operational in 2001. The company's competitive advantage is its strong financial backing to further its goal. Teledesic will primarily compete against Hughes Aircraft, which is targeting the same rural market, although the Hughes Spaceway plans to serve only the U.S., while the Teledesic system will be worldwide. Another competitior is Motorola's IRIDIUM project, targeted at the mobile executive with a pocket phone willing to pay premium prices to make and receive calls anywhere in the world. Additional challenges and risks include getting FCC approval in the U.S. and governmental approval around the world, and designing its network. Additionally there is the daunting task of actually building and launching satellites on a scale never attempted before—840 satellites over the course of only three years.

Other

Teledesic was announced in early 1994, although work on the project started in 1990. The company is headed by Russell Daggatt, an international lawyer who also owns about 30% of the company.

Primary VCs/Outside Financing

Messrs. Craig McCaw, Bill Gates, Edward Tuck, and Russell Daggatt.

KEY FACTS

Year Established:	1994
Employees:	15
Fiscal Year End:	n/a
Revenues FY '94:	$0.0
Revenues FY '95:	$0.0
Date of Next Financing:	n/a
Date of Last Financing:	n/a
Size of Last Financing:	n/a
Total Capital Raised:	n/a
Post Round Valuation:	n/a
Expected IPO Date:	n/a

TEXAS INSTRUMENTS

Product Description

Texas Instruments (TI) develops commodity chips and differentiated chips, including digital signal processors (DSPs) and microprocessors. The company, which is also involved in defense electronics and digital products, diversified into notebook PCs after developing the TI486 chip in 1992.

Market Strategy/Positioning

The company's mission is to create, make, and market useful products and services for customers throughout the world. Texas Instruments has strategic relationships with Apple, Kobe Steel, Lockheed Martin, Sprint, Hitachi, Canon, Microsoft, Hewlett-Packard, Sony, and Sun Microsystems. The company's competitive advantages are its DSP-based multimedia computing and its communications and consumer electronic chips, which enable companies to access various growth segments of the semiconductor industry. Texas Instruments primarily competes against AMD, Apple, Canon, Compaq, Fujitsu, Gateway 2000, GE, Hewlett-Packard, Hitachi, IBM, Intel, Micron Technology, Motorola, National Semiconductor, NEC, Oki, Siemens, and Toshiba. Additional challenges and risks include maintaining profitability in its defense systems business and capitalizing on client/server growth.

Other

Texas Instruments was founded in 1930 as Geophysical Service Inc. (GSI), which specialized in reflective seismology, a technology used to explore for oil and gas deposits. The company entered the defense electronics industry during WWII and changed its name to Texas Instruments in 1951. TI introduced the first commercial silicon transistor in 1954 and invented the integrated circuit in 1958. The firm diversified into consumer products during the 1970s but later abandoned such businesses. In 1991 TI joined Hitachi in developing a 256-megabit chip, and in 1994 the two companies announced plans to build a $500 million chip plant in Richardson, Texas. Chairman, president, and CEO Jerry Junkins joined TI in 1959. Mr. Junkins originally worked for the company's defense business.

Address:	13500 North Central Parkway
	P.O. Box 655474
	Dallas, TX 75265
Telephone:	214/995-2551
Fax:	214/995-3340
E-mail:	n/a
Web site:	http://www.ti.com
Industry:	Computers
Sector:	Semiconductors
CEO:	Jerry R. Junkins
CFO:	William A. Aylesworth
Stock Exchange:	NYSE
Stock Symbol:	TXN

425

KEY FACTS

Year Established:	1930
Employees:	57,600
Fiscal Year End:	December
Revenues FY '94:	$10.3b
Revenues FY '95:	$12.9b (estimate)
EPS '94:	$7.26
EPS '95:	$9.99 (estimate)
Shares Outstanding:	93.2b
Five-Year Growth Rate:	14%

THE DUCK CORPORATION

Address:	375 Greenwich Street
	Tribeca Film Center
	New York, NY 10001
Telephone:	212/941-2400
Fax:	212/941-3853
E-mail:	stan@duck.com
Web site:	n/a
Industry:	Computers
Sector:	Personal Productivity Software
CEO:	Stanley Marder
CFO:	n/a

Product Description

The Duck Corporation develops video solutions for multimedia, interactive TV, games, CD-ROM, electronic shopping, videoconferencing, and multimedia authoring. The company developed the first software-only video compression algorithm to allow full-screen TV quality. It also offers compression/rendering software for manipulation of real-time composited video images. Its software works across multiple platforms, including 3DO, DOS, Macintosh, Sega Saturn, Sony Playstation, and Windows.

Market Strategy/Positioning

The company's mission is to develop TV-quality video playback and interactivity on computer and video game platforms. The Duck Corporation has strategic relationships with Horizon Technologies, REV Entertainment, R/GA Digital Studios, Sega, and Intel. Significant customers include Sega, Accent Media Productions, CapCom USA, Crystal Dynamics, GameTek, Viacom New Media, Acclaim Entertainment, Simon & Schuster, GTE Interactive, Warner Music Group, and Sony Music. The company's competitive advantages are its patented technology that combines the compressing and artistic rendering of images, quality at all relevant data rates, full interactivity, and cross-platform compatability. The Duck Corporation primarily competes against Intel and Radius. Additional challenges and risks include maintaining neutrality amid platform contests.

Other

The Duck Corporation was founded by Stanley Marder, Dan Miller, and Victor Yurkovsky, who developed a software-only video architecture. Its first success came by using Duck's technology in compressing TV commercials for Multivail, a Miami-based ad insertion company. It announced a Sega licensing deal last year. CEO Stanley Marder has experience in the computer and media industries. Chief technology officer Dan Miller is a co-inventor of the company's video architecture and has worked in the audio and video post-production industries for a number of years.

Primary VCs/Outside Financing

100% internally funded.

426

KEY FACTS

Year Established:	1992
Employees:	15
Fiscal Year End:	n/a
Revenues FY '94:	$8.0–10.0m
Revenues FY '95:	n/a
Date of Next Financing:	n/a
Date of Last Financing:	n/a
Size of Last Financing:	n/a
Total Capital Raised:	n/a
Post Round Valuation:	n/a
Expected IPO Date:	n/a

TIME WARNER

Address:	75 Rockefeller Plaza
	New York, NY 10019
Telephone:	212/484-8000
Fax:	212/489-6183
E-mail:	n/a
Web site:	http://www.timewarner.com
Industry:	Entertainment & Information
Sector:	Film & Entertainment Production
CEO:	Gerald M. Levin
CFO:	Richard J. Bressler
Stock Exchange:	NYSE
Stock Symbol:	TWX

Product Description

Time Warner is the world's largest conglomerate entertainment group. It has film, TV programming, cable, book publishing, recorded music, broadcasting, theme parks, and interactive product divisions. It has studio libraries containing 2,300 features, 23,000 TV episodes, and 3,300 animated cartoons. Warner Bros. has been the number one film studio for the past three years, with an estimated 20% market share. It is also the number one supplier of TV programming in the world. The company operates several TV channels including HBO, Cinemax, and Comedy Central. HBO is the world's most successful cable channel, but it will see more competition from TCI and Viacom and may lose its exclusive licensing agreements with Paramount. Time Warner was a majority owner in the Six Flags amusement parks but sold its stake in 1995. Warner Bros.' presence in international countries is twice that of its nearest competitor; it reaches an audience of 5.1 billion people. Warner Bros. is building a digital post-production facility called Wabit to compete with Cineon. In September 1995 Warner Music announced that it would terminate its contract with Interscope Records, a record label known for its "gangsta rap" music, after several public figures criticized Time Warner's participation. Also in September 1995 Digital Marketing Group (DMG), a unit of Time Warner Cable, launched DreamShop, an electronic shopping mall on the World Wide Web. Merchants participating with Time Warner on this site include Eddie Bauer, The Bombay Company, Sharper Image, and Spiegel. It is found on the Web at www.pathfinder.com/DreamShop. The Pathfinder Web site is one of the most popular sites on the World Wide Web.

Market Strategy/Positioning

Time Warner has strategic relationships with AT&T, Itochu, Toshiba, and Silicon Graphics. Time Warner became a 10% owner in Interactive Digital Solutions, formed in June 1994 as a joint venture between AT&T and Silicon Graphics. Time Warner also acquired Cablevision Industries. It has a number of other investments, including Courtroom Television Network (55%), Comedy Central (50%), E! Entertainment TV (49%), Sega Channel (33 %), Black Entertainment Television (15%), 3DO (13%), Crystal Dynamics (10%), Savoy Pictures (3%), Whittle Communications (33%), Hasbro (14%), Atari (25%), and Catalog 1 (50%). The company's competitive advantages are its sheer size and its ability to monop-

KEY FACTS

Year Established:	1983
Employees:	50,000
Fiscal Year End:	December
Revenues FY '94:	$15.9b
Revenues FY '95:	n/a
EPS '94:	$(0.27)
EPS '95:	$(0.22) (estimate)
Shares Outstanding:	379.8m
Five-Year Growth Rate:	12%

TIME WARNER

olize programming. Time Warner primarily competes against Advance Publications, Bertels-mann, Walt Disney/Capital Cities/ABC, CBS, Comcast, Cox, GE, Hearst, Houghton Mifflin, Matsushita, McGraw-Hill, News Corp., Reed Elsevier, Sony, TCI, Thorn EMI, Times Mirror, Viacom, and Washington Post.

Other

Time Warner was created in 1989 when Time Inc. merged with Warner Communications Inc. Henry Luce founded Time Inc. in 1922 with Briton Hadden. In the 1930s the company added *Fortune* and *Life*. Mr. Luce died in 1967. The company continually expanded through the 1970s and 1980s, adding accomplishments such as HBO, *Money,* and *People.* In August 1995 it announced its intention to acquire Turner Broadcasting in an $8 billion stock swap.

TIVOLI SYSTEMS

Product Description

Tivoli Systems supplies systems management software and services for client/server environments. The company's solution consists of a comprehensive suite of products that reduces the cost and masks the complexity of managing widely dispersed UNIX and PC clients and servers in a distributed computing environment. This in turn has led to an acceleration in the deployment of client/server computing for mission-critical applications. Tivoli's open systems business model has led to the acceptance of its object-oriented framework as an industry standard.

Address:	9442 Capital Of Texas Highway North Arboretum Plaza One Suite 500 Austin, TX 78759
Telephone:	512/794-9070
Fax:	512/794-0623
E-mail:	webmaster@tivoli.com
Web site:	http://www.tivoli.com
Industry:	Computers
Sector:	Enterprise & Client/Server Software
CEO:	Frank Moss
CFO:	James Offerdahl
Stock Exchange:	NASDAQ
Stock Symbol:	TIVS

Market Strategy/Positioning

Tivoli has strategic relationships with Siemens and UNISYS, and database vendor relationships with Sybase, Informix, and PLATINUM Technology. Tivoli also has a licensing agreement with IBM. Significant customers include Cargill, Charles Schwab, Fidelity Systems, Merrill Lynch, Wells Fargo, AT&T, U S WEST, Florida Power, Motorola, National Semiconductor, Sybase, FedEx, and Hughes Aircraft. The company's competitive advantages are its being first-to-market with products tailored to manage resources in complex client/server environments, its cost-effective remote systems management, and its adoption as the standard by several prominent vendors. Tivoli primarily competes against IBM, Sun Microsystems, Hewlett-Packard, Microsoft, and Novell. Tivoli also competes against mainframe software vendors such as Computer Associates, and faces limited competition from point products from OpenVision, Boole and Babbage, and Novadigm. Additional challenges and risks include increased competition from the major players entering the client/server network management software market.

429

Other

Tivoli Systems was founded in 1989 with a focus on client/server network management that uses a bottom-up approach. It raised $30 million in its IPO in March 1995. Dr. Frank Moss joined Tivoli in 1991 as CEO and was formerly vice president at Lotus.

KEY FACTS

Year Established:	1989
Employees:	250
Fiscal Year End:	December
Revenues FY '94:	$26.9m
Revenues FY '95:	$47.8m (estimate)
EPS '94:	$0.07
EPS '95:	$0.22 (estimate)
Shares Outstanding:	16.4b
Five-Year Growth Rate:	45%

TOSHIBA

430

Product Description

Toshiba is one of the largest electronics firms in Japan. Its businesses include information and communications systems, electronic devices, consumer products, and heavy electrical apparatuses. It is the number one maker of large-scale memory chips. It has prototyped a 256 megabit DRAM chip in conjunction with IBM and Siemens. The new chip is at least 13% smaller and has an access time nearly twice as fast as other chips. The company will ship neural network-based chips for use in commercial applications in 1995. Toshiba is also one of the leading providers of portable PCs, for which demand is growing at twice the rate of desktops.

Address:	U.S. Headquarters
	1251 Avenue of the Americas
	41st Floor
	New York, NY 10020
Telephone:	212/596-0600
Fax:	212/593-3875
E-mail:	n/a
Web site:	http://www.toshiba.com
Industry:	Computers
Sector:	Semiconductors
CEO:	Fumio Sato (Japan)
	Takeshi Okatomi (U.S.)
CFO:	n/a
Stock Exchange:	Nikkei
Stock Symbol:	n/a

Market Strategy/Positioning

Toshiba has strategic relationships with IBM, Siemens, GE, Apple, and NEC. The company's strategic partnering plan has been a major part of Toshiba's success. The company's competitive advantage is its elaborate strategy of arranging joint ventures to defray the risk of researching expensive new technologies. Toshiba primarily competes against Ricoh, IBM, Siemens, GE, NEC, Sony, Matsushita, Compaq, Dell, Ericsson, Fujitsu, Nokia, Philips, Silicon Graphics, and Sun Microsystems. Additional challenges and risks include fluctuation of the yen and tougher global competition in its markets.

Other

Toshiba was founded in 1939 through the union of two Japanese electrical equipment manufacturers, Tanaka Seizo-sha and Hakunetsusha & Company. Toshiba became the first company in Japan to manufacture fluorescent lamps, radar, broadcasting equipment, and digital computers. In 1980 its new president, Shoichi Saba, focused the company on the information and communications businesses. Toshiba produced the first one-megabit DRAM chip in 1985, released the T3100 laptop in 1986, and formed joint ventures with Siemens in 1985 and with Motorola in 1986 to share microcomputer and memory-chip technology.

KEY FACTS

Year Established:	1939
Employees:	175,000
Fiscal Year End:	March
Revenues FY '94:	$46.7b
Revenues FY '95:	n/a
EPS '94:	$0.04
EPS '95:	n/a
Shares Outstanding:	3.2m
Five-Year Growth Rate:	n/a

TRANSWITCH

Address:	8 Progress Drive
	Shelton, CT 06484
Telephone:	203/929-8810
Fax:	203/926-9453
E-mail:	webmaster@transwitch.com
Web site:	http://www.transwitch.com
Industry:	Computers
Sector:	Semiconductors
CEO:	Santanu Das
CFO:	Michael Stauff
Stock Exchange:	NASDAQ
Stock Symbol:	TXCC

Product Description

TranSwitch is a semiconductor design company without manufacturing capabilities that designs digital and mixed-signal semiconductor integrated circuits for high-speed communications. Its VLSI devices are compliant with synchronous optical network (SONET), synchronous digital hierarchy (SDH), and asynchronous transfer mode (ATM) standards. The company's strategy is to leverage its mixed-signal expertise and to supply a broad family of chipsets that provides comprehensive solutions with desired analog and digital functionality. Applications of the company's products include multiplexors and DACS for public network equipment, cable TV systems equipment, as well as local-area network (LAN) and wide area network (WAN) equipment such as routers, switches, and hubs.

Market Strategy/Positioning

TranSwitch has a strategic relationship with Texas Instruments, OEM relationships with IBM and NET, and joint development contracts with AT&T, IBM, and Siemens. Significant customers include Alcatel, Cascade Communications, Cisco Systems, DSC Communications, FORE Systems, and Tellabs. The company's competitive advantages are its technological expertise in mixed-signal and digital design, and its early market penetration, design methodologies, and test tools. TranSwitch primarily competes against AMCC, Brooktree, Dallas Semiconductor, Crystal Semiconductor (a subsidiary of Cirrus Logic), PMC/Sierra, EXAR, National Semiconductor, Vitesse Semiconductor, LSI Logic, SGS-Thomson, and VLSI Technology. Additional challenges and risks include relying on external foundries; and intense competition from ASIC vendors, the semiconductor divisions of vertically integrated companies, and other semiconductor companies.

431

Other

Transwitch was founded in 1988 by former ITT Advanced Technology Center employees to take advantage of the worldwide telecommunications market. Its first product shipped in 1990, and the company went public in June 1995, raising $21 million. CEO and co-founder Santanu Das was previously president at Spectrum Digital. Before Spectrum, he was director of the applied technology division at ITT. Co-founder Daniel Upp was previously director of exploratory systems at ITT.

KEY FACTS

Year Established:	1988
Employees:	85
Fiscal Year End:	December
Revenues FY '94:	$5.6m
Revenues FY '95:	n/a
EPS '94:	$(0.28)
EPS '95:	n/a
Shares Outstanding:	9.26b
Five-Year Growth Rate:	30%

TRIBUNE

Address:	435 North Michigan Avenue
	Chicago, IL 60611
Telephone:	312/222-9100
Fax:	312/222-1573
E-mail:	n/a
Web site:	http://www.tribune.com
Industry:	Entertainment & Information
Sector:	Newspaper/Magazine Publishing
CEO:	John W. Madigan
CFO:	Donald C. Grenesko
Stock Exchange:	NYSE
Stock Symbol:	TRB

Product Description

The Tribune Company is a newspaper publisher as well as a radio, cable TV, and online information provider. Tribune's newspapers include the *Chicago Tribune*, the *Orlando Sentinel*, the Fort Lauderdale–based *Sun-Sentinel,* and the *Newport News*. Its New Media/Education branch owns Compton's Multimedia Publishing Group, Contemporary Books, and 10% of America Online. Tribune Broadcasting operates eight television stations, and six radio stations; it also produces and syndicates television and radio programming. In July 1995 Tribune initiated the first payment link-up between itself and Publicitas Advertising Services. The operation was created to speed up payments between newspapers and advertisers. It uses electronic data interchange (EDI) and e-mail. In addition, *XS Magazine*, owned by the *Sun-Sentinel*, introduced its own online service, XSO, last August. Among other features of this Internet service, customers can write their own movie reviews and see them published online for others to read.

Market Strategy/Positioning

The company's mission is to be the first place customers turn for news, information, and entertainment. Tribune has strategic relationships with America Online, CheckFree, Peapod, Picture Network International, StarSight Telecast, TV Food Network, Alternate Postal Delivery, PRC Realty Systems, and Knight-Ridder. Significant customers include national advertisers, local retailers, TV and radio audiences, readers, and schools. The company's competitive advantage is its media franchises in 12 major markets, reaching more than 60% of U.S. households. Tribune primarily competes against Advance, Associated Press, Capital Cities/ABC, CBS, Cox, Dow Jones, Gannett, GE, Hearst, King World, Knight-Ridder, Microsoft, *The New York Times*, News Corp., Reuters, Sony, Time Warner, Turner, United Press, Viacom, and Washington Post. Additional challenges and risks include making investments in products and services that leverage new technology, insuring these investments pay off, and exiting unprofitable operations. Tribune is unique in drawing on 148 years of journalistic experience and technological innovation to create content that can be adapted to many media forums.

Other

The company began in 1847 as the *Chicago Tribune*. In 1924 Tribune started radio station WGN, which

KEY FACTS

Year Established:	1847
Employees:	10,500
Fiscal Year End:	December
Revenues FY '94:	$2.1b
Revenues FY '95:	n/a
EPS '94:	$3.32
EPS '95:	$3.82 (estimate)
Shares Outstanding:	67.0m
Five-Year Growth Rate:	14%

TRIBUNE

first broadcast the World Series, the Indy 500, and the Kentucky Derby. In the 1940s the company began expanding its publishing and broadcasting outside Chicago. The Chicago Cubs were purchased from William Wrigley in 1981, and in 1983 Tribune went public. CEO John Madigan previously served as president of Tribune Publishing, as publisher of the *Chicago Tribune*, as vice president of corporate finance for Salomon Brothers, and as vice president in the investment banking division for Paine, Webber, Jackson & Curtis.

TRILOGY

Address:	6034 West Courtyard Drive
	Austin, TX 78730
Telephone:	512/794-5900
Fax:	512/794-8900
E-mail:	webmaster@trilogy.com
Web site:	http://www.trilogy.com
Industry:	Computers
Sector:	Enterprise & Client/Server Software
CEO:	Joseph Liemandt
CFO:	Wade Monroe

Product Description

Trilogy develops and markets tools to automate the product configuration and sales quotation process at point-of-sale. Its main product, SalesBUILDER, targets the computer hardware, electronic instrumentation, industrial equipment, and telecommunications industry. In addition, the company provides customer support programs, including product training, consulting, and technical support. Its tools run on all major platforms. Trilogy has a strong focus on object-oriented implementation.

Market Strategy/Positioning

Trilogy has strategic relationships with Intelligent Electronics, NCR, and Oracle. Significant customers include Hewlett-Packard, AT&T, Silicon Graphics, IBM, Boeing, and Rolm. The company's competitive advantages are its system, based on technology allowing relatively easy integration, and its strong reputation for configuration expertise. Additional challenges and risks include having to expand its system capabilities enough to justify relatively high costs.

Other

Trilogy was founded in 1989 by several former students of Stanford University. Three years later, the company released its software, SalesBUILDER. In 1993 it formed a software licensing agreement with NCR, and in 1994 it formed a similar agreement with Intelligent Electronics. Also in 1994 Trilogy announced an alliance with Oracle to develop a comprehensive solution for build-to-order manufacturers. CEO Joseph Liemandt left his undergraduate studies at Stanford University in order to found Trilogy with several classmates. At Stanford, he participated in researching the errors companies made in completing sales.

Primary VCs/Outside Financing

Greylock Management and New Enterprise Associates.

434

KEY FACTS

Year Established:	1989
Employees:	150
Fiscal Year End:	June
Revenues FY '94:	n/a
Revenues FY '95:	n/a
Date of Next Financing:	n/a
Date of Last Financing:	n/a
Size of Last Financing:	n/a
Total Capital Raised:	n/a
Post Round Valuation:	n/a
Expected IPO Date:	n/a

TURNER BROADCASTING

Address:	One CNN Center
	Atlanta, GA 30303
Telephone:	404/827-1700
Fax:	404/827-2437
E-mail:	n/a
Web site:	http://www.turner.com
Industry:	Entertainment & Information
Sector:	Broadcasters & Cable Networks
CEO:	R.E. (Ted) Turner, III
CFO:	Wayne H. Pace
Stock Exchange:	AMEX
Stock Symbol:	TBSA

Product Description

Turner Broadcasting is an entertainment conglomerate and a major distributor of news and entertainment products. Turner owns three production companies: New Line, Castle Rock Entertainment, and Turner Pictures. Turner spent $1 billion in 1993 to buy New Line Cinema and Castle Rock. The company also owns the Hanna-Barbera library of more than 8,500 cartoons; an additional 48 new cartoons are produced each year. Turner owns only one broadcast station (WTBS in Atlanta), and it operates six entertainment networks, three news networks, TNT, and CNN. The company has taken aggressive steps toward multimedia, the Internet, and interactive learning. Turner Home Entertainment has several divisons, including Turner New Media, Domestic Home, Turner Publishing, Licensing & Merchandising, and Turner Educational Services, which through Turner Adventure Learning, includes devising interactive electronic field trips for children. Turner Interactive, Hanna-Barbera Games, and Turner Games operate under the umbrella of Turner New Media.

435

Market Strategy/Positioning

Turner has strategic relationships with Moscow Independent Broadcasting, Time Warner, Sony Pictures Entertainment, and Westinghouse. The company's competitive advantage is its control of programming by providing more and acquiring more—from creation through distribution. Turner primarily competes against BET, CBS, GE, Heritage Media, Matsushita, News Corp., Orion Pictures, Sony, TCI, Time Warner, Tribune, Viacom, and Walt Disney/Capital Cities/ABC.

Other

Turner Broadcasting was started in 1970 with the purchase of Atlanta independent UHF Channel 17. In 1976 the channel became the first to be broadcast via satellite to cable homes. CNN premiered in June 1980 with 1.7 million subscribers. Headline News was added in 1982. Turner acquired MGM Entertainment Company in 1986 and introduced CNN Newsroom in 1989. It has been steadily built into one of the most powerful communications and entertainment companies in the world. In August 1995 Turner announced plans to be acquired by Time Warner in a stock swap valued at $8 billion. Time Warner will buy up the 82% of Turner that it does not already own. Chairman, president, and CEO Ted Turner began his empire by buying Chan-

KEY FACTS

Year Established:	1970
Employees:	8,200
Fiscal Year End:	December
Revenues FY '94:	$2.8b
Revenues FY '95:	n/a
EPS '94:	$0.14
EPS '95:	$0.43 (estimate)
Shares Outstanding:	282.4m
Five-Year Growth Rate:	15%

TURNER
BROADCASTING

nel 17 in Atlanta, after working as an account executive for Turner Advertising. In December 1976 he originated the concept of a "superstation" by transmitting his station's signal to cable systems nationwide via satellite. He purchased the Atlanta Braves in 1976, and launched CNN in 1980 and CNN International in 1985. CFO Wayne Pace took his current position in 1993, he formerly served as an audit partner with Price Waterhouse.

U.S. ROBOTICS

Address:	8100 North McCormick Boulevard
	Skokie, IL 60076
Telephone:	708/982-5010
Fax:	708/933-5800
E-mail:	salesinfo@usr.com
Web site:	http://www.usr.com
Industry:	Computers
Sector:	Peripherals
CEO:	Casey Cowell
CFO:	Mark Remissong
Stock Exchange:	NASDAQ
Stock Symbol:	USRX

Product Description

U.S. Robotics supplies information access products, including remote-access servers, desktop and portable modems, terminal servers, fax servers, and enterprise-wide communications systems. In addition to modems, the company makes local-area network (LAN) access products and wide-area network (WAN) hubs. The company is the second largest supplier of high-end modems, after Motorola. It is also working on voice, wireless PC, and cable-modem products that will increase the breadth of the company's offerings.

Market Strategy/Positioning

U.S. Robotics has a strategic relationship with Cisco Systems, with which it announced a three-year technology-sharing agreement in 1995. Significant customers include Advantis, Compu-Serve, MCI, and NETCOM. The company's competitive advantages are its core DSP-based technology, which controls the data pump design, and its focus on digital signal processing software instead of modem hardware. U.S. Robotics primarily competes against Motorola, Diamond Multimedia, and Global Village Communications. Additional challenges include absorbing the costs of its September 1995 acquisition of Palm Computing, a company that develops software for hand-held computers and communication devices.

Other

U.S. Robotics was founded in 1976 by CEO Casey Cowell, Steve Muka, and Paul Collard. The company first produced an acoustic coupler that connected computers over telephone lines through handsets. It started producing modems after an FCC ruling allowed non-AT&T products to be plugged into telephone lines. In 1995, U.S. Robotics acquired Megahertz, the largest provider of PC card modems for mobile computing. The two companies are now separate entities operating under the U.S. Robotics umbrella. CEO Mr. Cowell co-founded the company in 1976 at the age of 23. CFO Mark Remissong joined U.S. Robotics in April 1995 from Collins & Aikman, where he was senior vice president and CFO.

KEY FACTS

Year Established:	1976
Employees:	2,600
Fiscal Year End:	September
Revenues FY '94:	$473.4m
Revenues FY '95:	$857.7m (estimate)
EPS '94:	$2.18
EPS '95:	$3.30 (estimate)
Shares Outstanding:	40.5m
Five-Year Growth Rate:	35%

U S WEST

Address:	7800 East Orchard Road
	Englewood, CO 80111
Telephone:	303/793-6500
Fax:	303/793-6654
E-mail:	n/a
Web site:	http://www.uswest.com
Industry:	Communications
Sector:	Information Highway Services
CEO:	Richard D. McCormick
CFO:	James M. Osterhoff
Stock Exchange:	NYSE
Stock Symbol:	USW

Product Description

U S WEST provides telecommunications, information, and entertainment services. Through strategic relationships, the company is preparing itself for a multimedia future. Its growth in revenue reflects an increase in its number of access lines in service, and an increase in its number of cellular customers. The company is working on several international projects involving cable TV, cellular, and personal communications systems.

Market Strategy/Positioning

The company's mission is to be a leading provider of communications, entertainment, and information services over wired broadband and wireless networks. U S WEST has strategic relationships with Time Warner, Toshiba, ITOCHU, TCI, AirTouch, Bell Atlantic, and NYNEX. The company's competitive advantage is its being the first regional Bell operating company to merge three telecommunications units into one and to organize business around markets, not geography. U S WEST primarily competes against Ameritech, AT&T, Bell Atlantic, BellSouth, Cable & Wireless, RR Donnelley, GTE, WorldCom, MCI, NYNEX, Pacific Telesis, Southwestern Bell, and Sprint. Additional challenges and risks include competing to command content delivery and maintaining its presence in local markets, while expanding services outside its home territory. U S WEST is unique as the first (with TCI) to offer phone and cable TV service together.

438

Other

U S WEST is one of the seven regional Bell operating companies formed in 1984 when AT&T was split. The company was quick to move its Yellow Pages operations to a subsidiary and create a financial services arm. In 1988 it dropped the Bell name when it merged Pacific Northwestern Bell, Mountain Bell, and Northwestern Bell to form its U S WEST Communications subsidiary. U S WEST also began expanding internationally in 1988. Jack MacAllister was the former CEO of Northwestern Bell and became U S WEST's first CEO. Mr. MacAllister was responsible for moving the company into risky fields such as cable TV and equipment financing. He was also instrumental in changing the company's name, which was viewed as a bold move in the industry. Current president and CEO Richard McCormick was president of Northwestern Bell before joining U S WEST in 1985. He also worked as an engineer for AT&T.

KEY FACTS

Year Established:	1984
Employees:	60,800
Fiscal Year End:	December
Revenues FY '94:	$11.0b
Revenues FY '95:	n/a
EPS '94:	$3.15
EPS '95:	$2.76 (estimate)
Shares Outstanding:	441.0m
Five-Year Growth Rate:	7%

UUNET TECHNOLOGIES

Address:	3060 Williams Drive
	Fairfax, VA 22031
Telephone:	703/206-5600
Fax:	703/206-5601
E-mail:	info@uu.net
Web site:	whttp://ww.uu.net
Industry:	Entertainment & Information
Sector:	Online Services
CEO:	John W. Sidgmore
CFO:	Jeffrey G. Hilber
Stock Exchange:	NASDAQ
Stock Symbol:	UUNT

Product Description

UUNET Technologies was the first national provider of full commercial Internet access to corporate customers and individuals. UUNET offers a wide range of connection services, external connectivity, and technical expertise. It focuses is on high-quality service and believes value-added services will be a competitive advantage for the core business of Internet access. Product offerings include a 24-hour network operations center, UUCP mail, USENET news, World Wide Web services, security, and integration and training. In October 1995 it announced its AlterNet Tiered T-3, which provides more bandwidth and guaranteed Internet access of up to 45 megabits per second. It will build and operate TCP/IP network for Microsoft Windows 95, with full Internet access.

Market Strategy/Positioning

The company's mission is to allow users to easily and cost-effectively take advantage of the information revolution. UUNET wants to provide a dedicated, accessible, and reliable facility for international e-mail and electronic news, including access to the Internet through e-mail and news services. UUNET has strategic relationships with Compatible Systems, Interse, and Microsoft. Significant customers include AT&T, MCI, America Online, CompuServe, PRODIGY, *Chicago Tribune*, *The New York Times*, Dow Jones, Knight-Ridder, Citibank, American Express, Reuters, Intel, IBM, and Pizza Hut. The company's competitive advantages are a flexible "no-frills" network, its alliance with Microsoft, and a complete turnkey solution. UUNET primarily competes against AT&T, MCI, MFS, NETCOM, Performance Systems International, and BBN Planet. Additional challenges and risks include the acceptance and growth of the Internet. UUNET is unique in focusing exclusively on business use of the Internet. UUNET wants to be the "industrial strength" access provider. It is also the first Internet provider to offer a full range of multimegabit services.

Other

Founded in 1987, UUNET Technologies was recognized as the first Internet commercial provider. The company went public in 1995; for 1996 it set a goal of raising the total number of cities with local dial-access to the Internet to 200. Microsoft owns 15% of the company. CEO John Sidgmore was previously CEO of CSC Intelicom, where he engineered a performance turnaround. He also served at GE Information Services for 14 years and most recently held

KEY FACTS

Year Established:	1987
Employees:	250
Fiscal Year End:	December
Revenues FY '94:	$12.4m
Revenues FY '95:	$47.5m (estimate)
EPS '94:	$(0.35)
EPS '95:	$(0.41) (estimate)
Shares Outstanding:	29.2m
Five-Year Growth Rate:	50%

UUNET
TECHNOLOGIES

the position of vice president and general manager of GEIS North America. Founder, chairman, and CTO Richard Adams is responsible for several de facto standard networking protocols: SLIP (Serial Line Internet Protocol) and the "t" protocol for running UUCP (UNIX-to-UNIX Comm's Protocol) over TCP/IP connections. Mr. Adams also worked at the Center for Seismic Studies and served as a communications expert for the United Nations. CFO Jeffrey Hilber worked previously as corporate controller for Telebit, the first company to market a dial-up router. He also worked at Qume, most recently as corporate controller.

VERISIGN

Address:	100 Marine Parkway
	Suite 525
	Redwood City, CA 94065
Telephone:	415/508-1151
Fax:	415/508-1121
E-mail:	info@verisign.com
Web site:	http://www.verisign.com
Industry:	Entertainment & Information
Sector:	Online Services
CEO:	Stratton Sclavos
CFO:	n/a

Product Description

VeriSign's products secure electronic documents, financial transactions, and electronic mail transmitted over public and private computer networks. VeriSign's Digital ID technology will be embedded in a broad range of software products, including operating systems for PCs and Internet server computers providing users with "the driver's license for the Information Highway." The company's products enhance the security of encryption, and its technology also serves as a link to VeriSign's authenticating service. VeriSign plans to license other companies to provide this service as well.

Market Strategy/Positioning

The company's mission is to provide Digital IDs for all Internet applications. VeriSign has strategic relationships with Apple, Netscape, CommerceNet, Ameritech, Visa, RSA Data Security, and Mitsubishi. Significant customers include Open Market, Terisa Systems, Intel, Microsoft, Sun Microsystems, CommerceNet, CyberCash, Dun & Bradstreet, Premenos, and National Semiconductor. The company's competitive advantage is that it is the only Digital ID-issuing company ready to deliver Internet security. VeriSign primarily competes against the U.S. Post Office, which is introducing certified electronic mail. Additional challenges and risks include consumer acceptance of secure information exchange and electronic commerce on the Internet.

Other

VeriSign was founded in 1995 as a spin-off from RSA Data Security. Chairman and co-founder Jim Bidzos is president of RSA Data Security. Bessemer Venture Partners' David Cowan is a co-founder and director of VeriSign. CEO Stratton Sclavos was formerly vice president of worldwide marketing and sales for Taligent.

Primary VCs/Outside Financing

Bessemer Venture Partners, Visa, Ameritech, Mitsubishi, RSA Data Security, Netscape, Fischer International, and Security Dynamics.

KEY FACTS

Year Established:	1995
Employees:	25
Fiscal Year End:	December
Revenues FY '94:	$0.0
Revenues FY '95:	$0.0
Date of Next Financing:	n/a
Date of Last Financing:	n/a
Size of Last Financing:	n/a
Total Capital Raised:	$5.0m
Post Round Valuation:	n/a
Expected IPO Date:	n/a

441

VERSANT

Address:	1380 Willow Road Suite 201 Menlo Park, CA 94025
Telephone:	415/329-7500
Fax:	415/325-2380
E-mail:	davidb@versant.com
Web site:	http://www.versant.com
Industry:	Computers
Sector:	Enterprise & Client/Server Software
CEO:	David Banks
CFO:	Richard Kadet

Product Description

Versant develops language-independent object-oriented database software and related software products for connectivity to relational databases. It offers portability across several hardware platforms, including DEC, Hewlett-Packard, IBM, and Sun Microsystems. Its storage manager resembles base technology for relational databases, and its object manager gives databases object-oriented features. Versant focuses on document management, computer-integrated manufacturing, and network management systems. It supports existence between object-oriented database management systems and relational database management systems for different applications.

Market Strategy/Positioning

The company's mission is to provide database management systems and development tools for distributed object-oriented applications. Versant has strategic relationships with DEC, Miramar, Informix, and UNISYS. Significant customers include AT&T, Ameritech, Baker Hughes, British Telecom, Fujitsu, IBM, Nippon Steel, MCI, Sprint, Siemens, Texaco, and Bell Northern Research. The company's competitive advantages are its top-performing database software on independent market benchmarks and its strong development tools. Versant primarily competes against ODI, Illustra, and Servia. Additional challenges and risks include assuring successful deployment of Versant applications in the future.

Other

Versant was founded by six engineers from Oracle, Ingres, Informix, and object research projects. After a long period of architectural design and end-user feedback, they released VERSANT in September 1994. President and CEO David Banks was founding president and CEO of Cadre Technologies. Mr. Banks began his career at Hewlett-Packard, where he held positions in sales, marketing, and manufacturing. CFO Richard Kadet was vice president of finance and business management at InfoSpan and its interim CEO for a year. Before InfoSpan, Mr. Kadet also worked at Cadre as vice president of finance.

Primary VCs/Outside Financing

TA Associates, Bessemer Venture Partners, Trinity Ventures, Vertex, Atlas Ventures, Advent International, and Silicon Valley Bank.

KEY FACTS

Year Established:	1988
Employees:	80
Fiscal Year End:	December
Revenues FY '94:	$8.4m
Revenues FY '95:	$14.0m
Date of Next Financing:	n/a
Date of Last Financing:	April 1994
Size of Last Financing:	$4.5m
Total Capital Raised:	$23.5m
Post Round Valuation:	$18.0m
Expected IPO Date:	1996

VERTIGO
DEVELOPMENT GROUP

Address:	58 Charles Street
	Cambridge, MA 02142
Telephone:	617/225-2065
Fax:	617/225-0637
E-mail:	Vertigodev@aol.com
Web site:	n/a
Industry:	Computers
Sector:	Personal Productivity Software
CEO:	Robert Rosen
CFO:	Kimberly Howlett

Product Description

Vertigo Development Group develops enabling technology for next-generation interactive computer books. Its products combine the power of the PC and personal productivity software with the information found in traditional books. Vertigo's "books" are user-friendly and come "alive" to provide guidance, problem solving, and customized solutions to the user's specific needs. Its products include ActiveBook software technology titles such as *Your Mutual Fund Selector*, *Wall Street Journal Personal Finance Library*, *Your Best Money Moves Now*, and *Jonathan Pond's Personal Finance Planner*.

Market Strategy/Positioning

Vertigo has a strategic relationship with Intuit to co-publish interactive multimedia titles. It has other relationships with *Money* Magazine, Jonathan Pond, and Dow Jones. The company's competitive advantages are its proprietary technology, its comprehensive product vision, its fast time-to-market, and its relatively low cost. Vertigo primarily competes against MySoftware and Up Software.

Other

Vertigo Development Group was founded in 1991 by Martin J. Fahey and Robert Rosen to deliver the enabling technology for a new generation of interactive electronic books. Chairman and CEO Robert Rosen was formerly the development manager for the advanced spreadsheet group at Lotus. Before Lotus, he founded Resource Control Systems.

Primary VCs/Outside Financing

Matrix Partners, Aperture Associates, Applied Technology, Integral Capital Partners, Sequoia Capital, and Mr. Alex d'Arbeloff (President of Teradyne).

KEY FACTS

Year Established:	1991
Employees:	15
Fiscal Year End:	December
Revenues FY '94:	n/a
Revenues FY '95:	n/a
Date of Next Financing:	n/a
Date of Last Financing:	n/a
Size of Last Financing:	n/a
Total Capital Raised:	n/a
Post Round Valuation:	n/a
Expected IPO Date:	n/a

VIACOM

Address:	1515 Broadway New York, NY 10036
Telephone:	212/258-6000
Fax:	212/258-6597
E-mail:	n/a
Web site:	http://www.mcp.com
Industry:	Entertainment & Information
Sector:	Broadcasters & Cable Networks
CEO:	Frank Biondi
CFO:	George Smith
Stock Exchange:	NYSE
Stock Symbol:	VIA

Product Description

Viacom is one of the largest entertainment conglomerates in the world; its operations include Blockbuster Entertainment, MTV Networks, Paramount Parks, Paramount Pictures, Paramount Television, Showtime Networks, Simon & Schuster, and Viacom New Media. Viacom New Media works with outside hardware and software producers to develop, produce, distribute, and market interactive software. Viacom bought Blockbuster Entertainment in September 1994 and also acquired Spelling Entertainment as part of the agreement. However, in 1995 Viacom announced it would sell Spelling Entertainment and acquire Spelling's interest in Virgin Interactive Entertainment. Viacom is concentrating on becoming the best-capitalized global media company.

Market Strategy/Positioning

Viacom has a strong strategic relationship with BHC Communications. The company's competitive advantages are its successful bid for Paramount and its ability to fund its new interactive focus. Viacom primarily competes against Advance Publications, Bertelsmann, Walt Disney/Capital Cities/ABC, CBS, Cox, GE, Hearst, Heritage Media, Matsushita, McGraw Hill, News Corp., Pearson, E.W. Scripps, Sony, TCI, Time Warner, Turner Broadcasting, and all major entertainment software companies. An additional risk is that telephone companies may enter the business of creating and distributing program services, both inside and outside their respective service areas. Additionally, Viacom's ability to market its interactive entertainment products will be affected by the rapid development of new distribution technologies.

Other

Viacom was formed by CBS in 1970, after the FCC ruled that TV networks could not own cable systems and TV stations in the same market. In 1994 Viacom was the victor in the bidding war against QVC for Paramount. Before becoming president, CEO, and a director of Viacom, Frank Biondi served as chairman and CEO of Coca-Cola Television. CFO George Smith has been with Viacom since 1977 and was elected CFO in 1987.

KEY FACTS

Year Established:	1970
Employees:	5,000
Fiscal Year End:	December
Revenues FY '94:	$7.4b
Revenues FY '95:	$11.9b (estimate)
EPS '94:	$(0.62)
EPS '95:	$0.86 (estimate)
Shares Outstanding:	386.1m
Five-Year Growth Rate:	17%

VIRAGE

Address:	9605 Scranton Road
	Suite 240
	San Diego, CA 92121
Telephone:	619/587-4080
Fax:	619/587-4070
E-mail:	virage@virage.com
Web site:	http://www.virage.com
Industry:	Computers
Sector:	Personal Productivity Software
CEO:	Paul Lego (acting)
CFO:	Paul Lego

Product Description

Virage develops and markets image-management systems. Virage's flagship product manages multimedia assets by finding and storing images through a combination of content-based retrieval and keywords. It allows searches based on the "I-know-it-when-I-see-it" paradigm, which is the way humans look at images. It allows users direct interaction with images through a graphical user interface. Potential applications for its products include searching of police and FBI mug-shots to find criminals, checking identification for credit card transactions, screening blood samples, and visually selecting clothing types and colors in home shopping systems.

Market Strategy/Positioning

The company's mission is to become the leader in multimedia asset management using breakthrough visual information retrieval technology. Virage has a strategic relationship with Illustra Information Technologies. Significant customers include publishers, law enforcement agencies, and digital studios. The company's competitive advantages are its performance, its ease-of-use, and its intuitive heuristic searches. Most companies are focused on the front end of multimedia (chips, rendering tools, etc.) and not on the management of information and content coming out. Virage is working to overcome this problem and successfully manage text output. Virage primarily competes against IBM and Excalibur Technologies. Additional challenges and risks include keeping up with the pace of market development.

445

Other

Virage was founded in April 1994 to manage the vast amount of content generated by the information revolution. Founder and chairman Ramesh Jain brought together a technical team from the University of Michigan, Massachusetts Institute of Technology Media Lab, and Cornell to work on content-based retrieval. Mr. Jain is a professor of electrical engineering at UC San Diego. Mr. Jain previously founded Imageware and the Artificial Intelligence Laboratory at the University of Michigan. CEO Paul Lego is a partner with Sutter Hill Ventures and formerly served as COO of Digidesign.

Primary VCs/Outside Financing

Sutter Hill Ventures and Trinity Ventures.

KEY FACTS

Year Established:	1994
Employees:	15
Fiscal Year End:	March
Revenues FY '94:	n/a
Revenues FY '95:	n/a
Date of Next Financing:	n/a
Date of Last Financing:	April 1995
Size of Last Financing:	2.5m
Total Capital Raised:	n/a
Post Round Valuation:	n/a
Expected IPO Date:	n/a

VIRGIN INTERACTIVE
ENTERTAINMENT

Address:	18061 Fitch Avenue
	Irvine, CA 92714
	San Jose, CA 95131
Telephone:	714/833-8710
Fax:	714/833-8717
E-mail:	n/a
Web site:	http://www.vie.com
Industry:	Entertainment & Information
Sector:	Entertainment & Education Software
CEO:	Martin Alper
COO:	Thomas D. Allen

Product Description

Virgin Interactive Entertainment develops and publishes computer, video games, and CD-ROM software. Its headquarters also house Virgin Studios, an on-site development facility comprised of design studios, a state-of-the-art video production stage with digital betacam, and a 32-track digital music and post-recording studio. Virgin Interactive has additional offices in Las Vegas, London, Tokyo, Paris, Frankfurt, and Hamburg.

Market Strategy/Positioning

Virgin Interactive has strategic relationships with Converse, Nintendo of America, P.F. Magic, Sega of America, and Sony Computer. Virgin also has distribution agreements with EMI Records, LookingGlass Technologies, Northstar Studios, Papyrus Design Group, Parker Bros., and Trilobyte. The company's competitive advantages are its critically acclaimed titles, which include *The 7th Guest*, *Robocop vs. the Terminator*, Disney's *The Jungle Book* for Super NES, and *Demolition Man* for the 3DO System. Virgin primarily competes against Maxis, Id Software, Acclaim Entertainment, Electronic Arts, and LucasArts. Additional challenges and risks include increasing competition and soaring distribution channels in the entertainment software business.

Other

Virgin Interactive Entertainment was created in 1987 with the merger of Virgin Games and the Mastertronics Group, a distributor of budget PC titles. In 1991 Virgin Mastertronics was sold to Sega of Japan; however, the publishing division was retained. It expanded Virgin Games and was later renamed Virgin Interactive Entertainment to better adapt to new markets. In July 1994 Virgin Interactive was acquired by Spelling Entertainment, part of the Blockbuster Entertainment Group, a division of Viacom. In September 1995 Viacom announced its plans to sell Spelling Entertainment, but it wanted to buy back Virgin. CEO Martin Alper founded Virgin Interactive as Mastertronic Limited in the U.K. in 1983. He remains active in the acquisition of intellectual properties and in driving the direction of the company. COO Thomas Allen was previously employed at Fox Broadcasting.

Primary VCs/Outside Financing

100% owned by Spelling Entertainment.

KEY FACTS

Year Established:	1987
Employees:	230
Fiscal Year End:	December
Revenues FY '94:	n/a
Revenues FY '95:	n/a
Date of Next Financing:	n/a
Date of Last Financing:	n/a
Size of Last Financing:	n/a
Total Capital Raised:	n/a
Post Round Valuation:	n/a
Expected IPO Date:	n/a

VISIO

Address:	520 Pike Street
	Suite 1800
	Seattle, WA 98101-4001
Telephone:	206/521-4500
Fax:	206/521-4501
E-mail:	n/a
Web site:	http://www.visio.com.hk
Industry:	Computers
Sector:	Personal Productivity Software
CEO:	Jeremy Jaech
CFO:	Marty Chilberg

Product Description

Visio markets and develops drawing and diagramming software. It pioneered the efforts in the market with its release of Visio 1.0 in November 1992. Its software solves a wide range of problems for the user. The company markets its product line in North America, Europe, and Asia.

Market Strategy/Positioning

The company's mission is to simplify computer drawing and diagramming, making them more accessible to a wide range of users who need visual images with which to communicate. The company's major customers are business and technical professionals who use drawings and diagrams to communicate concepts. Visio has strategic relationships with Microsoft, Dell, and Storm Software. The company's competitive advantage is its user-friendly software, which gives the mainstream computer-user many capabilities. Visio mainly competes against Parametric Technology and Autodesk.

Other

Visio was founded in 1990 by Jeremy Jaech, Ted Johnson, and Dave Walter, all key developers of Aldus' desktop publishing software. Since its first product, it has released additional Window-based products designed for business, technical, and consumer users. President Jeremy Jaech also co-founded Aldus, which he left in 1989 to develop Visio. Before Aldus, Mr. Jaech worked at Atex and at Boeing Computer Systems. Vice president Ted Johnson previously worked at Aldus, at Atex, and at Carlisle Systems. Besides working with the other two founders at Aldus, chief architect Dave Walter worked at Atex with Mr. Johnson. CFO Marty Chilberg joined the company in 1992 from Symantec, where he was corporate controller.

Primary VCs/Outside Financing

Technology Venture Investors, Kleiner Perkins Caufield & Byers, and Integral Capital Partners.

KEY FACTS

Year Established:	1990
Employees:	150
Fiscal Year End:	September
Revenues FY '94:	$23.2m
Revenues FY '95:	$15.7m (6 months)
Date of Next Financing:	n/a
Date of Last Financing:	May 1995
Size of Last Financing:	$1.5m
Total Capital Raised:	$6.6m
Post Round Valuation:	n/a
Expected IPO Date:	n/a

WALNUT CREEK CDROM

Product Description

Walnut Creek CDROM develops and publishes CD-ROMs that cover topics from shareware collections, Unix, and programmer's tools to information, digital art, and entertainment. In addition, the company maintains an Internet site that offers over 52 gigabytes of data and hundreds of online support documents. Through this technology, it offers technical support, product information, and other services to its customers throughout the world. It also produces a direct-mail catalogue.

Address:	4041 Pike Lane
	Suite D
	Concord, CA 94520
Telephone:	510/674-0783
Fax:	510/674-0821
E-mail:	info@cdrom.com
Web-site:	http://www.cdrom.com
Industry:	Entertainment & Information
Sector:	Personal Productivity
CEO:	Robert Bruce (President)
CFO:	n/a

Market Strategy/Positioning

The company's mission is to devote itself to high-quality products and customer satisfaction. Walnut Creek has a strategic relationship with Publishers Group West, which helped Walnut Creek channel its products into bookstores. Significant customers include American Software, Ingram, and Frank Casper & Associates. The company's competitive advantages are its toll-free technical support system and its unconditional return policy. It claims to incorporate customer feedback into new editions of its CD-ROMs. The company has earned a reputation throughout the industry for quality products and responsive service. Additional challenges and risks include the shift from CD-ROM to online offerings and its short-term boost in profitability.

Other

Robert Bruce founded Walnut Creek CDROM in August 1991 to provide the general public with high-quality, cost-effective CD-ROMs. The company's first title was released in November 1991. Walnut Creek has expanded with the CD-ROM market by adding an average of one title per month to its catalogue. It now publishes fifty titles and has dozens more in development.

Primary VCs/Outside Financing

100% internally funded.

KEY FACTS

Year Established:	1991
Employees:	30
Fiscal Year End:	March
Revenues FY '94:	n/a
Revenues FY '95:	n/a
Date of Next Financing:	n/a
Date of Last Financing:	n/a
Size of Last Financing:	n/a
Total Capital Raised:	n/a
Post Round Valuation:	n/a
Expected IPO Date:	n/a

WALT
DISNEY

Address:	500 South Buena Vista Street
	Burbank, CA 91521
Telephone:	818/560-1000
Fax:	818/846-8726
E-mail:	n/a
Web site:	http://www.disney.com
Industry:	Entertainment & Information
Sector:	Film & Entertainment Production
CEO:	Michael D. Eisner
CFO:	Richard D. Nanula
Stock Exchange:	NYSE
Stock Symbol:	DIS

Product Description

The Walt Disney Company is a creative content producer and technology innovator. Walt Disney creates motion pictures, TV shows, and consumer products; it also operates theme parks. The company converted all of its animated business to a digital process nine years ago. Walt Disney's film library contains over 230 full-length, live-action features, 30 full-length animated features, and 530 cartoon shorts. The Disney Channel has over 14 million subscribers. Walt Disney has released over 450 titles to date on video, representing an estimated 40% of the total domestic business. Its new interactive division has sold more than 200,000 *Lion King* and 100,000 *Aladdin* CD-ROM titles. A Mickey Mouse CD-ROM was co-developed with Sony ImageSoft, and the *Lion King* release was co-developed with Virgin Interactive Entertainment. Walt Disney plans to publish titles for the Sega and Nintendo game machines, and will release 15 CD-ROMs, four video game titles, and numerous floppy disk products. Interactive educational products will be offered in 1996.

Market Strategy/Positioning

Walt Disney has strategic relationships with GTE, SBC Communications, 7th Level, Pixar, BellSouth, Telco, and Ameritech. Walt Disney, GTE, Ameritech, BellSouth, and SBC are partners in a venture created to provide video programming and interactive services for millions of U.S. households. The company's competitive advantage is its worldwide brand recognition. Walt Disney primarily competes against Bertelsmann, Dick Clark Productions, DreamWorks SKG, King World, Matsushita, Metromedia, News Corp., Orion Pictures, Sony, Time Warner, Turner Broadcasting, and Viacom. Additional challenges and risks include managing its growing empire (especially with the integration of Capital Cities/ABC) and competing in virtually every area of the entertainment industry. Walt Disney is unique in that its merger with Capital Cities/ABC will link a content developer with a distributor, creating the world's largest media firm.

449

Other

Walt and Roy Disney started a film studio in Hollywood in 1923 and produced their first animated feature film *Snow White* in 1937. Disneyland opened in Anaheim in 1955, and Walt Disney World followed in 1971 in Florida. In 1984 the Bass family bought a controlling interest, and Michael Eisner and Frank Wells joined top management. The

KEY FACTS

Year Established:	1923
Employees:	65,000
Fiscal Year End:	September
Revenues FY '94:	$10.1b
Revenues FY '95:	n/a
EPS '94:	$2.04
EPS '95:	$2.57 (estimate)
Shares Outstanding:	520.8m
Five-Year Growth Rate:	18%

WALT
DISNEY

Disney Channel was established in the 1980s, and in 1992 Euro Disneyland opened near Paris. The company bought Capital Cities/ABC in August 1995 for $19 billion. Chairman Michael Eisner formerly served at Paramount. President Michael Ovitz assumed his position in October of 1995. He is responsible for three divisions of the company and Capital Cities/ABC when the merger is completed. Mr. Ovitz was previously founder and chairman of Creative Artists Agency.

450

WHITETREE
NETWORK TECHNOLOGIES

Address:	3200 Ash Street
	Palo Alto, CA 94306
Telephone:	415/855-0855
Fax:	415/855-0864
E-mail:	mfo@whitetree.com
Web site:	http://www.whitetree.com
Industry:	Communications
Sector:	Computer Networking
CEO:	Maureen Lawrence
CFO:	Denise Savoie

Product Description

Whitetree Network Technologies develops high-value, cost-effective desktop local-area network (LAN) products based on asynchronous transfer mode (ATM) technology at 25 megabits per second. It will also offer a line of switches and adapters. The company focuses on the part of the network closest to the desktop computer, and will compete with switched and fast Ethernet alternatives. It is the first ATM-based solution that tightly integrates Ethernet.

Market Strategy/Positioning

The company's mission is to be the leading supplier of high-performance, high-value workgroup networking solutions based on ATM technology. Whitetree has strategic relationships with Madge Networks, Mitsui, and Toshiba. The company's competitive advantage is its unique positioning to lead the ATM market. Whitetree's products will accelerate the crossover from Ethernet to ATM through a smooth, relatively low-cost migration path. Whitetree primarily competes against First Virtual Corp., ATM Ltd., Cisco Systems, IBM, and Bay Networks. Additional challenges include meeting the demand for its product.

Other

Whitetree Network Technologies, founded in 1993, is a founding member of the Desktop ATM25 Alliance. CEO Maureen Lawrence was formerly at NET and Chipcom.

Primary VCs/Outside Financing

Greylock Management, Institutional Venture Partners, Matrix Partners, Madge Networks, and Stanford University.

KEY FACTS

Year Established:	1993
Employees:	20
Fiscal Year End:	n/a
Revenues FY '94:	$0.0
Revenues FY '95:	n/a
Date of Next Financing:	n/a
Date of Last Financing:	November 1994
Size of Last Financing:	5.0m
Total Capital Raised:	10.1m
Post Round Valuation:	15.0m
Expected IPO Date:	n/a

WIRED VENTURES

Address:	520 Third Street
	4th Floor
	San Francisco, CA 94107-1815
Telephone:	415/222-6200
Fax:	415/222-6289
E-mail:	info@wired.com
Web site:	http://www.hotwired.com
Industry:	Entertainment & Information
Sector:	Newspaper/Magazine Publishing
CEO:	Louis Rossetto
CFO:	Celeste Chin

Product Description

Wired Ventures provides information through its magazine, *Wired*, its online service, Hot-Wired, and its book-publishing division, HardWired, to managers, creators, and professionals in the computer, design, entertainment, media, and education industries. *Wired* magazine targets the leaders in the digital information revolution, and its editorial covers business, politics, media, art, and multimedia. Through its weekly newsletter, *HotFlash*, the company distributes product information to its subscribers.

Market Strategy/Positioning

The company's mission is "to track the overriding business, social, and cultural phenomenon of our times: the Digital Revolution." Wired Ventures has a licensing agreement with Dohosha Publishing to create a Japanese-language version of its products, and a relationship with Guardian Media Group (U.K.). Significant customers include IBM, NEC, AT&T, Schieffelin Distributors, Fujitsu, Microsoft, Motorola, Apple, Catapult Entertainment, and Origin Technology. The company's competitive advantages are its strong editorial product, reasonable advertising rates, consistent circulation, and advertising revenue growth. Wired Ventures primarily competes against CMP Publications, Fun City Megamedia, Flipside Communications, Hearst, Hypermedia Communications, International Data Group, Mecklermedia, Time Warner, and Ziff-Davis. Additional challenges and risks include increasing competition and the uncertain future of online services.

Other

Wired was founded in 1993 with an initial circulation base of 53,793 readers. HotWired was added in October 1994 with a startup subscriber base of 4,000 users. As of August 1995 the magazine's circulation had swelled to 240,000 and was estimated to top 300,000 by January 1996. Louis Rossetto and Jane Metcalfe attempted unsuccessfully to start a similar magazine in Europe in the 1980s. HotWired received approximately $15 million in funding from PacBell and others.

Primary VCs/Outside Financing

Messrs. Nicholas Negroponte, S.I. Newhouse, and Charlie Jackson.

KEY FACTS

Year Established:	1993
Employees:	150
Fiscal Year End:	December
Revenues FY '94:	n/a
Revenues FY '95:	n/a
Date of Next Financing:	n/a
Date of Last Financing:	n/a
Size of Last Financing:	n/a
Total Capital Raised:	n/a
Post Round Valuation:	n/a
Expected IPO Date:	n/a

WORLDS

Product Description

Worlds develops networked virtual reality applications that use standard PCs and analog phone lines, via the Internet. Its real-time rendering, compression, and authoring tools create photo-realistic, 3D cyberworlds with human motion simulation. The company is also developing voice capabilities.

Address:	510 Third Street
	San Francisco, CA 94107
Telephone:	415/281-1300
Fax:	415/284-9483
E-mail:	n/a
Web site:	http://www.worlds.net
Industry:	Entertainment & Information
Sector:	Online Services
CEO:	Dave Gobel
CFO:	Frank Murnane

Market Strategy/Positioning

The company's mission is to offer the world's most compelling 3D multiuser environments for the PC, both directly to consumers and for business-to-business applications. Worlds has strategic relationships with UB Networks (a division of Tandem Computer), Landmark Entertainment, Pearson, and Mr. Steven Spielberg. Significant customers include Visa, IBM, AT&T, Tandem Computer, and HarperCollins. The company's competitive advantages are its low-cost Internet backbone, effective compression, unique lifeforms motion technology, patents, the best 3D production studio in existence, and other undisclosed inventions that enhance 3D multiuser experiences. Worlds primarily competes against Fujitsu, Cultural Technologies, and Enter Television. Additional challenges and risks include evangelizing the concept of social computing and maintaining a market lead. The company is also aware of delayed growth of Internet use in the home.

Other

Worlds was formed in April 1994; its founders came from Knowledge Adventure, Kinetic Effects, Peregrine, and other U.S. and European software firms. The company invented a method to send articulated motion over analog telephone lines and the Internet providing software and server technology for the Starbright Pediatric Network, the first ATM network. Steven Spielberg's "Starbright World" allows children in pediatric hospitals who are seriously ill to socialize, play games, and interact with each other in a virtual playspace created by Worlds. In 1995 Worlds launched Worlds-Chat, the first multiuser 3D chat space on the Internet. The current managers bring experience from McKinsey, Paramount Technology Group, Microsoft, and Spectrum Holobyte.

KEY FACTS

Year Established:	1994
Employees:	70
Fiscal Year End:	n/a
Revenues FY '94:	n/a
Revenues FY '95:	n/a
Date of Next Financing:	n/a
Date of Last Financing:	March 1995
Size of Last Financing:	n/a
Total Capital Raised:	n/a
Post Round Valuation:	20.0m
Expected IPO Date:	n/a

Primary VCs/Outside Financing

Mr. Steven Spielberg and other strategic partners.

XAOS
TOOLS

Address:	600 Townsend Street
	Suite 270 East
	San Francisco, CA 94103
Telephone:	415/487-7000
Fax:	415/558-9886
E-mail:	info@xaostools.com
Web site:	http://www.xaostools.com
Industry:	Entertainment & Information
Sector:	Film & Entertainment Production
CEO:	Arthur Schwartzberg
CFO:	n/a

Product Description

Xaos Tools develops animation, authoring, and post-production tools for the Silicon Graphics and PC platforms targeted at the animation, multimedia, graphic design, desktop publishing, and film and video industries. The company is recognized for its flagship products, PANDEMONIUM and nTITLE, which run on Silicon Graphics workstations. One of its suites consists of an integrated environment based on an object-oriented scripting language. Content repurposing could open additional market opportunities for the company. For under $10,000 the company provides a complete software solution that incorporates paint, titling, 2D and 3D animation, special effects, image processing, and compositioning.

Market Strategy/Positioning

Xaos Tools has strategic relationships with NewTek, Apple, Silicon Graphics, Autodesk, Adobe, and Avid Technology. Significant customers include major broadcasters, post-production houses, and ad agencies. The company's competitive advantages are its technology, its employee expertise, and its desktop publishing and high-end animation tools architecture. Xaos Tools primarily competes against HSC and Discreet Logic. Additional challenges and risks include a volatile industry, falling software prices, competition from large companies poised to enter the market, and ability to access capital.

Other

Arthur Schwartzberg and Michael Tolson initially founded Xaos Inc. in 1988 to specialize in high-end animation and special effects. Chairman and CEO Arthur Schwartzberg and principal scientist Michael Tolson formed Xaos Tools in 1991 to concentrate on software product development. When Xaos Tools was spun off, all software property rights were given to Xaos Tools, and Xaos Inc. was granted a perpetual license to use the software.

Primary VCs/Outside Financing

Dillon Reed Venture Partners and CKS Venture Partners.

KEY FACTS

Year Established:	1991
Employees:	30
Fiscal Year End:	December
Revenues FY '94:	$3.0m
Revenues FY '95:	$6.0m
Date of Next Financing:	n/a
Date of Last Financing:	February 1995
Size of Last Financing:	$1.0m
Total Capital Raised:	$6.0m
Post Round Valuation:	$26.0m
Expected IPO Date:	1997

454

XEROX

Product Description

Xerox designs, develops, manufactures, markets, and services a range of document processing products and systems, including copiers, duplicators, electronic printers, optical scanners, facsimile machines, networks, and multifunction publishing machines. Xerox has eight business divisions. In 1993 the company decided to sell its insurance business and other financial services not involved in financing purchases of Xerox equipment. The company also operates Xerox Technology Ventures and Xerox Venture Capital, which both promote the growth of startup and existing technology-based ventures. In 1994 Xerox spun off LiveWorks, the company that manufactures and markets LiveBoard, the 67-inch interactive workstation and electronic chalkboard.

Address:	P.O. Box 1600
	800 Long Ridge Road
	Stamford, CT 06904
Telephone:	203/968-3000
Fax:	203/968-4312
E-mail:	n/a
Web site:	http://www.xerox.com
Industry:	Entertainment & Information
Sector:	Consumer Electronics
CEO:	Paul A. Allaire
CFO:	Barry D. Romeril
Stock Exchange:	NYSE
Stock Symbol:	XRX

Market Strategy/Positioning

Xerox has strategic relationships with Microsoft, Novell, NEC, Prism Software, AT&T, and Lotus. Significant customers include Compaq, Apple, and America Online. The company's competitive advantages are its substantial investment in research and development, and its extensive direct-sales and service forces. Xerox primarily competes against Canon, Eastman Kodak, Hewlett-Packard, Matsushita, Polaroid, Siemens, and Toshiba.

Other

Xerox was founded as The Haloid Company to manufacture and sell photographic paper. In 1949 Haloid announced the first xerographic copier, and in 1961 the company changed its name to Xerox. Xerox diversified into publishing and computers in the 1960s. In 1974 Xerox was forced to license its xerographic technology to other companies. From the 1980s onward Xerox concentrated on acquiring companies involved in optical character recognition, scanning and faxing, and desktop publishing. Chairman and CEO Paul Allaire joined Xerox in 1966 as a financial analyst. He was elected president and member of the board in 1986, CEO in 1990, and chairman in 1991. CFO Barry Romeril joined Xerox in 1993. He was previously finance director at British Telecom, before which he spent 14 years with Imperial Chemical Industries.

KEY FACTS

Year Established:	1906
Employees:	103,300
Fiscal Year End:	December
Revenues FY '94:	$17.8b
Revenues FY '95:	n/a
EPS '94:	$6.73
EPS '95:	$8.66 (estimate)
Shares Outstanding:	107.0m
Five-Year Growth Rate:	11%

455

XILINX

Address:	2100 Logic Drive San Jose, CA 95124-3400
Telephone:	408/559-7778
Fax:	408/559-7114
E-mail:	n/a
Web-site:	http://www.xilinx.com
Industry:	Computers
Sector:	Semiconductors
CEO:	Bernard V. Vonderschmitt
CFO:	Gordon M. Steel
Stock Exchange:	NASDAQ
Stock Symbol:	XLNX

Product Description

Xilinx develops programmable logic for the semiconductor industry. Its main products are programmable logic devices (PLDs) and application-specific integrated circuits (ASICs). In October 1995 the company announced its plans to invest $150 million to build a semiconductor manufacturing facility in Taiwan with United Microelectronics (UMC). UMC and other select partners will invest another $1 billion to complete the project. This is the first manufacturing facility in which Xilinx has taken part.

Market Strategy/Positioning

Xilinx has strategic relationships with Seiko Epson, Yamaha, Taiwan Semiconductor, Synopsys, UMC, and IC Works. Xilinx has also established global marketing and distribution networks in Hong Kong, England, Germany, France, Canada, and Japan. Significant customers include AT&T, Apple, Compaq, DEC, IBM, NEC, Newbridge Networks, Northern Telecom, Siemens, Stratacom, and Sun Microsystems. The company's competitive advantage is its leading position in field programmable gate array (FPGA) semiconductor devices. The company primarily competes against Altera, Adaptec, AMD, Cypress Semiconductor, LSI Logic, Motorola, NEC, and QuickLogic.

 456

Other

Xilinx was founded in 1984 by CEO Bernard Vonderschmitt, Jim Barnett, and Ross Freeman. The company opened a Japanese subsidiary in 1988 and went public in 1990. Before founding Xilinx, Mr. Vonderschmitt worked at Zilog for three years and at RCA for over 20 years. He holds 13 issued patents. CFO Gordon Steel joined Xilinx in 1987; he was previously with Pyramid Technology and co-founded EVOTEK.

KEY FACTS

Year Established:	1984
Employees:	1,100
Fiscal Year End:	March
Revenues FY '94:	$256.4m
Revenues FY '95:	$355.1m
EPS '94:	$0.57
EPS '95:	$0.79
Shares Outstanding:	70.5m
Five-Year Growth Rate:	35%

XING TECHNOLOGY

Address:	1540 West Branch Street
	Arroyo Grande, CA 93420
Telephone:	805/473-0145
Fax:	805/473-0147
E-mail:	streams@xingtech.com
Web site:	http://www.xingtech.com
Industry:	Entertainment & Information
Sector:	Entertainment/Education Software
CEO:	Howard R. Gordon
CFO:	Eric W. Markrud

Product Description

Xing Technology produces software for delivering live and on-demand audio and video over the Internet. It uses a process called "streaming media" to deliver audio and video in real-time, eliminating the need to first download content to a hard drive. Ultimately, users will be able to follow local sports teams, political issues, or financial information regardless of their location. The company also creates software-based MPEG products. It's currently working on software that would allow "live" video on the World Wide Web.

Market Strategy/Positioning

Xing Technology has strategic relationships with Silicon Graphics, Microsoft, Intel, Bellcore, NTT, Fujitsu, Samsung, Hewlett-Packard, and IBM. Significant customers include NBC and Reuters. The company's competitive advantages are its adherence to industry standards and high-performance, scalable products. Xing Technology primarily competes against Progressive Networks. Additional challenges and risks include existing in a constantly changing market which makes long-term product strategy difficult, and having technology that requires more bandwidth than most users currently have.

Other

Xing Technology was incorporated in 1989. In 1991 it licensed its JPEG technology to Microsoft and in 1992 it licensed its MPEG video technology to Intel. Xing CD was introduced in 1994; followed by StreamWorks in 1995. Founder, chairman, and CEO Howard Gordon founded Network Research, a company based on vendor-independent local-area network software, in 1982. Executive vice president Eric Markrud joined the company in 1993. Before Xing, Mr. Markrud served as CEO of National Micronetics and spent 12 years working at GE.

Primary VCs/Outside Financing

Not disclosed.

457

KEY FACTS

Year Established:	1989
Employees:	35
Fiscal Year End:	June
Revenues FY '94:	n/a
Revenues FY '95:	$2.0m
Date of Next Financing:	n/a
Date of Last Financing:	November 1995
Size of Last Financing:	n/a
Total Capital Raised:	n/a
Post Round Valuation:	n/a
Expected IPO Date:	n/a

Address:	26679 West Agoura Road Suite 100 Calabasas, CA 91302
Telephone:	818/880-3500
Fax:	818/880-3505
E-mail:	info@xylan.com
Web site:	http://www.xylan.com
Industry:	Communications
Sector:	Computer Networking
CEO:	Steve Kim
CFO:	Peter Vazzana

Product Description

Xylan provides local-area network (LAN) switches that facilitate technology migration to switched, dedicated, high-speed connections. The Xylan switch automatically switches and translates among Ethernet, token ring, FDDI, CDDI, 100BaseT, and ATM, and also provides switching within virtual LANs, as well as routing between them. The company focuses on powerful and inexpensive products so that corporate networks can migrate rapidly and easily to switched connections.

Market Strategy/Positioning

The company's mission is to enable the transformation of computer networking by providing powerful yet inexpensive switches as the basic building blocks of corporate networks. Xylan has strategic relationships with Alcatel, Network Systems, and Hitachi. Significant customers include ADP, Bell Atlantic, Canadian Broadcasting, Data General, and Time Warner. The company's competitive advantages are its heterogenous LAN switching technology, switching and routing within virtual LANs, and reliability. Xylan primarily competes against Cisco Systems, Cabletron Systems, Bay Networks, 3Com, Alantec, Plaintree, and Agile Networks. Additional challenges and risks include intense competition, particularly from established industry giants, and the constant pressure to bring a broad set of technologies to market rapidly.

Other

Founded in July 1993, the company first received venture capital funding in December of 1993 and released its first product in September of 1994. CEO Steve Kim was previously the founder and CEO of Fibermux, a networking company with revenues of $50 million. Before founding Fibermux, he held management positions at Phalo Optical Systems, Litton Data Systems, and Burroughs.

Primary VCs/Outside Financing

Brentwood Associates, Crosspoint Venture Partners, U.S. Venture Partners, and Norwest Venture Capital.

458

KEY FACTS

Year Established:	1993
Employees:	45
Fiscal Year End:	September
Revenues FY '94:	n/a
Revenues FY '95:	n/a
Date of Next Financing:	n/a
Date of Last Financing:	November 1994
Size of Last Financing:	$6.2m
Total Capital Raised:	$11.6m
Post Round Valuation:	$26.2m
Expected IPO Date:	n/a

YAHOO!

Product Description

Yahoo!, a comprehensive online guide for the Internet, categorizes and provides links to tens of thousands of online resources and sites on the Internet's World Wide Web. Yahoo!'s guide lets users navigate their way through the Internet to gather diverse information. Numerous Web sites are created every day, with no real centralized way for the user to find out about them. Yahoo!'s site gets approximately 3 million "hits" per day, with 1,000 submissions per day for new links from companies who want its Web site listed on Yahoo!'s directory. Amazingly enough, Yahoo!'s service is free to the end-user.

Address:	110 Pioneer Way
	Suite F
	Mountain View, CA 94041
Telephone:	415/934-3230
Fax:	415/934-3248
E-mail:	pr@yahoo.com
Web site:	http://www.yahoo.com
Industry:	Entertainment & Information
Sector:	Online Services
CEO:	Timothy Koogle
CFO:	n/a

Market Strategy/Positioning

Yahoo! has strategic relationships with Netscape, Reuters (which integrated Reuters Online News Service into Yahoo!), MCI, Mastercard, NECX, Worlds, and Internet Shopping Network. Significant customers include "all Net surfers." The company's competitive advantage is being one of the most popular directory sources on the Web, and directory services are thought to be the latest big boom in the Internet business. Yahoo! primarily competes against Global Network Navigator (O'Reilly & Associates), EINet Galaxy, Architext, America Online, Microsoft, AT&T, and PRODIGY. Additional challenges and risks include future competition from large companies that could gain a monopoly.

459

Other

Yahoo! (Yet Another Hierarchically Officious Oracle) was started by two Stanford graduate students as a hobby, because "anything was more interesting" than their Ph.D. studies, according to co-founders David Filo and Jerry Yang. In April 1994 they began categorizing their favorite sites on the Web and, by word of mouth, now include tens of thousands of sites. The company received funding from Sequoia Capital, mainly because of the support of general partner Michael Moritz, who was impressed by Yahoo!'s apparent overnight success. Both founders were pursuing Ph.D. degrees at Stanford, which are now on hold so they can run Yahoo! full-time.

Primary VCs/Outside Financing

Sequoia Capital.

KEY FACTS

Year Established:	1994
Employees:	15
Fiscal Year End:	December
Revenues FY '94:	$0.0
Revenues FY '95:	n/a
Date of Next Financing:	n/a
Date of Last Financing:	April 1995
Size of Last Financing:	$1.0m
Total Capital Raised:	$1.0m
Post Round Valuation:	n/a
Expected IPO Date:	n/a

ZILOG

Address:	210 East Hacienda Avenue Campbell, CA 95008
Telephone:	408/370-8000
Fax:	408/370-8056
E-mail:	n/a
Web site:	http://www.zilog.com
Industry:	Computers
Sector:	Semiconductors
CEO:	Edgar A. Sack
CFO:	William R. Walker
Stock Exchange:	NYSE
Stock Symbol:	ZLG

Product Description

Zilog designs, develops, manufactures, and markets application-specific standard products (ASSPs) for the consumer electronics, data communications, and peripherals markets. It also works closely with major peripheral manufacturers to add its microcontroller intelligence to laser printers, modems, keyboards, and disk drives. In August 1995 the company announced its V-chip, which offers TV programming control capability. The company's assembly and testing operations are located in Malaysia, the Philippines, and Indonesia, and it has been aggressively branching out into international business. In 1995 Zilog sealed an agreement with semiconductor distributor Memec to sell its products in Asia.

Market Strategy/Positioning

Zilog has strategic relationships with Apple, Gulbransen, StarSight Telecast, and Interlink Electronics. The company's competitive advantage is its leadership position in multiprotocol controllers for local-area network and wide-area network markets. Zilog primarily competes against AMD, Atmel, Intel, IBM, Motorola, National Semiconductor, NEC, Siemens, Sony, and Texas Instruments.

Other

Zilog was founded in 1974 by Ralph Ungermann and Frederico Faggin, both former Intel employees. It became a wholly-owned subsidiary of Exxon in 1980. Zilog's management purchased the company from Exxon in 1989, and Zilog went public in 1991. CEO Edgar Sack was hired in 1984 to help turn the company around, since it was losing money at the time. Mr. Sack led the management buyout in 1989 from Exxon. He was previously employed at General Instrument for 15 years. CFO William Walker previously worked at Exxon for over 20 years.

KEY FACTS

Year Established:	1974
Employees:	1,600
Fiscal Year End:	December
Revenues FY '94:	$233.3m
Revenues FY '95:	n/a
EPS '94:	$1.80
EPS '95:	$2.04(estimate)
Shares Outstanding:	n/a
Five-Year Growth Rate:	n/a

473

491

Editor-in-Chief — Anthony B. Perkins
Executive Editor — Christopher J. Alden
Senior Author — Michael C. Perkins
Company Profiles Editor — Anne T. Linsmayer
Managing Editor — Nina J.A. Davis
Contributing Editors — Jonathan G. Burke / Alexander B. Gove
Seth Kenvin / Virginie S. Pelletier
Research Assistants — Raj Gollamudi / Nikki C. Goth
Somaya A.G. Larson / Jeffrey R. Whittaker
Editorial Advisors — Jim Breyer / Sandy Climan / Kevin Compton
Fred Davis / Pierre Lamond / Gary Lauder
Bob Metcalfe / Avram Miller / Steven Milunovich
Carl Rosendahl / Tom Waldrop / Alex Vieux

Book Design — Bart Nagel's Brain
Production/Layout Team — Pete Ivey / Karen M. Huff / Marcy J. Walpert
Contributing Artists — Tim Brock / Steve Curley / Robert B. Gerber
Pete McDonnell / J. Garett Sheldrew / Eric White
Contributing Photographers — Anne Knudsen / Mary Merrick

Project Consultants — Andrea Gregg / Roger Siboni
KMPG Peat Marwick
Project Counsel — Brobeck, Phleger & Harrison
First Amendment Counsel — Nasty, Brutish & Short

493

The Lore of THE RED HERRING In the 1800s, wily British fugitives discovered that rubbing a herring across their trail would divert the bloodhounds hot in their pursuit. Later, in debate and detective mysteries, the "red herring" described any clever device used to distract people from the main issue. In the 1920s, equally clever American investment bankers began calling preliminary investment prospectuses "red herrings," as a warning to investors that the documents were not complete or final. These documents were distinguished by covers printed largely in red. Today, one Wall Street curmudgeon describes a red herring as "the one shining example of truth in advertising in the securities industry." In the spirit of truth in financial reporting, the founders of this publication felt THE RED HERRING an appropriate name for a monthly dedicated to providing a first look at business information in a style that is at once accurate and provocative.